D1351399

Independents in Irish party democracy

MANCHESTER
1824

Manchester University Press

Independents in Irish party democracy

Liam Weeks

Manchester University Press

Published by Manchester University Press
Altrincham Street, Manchester M1 7JA

www.manchesteruniversitypress.co.uk

British Library Cataloguing-in-Publication Data
A catalogue record for this book is available from the British Library

Library of Congress Cataloging-in-Publication Data applied for

ISBN   978 0 7190 9960 1 hardback

First published 2017

Typeset by
Servis Filmsetting Ltd, Stockport, Cheshire
Printed by Lightning Source

Table of contents

List of figures	*page* vi	
List of tables	ix	
Acknowledgments	xii	
List of abbreviations	xiv	
1	Introduction	1
2	A typology of independents	23
3	Independents' electoral history	54
4	Independent parliamentarians	91
5	The independent voter	147
6	Independents and the electoral system	172
7	Independents and government	205
8	Why are there independents in Ireland?	252
9	Conclusion	269
Appendix		286
References		293
Index		308

Figures

1.1 Independents elected at general elections, 1950–2016.
Author's figures calculated from Brancati (2008); Ehin
et al. (2013); national electoral authorities. *page 3*

2.1 Support for independent families, 1922–2016. Author's
figures calculated from various issues of *Election results
and transfer of votes for Dáil and bye-elections*. Dublin:
Stationery Office; Gallagher (1993); Walker (1992);
www.electionsireland.org. 31

3.1 National elections with an aggregate independent vote
above 5 per cent, 1950–2016. Author's figures calculated
from Brancati (2008); Ehin et al. (2013); national
electoral authorities. 60

3.2 National vote for independents in Australia, Ireland and
Japan. Author's figures calculated from Australian Politics
and Elections Database accessed at www.elections.uwa.
edu.au; Klein (2001); www.electionsireland.org. 61

3.3 Independents as a proportion of votes, seats and
candidates, Dáil elections 1922–2016. Author's figures
calculated from various issues of *Election results and transfer
of votes for Dáil and bye-elections*. Dublin: Stationery
Office; Gallagher (1993); Walker (1992);
www.electionsireland.org. 68

3.4 Mean and median first-preference vote per independent
candidate at Dáil elections, 1922–2016. Author's figures
calculated from various issues of *Election results and
transfer of votes for Dáil and bye-elections*. Dublin:
Stationery Office; Gallagher (1993); Walker (1992);
www.electionsireland.org. 74

3.5 Percentage vote for independents per province, 1923–2016.
Author's figures calculated from various issues of *Election
results and transfer of votes for Dáil and bye-elections*. Dublin:

Stationery Office; Gallagher (1993); Walker (1992); www.electionsireland.org.   86

5.1 Levels of party detachment, 1978–2013 (%). Author's figures calculated from Eurobarometer surveys 1978–1994; Comparative Study of Electoral Systems (CSES) database 1996–2013.   159

6.1 Number of independent candidates per constituency at Dáil elections in Ireland, 1923–2016. Author's figures calculated from various issues of Department of the Environment and Local Government. *Election results and transfer of votes in general election for Dáil and bye-elections.* Dublin: Stationery Office, 1948–2016; Gallagher (1993).   180

6.2 Percentage of seats won by independents at Dáil elections in Ireland, 1923–2016. Author's figures calculated from various issues of Department of the Environment and Local Government. *Election results and transfer of votes in general election for Dáil and bye-elections.* Dublin: Stationery Office, 1948–2016; Gallagher (1993).   181

6.3 Seat–vote deviation by district magnitude at Dáil elections in Ireland, 1923–2016. Author's figures calculated from various issues of Department of the Environment and Local Government. *Election results and transfer of votes in general election for Dáil and bye-elections.* Dublin: Stationery Office, 1948–2016; Gallagher (1993).   182

6.4 Effect of transfers on independents' performance at Dáil elections in Ireland, 1948–2016. Author's figures calculated from various issues of Department of the Environment and Local Government. *Election results and transfer of votes in general election for Dáil and bye-elections.* Dublin: Stationery Office, 1948–2016; Gallagher (1993).   185

6.5 Mean vote for independents at lower- and upper-house elections in Australia, 1950–2015. Author's figures calculated from Australian Politics and Elections Database accessed at www.elections.uwa.edu.au; Rodrigues and Brenton (2010).   188

6.6 Commonwealth Senate STV ballot paper. Source: Australian Electoral Commission.   191

6.7 ACT STV ballot paper. Source: ACT Electoral Commission.   193

6.8 Irish STV ballot paper. Source: Department of Housing, Planning, Community and Local Government, Dublin.   194

7.1 Cohesion rates of independents in Dáil, 1937–2015. Author's figures calculated from Hansen (2009; 2010).   212

7.2 Participation rates (%) of independent TDs in Dáil votes, 1937–2015. Author's figures calculated from Hansen (2009; 2010).   244

7.3 Support rates (%) of independent TDs for governments, 1937–2015. Author's figures calculated from Hansen (2009; 2010).   245

Tables

2.1 Typology of independents, 1922–2016. Author's analyses from the *Irish Times* 1922–2016 accessed at www.irishtimes.com and local newspapers from *Irish Newspaper Archive* accessed at www.irishnewsarchive.com.   *page* 30

2.2 Candidates and seats by independent category. Author's figures calculated from various issues of *Election results and transfer of votes for Dáil and bye-elections*. Dublin: Stationery Office; Gallagher (1993); Walker (1992); www.electionsireland.org.   32

2.3 Performance of party TDs as apostate independents at succeeding elections, 1922–2016. Author's figures calculated from various issues of *Election results and transfer of votes for Dáil and bye-elections*. Dublin: Stationery Office; Gallagher (1993); Walker (1992); www.electionsireland.org.   50

3.1 Independents elected since 1990. Author's figures calculated from Nohlen (2001; 2005; 2010).   57

3.2 Independents elected at national elections in Australia and Japan, 1945–2015. Author's figures calculated from Australian Politics and Elections Database accessed at www.elections.uwa.edu.au; Klein (2001).   62

3.3 Numbers and shares of votes and seats for independents, and numbers and proportion of candidates comprising independents at Dáil elections, 1922–2016. Author's figures calculated from various issues of *Election results and transfer of votes for Dáil and bye-elections*. Dublin: Stationery Office; Gallagher (1993); Walker (1992); www.electionsireland.org.   69

3.4 Independents' performance at local, European Parliament, presidential and by-elections in Ireland. Author's figures calculated from Weeks and Quinlivan (2009); www.electionsireland.org.   81

3.5 Mean level of support (%) for independents per
constituency at Dáil elections, 1923–2016. Author's
figures calculated from various issues of *Election results
and transfer of votes for Dáil and bye-elections.* Dublin:
Stationery Office; Gallagher (1993).   83

3.6 Correlation of independent vote per county, 1923–48.
Author's figures calculated from Gallagher (1993).   87

3.7 Correlation of independent vote per county, 1948–2016.
Author's figures calculated from various issues of *Election
results and transfer of votes for Dáil and bye-elections.*
Dublin: Stationery Office.   88

5.1 Support for independents (%) by socio-economic status.
Author's figures calculated from INES 2002–11 and a 2016
exit poll conducted by Behaviour and Attitudes for RTÉ in
partnership with the School of Politics and International
Relations in UCD, the Department of Government in UCC,
the School of Politics, International Studies and Philosophy
in Queen's University Belfast, and Trinity College Dublin.   154

5.2 Models of independent vote. Author's figures calculated
from INES 2002–11.   165

5.3 Models of independent vote. Author's figures calculated
from INES 2002–11.   170

6.1 Independent seats won at upper and lower house elections
in Australia, 1950–2015. Author's figures calculated from
Australian Politics and Elections Database accessed at
www.elections.uwa.edu.au; Rodrigues and Brenton (2010).   188

6.2 Mean vote for independents before and after the
introduction of STV and STV ticket voting, 1950–2013.
Author's figures calculated from Australian Politics
and Elections Database accessed at www.elections.
uwa.edu.au   189

6.3 Performance of independents at STV elections, 1945–2016.
Author's figures calculated from Australian Politics and
Elections Database accessed at www.elections.uwa.edu.
au; various issues of *Election results and transfer of votes
for Dáil and bye-elections.* Dublin: Stationery Office;
Gallagher (1993).   197

6.4 OLS (Ordinary Least Squares) regression of independent
vote on STV, Australia and Ireland, 1945–2016. Author's
figures calculated from Australian Politics and Elections
Database accessed at www.elections.uwa.edu.au; various
issues of *Election results and transfer of votes for Dáil and*

bye-elections. Dublin: Stationery Office; Gallagher
(1993).   199

6.5 OLS regression of independent vote on STV, Australia
and Ireland, 1945–2016. Author's figures calculated from
Australian Politics and Elections Database accessed at
www.elections.uwa.edu.au; various issues of *Election
results and transfer of votes for Dáil and bye-elections.*
Dublin: Stationery Office; Gallagher (1993).   203

7.1 Minority governments needing the support of independents
in Ireland, 1922–2016   208

7.2 Length of type of government (in days) in Ireland,
1922–2016. Author's figures calculated from Gallagher and
Weeks (2010).   243

8.1 Hypotheses on an independent presence   257

8.2 Summary of hypotheses   262

8.3 Summary statistics per constituency level, 1981–2011.
Author's figures calculated from various issues of *Election
results and transfer of votes for Dáil and bye-elections.*
Dublin: Stationery Office; Central Statistics Office accessed
at www.cso.ie   267

8.4 Models of independent significance. Author's figures
calculated from various issues of *Election results and
transfer of votes for Dáil and bye-elections.* Dublin:
Stationery Office; Central Statistics Office accessed at
www.cso.ie   267

Acknowledgments

This book is a culmination of fifteen years of research on the subject of independents. It stems from an interest first sparked by a PhD on the topic in the Department of Political Science at Trinity College, Dublin, and it was later the subject of a postdoctoral fellowship. I am extremely grateful to the Irish Research Council for funding both these projects. The first was in the form of a Government of Ireland postgraduate scholarship (2002–5), and the second a Marie Curie CARA fellowship at Macquarie University, Sydney and University College Cork (2010–13).

A number of other institutions also provided crucial support, including the Royal Irish Academy, the Institute of Social Research at Swinburne University of Technology in Melbourne and the Waseda Institute for Advanced Study at Waseda University in Tokyo.

Of course this book would not have been possible without the advice I received along the way. In particular, Michael Gallagher deserves special thanks for supervising the original PhD dissertation, as does Michael Marsh, and Murray Goot for his counsel in Sydney. I am extremely grateful to Nicole Bolleyer, Fiona Buckley, Ken Carty, Michael Gallagher, Shane MacGiollabhuí and Mícheál Ó Fathartaigh for reading and commenting on various draft chapters. I would also like to thank Martin Hansen for providing the roll-call data used in Chapter 7, and for always responding so promptly to my many queries.

Others deserving of at least a mention include Clive Ahern, Eddie Campbell, John Coakley, Neil Collins, Stephen Collins, Richard Colwell, Brian Costar, Anthony Egan, David Farrell, Kieran Galvin, Anika Gauja, Anthony Green, Martin Hansen, Airo Hino, Willy Jou, Muiris MacCarthaigh, Shane Martin, Ian McAllister, David McEllin, Ian McShane, Catherine Murphy, Yvonne Murphy, Eunan O'Halpin, Maureen O'Sullivan, Roderick Pace, Steven Reed, Campbell Sharman, Kathy Sheridan, Rodney Smith, Peter Tucker, Tony Varley and Noel Whelan.

I have also benefited from the sage advice of colleagues at departments who have hosted me, especially the Department of Government and International Relations at the University of Sydney, the Institute of European Studies at Valetta, Malta, the School of Political Science and Economics at Waseda University, Tokyo, and the Department of Political Science at the University of Nebraska-Lincoln. I am indebted to my colleagues at the Department of Government, University College Cork, for their support in this journey.

I am grateful for the expert advice provided from members of the various electoral commissions and parliamentary libraries across Australia, in particular Colin Barry, Philip Greene, Michael Maley, Terri Newman, Jenni Newton-Farrelly, Brian Stait, Steve Tully and Walter van der Merwe.

I thank all the team at Manchester University Press for believing in, and supporting, this project. This includes, in particular, Tony Mason and Dee Devine. I am also very grateful to the two anonymous referees who provided a number of extremely useful suggestions.

Some work in this study has drawn upon material from within: Liam Weeks (2015), 'Why are there Independents in Ireland?', (adapted), *Government and Opposition*, FirstView Article, Cambridge University Press 2015; Liam Weeks, 'Crashing the party. Does STV help Independents?', *Party Politics* 20(4): 604–16; Liam Weeks (2011), 'Rage against the machine: who is the independent voter?', *Irish Political Studies*, 26 (1): 19–43; and Liam Weeks (2009), 'We don't like (to) party. A typology of Independents in Irish political life, 1922–2007', *Irish Political Studies*, 24 (1): 1–27. Thanks also to the Australian Electoral Commission and the Department of Housing, Planning, Community and Local Government for permission to reproduce the ballot papers in Chapter 6.

As ever, my family were a bedrock of support along the way. Special thanks are due to my parents Graham and Margaret, and my sister Caoimhe.

Finally, this book could not have been produced without the assistance of the independents themselves, who put up with my many requests and questions. They were always extremely generous with their time and patience. This book is dedicated to them.

Abbreviations

ACT	Australian Capital Territory
AV	Alternative Vote
CSES	Comparative Study of Electoral Systems
IFF	Independent Fianna Fáil
IMF	International Monetary Fund
IPP	Irish Parliamentary Party
INES	Irish National Election Study
IRA	Irish Republican Army
LDP	Liberal Democratic Party
MP	Member of Parliament
PD	Progressive Democrats
PR	Proportional Representation
PR-STV	Proportional Representation by the Single Transferable Vote
SNTV	Single Non-Transferable Vote
STV	Single Transferable Vote
TCD	Trinity College Dublin
TD	Teachta Dála (member of parliament)
VAT	Value Added Tax

1

Introduction

Independents

This is a study of mavericks, of the independent politicians who go it alone. They are the metaphorical equivalent of sheep who stray from the flock, who would rather discover fresh pastures than graze on their own. In most political systems, there are very few incentives to take such a deviant path. The few sheep that wander tend to be quickly picked off by the preying wolf that is the party system. In Ireland things are a bit different, however, as the maverick path does not imply political termination. Life outside of the flock can bring its rewards, and for some can be the rational path to pursue. This study is a detailed analysis of these independents, primarily of the factors that explain their presence and survival in the midst of one of the longest enduring party democracies in the world.

With this in mind, the result of the electoral count for the rural constituency of Kerry at the February 2016 Dáil (lower house of parliament) elections in Ireland would have seemed highly unusual to an international observer. Michael Healy-Rae, an independent candidate first elected to the Dáil in 2011, comfortably won a seat again with 20,378 first-preference votes, almost 26 per cent of the total valid constituency poll. This was the largest vote won by any of the 551 candidates in all of the forty constituencies at that Dáil election, and the fifth largest first-preference vote ever won at a general election in post-independence Ireland. That an independent was elected to national parliament was unusual enough from a comparative perspective; that he received the largest vote in the country was even more unusual; but perhaps the most unusual event of the night was the unprecedented election of his brother, Danny Healy-Rae, as an independent in the same constituency. Between them, these two brothers won almost two and a half electoral quotas in first preferences alone, a vote total that suggested had another member of the family run, he or she could also have been elected. Michael and Danny Healy-Rae continue a family tradition in politics, as their father, Jackie, also held a seat as an independent in the Dáil between 1997 and 2011. A third generation of this family entered politics in 2014, when Danny's son, Johnny, was elected to the local council. Danny's daughter, Maura, was later co-opted to the same council to take the seat her father had to vacate on his election to the Dáil in 2016. To many, the election of the Healy-Raes symbolises the enduring importance of localism and parish-pump politics in Ireland, where politicians are elected to deal with issues in their respective constituencies, and not because of their ideology, policy platforms or representation of social groups, as can be the practice in other countries. While some question the value of having a national parliament comprising such local politicians, Danny Healy-Rae made no bones on election night about where his or his brother's priorities lay: 'There's been a lot of talk of representing the nation and that we're not good for the nation, but the people of Kerry are part of the nation. And we'll have to fight for those people and we make no apologies for that' (Daly 2016).

Independents' electoral success was not restricted to the Healy-Raes that February weekend. Of the 157 contested seats in the 2016 Dáil election, twenty-three were won by independents. Occupying almost one in six seats in the new Dáil, this was proportionally the highest level of elected independent representation in the national parliament of any established democracy since 1950. Aside from this electoral performance, what would have seemed additionally unusual to an international observer was the role many of these independents went on to play in the formation of the next government, a process which took over two months. With there being no clear winner of the election, these independent deputies were courted by the two largest parties: Fine Gael and Fianna Fáil. This culminated in an unprecedented partnership minority government involving Fine Gael and a number of independents, supported from the outside by Fianna Fáil. Three independent TDs were appointed to cabinet, another made a 'super-junior' minister who could sit – but not vote – at cabinet, and two others were appointed junior ministers. Although non-party technocrats have participated in government in some Mediterranean democracies, it is highly unusual from an international perspective for an independent MP to be a member of cabinet. Independents also had unprecedented success at the Seanad (upper house of parliament) elections in April 2016, winning four seats on the vocational panels and five seats on the university panels. With the Taoiseach (prime minister) appointing another five independents to the Seanad, this meant they occupied fourteen of sixty seats, the largest ever number of independent senators in the house.

This influence wielded by independents both at the elections and in government would have seemed unusual to external observers because in most countries political competition at the national level is all about parties. Few politicians wander from the party path and, for those that do, there is rarely life outside the party. For example, at the same time as twenty-three independents were elected to the Dáil, across the other thirty-six industrial democracies there were only eighteen elected independents in total, sitting in just six parliaments.[1]

This presence of independents in the Irish parliament as an unusual international outlier is not unique to the 2010s. Between 1945 and 2016, 3,130 TDs were elected to the Dáil, of whom 137 were independent (i.e. 4.4 per cent). This represents fifty-nine times the proportion that were elected during this period in Britain, thirty-two times the proportion that were elected in the United States, ten times the proportion that were elected in Canada, six times the proportion that were elected in Australia and seventy-seven times the proportion elected in New Zealand. These are a select range of democracies that have also had independent members of parliament in the same time period. There are not too many of these jurisdictions, as is detailed in Figure 1.1 which indicates the total number of elected independent parliamentarians across all industrial democracies since 1950. It is only in Japan that independents have experienced similar levels of electoral success as in Ireland. Even then, as is discussed in Chapter 3, the Japanese case is somewhat different because the genuine independence of these

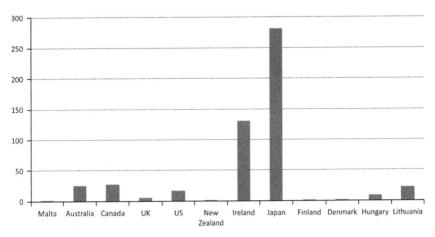

Figure 1.1 Independents elected at general elections, 1950–2016.

Note: This chart indicates the total number of independents elected at general elections in each democracy since 1950. It does not include by-election victories. Only those democracies with independent MPs are included.

independents is questionable, since most of them originate in parties and join them again following their election.

Figure 1.1 includes only those countries where independents have been elected to the lower house of national parliament, so what is evident from the inclusion of just twelve countries is that independents are a rare breed. In most democracies, independent candidacies are either not possible (because of the operation of closed list electoral systems that restricts elections to parties) or, where they are, support for them is negligible and they have never been elected (Brancati 2008). This comparative weakness of independents makes their signifi-cance in Ireland all the more puzzling. Coakley describes this presence as 'the most distinctive phenomenon on the Irish electoral landscape' (2010b, 28), and the aim of this book is to explain this puzzle – why are there independents in Ireland?

The political systems where independents are usually successful are those where party organisations are very weak or they are prohibited (Norris 2006, 91). Examples of the former are in some post-communist polities – for example, Kazakhstan and Ukraine – and small island states, particularly in the south Pacific, while examples of the latter are prevalent in the Arabian Gulf, where parties are seen as an unnec-essary intermediary between the rulers and the ruled. The presence of independents in these systems, however, is more to do with their respective stages of development. They are not party democracies, and so by implication most politicians in these systems are not necessarily independents by positive choice; simply, in the absence of parties this is their de facto status. What makes the Irish case unusual is that it is one of the longest surviving continuous democracies with a stable party system, and yet independent parliamentarians have persisted as rel-evant political actors. The process whereby parties monopolise political representation was never completed in Ireland. This anomaly is the subject of this book.

This chapter comprises a general introduction to the topic of inde-pendents. It begins with a discussion as to the meaning of the concept, and what is understood by an independent for the purposes of this study. There then follows a rationale for a book on this topic, before the international and Irish experience of independents is briefly exam-ined. The final section outlines the central premise of this study and its structure, detailing how the question of an independent presence can be explained. Before delving any further into this topic, the first issue to consider is: what is meant by an independent?

What is an independent?

The term 'independent' is itself an essentially contested concept whose meaning can vary across time, context and jurisdiction. This lack of uniformity does not help systematic and comparative analysis. While it is easy to describe what an independent is not – that is, not a party – a positive definition is a little bit more difficult. A necessary first step before defining an independent is to trace its evolution.

For some, a key question as to the meaning of 'independent' is: 'independent' of what (Sharman 2002, 53)? When a former independent candidate in Ireland took a court case in 2005 because he was not allowed to describe his political affiliation as 'independent' on the ballot paper (the choice is between 'non-party' or simply no description at all), the presiding judge struck down his claim on the grounds that 'if a candidate became entitled to describe himself as "independent" I have no doubt the next step would be a claim to set forth, no doubt at some length, what he was "independent" of' (*Irish Times*, 24 February 2005, 7). Typically, 'independent' has implied that a political candidate or politician is independent of parties. However, this has not always been the case. Before the evolution of parties in Britain into their current form in the nineteenth century, independence meant independent of the monarch and of the great families, and later, in the eighteenth century, independent of the government. In that pre-nineteenth century era, independence therefore implied that a politician had a sufficient level of financial resources, which meant that he neither had to kowtow to the aristocracy nor leave himself open to the corrupting influences of parliament (King-Hall 1951, 104). For this reason, before the emergence of the party as the principal organisational unit in the nineteenth century, independents had a laudable role in the House of Commons. While many professing independence ultimately supported either the Whigs or the Conservatives, this was an era when party was still little more than an ideological label; consequently, these MPs were independent both in terms of organisation and what motivated their stance in parliament.

The contemporary understanding of an independent is only as old as that of parties as a concept, because without parties it can be difficult to see of what such individuals are independent. It is therefore only with the emergence of parties that independence took on a clear identity. In the early years of parties, independence was seen as a virtue, primarily because the former – or more accurately their precursor, factions – were much reviled. The source of this animosity stemmed from the tendency of factions as mobilised groups to promote sectional interests to the detriment of national welfare (Sartori 2005, 3–5), a sentiment echoed in many political texts including, famously, by James Madison in *The Federalist* number ten (Hamilton et al. 2003, 46–51). As Belloni and Beller note, 'party spirit was viewed as the antithesis of public spirit' (1978, 4). In such a climate the 'private' members of parliament – the independents – were celebrated (Beales 1967, 3), because being independent was more than just a label; it was heralded as the highest state of being for any true political representative. It implied that an MP could make a decision based on his or her own personal judgement, which would be free of pressure from any external influence such as parties or interest groups.

When parliamentarians lacked the resources to remain independent of external influences (most notably party influences), and once they realised the advantages of working in unison on a more permanent basis, the modern, disciplined political party was born. With an acceptance that they were not detrimental to society, parties had taken a stranglehold upon political power in all Western democracies by the end of the nineteenth century, resulting in the rapid decline of the independent politician. With the emergence of the complexities associated with modern government, it became an accepted premise that parliamentary democracy could not survive without parties. The esteem with which independents were held took a steep nosedive as a result; they were seen as irresponsible fence-sitters, who avoided making the key political decisions. They became equated with a similar type of fictional independents – 'the neutrals' in Dante's *Inferno*, who were the most hated creatures in hell because they refused to take a side in the battle between Lucifer and God (Alighieri 1996). It was only in candidate-centred systems that independents persisted, primarily in the Anglo-Saxon democracies. Even then, the vast majority attracted few votes and, as has been stated, independent electoral victories would become infrequent occurrences.

Today, an independent usually refers to someone who is neither a member of, nor affiliated to, any political party. However, this is not a sufficiently specific definition because there remains something intangible regarding the independence of such politicians (Ehin et al. 2013, 11). In many European countries, independents can run on lists and can form their own lists. There are also parties or movements of independents, and MPs who have been expelled from parties but have never contested an election as an independent. Aside from these institutional differences regarding the nature of independents, independence can also be thought of as a qualitative term that assesses the extent to which individual MPs follow the directives of an affiliate organisation, be it a political party or an interest group. For example, there are many cases in the US of party mavericks with their own personal machine who do and say what they want, largely independent of their party executive. These can be more independent in the qualitative sense than some independents nominated to run by interest groups, who may be little more than the latter's mouthpiece. For this reason, some party MPs resent the label adopted by independents because it implies that they are somehow more virtuous. In a Dáil debate in the 1960s over whether independents could describe themselves as such on the ballot, Fine Gael TD Anthony Barry said: 'the word independent always had for me a connotation of superiority which my experience of independents does not justify ... I do get tired occasionally of those who sit on the sideline with that smug superiority over those who have to sit behind or in the front bench and bear a party label' (Dáil debates 200: 484, 27 February 1963). This explains why, in 2005, one opposition party TD, Michael Ring of Fine Gael, felt compelled to declare himself the only true independent in the Dáil (at a time when there were fourteen independent TDs) (Dáil debates 602: 460, 11 May 2005). In the ideological sense, independent need not imply the holding of either a centrist or neutralist position; it simply means that an individual's political stance stems from his or her own original position – a position that was not forced on them by an external group, such as a political party. In light of the many potential difficulties that could arise when attempting to undertake a qualitative analysis of the independence of politicians, the working definition for this study is King-Hall's minimalist version: 'a person independent of the party machines' (1951, 54); that is, someone not affiliated with a political party. Marsh et al.'s study of Irish voters uses a similar classification, defining independents as 'simply electoral candidates who are not associated with any particular party' (2008, 49). This means that any candidates with an ambiguous party background are excluded from this study. Only those who do not maintain links to a party, and who contest elections on their own, are included. This excludes independents who are part of an electoral list, and whose nomination requires the endorsement of a political party. It is also worth noting that independence is not a permanent status. For some, it is akin to a form of limbo: a temporary position based on particular circumstances until they decide on the next stage of their respective political careers.

Why independents?

Independents are a relevant political actor in the Irish case. As well as maintaining continuous representation in the Irish parliament since the foundation of the state in 1922, they have also frequently held the balance of power in the Dáil, resulting in the political parties relying on the support of independents when attempting to form a government. This has motivated newspaper headlines such as:

> 'The future of the government is in the hands of six independents' (*Irish Times*, 4 June 1951).
>
> 'Independents and others to hold balance in Dáil' (*Irish Times*, 13 June 1981).
>
> 'Government falls as independents revolt against budget measures' (*Irish Times*, 28 January 1982).
>
> 'Haughey's [Taoiseach; prime minister] fate rests on Gregory [independent] vote' (*Irish Times*, 10 March 1987).
>
> 'The government … will remain in office only so long as it keeps independents happy' (*Irish Times*, 12 December 1998).
>
> 'Independent MPs to ensure victory for coalition in bailout vote' (*Irish Times*, 13 December 2010).
>
> 'Independents hold nation to €13bn ransom' (*Sunday Independent*, 17 April 2016).

Such influence exercised by independents has stimulated a lot of discussion about the democratic validity of the power that independents have been able to exert as 'kingmakers', especially in relation to their influence on distributive policy, as patronage tends to be the common currency used to buy their support (FitzGerald 2003, 63). Former Taoiseach Garret FitzGerald highlighted these concerns during the term of one such government (the 1997–2002 administration) reliant on the support of independents:

> The packages of special measures to benefit four constituencies represented by pro-government independents … demonstrate unequivocally the scale of the distortions in public policy priorities which now prevails … from the point of view of the common good of the state as a whole, the interests of which national parties are elected to serve, the consequences of this government dependence on independents have been deplorable. National resources, provided by the taxpayers of the state as a whole, have been deployed in a highly skewed manner without regard to any assessment of where needs are greatest (FitzGerald 2000).

In addition, independents' influential position is sometimes deemed to be detrimental to political stability, because their support 'may be delivered at a disproportionate price and even then may or may not be durable' (Sinnott 2010, 127). An example regularly cited of such instability in Ireland is the 1981–82 period, when there were two short-lived governments dependent on independents, both of which lasted less than ten months. Likewise, in Australia, in 1999 the ratings agency Moody's threatened to downgrade the credit rating of the state of Victoria when its premier, Steve Bracks, looked to form a government dependent on an alliance of independent MPs (Costar and Curtin 2004, 39). Such governments reliant on independents are deemed unstable because party discipline cannot be enforced on them, with the implication that the government could be defeated at any time. This in part explains why independents are portrayed as an atavistic form of representation, who can promote legislative gridlock, reduce accountability and generally lower interest in politics (Moser 1999; Reilly 2002; Sherrill 1998; Wright and Schaffner 2002).

While the merits of these arguments are discussed in more detail in Chapter 9, for now it should be noted that most scholars agree on the necessity of political parties. They claim that parties fulfil a number of important roles that independents cannot realise, including the aggregation of interests, the structuring of preferences, the provision of a 'brand name' to make the voting decision easier for voters, the provision of a linkage between the ruling and the ruled and the recruitment and socialisation of the political elite (Gallagher, Laver and Mair 2011, 327–8). Parties achieve these functions because they involve politicians coming together to offer common policy packages. In this way, parties structure the political world, which revolves around competition between the different packages on offer, and they make life easier for voters, who do not need take a position on every political issue but can instead go with that of their preferred party. If matters go awry, voters know which parties to hold accountable – unlike what might be the case in a parliament of independents, where it could be difficult to identify responsibility. Parties also structure the political world for the elites as they act as a form of training ground, recruiting people to political office and socialising them about how politics works. Aldrich (1995, 21–4) further claims that without parties, politicians would also not know what policies were preferred by voters as a whole, nor would they be able to achieve policy majorities. Parties thus solve the problems of how to make decisions for society and of collective action, because their offering of policy proposals enables them to determine the preferences of the electorate and the whip ensures they can get such policies implemented if they have the necessary majority. In this way, parties also help prevent the instability that can result from cyclical majority rule, whereby in the absence of a party whip binding parliamentarians collectively, governments might regularly form and fall (Aldrich 1995, 39–41; Brennan and Lomasky 1997, 81–6). The final problem identified by Aldrich that parties help resolve is that they facilitate politicians winning – in terms of achieving their policy preferences – more often. Referring to the classic case of the prisoner's dilemma, he shows how parliamentarians acting individually will achieve fewer of their interests than if they cooperate (Aldrich 1995, 29–37).

Parties are therefore a rational construct for politicians, voters and democracy. In their absence, it is claimed that an accountable, transparent and functioning political system would be almost impossible to achieve. This explains why a textbook on European politics states 'if there were no parties – in other words, if every member of parliament was an independent, with no institutionalised links with other members – the result would be something close to chaos' (Gallagher, Laver and Mair 2011, 327). The case of Papua New Guinea highlights what can happen when there are a large number of independents in a parliament. Since independence in 1975, Papua New Guinea has had an unstable political system, with no parliament lasting a full term and every government defeated by a no-confidence vote (Reilly 2002, 707). In part this was due to a considerable presence of independents, who won a plurality of seats at both the 1992 and 1997 general elections (Reilly 2002, 706). This eventually resulted in a reform of its political institutions in 2001, with one of the aims being to discourage independent candidacies. Similar fears about independents were echoed in the run-up to the February 2016 election in Ireland, when political parties and commentators queried how the parliament would function if a large number of independents were elected, as was being predicted by the opinion polls. This is why parties are the agents of democracy and why, when democratisation occurs, it usually takes place through their institutional injunction (Gallo 2004, 18).

Of course, most of the arguments made in defence of parties are to counter a hypothetical scenario in which parties are completely absent. The presence of independents does not necessarily imply the absence of parties. Consequently, while some of these points might not carry as much weight in a system where both parties and independents are present, they are still pretty relevant and have been frequently raised in the Irish case. Given all these claims concerning the necessity of political parties, and concerns about the dangers of independents for the health and vitality of a democracy, why then do they have an exceptional presence in the Irish political system? Answering this question is the focus of this study, but it is a question of relativity, as a claim to exceptionalism depends on the fate of independents elsewhere. The next section examines the international experience of independents as a prelude to a discussion of their fate in Ireland.

Independents – the comparative experience

The immediate post-World War II period saw the near extinction of the independent parliamentarian. With the consolidation of party systems, the opportunities for independents became extremely limited. Consequently, since 1950 there have been no independents elected to most European parliaments. Outside of Ireland and the UK, Jacob Haugaard in Denmark in 1994 is a rare exception of an elected independent MP in Western Europe. Even in the systems where independents could run, very few of them were elected. Of the Anglo-Saxon systems, Canada had the most independent MPs (twenty-three between 1950 and 2016), but almost all of them had first been elected for a party. Only one independent was elected between 1950 and 1990 to the Australian House of Representatives (Costar and Curtin 2004), three to the US House of Representatives, three to the British House of Commons and none in either New Zealand or Malta.

Things did change slightly in the 1990s, though, and since then independents, albeit only a handful, have been elected regularly in Australia, Canada, the US and the UK. Outside of the Irish case scrutinised in this study, Japan is the only other industrial democracy that has consistently had a regular cohort of independents elected to its national legislature. That most of them forgo this independence when in parliament is discussed in greater detail in Chapter 3. This emergence of independents may reflect a growing personalisation of politics, whereby individual actors become more important than parties or other such collective identities (Karvonen 2010). Personalisation can be reflected in voters basing their choices on a candidate rather than on a party; on politics being perceived as a competition between individuals rather than collective entities; in campaigns being centred on leaders and candidates instead of on parties; and on institutions stressing individuality over organisation (Karvonen 2010, 5).

At the same time as independents re-emerged in some Western democracies in the 1990s, so too they were elected in some post-communist states in central and eastern Europe. This was in part a reflection of newly emergent party systems looking to find their feet, and is a pattern typical of most transition democracies. It was also a product of considerable levels of anti-party sentiment following decades of one-party rule. There have been independents elected to the

Hungarian National Assembly, the Slovakian National Council (as part of the 'Ordinary People and Independent Personalities' list), the unicameral Seimas in Lithuania and Sabor in Croatia, the Russian Duma (Gallo 2004; Hale 2005; Moser 1999) and the Czech and Polish senates (Ehin et al. 2013). Independent candidates have also been elected to the European Parliament from Hungary, Romania and, in particular, Estonia, where Indrek Tarand was elected with 26 per cent of the national vote in 2009 and 13 per cent in 2014 (Ehin and Solvak 2012).

Success in such second-order elections is not unusual for independents. Independent presidents, mayors and governors are not uncommon. This prevalence at the lower levels of government happens for a number of reasons. The first is that there is no decision on the formation of a government at stake, and this usually acts as an impediment to independents. Second, incumbent parties and governments are more likely to be punished in these second-order elections. Third, because there is less at stake, parties devote fewer resources to their electoral campaigns. Fourth, there is an historical tradition of independent representation (although this is more of a product of party weakness than independent strength) at these lower levels, particularly in local government, where it is believed that parties are superfluous. As has been argued in the UK, 'there is no socialist or conservative way to dig a ditch' (Copus et al. 2012, 210). Likewise, although perhaps different to the traditional independent candidate standing on his or her own under candidate-centred electoral rules, local independent lists are present in a number of European countries (Åberg and Ahlberger 2013; Gendźwiłł 2012; Reiser and Holtmann 2008). These are nonpartisan lists of candidates who do not contest national elections and are not connected with a national party (Aars and Ringkjøb 2005, 215). Nonpartisan can have a wide meaning, varying from the absence of party on the ballot being a mere legal formality, to the absence of parties as institutions, with the degree of nonpartisanship depending on the context. For example, historically parties were absent in many local government jurisdictions, such as in parts of rural Scotland in the UK. In other arenas, such as some state and local government in the US, nonpartisan means that parties are not on the ballot and there are no caucuses in the legislative arena, but most politicians are publicly affiliated with parties. This type of nonpartisanship has a long history in the US (Adrian 1959; Wright 2008). Two states have had nonpartisan legislatures: Minnesota, between 1913 and 1974, and Nebraska, since 1935 (Berens 2005; Wright and Schaffner 2002), with nonpartisan elections more prevalent at the level of small cities (Olson 1965). Although not a direct example of such a nonpartisan regime, this type of politics can be traced back to the 'Era of

Good Feelings', a period in the early nineteenth-century US when party conflict was less to the fore. It was a short-lived era that coincided with James Monroe's presidency between 1817 and 1825 and the collapse of the Federalist party, although the extent of the actual harmony is questionable (Dangerfield 1952). The idea that parties can disrupt the nation echoes some of Madison's aforementioned writings against factions in *The Federalist* number ten, and was one of the factors motivating the absence of parties in the secessionist Confederate States (1861–65).

While few politicians in such nonpartisan regimes are independents in the sense defined in this study, there are a number of genuine nonpartisan systems where parties are absent. At the national level these comprise six small island states in the Pacific: Kiribati, Nauru, Tuvalu, the Marshall Islands, the Federated States of Micronesia and Palau. Although attempts have been made to form more concrete alliances and parties in some of the islands, they have never endured, and independence remains the primary form of representation (Anckar and Anckar 2000). 'Big man politics' predominates in these island states (Alasia 1984), where the political world is structured around significant individuals who have an ability to provide resources for their followers. This follows the logic of Aldrich, who stated that although democracy is unworkable without parties (1995, 3), there is no reason why politicians must turn to parties if it does not help them realise their goals (1995, 286). For example, Veenendaal (2013, 8) describes political life in Palau as one of 'attitudinal homogeneity, personalised politics … lack of ideologies and particularistic relations between politicians and citizens'. In such an environment, there is little need for clans or political leaders to form parties.

Some territorial governments, also small islands, have no parties. These include American Samoa, Guernsey and the Falkland Islands. In addition, parties have only recently made a breakthrough in the Isle of Man and in Jersey, where the legislatures have always been dominated by independents. Two other prominent examples of nonpartisan regimes are the Canadian territories of Nunavut and the Northwest Territories, both of which are 'consensus' democracies. Apart from a short period of party rule at the turn of the twentieth century (G. White 1991, 2006), nonpartisan politics has been to the fore in these regions, without the need for parties. What these jurisdictions have in common with the aforementioned Pacific islands is that they are small in size and have a cultural resistance to parties. Smallness contributes to a high element of personalism, lessens the significance of ideology and is associated with attitudinal homogeneity (Veenendaal 2013, 2). This results in few political divisions, meaning that parties are not needed.

Smallness also results in closer links between representatives and citizens, again lessening the necessity for parties. The cultural resistance to parties can stem from an opposition to the conflict associated with the latter, which explains the consensus system in the two Canadian territories. Although the latter are not small geographically, they too have a small population, a combined total of just over 80,000. The third factor given for the absence of parties in some parts of the Pacific is archipelagic geography, in that many of the states comprise groupings of scattered islands, making it more difficult for parties as unitary organisations to mobilise (Anckar and Anckar 2000).

There is a range of other political bodies where independents have been prevalent; many of these are at the level of local government, as has been discussed. Some are unelected, such as the British House of Lords, which possibly has more independents than any other parliament in the world (Russell and Sciara 2009, 40). Others have questionable democratic credentials, such as the Russian Duma (Hale 2005), or are in developing countries, such as Uganda, where political party activity in the National Assembly was banned between 1986 and 2005 (Carbone 2003). Ireland is the only mature party democracy where genuine independents have had a constant presence and a considerable influence at the national level.

Independents in Ireland: a background

As is evident, independents have a mixed international experience. They are absent in the national parliaments of most industrial democracies, but they are present elsewhere – including in newly emergent independent states, at the regional level, or in very small jurisdictions. What this suggests is that independents may be associated with certain stages of development. Where party systems have not been fully established, we may expect to see some independents, as in some central and east European states in the early 1990s, or in some Pacific island states. In addition, because party systems sometimes do not permeate down to subnational levels of government, we might also expect to see independents present in such bodies as local councils. This comparative experience of independents makes their presence in Ireland all the more curious. It is one of the oldest surviving democracies in the world, has a mature and enduring party system, and yet independents have been a persistent presence in the national parliament. This is discussed in more detail in Chapter 3 but, before doing so, what is implied by the term 'independent' in Ireland needs to be clarified. As already discussed, its meaning can vary across culture and contexts, being very much dependent on what is meant by a 'party'. Defining an independent in the Irish sense is a starting point to an understanding of the presence of this phenomenon.

The working definition of an independent already outlined – as a politician independent of a party machine – is not a specific enough a guideline. As Chubb (1957, 131) acknowledges, an independent 'does not necessarily call himself an "independent". He may not be a "true" or "pure" independent who fights his own election battle ... (he may) belong from time to time to a party ... (he may) be a virtual camp-follower of one of the parties.' Because some independents run under self-adopted 'party' names, defining an independent does not simply involve identifying all those who run under the 'independent' brand. Candidates running under minor party labels could also be categorised as independents if it is the case that these minor parties are little more than the personalised political machines of individual candidates. To resolve this issue, Chubb (1957, 132) defines an independent based on two characteristics: (1) the candidate does not have the resources of a party behind them at election time; and (2) the candidate does not take a party whip in the Dáil.

Since most independent candidates are not elected, the lack of a party whip is not all that significant a criterion as the issue does not arise for them. The key component in defining an independent is whether or not they are standing for a party. It is therefore how a party is defined which determines how an independent is defined. While it is relatively straightforward to differentiate between a major party and an independent, this is not the case with minor parties. Pedersen (1982, 5) defined a minor party as 'an organisation – however loosely or strongly organised – which either presents or nominates candidates for public elections, or which, at least, has the declared intention to do so'. However, as is detailed in Chapter 2, there are a lot of examples of independent candidates standing for election who are nominated by organisations, such as farmers' bodies and religious associations, who would all be classified as minor parties according to Pedersen's defini-tion. This has been a source of conflict in the literature when it comes to defining independents because it is not always clear how to distinguish a minor party from a grouping of independents (Coakley 2012, 46–50). Consequently, tables of votes and seats for independents differ across various sources, as there is no agreed definition of an independent. As Sinnott (1995, 64) notes, 'the category of "independents" is a residual and shifting one, its size depending on how much substance one attrib-utes to ephemeral party labels'.

To clarify what constitutes a minor party, the legal definition of a party can be used. However, up until the 1963 Electoral Act, there was no official registry of parties and party affiliations were not stated on ballots. Where minor party organisations existed before 1963, it is often a subjective decision to categorise these as genuine parties or to see them merely as the personal organisations of independents. There are many examples of candidates with a well-mobilised organisation naming their groups as parties, even though they were, to all intents and purposes, independents.

Even the state registry of parties does not wholly clarify matters. Any group seeking to qualify must have 300 recorded members or at least one TD or three local authority members. It must also have a written constitution and an annual conference of the party. Consequently, should any independent win a seat in the Dáil, all he or she needs to do to form a party is draw up a list of rules and hold a meeting once a year. For example, Neil Blaney's personal political machine, Independent Fianna Fáil, qualified as a minor party after he was expelled from Fianna Fáil in 1972; yet he is still treated as an independent for the purposes of this study. Ultimately, there is no foolproof means of defining a minor party or an independent, but the method used here is to apply a set of criteria as to what defines a party to all of the micro-parties that contested Dáil elections. Any candidate standing for such a group that does not meet these criteria is categorised in this study as an independent. This approach clarifies exactly what an independent is: a non-party. More details of this method and the classification of micro-parties are provided in Chapter 2.

Having defined an independent, who are the individuals of note who wore this label in Irish politics? They include Alfie Byrne, who was elected to the British House of Commons, Dublin Corporation, the Dáil, the Seanad and the mayoralty of Dublin. They also include the likes of Barbara Hyland, who was a single-issue candidate who ran for the National League Justice Action Group in five general elections between 1987 and 2002. In 1987, she ran in thirteen constituencies, but her highest first-preference vote was 217 (less than half of 1 per cent). The case of Hyland is highlighted because no-hope independent candidates run in many countries, but very few Alfie Byrnes are elected.

Independent politicians are an eclectic bunch, with candidates elected under this label in Ireland ranging from former government ministers and grand masters of the Orange Order to bonesetters. Although independents represent for some people the corollary of the sheer localism inherent in Irish politics, their ranks also include the likes of James Dillon, who represented two counties – Donegal and Monaghan – neither of which he actually ever lived in. To some, independents are the corollary of clientelism, but also they include the likes of Tom Burke, a bonesetter from county Clare who refused to engage in parish-pump politics to the extent that he never sought to get the local council (on which he sat for forty years) to repair the road to his house – even though patrons of his services regularly had to have their cars towed from it, so bad was its surface (White 2009b). Although, to some people, independents represent the populist 'clever man who cries the catch-cry of the clown' ('The Fisherman'; Yeats 1990, 197), they also include individuals such as Jim Kemmy, who preached anti-nationalism, anti-clericalism and socialism at a time when to do so was not electorally beneficial. To others, independents are the product of a preferential voting system that allows fence-sitters to scrape home with the last seat, but they also include Alfie Byrne and Oliver J. Flanagan, who got more first preferences than anyone else in the country in the 1932 and 1948 Dáil elections, respectively.

These 'non-party' candidates are an amorphous collection, which is classified under the generic title of 'independents'. To date, there has been little analysis of their common characteristics. One common thread is that many of them have had a prior affiliation to a political party. Forty-nine of the seventy-two individual independent TDs elected between 1948 and 2016 had a party background, having in the past been either a prominent advocate of a particular party or an official party candidate. This does not necessarily lessen their independence, nor the merits of studying them, because they were all elected as independents in their own right. Unlike in other jurisdictions, where some independents maintain an affiliation with a party, this is not possible in Ireland, where parties do not sponsor independent candidates at Dáil elections. It is also very rare that an independent TD rejoins a party – only three of the sixty-four independent TDs in the history of the Irish state who came from parties have done so. Despite their party political past, all independent TDs (and indeed all independent candidates) are what have been described in other jurisdictions as 'pure' (Hijino 2013, 71) or 'true' (Nicolson 1946) independents – they are standing on their own, independent of political parties.

Independents have been successful in all types of elections in Ireland. As is detailed in Chapter 3, there have been considerable numbers of them elected to local government – both city and county councils. Independents, who almost exclusively represent the universities, have also been a fixture in the Seanad. Considerably more independents were elected to the Free State Senate (1922–36), which was directly elected, and which worked almost entirely on a non-party basis for the first six years of its existence (O'Sullivan 1940, 266). Independents getting elected to local bodies and to university seats is not an unusual comparative occurrence, however, and so they are not the primary focus of this study. It is their continuous presence at the national level, in the Dáil, which is almost exceptional and which warrants analysis.

Why are there independents in Ireland?

Given their failure to challenge parties in most jurisdictions, it is not surprising that the comparative literature on independents is rather limited. It tends to comprise case studies from the US (Avlon 2004; Collet 1999; Owen and Dennis 1996; Sifry 2003), Russia (Gallo 2004; Hale 2005; Moser 1999), the UK (Berry 2008; Cowley and Stuart 2009; Russell and Sciara 2009), Japan (Hijino 2013), and, particularly, Australia (Bean and Papadakis 1995; Costar and Curtin 2004; Papadakis and Bean 1995; Rodrigues and Brenton 2010; Sharman 2002; Singleton 1996; Smith 2006). There has also been some research on independents in local government (Aars and Ringkjøb 2005; Bottom and Copus 2011; Copus et al. 2009; Junzhi 2010; Kukovic and Hacek 2011; Reiser and Holtmann 2008) and in European Parliament elections (Ehin and Solvak 2012). Cross-country studies even in these areas are few, however, although they include an analysis of the effect of electoral systems on independents in thirty-four countries (Brancati 2008), in Australia and Ireland (Weeks 2014), in three African polities (Ishiyama, Batta and Sortor 2013), and a comparative examination of independents in Europe as a whole (Ehin et al. 2013).

Most of the research on independents in Ireland has been conducted by this author (Bolleyer and Weeks 2009; Weeks 2008a, 2009, 2011, 2014, 2016), prior to which the main study in this area was an overview of independents by Chubb (1957) in the 1950s. There are occasional references to them in various texts on Irish elections, but these are generally in basic agreement on the factors that explain the significance of independents. These include the presence of a personalistic and localistic political culture working in tandem with a candidate-centred electoral system (Busteed 1990, 40–1; Carty 1981, 58–61; Weeks 2010b, 146–7). Other factors cited include the relatively low number of votes needed to win a seat to the Dáil, and the benefits that independents can deliver for their constituencies when they hold the balance of power in parliament. There is little need to discuss these further here as they are covered in greater detail throughout this study.

In the national parliaments of most democracies there is very little life outside party politics. A brief overview of the 106 directly elected legislatures in the 89 free democracies in 2011 found that – excluding the 6 Pacific island states, where there are no parties – there are no

2

A typology of independents

Introduction

The difficulty in identifying the type of political actor with which this study is concerned was alluded to in the introductory chapter. The term 'independent' can be used loosely in public and media references, and is sometimes taken to include solitary representatives of parties in parliament or members of small parties. Others bemoan the use of this label for parliamentarians who align with a political party, who may have their origins in the said party and still vote for them in parliament. Some critics of independents seem to be of the opinion that the latter should almost be neutral or non-aligned, and thus do not see those who pursue a political ideology as genuinely independent. So, in some ways, the use of the term independent is a bit misleading, since it implies that they are a unitary grouping, almost akin to a party. It is misleading because, by definition, a party is exactly what independents are not. In most countries independents comprise a generally heterogenous bunch of candidates, almost a residual group of those who do not fit into parties or a party system. Consequently, there can be considerable differences between these candidates, in terms of their socio-economic background, their ideology and their political motivations. In fact, there may be as much difference between individual independents, if not more, than there is between political parties. For this reason, when we refer to independents, there is not really a typical independent to speak of. Their one common characteristic is that they are not parties, but beyond this it is difficult to define what exactly constitutes the average independent politician. There are, and have been, different types of independents, and providing a systematic classification of them is the aim of this chapter.

In the Irish case, the level of heterogeneity between independents has varied. In the early decades of the state, independents in parliament were a relatively homogeneous group. Most of them came from a conservative, constitutional stock, and were anti-Fianna Fáil. They were also referred to in the Dáil as the 'Independent party', and reaped the benefits of such a status, having a party room in parliament buildings and being allocated places on parliamentary committees in accordance with their collective strength (Chubb 1957, 137). A similar independent group prevailed in the Free State Senate before the abolishment of the latter in 1936. However, this homogeneity did not last, as more diverse independents emerged, acknowledged by independent TD Frank Sherwin in the Dáil in 1963: 'There is the difference between chalk and cheese between independents. There are independent ratepayers, independent tenants' representatives. They may be out for each other's blood' (Dáil debates 201: 522, 27 March 1963). In spite of this, independents are still spoken of in the collective sense, an erroneous reference because, by their very nature, they are not collective, but rather individual, units. In part this is done for reasons of convenience, but it also reflects a lack of knowledge about independents and an attitude that treats them as outliers, as political cranks outside of the establishment. Their being individual units has not prevented independents from working together, however, as has been evident in alliances and electoral lists in some European polities, and also in technical groups and other arrangements in Ireland, including a number of alliances of independents that emerged around the 2016 Dáil election.

So, what exactly does 'independent' mean? Notwithstanding the aforementioned arrangements, the independent label is not very revealing. It does not illuminate the policies, organisation or ideologies of the candidates wearing such political attire. It is a catch-all uniform that indicates little else other than that the wearer does not belong to a political party (and even then this may not be wholly accurate), which is the definition applied in Chapter 1. A deeper analysis of the individuals who choose to wear this label is necessary in order to understand the meaning of 'independence'. To do so, this chapter constructs a typology of independents that examines their nature, the support they attract and their electoral fate. Going back to the first elections in post-independence Ireland in 1922, what follows is an analysis of how independents have evolved and who they have represented. This is necessary because, lacking a specific brand, the support they attract can be quite contextual, and can be dependent on the ideological nature of the independent. For example, as is detailed later in this chapter, independents in the border region of Donegal attracted a protestant vote until the 1950s, but from the 1970s to the 1990s they attracted a nationalist, republican vote. This was not because of a sudden change in the ideological orientation of independent voters, but was due to a change in the type of independent candidate.

There are a range of different categories of independents, across both geography and time. However, this does not mean they are an unclassifiable phenomenon. Independents can be analysed in much the same way parties are grouped by family, organisation, structure or ideology. This facilitates placing an apparently deviant phenomenon into a comparative context. In addition, constructing a taxonomy helps focus attention on what explains the presence of independents, reduces complexity and allows for more comparison and differentiation between cases (Bailey 1994, 12–14). The structure of this chapter is as follows. First, the working definition of an independent is clarified, in particular how they differ from micro-parties. A taxonomy is constructed, which identifies six clear families of independents and six further sub-categories. Details of their electoral performance back to 1922 are provided, before each family and category is examined in depth, using examples of each type of independent. Aside from the intrinsic value of this classification, the other aim of this chapter is to indicate the Downsian (1957), or rational, fashion by which independents represent issues and social groups not catered for by the political parties. This concerns the first hypothesis of this study – that the presence of independents is positively related to the openness of the party system. If a gap emerges in the party system, independents can easily move to fill it, in a way that parties cannot because it may lose the established parties face or votes and because of the logistics and time involved in setting up a new party to cater for such an issue. An independent campaign can be launched overnight, and indeed whenever a controversial issue crops up in a constituency that the parties have not resolved, one of the first threats heard from local interest groups is to run as an independent at the next election to challenge the parties. There is not a wide range of flavours in the Irish party system, with most parties converging on the median, or middle, voter. This regularly leaves a number of vacancies for independents to occupy, and is one of the contributory factors to their significant presence in the Irish political system.

What is an independent?

The first step in the construction of a typology of independents involves distinguishing independents from minor parties. As outlined at the beginning of this study, the working definition of an independent is that used by the electoral authorities: a non-party (or at least, non-registered party) candidate. For the period prior to 1963 in Ireland (when there was no state registry of parties), the task of identifying independents is a bit more difficult, as some such candidates did not need to necessarily call themselves an independent, running instead under a party label (Chubb 1957, 132). Defining an independent under such circumstances requires a clarification of what an independent is not; that is, a party. LaPalombara and Weiner's (1966, 6) definition of a party is used here, which identifies six key characteristics such an organisation must exhibit. They must:

- demonstrate continuity in organisation, where the life of the party is not dependent on the political life of the leader
- have a 'manifest and ... permanent organisation at the local level'
- have an aspiration to attain power in office
- have an explicit desire for votes
- not be a personalised machine of a dominant individual in the group
- run more than one candidate (unless this candidate is not the party leader).

Based on the assumption that all parties outside of the established trio of Fianna Fáil, Fine Gael and Labour are minor parties (Weeks and Clark, 2012), a qualitative analysis of all such parties that contested general elections before 1963 is employed; the candidates of any group that do not possess all of the above six characteristics are treated as independents. The data used for this classification stemmed from an analysis of contemporary newspapers and some secondary literature, in particular Coakley (2012a); where conflict arises concerning the 'independent' nature of a candidacy, the more commonly cited description is used. Based on these criteria, the following groups do not qualify as parties, and their candidates are included as independents at elections listed. They are categorised based on their missing features:

1. The following organisations are simply ad hoc electoral machines of interest groups, and cannot be defined as parties:
   Ratepayers' Association (1922–23, 1957)
   Town Tenants' Association (1923–September 1927)
   City Workers' Housing Association (1923) (it also ran only one candidate)
   Workers' Farming Association (1923) (it also ran only one candidate)
   Unpurchased Tenants' Association (1923) (it also ran only one candidate)
   Evicted Tenants' Association (1923) (it also ran only one candidate)
   Blind Men's Party (June 1927)
   Irish Women's Citizens' Association (June 1927) (it also ran only one candidate)

    Cine Gael (1954) (it also ran only one candidate)

    Irish Housewives' Association (1957).

2. The following groups were little more than the personalised machine of an individual who was the group's sole candidate:

    Irish Workers' League (1951–54, 1961)

    National Action (1954).

3. Although these groups ran several candidates, they cannot be included as parties since the contemporary newspapers described them as independent business or 'commercial' candidates (see, for example, *Irish Times*, 18 June 1922, and other dates), with most of these candidates, especially in Cork, conducting independent campaigns:

    Business and Professional Group (1922)

    Cork Progressive Association (1923).

4. Although these groups may have run more than one candidate, they were little more than the personalised machines of a dominant individual that wound up on his departure from the association:

    'Irish Worker' League (September 1927–32)

    Monetary Reform (1943–48)

    Christian Democratic Party (1961) (it also ran only one candidate).

5. These groups exist post-1963 but were not registered as political parties for Dáil elections, and all their candidates had a blank or non-party affiliation on the ballot:

    Christian Democratic Party (1965–73)

    Women's Progressive Association (1973; Feb. 1982)

    Irish Republican Socialist Party (Feb. 1982)

    Sinn Féin (Feb. 1982)

    Ecology Party (Nov. 1982)

    National League Justice Action Group (1987)

    Tax Reform League (1987)

    Army Wives' Association (1989)

    Transcendental Meditation (1992)

    Natural Law Party (1992)

    Donegal Progressive Party (1992–97)

    Immigration Control Platform (1997–2011)

    Fathers' Rights Responsibility Party (2007)

    People Before Profit Alliance (2007)

    Workers' Unemployed Action Group (2002–16)

    United Left Alliance (2011)

    New Vision (2011)

    Fís Nua (2011)

    People's Convention (2011)

Irish Democratic Party (2016)
Identity Ireland (2016)
Independent Alliance (2016).

Categorisation of independents

The difficulty in providing a typology of independents has been noted, with claims ranging from 'classifying deputies as independents is not always easy' (Coakley 2003, 515) to 'independents are by definition almost impossible to categorise' (Busteed 1990, 40). Despite the considerable number of independents in Australia, there is no known typology of them; in Japan, Hijino (2013, 71–2) identifies two categories at local municipal level – pure independents and those with an affiliation to a party; the latter group he subdivides into five types based on their motives for avoiding a partisan label. In New Zealand, in the early twentieth century, there were 'simple independents', who had no coherent or comprehensive ideology; ideological independents; 'wrecking independents', who wanted to put a spanner in the works of a major party; interest group independents and tactical independents (Milne 1966, 73–5). Nicolson (1946) identified five types of independents in the UK: fortuitously independent (those elected when there is a party truce); academic independent (representing university seats); temperamental independent (who flitted in and out of parties); forlorn independent (remnants of defunct parties) and true independents (those standing on their own). A more recent categorisation of independent councillors in England identified three types of independents involved in local politics: the 'fully independent', who has no organisation behind him or her; the 'revealed-party independent' who uses a party label in the title of his or her candidacy and the 'conjoined independent', who belongs to a loose alliance of independents (Copus, Clark and Bottom 2008).

In the Irish context, it is impossible to achieve universal agreement for a categorisation of over 1,100 Dáil candidates, but what can be done is to employ an objective and replicable method. To satisfy these criteria, a combined conceptual/empirical taxonomy is employed (Bailey 1994, 31–2, 79), which utilises both inductive and deductive logic. It is conceptual in that some of the taxa were constructed a priori – before the data were analysed to check for their existence; it is empirical in that many of the independents were only classifed a posteriori – once the data were gathered, following which more categories were added to the taxonomy. The conceptual classification was aided by occasional references in the literature to a number of different types of independents; these include independent farmers, business candidates, party

South in 1910, Cooper was also (1912–14) honorary secretary of the Irish Unionist Alliance (Maume 2009a). His experiences in World War I significantly mellowed his unionism (Robinson 1931, 110), and during the war of independence Cooper encouraged a rapprochement with Sinn Féin. Following partition, he adopted a constructive attitude towards the new state and was elected to the Dáil in 1923, where he became the unofficial leader of the business and unionist independents (Maume 2009a). Held in high regard by his fellow TDs, one government minister labelled him his 'moderator of undue rigidity' (M. Kelly 2006). Cooper urged southern unionists to take part in the political process lest their interests be ignored in the new government (he himself joined Cumann na nGaedheal in 1927).

The number of independent unionists contesting Dáil elections was ten in 1923, and held at a figure between seven and nine until 1937. During this period, they won on average over 29,000 votes, attracting 27 per cent of the overall independent vote. A significant decline began in 1937, from which point on no more than three independent unionists ran at one election. Their vote followed suit, averaging just over 14,000 first preferences from 1938 until 1961. One reason accounting for the decline in candidates was the transferral, under the 1937 constitution, of the three University of Dublin (Trinity College) seats (which were always filled by independent unionists) to the Seanad. The decline in the vote is best explained by the dwindling protestant population, who transferred their allegiance to Cumann na nGaedheal (King 2000, 89), which attracted two independent unionist TDs into its ranks in 1927 and 1937.

These trends differed in the border counties, where there remained a social and cultural divide between the catholic and protestant communities. Indeed, from 1937 on, all the independent unionist candidates (bar two minor figures in the 1980s) were from the three border counties, each of which was represented by a prominent unionist until the late 1950s (primarily the aforementioned independent unionist and farmer candidates). Chubb put this persistence down to a different social make-up in the region, claiming 'a class of small, conservative, highly independent farmers (some of them protestant) dominates and the parties have never satisfied or attracted the support of some of its members' (1957, 136). The independent status of border protestants was confirmed by the findings of other research of a 'consistently strong relationship' between support for independents and the number of non-catholics in an area from 1927 to 1957 (Gallagher 1976, 59; King 2000, 90; Sacks 1976, 153–60). Independent unionist candidates at Dáil elections pretty much disappeared in the 1960s. Both Gallagher (1976,

62) and Sacks (1976, 53–4) claim that an important factor was the 1961 Electoral (Amendment) Act, which saw Cavan and Donegal East, independent unionists' strongest areas of support, each losing a seat. The increase in the electoral quota severely dented independent unionists' chances of election, since they needed to attract a wider vote from beyond the protestant community – something a unionist candidate would find difficult in a nationalist-dominated political system. A mild reprieve was offered to the protestant community by the appointment of John Copeland Cole and William Sheldon (in 1961 and 1965) to the Seanad. Most of these independents' former supporters drifted to Fine Gael (Gallagher 1976, 62–3), which sometimes appeared more sympathetic to protestants, and was not as overtly nationalist as Fianna Fáil (and indeed selected protestant candidates to attract such support). Protestant representation did not completely vanish, however, and continued primarily at the local government level, particularly in the form of quasi-parties. These included the Monaghan Protestant Association and the Donegal Progressive Party, both of which won seats on local councils up until the 1990s.

Corporatist independents

There have been two types of corporatist independents: independent business candidates and independent farmers. The term 'corporatist' is used because these independents are representative of professional and industrial sectors, with the aim of exercising influence over the political system.

Independent business

Described as the 'urban counterpart' of the independent farmer (Chubb 1957, 135), independent business candidates were predominantly concerned about the future of the economy in the immediate post-independence era in the 1920s. This title is adopted because it was the label these independents used to identify themselves during their respective election campaigns. Some business candidates also called themselves 'independent progressives' and are included within this family, as are those who ran under quasi-party business labels, including the Cork Progressive Association (a grouping of professionals and businessmen mobilised to promote industry in the Cork region) and the Business and Professional Group. Because these independents were primarily wealthy businessmen (they include Richard Beamish, chairman of the Beamish brewery; James Xavier Murphy, former governor of the Bank of Ireland; and Andrew O'Shaughnessy, a prominent wool manufacturer) dependent on foreign trade, and because many of them hailed from ex-unionist stock (Chubb 1957, 135), they openly supported Cumann na nGaedheal in government (both TDs elected under the Cork Progressive Association mantle took the Cumann na nGaedheal whip in 1924 (Regan 1999, 223)). Sometimes these independents formed a micro-party, an example being the Business Men's Party formed for the 1923 election by the Dublin Chamber of Commerce; but more generally they tended to run individual campaigns as independents.

Despite their ideological disposition, these candidates were keen to stress that they were above the squabbles of partisan politics. At the 1923 election they took out a front page advertisement in the *Irish Times* that read 'We stand by the Treaty but do not seek office. We want to be there to help the government of the country' (*Irish Times*, 25 August 1923). Likewise, those involved in the Progressive Association claimed 'they were not politicians', and that they 'had no desire to enter into useless discussion of the pros and cons of the differences between those who should be working together for the benefit of the country' (*Irish Times*, 10 September 1927). Standing as an independent constitutionalist (Coleman 2009a), one of Xavier Murphy's campaign slogans in 1927 was, 'Drop Politics for a while and get on with the work' (*Irish Times*, 10 September 1927). He claimed that he was not campaigning against the government, but that he could be a valuable addition to the Dáil with his business experience. Murphy's election was described by the *Irish Times* as 'one of the few encouraging features' of the September 1927 poll (Coleman 2009a). After serving one term, Murphy's local electorate in the Dublin County constituency thought otherwise, as in 1932 his first-preference vote fell by almost 50 per cent, losing Murphy his seat. The Dublin County voters were not deprived an independent business representative, however, as John P. Good held his seat at the same election – first won for the aforementioned Business Men's Party in 1923, and held as an independent at four subsequent elections until his retirement in 1937. Good had previously run for the Unionist Party in the Dublin Pembroke constituency in 1918, highlighting the pro-union leanings of this type of independent.

While the altruism of the independent business candidates might be questionable, in the 1920s there were justified fears over how a group of former revolutionaries, with little or no political experience, would be able to properly manage the finances of a fledgling state. As a result, the *Irish Times* (whose unionist leaning may be another factor why it supported these candidates) strongly encouraged voters to back the business candidates to bring some much-needed expertise into the Dáil, noting that: 'The constructive criticism of the independent members, who include men of great experience not only in parliamentary, but also in financial and economic affairs, will be of much assistance to Ministers' (*Irish Times*, 1 September 1923). In a separate editorial, it was claimed:

> These business men appeal neither to passion nor to prejudice ... their chief appeal is to the increasing number of thoughtful Irishmen who prefer an ounce of industry to a pound of eloquence. If the business candidates are elected – and many of the other independent candidates are well qualified to help them – they will devote themselves to the task of enforcing economy and clear thinking in every department of national affairs. (*Irish Times*, 8 August 1923).

Again in September 1927, the newspaper urged the 'educated electorate ... not [to] overlook the special claims of Mr. John Good and of that new and excellent candidate, Mr. Joseph X. Murphy' (*Irish Times*, 15 September 1927).

However, once it was clear that neither the country nor the economy were going to collapse in ruin, and once the business candidates' dreams of non-partisan, meritocratic political competition were well and truly shattered by the 1930s, these independents flitted out of the political scene, with most of their supporters drifting to Cumann na nGaedheal. Apart from the apostate independent, William Dwyer, in the 1940s, this type of candidate did not re-appear. These independent business candidates were an ad hoc interest group who might have prospered had political competition taken on a vocational pattern, which some feared might be a product of the newly adopted STV electoral system.[1]

Independent farmers
Despite the importance of agriculture in Ireland, there has never been a major farmers' party representing all agricultural interests (Varley 2010). Instead, various short-lived organisations have appeared on behalf of sectional farming interests, and while they have sometimes formed parties, such as the Farmers' Party in 1922, these were often little more than loose collections of independent farmers, selected by separate farmers' unions, but united in an ad hoc electoral group to maximise their profile (Manning 1972 passim.).

Independent farming candidates were usually selected at conventions organised by local farmers' unions; for example, in 1954 the Cork County Farmers' Association ran a candidate in each of the four rural Cork constituencies. At times there was no clear line of demarcation between independent farmers and farmers' parties' candidates, in part because of the loose structure of the latter organisations. For example, some TDs (including William Sheldon in Donegal and Denis Heskin in Waterford) included as part of Clann na Talmhan's (a farmer's party) parliamentary numbers in the 1940s acted as, and called themselves, independents (Ó Fathartaigh 2001). Another group, the National Farmers' and RatePayers' League of the 1930s, has been described as little more than 'a loose federation of independent deputies' (Sinnott 1995, 61). This ambiguity has created some confusion in the literature, so all candidates using the label 'independent farmers' at some stage in their campaign are included.[2] By implication this also includes representatives of farming associations, such as Frank MacDermot, who won a seat for the National Farmers' and Ratepayers' League in 1932 despite a limited knowledge of farming (which earned him the nickname 'the Paris farmer') (Manning 1999, 61).

A particularly prominent example of an independent farmer was Thomas Burke from Clare (L. W. White 2009b). First elected to the Dáil for the Clare Farmers' Party (a local interest group) in 1937, he went independent in 1943 after the organisation was subsumed into Clann na Talmhan, and retained his seat at three further elections. Similar to other farming candidates, Burke proclaimed himself as 'non-political', and eked out a personal following based on his renown as a bonesetter (an occupation which he described as his party affiliation, a reminder to his electorate to compensate him with a vote for the free service he provided mending bones). Burke's non-political stance was evident in his lack of participation in parliament. Having spoken on six different days in the Dáil in the first two years of his parliamentary career, he uttered not another word in the remaining twelve, eight of which he served as an independent. In those eight years he cast just one vote, for the nomination of his constituency colleague, Éamon de Valera, as Taoiseach in 1948.

Independent farmers were not a cohesive bunch, as they represented a diversity of interests within the agrarian community. In addition to the 'independent unionists and farmers' from the border counties (included in the category of independent unionists), there existed 'protectionist farmer' candidates in the 1920s, who were nominated by unions of small farmers to campaign for tariffs to protect Irish farmers from cheaper foreign imports. Besides these independents, larger farmers, who favoured free trade policies, were also represented by independent farmer candidates (as well as by Fine Gael and its precursor (Gallagher and Marsh 2002, 62, 70)), especially in the 1920s, when they united to form the pro-government Farmers' Party.

Farmers, particularly those with small holdings, turned towards these candidates because of 'a deep sense of betrayal' (Varley 1996,

591), a sentiment directed at the civil war parties (particularly Fianna Fáil), who they blamed for not arresting the declining economic fortunes of the agricultural sector in post-independence Ireland. Following a pronounced shift in government policy in the late 1950s, with a focus on industrial expansion and foreign direct investment, the importance of agriculture to both the Irish economy and society steadily declined. This trend, combined with the rise to prominence of a powerful farmers' interest group (the Irish Farmers' Association), meant the support, and the need, for independent farmers waned. While they regularly gained between one-quarter and one-third of the independent vote from the 1920s to the 1960s, since the latter period independent farmers have been virtually non-existent as electoral competitors – with one sole exception, T. J. Maher, who was also elected to the European Parliament in 1979.

Ideological independents

These independents are labelled 'ideological' because they are very much policy-oriented candidates, whose main aim in running for office is to achieve, or at least to highlight, particular policy goals.

Left-wing independents

Left-wing independents are defined as those whose policy platforms adopt a classically left-wing position. This includes favouring greater redistribution of wealth via an equitable taxation system, nationalisation of important industries, and generally high levels of state intervention in society, including increased expenditure on services by the government. This category includes former members of left-wing parties who are no longer classified as apostate independents, those who ran on behalf of a left-wing movement, those who ran on an 'independent Labour' ticket (but not including those who had run for Labour at a preceding election) and those who ran on an openly socialist ticket. Although such candidates do not necessarily run under a 'left-wing independent' label, their ideological stance is a defining feature of their political life and they usually identify with left-wing parties, either by working in cooperation with them or by joining them at some stage in their political career. An archetypal example of this category of independent is Tony Gregory, a self-defined republican socialist who represented a disadvantaged area in Dublin's inner city from the 1970s until his death in 2009 (Gilligan 2012; Hanley 2014). At separate times a member of three far-left parties, Official Sinn Féin, the Irish Republican Socialist Party and the Socialist Labour Party, Gregory was also active in a community organisation, the North Central Community

Council (C. Curtin and Varley 1995, 397–9). First elected to the Dáil in 1982, Gregory's left-wing orientation was obvious from the outset; he himself confirmed: 'I think it is fairly clear that my vote is the left-wing vote' (*Irish Times*, 19 February 1987). It was also evident in his numerous failed attempts to form a left alliance with other independents and parties in the Dáil, and in his antipathy to the centre-right parties that dominated Irish politics. Some of Gregory's left-wing agenda was reflected in the particulars of the eponymous deal he negotiated in 1982 with Charles Haughey (leader of Fianna Fáil) in return for his supporting Haughey's nomination as Taoiseach. These included public authority housing, the nationalisation of a large paper mill and measures to tackle unemployment (see Chapter 7 for more details) (Gilligan 2012, 196–223).

In the early decades of the state, most left-wing independents were Labour Party members who disagreed with the party's non-confrontational conservative approach in the Dáil arena, or campaigners for interest groups – such as the Town Tenants' Association. Consequently, the presence of left-wing independents appears correlated to the level of harmony within the Labour Party, the latter of which was continually open to divisions. Many of these were the product of personality clashes between left-wing leaders, whether between Jim Larkin and William O'Brien from the 1920s to the 1940s, or Noël Browne and Brendan Corish in the 1970s. A row over coalition strategy in the 1970s produced another batch of Labour dissidents, but the main change in left-wing candidates came that same decade with the emergence of a new type of left-wing independent – that of a socialist community candidate. These independents were often nominated by local community action groups, and tended to focus their campaign on social issues, Gregory and his North Central Community Council being an example (C. Curtin and Varley 1995, 397–9). One reason accounting for the presence of these independents may be the waning of a conservative political culture, which led to the emergence of what Garvin calls a 'new left' in the 1980s (1987, 4), that included a new urban intellectual Labour Party, a Marxist Workers' Party and left-wing independents. In addition, the subsequent decline of the Workers' Party, and the absorption of Democratic Left into the increasingly centrist Labour Party, created a gap in the market on the left of the political spectrum, which in a Downsian fashion[3] left-wing independents have sought to occupy. The number of left-wing independents in the 2010s is larger than it appears in Table 2.2 because some of them are included in other independent categories, most particularly quasi-parties.

Independent republicans

Running under a self-adopted label, independent republicans' main ideological preoccupation is with partition of the island. There have been several different types of these candidates. In the early years of the state, they comprised those who were divided over the Anglo-Irish treaty of 1921, which granted Ireland a form of independence. These independents did not wish to align with either of the dominant Sinn Féin fragments, largely as a consequence of their disillusionment over the party split. Darrell Figgis was the most prominent pro-treaty independent republican, winning over 15,000 first-preference votes (29 per cent) in Dublin County in 1922, when standing on the single issue of the Anglo-Irish treaty. The anti-treaty republicans were those who grew disillusioned with the abstention from the Dáil by anti-treaty Sinn Féin, and ran as independents before joining Fianna Fáil – Daniel Corkery and Dan Breen being two such examples. With the realisation that the Irish Free State was here to stay, this category faded from the scene until 1937, when seven independent republicans ran, winning over 12,000 votes between them.

Up until the so-called 'arms crisis' in 1970, which concerned a plot to illegally import arms into Northern Ireland, the vast majority of independent republican candidates (over 75 per cent) ran in areas where nationalist sentiment still ran high, predominantly the border areas and the traditionally republican midlands region centred on the counties of Roscommon, Longford and Westmeath. As the main focus of these independents' campaigns was on republican issues, their primary source of support was from republican sympathisers, who were also usually ideologically left wing. While many of these independent republicans attracted significant levels of support, the only two elected were both apostate independents (Ben Maguire in Sligo-Leitrim (1943–48; 1954–57) and Jack McQuillan in Roscommon (1951–65)), which reflected the electorate's lack of major concern about the 'national question'.

The arms crisis resulted in the emergence of a new wave of independent republicans. It threatened a serious split in Fianna Fáil, as two government ministers were sacked over their role in the scandal, and another resigned. Some left the party in protest over what they perceived was a failure to adopt a more hard-line policy on Northern Ireland. A number of prominent ex-Fianna Fáilers running in 1973 won 20,000 first preferences between them, 55 per cent of the total independent vote. If the 4,000 votes for other independent republican candidates at that election are included, in total they received two-thirds of the support for independents, which signifies the importance of the protest element to this vote.

The only one of these candidates elected, however, was Neil Blaney, one of the sacked ministers. When he was expelled from Fianna Fáil in June 1972, Blaney brought with him his personal machine, the so-called 'Donegal Mafia' (Sacks 1976), to create an 'Independent Fianna Fáil' (IFF) organisation. Attracting up to 3,000 members at one stage, it regularly secured four or five local council seats, briefly held a second Dáil seat (Paddy Keaveney, 1976–77) and also got Blaney elected to the European Parliament (1979–84, 1989–94) (Maume 2009b). Like other independent republicans, Blaney believed that partition was the source of most of Ireland's ills, and that the country could not develop until this (perceived) obstacle had been overcome. Consequently, this was the central plank of all Blaney's election campaign platforms – a pattern continued after his death by his brother, Harry Blaney, and later his nephew, Niall. When Charlie Haughey and Bertie Ahern separately needed the support of the Blaneys to form a government (see Chapter 7), one of the main assurances thus sought was the pursuance of a republican policy in relation to Northern Ireland.

The H-Block protests by republican prisoners in Belfast's Maze prison in 1981 stirred up a wave of republican discontent that motivated another raft of independent republicans. The nine candidates run by the National H-Block Committee at the 1981 Dáil elections are not included as independents because they ran on a common platform under a national organisation that was orchestrated by two parties: Sinn Féin and the Irish Republican Socialist Party (IRSP). However, other genuinely 'independent' republicans who campaigned on the issue of the hunger strikers, but were to all intents and purposes independent of a political party, are included. While these candidates won over 22,000 votes, this proved to be the high point of independent republicanism, which abated following the end of the H-Block protests and the decision by Sinn Féin and the IRSP to contest Dáil elections. From the mid 1980s on, apart from a few solitary figures, the sole independent republican candidates were members of the Blaneyite organisation. This was merged into the Fianna Fáil fold in 2006 which, combined with the development of the peace process in Northern Ireland, suggests the end of the independent republican.

National-issue independents
The final sub-category of ideological independents is those standing on national issues. As the title suggests, these candidates run their campaign on a national (often single) issue, ranging from immigration rights, to reform, to women's rights. Because their concern is a national policy as opposed to a constituency issue, they are deemed ideological,

as opposed to localistic (which applies to those running on a local single issue; that is, community independents). These independents are a relatively recent phenomenon, with only a few such candidates running before the late 1970s. Sometimes these independents are organised in groups, hoping that a collective campaign will increase the awareness of the issue they are trying to highlight. Examples of this include the pro-life candidates (who were picked at selection conventions) and the 'independent health alliance' in 2002. Others run what Gallagher calls 'one-person crusades' (1985, 119).

One of the most high-profile national-issue independents has been Dana Rosemary Scallon, a well-known singer and chat show host on a catholic television station in the US. She ran on the issue of 'family values' and was especially vociferous in her opposition to abortion. Running for the presidency in 1997, she won over 13 per cent of the national vote (beating the Labour Party candidate into third place), and was elected to the European Parliament in 1999. Scallon came into conflict with the catholic church hierarchy in 2002 when she opposed an abortion referendum that had the backing of the bishops. This cost her some electoral support, because when she contested her first general election in 2002, Scallon's first-preference vote was less than 4 per cent. It may also have been the case that despite the strong tradition of catholicism in Ireland, religion plays only a small role in how Irish voters decide at first-order elections, a theory which is supported by the poor electoral performance of the pro-life candidates in 1992 (when only one of twenty-two retained her deposit).

The number of national-issue candidates has increased in recent years, but most of them have had a very limited electoral impact. In the midst of a severe economic recession in 2011, a large number of this type of independent ran, primarily to voice their concern about the national economy. They are also keen to stress their differences from the usual, parish-pump type of independent politician. Despite the pressing nature of the economic crisis, most of these candidates continued the tradition of low electoral support for this type of independent. There were a few notable exceptions, however, including Shane Ross in Dublin South and Stephen Donnelly in Wicklow, both of whom were elected to the Dáil. Although these types of independents are national-oriented, an interesting sidenote is that such is the importance of localism in Irish politics, even the likes of Ross still had to stress his local credentials on his election literature. It read: 'A native of Dublin South. I was born in Sandyford, reared in Stepaside, at school in Dundrum and lived in Dublin South's Carrickmines until four years ago.'[4]

Community independents

Community independents' title (a label with which some of these independents are christened either by the media or themselves) derives from their candidacy being entirely focused on representing their local community. They tend to have little interest in the national political arena, except as a forum to promote their locality. Especially prevalent at local elections, this category includes candidates – who may or may not have been selected by an ad hoc electoral interest group – running a campaign centred on a single local issue. Those running on behalf of the Roscommon Hospital Action Committee are a typical example of community independents. Campaigning for the retention of their local hospital, this group has contested every local and general election since 1985 (C. Curtin and Varley 1995, 390–2). One of their candidates, Tom Foxe, was elected to the Dáil in 1989 and 1992, a position he used to secure the future of Roscommon hospital (see Chapter 7). The localistic mindset of community independents was emphasised by a response Foxe gave when reporters questioned what role he could play in national politics, given that the issue he stood on was purely a local matter. 'Not at all', he replied, 'the whole county's concerned about it' (Gallagher 1989b, 78).

This category of independents also includes residual candidates who received a minuscule vote and about whom there is not enough information to classify the nature of their candidacy. The latter group tend to focus on some pressing local issues, which they do not address in an in-depth fashion; this is usually based on a realisation that their chances of being elected are extremely limited. Community independents with a history of association with a party are included in this category provided they do not continue to identify their candidacies according to such an association, and provided they are contesting at least their second election as an independent since leaving the party (but not their first – in which case they are categorised as apostate independents). For example, Michael Lowry, a former Fine Gael minister, is treated as an apostate independent for his first election as an independent in 1997, but for every election after as a community independent because he did not adopt an 'independent Fine Gael' label.

Community independents highlight the disparities between their local area (often portrayed as a periphery) and the centre, emphasising the claim that government resources, be it jobs, infrastructure or investment, are disproportionately distributed in favour of the latter. These candidates tend not to have any ideological platform, nor are they concerned with national policy issues. They have been aptly described as 'friends and neighbours' independents (Gallagher 1985, 119), as they rely almost wholly on the strength of their local profile to attract votes. One such independent, Joe Sheridan, ran on the slogan 'Vote for Joe, the man you know', which during election campaigns was painted on roads throughout his constituency of Longford–Westmeath (Collins 1991). Of course it was not the case that the local electorate did not know the other men in the electoral race, but lacking a party label Sheridan needed to emphasise that he was more local than any of them. Being born in one of the counties (Longford) in his constituency, and living and working in the other (Westmeath), might well have helped him advance this position, since the traditional pattern of electoral behaviour in two-county constituencies is that votes tend not to leave counties. Throughout Sheridan's career, he promoted the image of himself as the go-to guy to get things done. This came in the form of buying a pair of glasses for a farmer who was intending to apply through the health service, to getting the widow's pension for a gay man whose partner had died (Collins 1991). Of course, most candidates, whether party or independent, have this localistic focus and practise an element of brokerage if elected, but what distinguishes this type of independent is that these features are their sole, or at least most distinguishing, attribute. Community independents have consistently been by far the most successful type of independent candidate, winning on average 25,700 votes and 31 per cent of the overall independent vote at each Dáil election. This is probably because they are the very epitome of what it implies to be an independent, appealing to the cultural features that support the persistence of independents, chiefly localism, particularism and personalism.

Apostate independents

Despite the presence of disciplined party organisations, there have always been individuals who have flitted between party and independent status. This abandonment of previous loyalties explains their being categorised as apostates. A number of factors account for the presence of these independents, including their resigning or being expelled from a party (these can be called 'exiles'), failing to secure a nomination (this group are 'reluctants'), or because they are tolerated by a party owing to an acknowledged preference for the latter on the part of the independent (they are 'abstainers'). These apostates may also be using an independent status as a stepping-stone to joining another party (this group are 'renegades'). This category of apostate independent specifically includes those who had run as a party candidate at a preceding election, those who campaigned on a history of association with a party and those who unsuccessfully sought a party nomination for the same election. One caveat is that this definition refers only to those dissidents who are running as an independent for the first time since leaving their respective party. For any election after this, such candidates are classified according to the central plank of their campaign (that is, whether independent republican, community independent and so on), because their dependence on the party label should dissipate over time. Exceptions to this rule are when candidates continue to campaign on the record of their prior party affiliations. This method is necessary, because it would otherwise be impossible to establish how long an apostate independent retains this label. The sole exception to the inclusion of those running on a record of prior party association within this category is Neil Blaney. Although he continued to campaign under an 'Independent Fianna Fáil' platform, Blaney had his own personal machine and was clearly identifiable as an independent republican. The rationale behind this categorisation is that it was this machine and Blaney's republican stance that were the main source of his support, rather than his previous affiliation to Fianna Fáil.

One factor explaining the presence of apostate independents is the candidate selection system within parties; a centralised process can result in cases of disgruntled members who blame the party executive for their failure to acquire a nomination. Mair claims that the electoral system is partly responsible, because voters can cast a preference for such a dissident without having to desert their favoured party (1987, 67). The numbers of dissidents running has increased at elections since the 1990s, but this is markedly so in Fianna Fáil (Weeks 2009, 20), which has a more centralised selection process than the other parties and was the last party to adopt the one-member one-vote system to pick its candidates. One factor in the rise of dissidents is the increasing importance of personal vis-à-vis party organisation. Candidates within parties develop their own personalised organisations that guarantee their electoral popularity and shield them from the varying fortunes of their respective parties. This makes them more independent, with the implication that leaving the party has fewer negative electoral consequences than it would have in the past.

Internal divisions within Labour were a frequent contributor to the apostate independent ranks. In October 1931, Dan Morrissey and Richard Anthony were expelled from the party for defying the whip to vote with the Cumann na nGaedheal government on a bill establishing a military tribunal. Both were elected as independents the following year. Morrissey joined Cumann na nGaedheal soon after and then Fine Gael, whom he represented in the Dáil until the 1950s (L. W. White 2009a). Anthony was elected for a further five terms on an independent Labour

Table 2.3 *Performance of party TDs as apostate independents at succeeding elections, 1922–2016.*

Party	N	Vote as party candidate	Vote as Ind. candidate	% Vote as party TD	% Vote as Ind. candidate	Change in vote (%)	% Holding seat as Ind.
Fianna Fáil	13	7,208	4,338	18.9	11.5	–39.2	39
Fine Gael	15	6,927	4,131	15.4	10.0	–35.1	27
Labour	12	6,694	4,239	19.2	9.3	–51.6	58
Minor Parties	13	4,433	4,248	13.5	12.8	–5.2	77
Total	53	6,148	4,164	17.0	10.6	–37.6	48

Note: Change in vote notes decline in percentages, not raw support. Author's figures calculated from various issues of *Election results and transfer of votes for Dáil and bye-elections.* Dublin: Stationery Office; Gallagher (1993); Walker (1992); electionsireland.org.

ticket, not rejoining the party ranks until the late 1940s (Dempsey 2009).

The fate of party TDs as independents, as described in Table 2.3, shows that they lose support, and in many cases lose their seat, when they cross the Rubicon by leaving their party. While 25 of 53 (48 per cent) dissidents held their seats as independents, most of these TDs were from Labour or the smaller parties. Only five of the thirteen Fianna Fáil dissidents (39 per cent) and three of the twelve Fine Gael TDs (25 per cent) held their seats. This is in the context of a re-election rate of 80 per cent for all TDs running between 1927 and 1997 (Gallagher 2000, 94). On average, party dissidents lose one-third of their first preference support when they run as an independent.

Quasi-parties

The final category of independents to consider is candidates standing under a quasi-party label. These are already identified as not necessarily 'pure' independents, but are included within the framework of this research because their affiliate organisations do not fulfil the criteria to qualify as parties; in effect, they are also non-party candidates.

This refers to the pre-1963 era when there was no register of parties. For the time since, it includes all movements and groups that were not registered for Dáil elections (some of them may have been registered for local elections, such as the Donegal Progressive Party). The organisations included within this category are all those listed at the beginning of this chapter who do not qualify as parties. Some of these quasi-parties were semi-permanent organisations (existing outside of election periods), while others were what have been called the 'personal vehicle' parties of dominant individuals (Rochon 1985). The latter type of movement was usually founded by the said personality, who was its sole elected (or nominated) representative, who moulded the organisation around his or her policy preferences and whose interest in maintaining the movement determined the latter's lifespan. The Monetary Reform Association (MRA) in the 1940s was a classic example of a personal vehicle party. It was established and dominated by Oliver J. Flanagan, the party's sole TD. Although the MRA held selection conventions to officially ratify Flanagan's candidacy, and although branches of the organisation existed outside of his local constituency, there was never any doubt that he was the personification of the organisation, especially considering the large vote he attracted (over 30 per cent of the constituency vote in 1948). The central policy of the MRA was economic self-sufficiency, although its programme had an anti-semitic tone, referring to Jewish conspiracy theories concerning the financial system (Ferriter 2009). Indicating its personal vehicle nature, the movement came to an end when Flanagan joined Fine Gael in 1952.

Up until the twenty-first century, the MRA was the only one of these quasi-parties to secure parliamentary representation, which is not surprising because, if any of them were capable of winning a seat, they would most likely have qualified as full parties. The fortunes of these movements changed in the 2000s with, first, the electoral successes of Séamus Healy's Workers' Unemployed Action Group in Tipperary, followed by Luke Ming Flanagan for New Vision in Roscommon in 2011. These groups, or alliances, became the flavour of the month for independents in 2016, as the Independent Alliance (which ran twenty-one candidates) had six members elected, the Independents 4 Change movement had four TDs, with two more joining it in May 2016,[5] while a group of five independent TDs formed the self-styled 'Rural Alliance' after the February Dáil election. One common characteristic these groups all share is that they tend to be fleeting organisations that barely survive one election; of the approximately twenty-five quasi-parties, only six contested more than one general election, and none contested more than three.

Conclusion

Approximately 1,250 independent candidates contested Dáil elections between 1922 and 2016. They are a very heterogeneous category, ranging from representatives of the protestant community to catholic defenders of pro-life interests, from socialist independents to right-wing business candidates. The ideological nature of independents has proven very flexible, having gone from generally being pro-establishment in the early years of the state to an anti-establishment position since the 1970s. One trend that has been persistent, however, is that independents mobilise on issues that parties are perceived to be unable to adequately deal with, whether it is the representation of the protestant community in the 1920s, or the provision of adequate health facilities in the early twenty-first century. This seems to indicate some level of strategic rationale behind the motivations of independent candidates – in contrast to their image in other systems, where independents' minimal chances of electoral success results in those choosing the non-party route being portrayed as irrational, expressive actors. For example, the subtitle of Collet's study of independents in the US (1999) is *Can they be Serious?* and Sifry's (2003) is *Spoiling for a Fight*. In Ireland, independents occupy a lacuna in the political market. When there was no party for unionists or farmers, they stepped in. Likewise when Fianna Fáil was perceived to have drifted from its republican origins, or when Labour oriented to the centre of the political spectrum. So too when there was no party catering for a particular position on an issue, whether of a national dimension such as abortion, or a constituency matter such as the retention of a local hospital. The presence of different categories of independents is not a random occurrence, but can be as much an insight into the dynamics of the party system as it is into the motivations of the independents themselves. Overall, this supports the first premise of this study – that the presence of independents is positively correlated to the openness of the party system; the more open the system, the more likely independents are to emerge.

There are six general types of independent families: vestigial independents, corporatist independents, ideological independents, community independents, apostate independents and quasi-parties. While not all of these are 'pure' independents in the classical sense (if such a type of politician ever existed), they correspond to the three other common types of non-party candidates: gene pool independents, interest group representatives and quasi- or localised parties. Within these six families exist nine categories of independents: independent unionists, independent farmers, independent business candidates, left-wing independents, independent republicans, single-issue independents, community independents, apostate independents and quasi-parties. These categories have not experienced consistent levels of success since 1922, but have tended to ebb and flow in line with the fortunes of the parties and the salience of the issues they represent. Just as the parties of today are different to those present in the 1920s, so too are independents different. The latter are a reactionary category, who emerge when a particular issue or crisis arises, be it the loss of a local service or the failure of a politician to secure a party candidacy. While their existence can be dependent on the ability of parties to deal with the respective issue, the importance of personal factors for independents should not be underestimated. They cannot compete with parties in terms of both resources and organisation, and the disappearance of some independents from political life may simply reflect the difficulty of maintaining a lone crusade in a party democracy.

Overall, this chapter lays the groundwork for this study and suggests a number of areas that warrant further examination to understand the significant presence of independents in Irish politics. These concern the motivations of independent candidates and voters, the influence of the electoral system, the nature of the party system and their role in the process of government formation. They are all examined in later chapters, before which is an analysis of their electoral performance from a temporal and comparative perspective.

Notes

1 For example, Minister for Home Affairs Kevin O'Higgins warned in a parliamentary speech in 1922: 'We will have groups here – small groups of seven or eight. We will not have parties on definite lines of political cleavage; we will rather have a representation here and the reflection here of interest – particular interests in the community; and as there are many varieties, of interests in the community, we are likely to have representatives here of all these interests' (Dáil debates 1: 1560, 12 October 1922).
2 This excludes independent farming candidates who are remnants of defunct parties, and are included in the category of vestigial independents.
3 This refers to the spatial model of electoral competition proposed by Anthony Downs (1957), which theorises that political actors occupy space that maximises their electoral gains.
4 See https://irishelectionliterature.wordpress.com/2011/02/05/flyer-from-shane-ross-independent-dublin-south-2011-general-election/.
5 Independents 4 Change was originally formed by independent TD Mick Wallace as the 'Independents for Equality Movement' for the 2014 local elections, when it ran four candidates. In 2015 the group changed its name to Independents 4 Change, and it is the one exception of a registered party treated as independents in this study. The rationale is because its members all identified themselves as independents and there was no whip or overarching central organisation. The movement was formed to get the label 'independent' on the ballot paper and to highlight its members' participation in the Right 2 Change anti-water charges movement. Quite simply, its members remained independents.

3

Independents' electoral history

Introduction

Independents have been a constant feature of the Irish electoral landscape. They have maintained a continuous presence in the Dáil right
back to the 1922 elections, the first in the Irish Free State.[1] This is in
contrast to their electoral performance in other established democracies, where independent candidates struggle to win votes, let alone
seats. At the same time, independents' success rates in Ireland have
not been consistent, as sometimes (particularly in the 1960s and
1970s) their representation dipped to as low as a handful of deputies.
At other times, such as in the 1920s, 1940s and the 2010s, independents won as many as one in ten Dáil seats. An analysis of this variation in electoral fortunes is necessary to understand their significance
in Ireland, and it facilitates some inductive theorising to explain this
exceptionalism.

This comprises the context for this chapter, which examines independents' electoral history from three aspects. The first is the comparative performance of independents in countries outside of Ireland,
with particular attention given to Australia and Japan, the two other
established democracies where independents have been prominent at
national parliamentary elections. As well as placing Irish independents
in an international context, the comparative dimension also assists an
analysis of the factors behind their significance. The second focus is on
the Irish case, with an outline and analysis of independents' history at
Dáil elections back to 1922. The final section is a cursory enquiry into
the geography of their electoral history.

In terms of the overall perspective of this study, its second key
premise is that independents have a strong electoral tradition in
Ireland, which is the focus of this chapter and is a factor in their
continued levels of electoral success. The ability of independents to
regularly attract votes indicates that there is a permissive tradition in
their favour in Ireland. While in other countries the rationality of a

vote for independents might be questioned, given the weight of history against them in terms of the difficulty in winning a seat, there is no such suppressive culture in Ireland. An independent candidacy is a viable option which has a knock-on effect, encouraging more capable candidates down this electoral path, which in itself should increase support for independents.

In Chapter 2 the role of a party system was discussed in terms of its tendency to suppress independents. It was shown that the Irish party system leaves gaps in the electoral market for independents. However, this effect is not constant and contributes to the fluctuations in support for independents. This is the prism through which independents are examined in this chapter and concerns the first key argument of this study about the presence of independents in Ireland, namely that their support varies in line with the openness of the party system. When the latter was in the process of formation in the 1920s and 1930s, independents had the opportunity to be a real electoral force. Party attachments among the electorate had not yet solidified, and it was an open market, with parties coming and going, and higher levels of electoral volatility. Once the party system consolidated into a two-and-a-half-party model from the 1950s, it was very much a suppressive force and independents faded away into what seemed like a terminal decline during this period. They only re-emerged when dealignment began in the 1980s and the party system opened up once more. So the electoral fortunes of independents follow a rational path vis-à-vis the party system. Under conditions conducive to their development, independents emerge; when such conditions disappear, they follow likewise.

Electoral performance of independents:
the comparative evidence

At the first set of general elections held across Europe in the 2010s, independents did not fare well. Of the eighteen EU democracies that permit independent candidacies at lower house elections, it was only in Ireland, Lithuania and the UK that independents were elected. Lady Sylvia Hermon in Northern Ireland was the sole independent MP after the 2010 UK House of Commons elections (a status re-affirmed at the 2015 elections), while three independents were elected to the unicameral Seimas in 2012, maintaining a trend of representation in the Lithuanian parliament that has persisted since the Baltic state gained independence in 1990. The numbers elected to the Irish Dáil in 2011 were much greater – fifteen in total, a figure exceeded only by the next set of Dáil elections in 2016, when twenty-three independents were elected. Consequently, the vast majority of independent MPs in Europe sit in the Irish parliament.

Another arena in which to compare representation is the European Parliament. Since elections to this legislature are of a mid-term, second-order nature, where governments are often punished, we might expect independents to have greater opportunities for electoral success than at first-order, national elections where formation of government is at stake. Direct comparison across all EU member states is not wholly possible because only seven explicitly permit independent candidacies – Bulgaria, Cyprus, Estonia, Malta, Ireland, Romania and the UK. The other member states use list-based electoral rules that do not allow single-candidate lists, although in Austria, Finland and the Netherlands these are not explicitly prohibited (Ehin et al. 2013, 24). Since the first direct elections to the European Parliament were held in 1979, independents have been elected on seventeen separate occasions – twice in Estonia, thrice in Romania, but twelve times in Ireland. So more than two-thirds of elected independent MEPs have been Irish, a remarkable statistic considering Ireland (in 2016) elects just eleven seats to the parliament of 751.

Extending the focus to democracies beyond the Mediterranean Sea and the Ural mountains, there were also independents elected to the US Senate in 2012 (Angus King in Maine and Bernie Sanders in Vermont), and both houses of the Australian (in 2013) and Japanese parliaments (2014). In Australia, two independents were elected to the House of Representatives and one to the Senate. The equivalent numbers in Japan were eight in the House of Representatives and two in the House of Councillors. Including these with the European data brings the total number of independents elected to the lower houses of parliament across all thirty-six industrial democracies (excluding Ireland) in the first elections of the 2010s to fourteen, close to the same number elected to the Dáil in 2011, and just over half that elected to the Dáil in 2016.

This finding of Irish significance is not unique to the 2010s. Table 3.1 details the numbers of independents elected since 1990 in the same thirty-seven established democracies, and it is apparent that independent parliamentarians tend to be few and far between. In this period there were no independents elected in Bulgaria, Cyprus, Estonia, France, Germany, Greece, Malta, New Zealand and Romania. The exceptions in continental Europe include Denmark, Hungary and Lithuania. Independents have also won seats in the directly elected Czech and Polish senates (they cannot contest lower-house elections in these countries). In the other democracies not listed – such as Belgium, Israel, Italy, Latvia, Portugal,

Table 3.1 *Independents elected since 1990*

Australia (HoR)	Canada	Denmark	Hungary	Lithuania	UK	US (HoR)	Japan	Ireland
2 (2013)	0 (2015)	0 (2015)	0 (2014)	3 (2012)	1 (2015)	0 (2014)	8 (2014)	23 (2016)
4 (2010)	0 (2011)	0 (2011)	1 (2010)	5 (2008)	1 (2010)	0 (2012)	5 (2012)	15 (2011)
2 (2007)	2 (2008)	0 (2007)	0 (2006)	6 (2004)	2 (2005)	0 (2010)	6 (2009)	5 (2007)
3 (2004)	1 (2006)	0 (2005)	0 (2002)	3 (2000)	1 (2001)	0 (2008)	18 (2005)	13 (2002)
3 (2001)	1 (2004)	0 (2001)	1 (1998)	4 (1996)	1 (1997)	0 (2006)	11 (2003)	6 (1997)
1 (1998)	0 (2000)	0 (1998)	0 (1994)	1 (1992)	0 (1992)	1 (2004)	15 (2000)	4 (1992)
5 (1996)	1 (1997)	1 (1994)	7 (1990)			1 (2002)	9 (1996)	
2 (1993)	1 (1993)	0 (1990)				2 (2000)	30 (1993)	
1 (1990)						1 (1998)	21 (1990)	
						2 (1996)		
						1 (1994)		
						1 (1992)		
						1 (1990)		

Note: Year of election indicated in parentheses. Only democracies with elected independent MPs since 1990 included. The thirty-seven democracies include: the twenty-eight EU members, Australia, Canada, Iceland, Israel, Japan, New Zealand, Norway, Switzerland and the US. HoR denotes House of Representatives. Author's figures calculated from Nohlen (2001; 2005; 2010).

Slovakia, Slovenia, Spain and Sweden – independent candidacies are not permitted under the respective electoral rules. In some of these parliaments MPs occasionally leave their party to sit out the remaining parliamentary session as an independent. The make-up of a parliament on dissolution can consequently often contain a number of independents, but very few – if any – of these are re-elected as independents. For example, there were sixteen independents in the Bulgarian National Assembly of 240 MPs at the beginning of 2013. At the parliamentary elections in May of that year there were no independents elected. More fracturing occurred in the new parliament, so that when early elections were called for October 2014, there were five outgoing independent MPs. While independent candidacies are possible in Bulgaria, the conditions for them are very onerous, including – before electoral reform in 2010 – a requirement of 10,000 signatures and a deposit of €7,500 to run, in addition to the use of a closed-list electoral system with a national threshold of 4 per cent. For this reason, just three independent candidates contested the 2014 parliamentary elections. This scenario is repeated across a number of European democracies where independent candidacies are theoretically possible, but in practice a non-runner because of the institutional obstacles against electoral success down such a path. So, while independent MPs are not necessarily an unknown phenomenon across Europe, elected independents generally are, and it is only the latter in which this study is interested. Anyone can choose to leave their party to be an independent, but very few can be elected an independent, and this study's definition of independence is limited to those who choose to wear these colours at an election.

The example of Bulgaria highlights the importance of electoral rules in affecting the presence of independents. The non-permissive nature of such rules towards independents is one of the primary factors for their absence in most European parliaments, which are generally elected under party-list voting systems. As already mentioned, only half of EU member states permit independent candidacies at parliamentary elections. Nine prohibit them, while another five – although not expressly prohibiting independents – require them to form single-candidate lists. It is generally only in jurisdictions using single-member districts (Ireland being an exception) that independents are elected. This supports the theory that permissive institutions are a key factor behind the emergence of independents. Where they are not permitted, aspirant independents are compelled to pool their resources into, or with, a party. An example of this was MOST (the Bridge of Independent Lists), a party that included independents on its national ticket for the Croatian parliamentary elections in 2015, in which it won nineteen seats.

At the same time, under electoral rules that are more permissive of independents, we are more likely to see them elected to parliament. For example, one of the common links between the countries with independent MPs in Table 3.1 is that they almost all have an element of candidate-centred electoral rules. This is discussed in more detail in Chapter 6, but the general significance of such rules is that they facilitate a more individualistic form of political competition, which puts independents at less of a disadvantage vis-à-vis parties as they would be under a party-oriented voting system. Returning to the countries listed in Table 3.1, Canada, the US and the UK use single-member plurality voting, where candidates of different parties compete against each other. Australia and Ireland use preferential voting, where voters rank candidates. Until 1995 Japan used a similar system, except that votes were non-transferable. Since then it has employed mixed-member electoral rules; as do Hungary and Lithuania, where independents have an opportunity of being elected in the single-member districts. Denmark has an open list system, which encourages intra-party candidate competition, unlike the closed-list systems used elsewhere in Europe.

Expanding beyond cases of elected independents to overall patterns of support for all independent candidates, significant examples of this are also limited to a few countries. At most elections in most established democracies, the vote for independents is historically so low that there is little point including a graph to demonstrate this, as the trend line would correspond to the x-axis. In their analysis of independents' performance at national elections in EU member states since 1945, Ehin et al. (2013, 29) found that in two-thirds of cases support for independents is less than 1 per cent of the national vote.

Using data from the same study (2013), building on the work of Brancati (2008) and including election results from other democracies where independents are allowed to run – Australia, Canada, Japan, New Zealand and the US – the vote for independents can be detailed as far back as 1950. Thirteen of these thirty-seven countries do not allow independents to run on their own, but this still leaves hundreds of cases of elections where independents are allowed to compete. Examining the national vote for independents, there are fifty-seven cases since 1950 where independents won at least 2 per cent. Apart from solitary exceptions in Estonia in 2011 and Romania in 1996, these cases are limited to four countries: Australia (9), Ireland (18), Japan (23) and Lithuania (5). Narrowing the focus further, there are just twenty cases of a national independent vote of 5 per cent or greater: eleven in Ireland and nine in Japan. As Figure 3.1 indicates, the 2011 Dáil election was the first time independents won more than

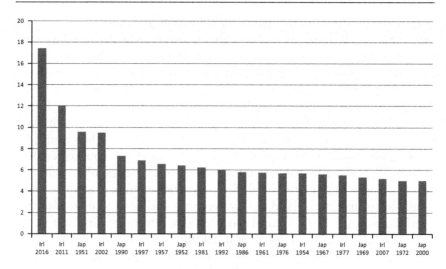

Figure 3.1 National elections with an aggregate independent vote above 5 per cent, 1950–2016.

Note: Irl denotes Ireland, Jap is Japan.

10 per cent at any national parliamentary election held since 1950, a feat repeated in 2016.

From this analysis of seat and vote returns it is apparent that there are just three established democracies where independents have had a consistent presence across the post-war decades: Australia, Japan and Ireland. While the overall focus of this study is on Ireland, it is nevertheless useful to briefly examine the electoral performance of independents in the two other cases. To this end, Figure 3.2 details the national vote for independents in each of the three countries back to the 1920s. This indicates that support for independents declined across all three in the post-war era, not rising again until the 1980s. However, Ireland has diverged in recent years as support for independents continued to grow, unlike in Australia and Japan where it slipped back again in the twenty-first century.

Australia

Examining the Australian case in greater detail, the presence of independents has at times been sporadic, but independents have been represented at all levels of government across all states and territories. Table 3.2 details the level of representation at the federal level, where it is only in recent decades that independents have had a renewed presence. Having won just one seat at seventeen elections to the House of

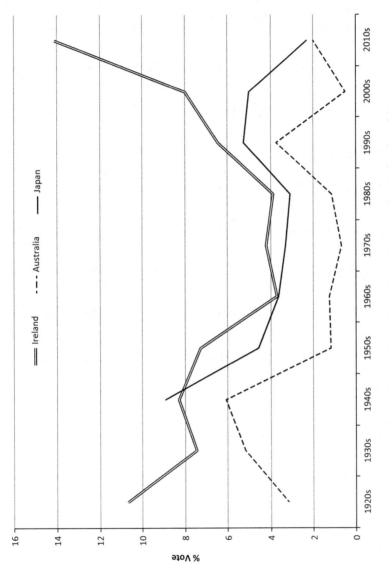

Figure 3.2 National vote for independents in Australia, Ireland and Japan.

Note: Results from House of Representatives elections.

Table 3.2 *Independents elected at national elections in Australia and Japan, 1945–2015*

Australia			Japan			
Year	**House of Representatives**	**Senate**	**Year**	**House of Representatives**	**Year**	**House of Councillors**
1946	0	0	**1946**	26	**1947**	21
1949	0	0	**1947**	12	**1950**	15
1951	0	0	**1949**	12	**1953**	20
1953	0	0	**1952**	19	**1956**	9
1955	0	0	**1953**	11	**1959**	7
1958	0	0	**1955**	6	**1962**	0
1961	0	1	**1958**	12	**1965**	5
1964	0	0	**1960**	5	**1968**	3
1967	1	1	**1963**	12	**1971**	4
1970	0	3	**1967**	9	**1974**	5
1974	0	1	**1969**	15	**1977**	2
1975	0	1	**1972**	14	**1980**	7
1977	0	0	**1976**	21	**1983**	3
1980	0	1	**1979**	19	**1986**	2
1983	0	1	**1980**	11	**1989**	2
1984	0	0	**1983**	16	**1992**	1
1987	0	2	**1986**	9	**1995**	5
1990	1	0	**1990**	21	**1998**	20
1993	2	1	**1993**	30	**2001**	2
1996	5	0	**1996**	9	**2004**	3
1998	1	1	**2000**	15	**2007**	7
2001	3	0	**2003**	11	**2010**	0
2004	3	0	**2005**	18	**2013**	2
2007	3	1	**2008**	6		
2010	4	0	**2011**	5		
2013	2	1	**2014**	8		

Note: Author's figures calculated from Australian Politics and Elections Database accessed at www.elections.uwa.edu.au; Klein (2001).

Representatives between 1949 and 1990, independents won twenty-four seats at the next nine elections between 1990 and 2013. Perhaps the culmination of independents' resurgence was their holding the balance of power after the 2010 election, when neither Labor nor the Liberal–National coalition won a majority. Although similar outcomes have often occurred at the state and territorial level in Australia, it was the first time since the 1940s that independents got to influence which party held the reins of power at the federal level. While fewer numbers have been elected to the federal Senate, there too independents have held the balance of power, including Brian Harradine in the 1990s and Nick Xenophon in the 2010s. In total, though, the number of individual independents elected to both houses since 1950 is pretty small – twelve to the House of Representatives and five to the Senate. It is perhaps no coincidence that three of the five senators represented Tasmania, by far the smallest state, and therefore a much easier constituency for an independent to contest than the other, far larger, states.

Three key factors have been cited to explain the mild resurgence of independents in Australia (Costar and Curtin 2004, 9–10). They include the increasing neglect of regional and rural areas by the main parties, which has created a social and economic divide and propelled disillusioned party voters into the hands of independents. The second factor is the increasing level of centralisation within the two big parties, which both forced MPs to back national policies that were unpopular locally and in some cases resulted in them leaving the party to run as independents. Consequently, many of the independents elected in Australia first began life as party representatives. This includes Tony Windsor and Rob Oakeshott, two of the three independents who supported Julia Gillard's minority Labor administration at the federal level in 2010. The third factor facilitating independents is preferential voting, which has pushed some disaffected party voters towards independents. This theme is further explored in Chapter 6.

At the state and territorial level in Australia, independents have had greater levels of electoral success (this is discussed in more detail in Chapter 6) but, as in the Commonwealth parliament, this has primarily been in recent decades. The Tasmanian Legislative Council is an exceptional case that has always had a majority of independents, making it one of the few directly elected parliaments in the Western world that has never been controlled by political parties (Sharman 2013). Of the 159 members elected between 1909 and 2015, 132 have been independents. In contrast, independents won just thirty-five (this includes the twelve seats won by the Independent Greens – the precursor to the Tasmanian Green Party – in the 1982–92 period) of the 1,000 seats contested in the lower House of Assembly over the same time period. The vote for independents at Legislative Council elections has ranged between 50 and 90 per cent, while it has exceeded 10 per cent in the lower house on only two occasions since the 1940s (both times for the Independent Greens). In many ways, the Legislative Council is perhaps the closest existing resemblance to a nineteenth-century 'gentlemen's club'-style parliament, one that functioned as a house of review before the emergence of modern political parties. There are a number of reasons for the distinctiveness of Tasmania's upper house, including the use of small single-seat constituencies with a mean electorate of 23,000, a stringent restriction on campaign expenditure and the use of staggered elections to elect two or three members annually – which reduces the intensity and level of interest that might otherwise be present in a general election. This helps maintain an extremely high rate of re-election for incumbents, ensuring that independents have managed to retain control of the Council.

Japan

The only other democracy to match Ireland for its national presence of independents is Japan. As shown in Figure 3.2 and Table 3.2, although the aggregate vote for independents is usually below that of Ireland, the numbers elected have often been greater (in part due to a larger parliament – the House of Representatives comprises 480 members, with independents eligible to contest the 300 single-member district seats). Fewer independents are elected in the House of Councillors, one of the reasons being fewer seats available for them to contest at elections. With 126 councillors elected every three years, independents can contest the seventy-six seats that are run under the Single Non-Transferable Vote (SNTV). Prior to the electoral reforms of the mid 1990s, all seats in both houses were elected under this system.

Table 3.2 shows that the number of independent MPs in Japan has varied considerably, and in recent years has begun to decline from a high in the early 1990s of thirty to eight in 2014. One reason why Japanese independents have not attracted more academic atten-tion is because of the questionable nature of their independence. Traditionally, most elected independents in Japan are affiliated with a political party, in particular the Liberal Democratic Party (LDP). They tend to comprise dissidents who failed to secure a party nomination, but were told by the LDP 'if you win you are LDP' (Reed 2009, 298). In other words, they are re-admitted to the party on election. This policy also applied to the cases where the LDP could not agree on a candidate and its aspirants ran as independents, with the winner(s) securing the party nomination. The election of independents in Japan is due to the importance of the personal machines (*koenkai*) of individual politi-cians, and the prevalence of candidate-centred voting, both of which are related. Lacking a powerful central party organisation, the LDP had little option but to tolerate the existence of these 'Liberal Democratic Independents' (Reed 2009) in order to avoid intra-party factional con-flict. Rather than indicating a predilection for independents on the part of the Japanese voter, the numbers of independents elected instead reflects the level of this conflict. When it is particularly high, a great many more independents run and are elected. A prime example was in 2005, when thirty-seven LDP MPs opposed their own government's plans to privatise the postal system. Failing to secure a party nomination at the ensuing election, many ran as independents. The LDP hierarchy picked twenty 'assassin' candidates to run against these 'traitors', but less than half of them were successful. Thirty independents were elected, the highest number in post-war Japan, but all of the elected traitors were re-admitted to the LDP (Reed 2009, 312).

As is apparent, these Liberal Democratic Independents (LDI) are independent in name only, as not only do they seek an LDP nomination, but they are also from the same gene pool as official LDP nominees. They tend to belong to the LDP legislative grouping at the local assembly level, and are often the sons of retiring LDP MPs (Reed 2009). If elected, almost all of them join the party even before parliament meets. For this reason, Reed (2009) considers independents in Japan as more an electoral than a legislative phenomenon.

There is also a considerable number of independents elected at the local municipal level in Japan, far more than in most other Western democracies (Hijino 2013). However, as with the independents at the national level, a large majority are affiliated to a party, which they conceal at election time. In part this can be due to the unpopularity of their party at the local level, but it is also a product of institutional factors, as parties both allow their candidates to hide their affiliation and to receive different grades of nomination, including a party 'recommendation' or 'support' (Hijino 2013, 70).

The SNTV electoral system was often cited as one reason for the election of independents in Japan (Hijino 2013). This system entailed multi-seat constituencies, which resulted in high levels of patronage and candidate-centred politics as candidates of the same party sought to distinguish themselves from each other. This is quite similar to the argument often given on how STV helps independents in Ireland (see Chapter 6 for more detail). The LDP was particularly keen to get rid of SNTV because of the manner in which it facilitated independents. It was in favour of a move to a more party-centred electoral system that would increase the importance of party label and lessen the prevalence of intra-party tension and of LDIs. In 1994, when electoral reform happened in favour of a mixed system of plurality and proportionality, some might have imagined (or indeed hoped) that this would have been the death knell for independents in Japan. However, the new system was not as party oriented as some desired, and so, while the numbers of independents in Japan did fall, they continue to persist.

The average number of independents elected under the new rules is ten in the seven elections between 1996 and 2014. This compares with an average of thirteen under SNTV between 1952 and 1996.

The LDP had a partial victory with electoral reform in that there are now fewer LDIs elected. There are now more independents from other parties. For example, some parties collaborate to support a single independent, known as a 'fusion' candidate, against an LDP incumbent. This is often the product of district bartering, where the parties act strategically to support whichever of the opposition parties has the greatest opportunity of ousting the sitting LDP MP.

It can still be said, however, that almost all the independents elected to the Japanese Diet are independent in name only. While some might see similarities between gene pool independents in Ireland and the LDIs in Japan, there is quite a clear distinction between the two. The former are not the product of party strategy, are not approved by the party headquarters and do not have the backing of local party organisations. Unlike in Japan, there are no affiliation links between gene pool independents in Ireland and their parties of origin. It is for this reason that although there may be more independents elected in Japan, there are more legislative independents in Ireland, making the latter a more distinctive case of independent success. This, and more specifically their electoral history, is the focus of the remainder of the chapter.

Independents: the Irish evidence

Independents were not always a permanent feature of the Irish political landscape. Mirroring the British House of Commons, the Irish parliament was divided almost wholly along Whig and Tory lines in the early eighteenth century. The disintegration of this two-party system following the death of Queen Anne in 1714, and the resultant Whig supremacy in London, resulted in a parliament of factions in Ireland for much of the 1700s, until the emergence of the Irish Patriot Party in the latter half of the century. While some of these factions were organised around individuals or families, there were also 'country gentlemen' in parliament who saw themselves as independents (Hayton 2004, 119–20). The absence of clear party structures in this period, however, makes it difficult to classify and identify independents in the sense of those independent of organisation or faction.

When Irish MPs took their seats in the British House of Commons following the dissolution of the Irish parliament under the Act of Union in 1800, most of them aligned with either the Whigs or Tories. The number of non-aligned MPs (which at the time bore the closest resemblance to an independent) was greatest in the years immediately after the union, but dwindled quickly, so that by the election of 1807 the number of non-aligned MPs had fallen to nine, from thirty-nine in 1801 (Coakley 2010a, 437–8). Following catholic emancipation in 1829 and the emergence of Daniel O'Connell's Repeal Party, the non-aligned MP disappeared in Ireland, both because of sectarian polarisation between protestant and catholic, and possibly because of the increasing size of the electorate, which had begun with the Catholic Relief Act of 1793 (Coakley 2010c, 10–11). Independent parliamentarians did not appear again until Ireland achieved independence in 1922, in the third Dáil elected in June of that year. Consequently, despite the portrayal of independents as an atavistic, almost premodern phenomenon of a bygone peasant age, the reality is that the presence of independent members of parliament in Ireland is largely a genuinely twentieth- (and now twenty-first) century phenomenon. This emergence of independents in a nascent party system was a not an experience unique to Ireland, as it was also a pattern of political life in other Anglo-Saxon democracies, such as Australia, Canada and New Zealand. Where the Irish experience differs is that independent MPs did not disappear once parties consolidated their position, unlike in the other Anglophone systems.

The performance of independents at Dáil elections is summarised in Figure 3.3 and Table 3.3. Both detail the proportion of first-preference votes and seats won by independents, as well as the proportion of candidates that comprised independents. As is evident, independents more than held their own in the first three decades of the new state, before entering a decline in the 1950s. A gradual recovery started in the 1980s, while a considerable surge for independents began in the 2000s. These mark four distinct electoral phases for independents.

1920s–1950s
The first phase was in the early decades of the state, when the numbers of independent TDs regularly reached double digits. For example, at the four Dáil elections in the 1920s there were nine, fifteen, sixteen and thirteen independent candidates elected. At the June 1927 election, three of the ten highest poll-toppers in the country were independents: Alfie Byrne in Dublin North, John F. O'Hanlon in Cavan and Bryan Cooper in Dublin County (Gallagher 1993, 89). It was not just the case that there was a core group of independents consistently re-elected over this period. Certainly there were some, such as Byrne and many of the independent unionists. However, there was also a new crop of independents returned at every election and this continued on to the 1950s. In 1923, nine new independents were elected to a Dáil of 153;

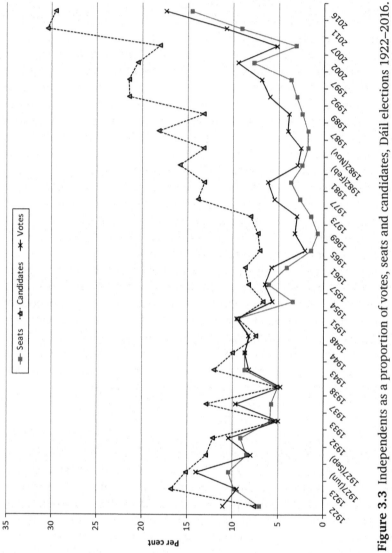

Figure 3.3 Independents as a proportion of votes, seats and candidates, Dáil elections 1922–2016.

Table 3.3 *Numbers and shares of votes and seats for independents, and numbers and proportion of candidates comprising independents at Dáil elections, 1922–2016*

Year	Total votes	% Total votes	No. of seats	% Total seats	No. of candidates	% Total candidates
1922	65,797	11.1	9	7.0	21	7.6
1923	96,877	9.4	15	9.8	63	16.8
1927 (June)	158,004	14.0	16	10.5	57	15.2
1927 (Sept.)	106,224	8.1	13	8.5	34	12.9
1932	140,298	10.5	14	9.2	34	12.2
1933	68,882	5.0	9	5.9	13	5.3
1937	129,704	9.7	8	5.8	33	13.0
1938	60,685	4.7	7	5.1	11	5.1
1943	120,471	8.3	12	8.7	43	12.1
1944	104,708	8.7	12	8.7	25	10.0
1948	109,089	8.3	12	8.2	30	7.4
1951	118,714	9.6	14	9.5	28	9.5
1954	75,896	5.7	5	3.4	20	6.6
1957	80,402	6.6	9	6.1	24	8.3
1961	67,372	5.8	6	4.2	26	8.7
1965	26,460	2.1	2	1.4	20	7.1
1969	42,230	3.2	1	0.7	27	7.3
1973	38,082	3.0	2	1.4	27	8.1
1977	87,527	5.5	4	2.7	52	13.9
1981	106,632	6.2	6	3.6	53	13.2
1982 (Feb.)	50,713	2.9	4	2.4	58	15.9
1982 (Nov.)	42,451	2.5	3	1.8	48	13.2
1987	72,217	4.0	3	1.8	85	18.2
1989	57,982	3.9	4	2.4	49	13.2
1992	99,243	6.0	5	3.0	103	21.4
1997	124,490	6.9	6	3.6	104	21.5
2002	176,304	9.5	13	7.8	95	20.5
2007	118,951	5.8	5	3.0	90	19.1
2011	273,318	10.8	15	8.4	173	30.5
2016	369,763	17.4	23	14.6	163	29.6

Source: Author's figures calculated from various issues of *Election results and transfer of votes for Dáil and bye-elections*. Dublin: Stationery Office; Gallagher (1993); Walker (1992); www.electionsireland.org.

in June 1927 the number was eight; four in 1932, 1937 (to a Dáil reduced in capacity to 138) and 1943; five in 1948 (to a Dáil of 147); and six in 1951. The exceptions were the snap elections of September 1927 (one new independent TD – Joseph Xavier Murphy), 1933 (no new independent) and 1938 (one new independent – Patrick Cogan in Wicklow), all called less than one year into the lifetime of a new Dáil.

While the number of independent TDs slipped back into single figures in the 1930s, it increased again in the 1940s even though the Dáil was reduced in size. One particular pattern over this period was that whenever an election was called within a year of the previous one, fewer independents had the resources to mobilise a candidacy. In September 1927 there were thirty-four independent candidates, down from fifty-seven at the June election a few months earlier. In 1933, thirteen independents ran, down from thirty-four the previous year. There was a similar drop from thirty-three to eleven independent candidates between the 1937 and 1938 elections. What is perhaps remarkable is that these low numbers did not prevent independent electoral victories, as nine of the thirteen were elected in 1933 and seven of the eleven in 1938.

What explains this successful era for independents? As detailed in Chapter 2, the new party system did not cater for all interests, ranging from agrarian to business to protestant communities, who nominated independent candidates to represent their views. For many not attracted by either nationalist or socialist politics, independents constituted one of the few, if not the only, alternative(s). Most of the independent TDs were of a conservative, pro-establishment leaning, certainly far different to many of the more left-wing and anti-establishment independents elected since the 1980s. There was also a sense that they could have genuine input. In one of the earliest contributions to Irish political science, Hogan says of independents:

> There is much to be said for having in parliament at least a few Independents, who, because they have minds of their own and are free to speak them, can become the medium for expressing unpalatable but salutary truths and opinions … such plain speaking is essential to the elasticity of thought which is an indispensable condition of an alert, fearless, and freely developing public opinion (1945, 92).

These independents were elected because there was a fear that former revolutionaries in the two main parties of Cumann na nGaedheal and Fianna Fáil would be incapable of running the new state. In particular the *Irish Times* newspaper was a firm advocate of the merits of independents, in part due to the latters' conservative leanings. During the 1938 election campaign, an editorial in the *Irish Times* said 'they [independents] ought to be supported wherever they are standing' (17 June), and in 1944 it stated 'an encouraging feature of the polling is the fact that a large number of independent candidates has been returned' (2 June 1944). An op-ed in 1937 outlined why the newspaper favoured independents:

> There is one strong reason why the competent Independent should be preferred to the equally competent party nominee. Parliamentary records show that Independent deputies have contributed much more than their share to the interest and the constructive value of Dáil debates. Their influence on legislation has consequently been far in excess of their numerical strength. More than once they have succeeded in "leavening the loaf" of discussion, which otherwise would have been flat, stale and lacking in nutriment … the value of deputies who are free from castigations by party whips may be even greater than it has been in the past (Politicus, *Irish Times*, 24 June 1937).

Both Manning (1972, 85–6) and Chubb (1957, 133) point to the newly adopted electoral system (STV) as a causal factor in the initial success of independents. They claim the presence of Proportional Representation (PR), especially the introduction of the multi-seat constituency, encouraged candidates to run and that an over-estimation of its inclusivity (largely based on an ignorance of the workings of the new system) led to 'an optimistic rush of independent candidates' in the early elections (Chubb 1957, 133). However, STV did not prove to be the Pandora's box that the parties had feared and, once this was realised, the number of independent candidates fell to just over thirty in the 1930s – around which figure the average number of candidates hovered until the late 1970s.

As mentioned earlier, the success of independents at elections in the early years of a new party system is not an experience unique to Ireland. Because it takes time for a party system to settle on an established pattern of competition, for parties to establish identities and for voters to forge concrete attachments to parties, the infant period of most party systems witnesses volatile electoral behaviour, a pattern that suits non-partisans such as independents. Once the political climate settles down, and voters have decided which party best suits their interests, the parties gain a stranglehold on the political system and independents fall by the wayside.

This pattern appeared to be on the verge of happening in the Irish party system in the 1930s. After the volatility of the 1920s, when nine different parties contested elections, electoral politics stabilised in the following decade, as both Fianna Fáil and Fine Gael broadened their support base, and a bipolar party system evolved. This appeared to squeeze out independents, as the number of independent candidates fell from a high of sixty-three in 1923 to eleven in 1938. The number of independent TDs also declined in these years, from fifteen to seven, as did their vote share, falling from just under 10 per cent to 5 per cent. However, independents did not disappear, and they bucked the comparative trend by recovering in the 1940s, winning an average of over twelve seats in the four elections between 1943 and 1951.

Even though this first phase for independents was one of electoral strength, there was a continuous series of ups and downs in their vote. It was not until 1944 that support for independents increased at consecutive elections. A number of reasons can be hypothesised to account for this topsy-turvy performance. The first is due to independents' lack of a party label, which makes it difficult for voters to establish a firm attachment to them. The independent vote is often a floating protest vote. A second reason is related to the discussed fluctuating number of independent candidates. For example, a 62 per cent decline in independent candidacies from 1932 to 1933 was matched by a 51 per cent fall in their aggregate vote. A simple correlation between the number of candidates and vote share for independents for the period 1927–44 confirms the strength of this relationship, since it produces a very high coefficient of +0.93, where a figure of 1 would imply a perfect relationship and 0 no relationship. Expanding this correlation to all elections between 1927 and 2016 produces a far lower coefficient of +0.25. This suggests that the number of candidates affected the overall vote for independents during the early years of the state when there was no established independent vote, but that its significance declined once a certain pattern of independent voting emerged.

During this same period, there was something of a cyclical pattern about independents' electoral performance, which replicates a model used for the Labour Party (Gallagher 1982, 155–6). At an election after a long Dáil, independents usually fared quite well, increasing their vote (and usually their seat) share at every such election within this time-frame. This resulted in difficulties for the main parties in forming a stable government, leading to an early election where independents lacked the resources to compete and may also have been punished by an electorate that favoured a stable government. This in turn led to the major parties making gains at such elections, forming a stable government – and hence a long Dáil. This led back to a rise in support for independents, which re-iterated the cycle. Table 3.1 confirms this pattern of events, where independents prospered at the June 1927 election, fell back at the next election three months later, experienced gains in 1932 and losses in 1933, a pattern that continued until the 1943 election.

1950s–1970s

Apart from a blip in the 1930s, the number of independents elected to the Dáil remained in double figures until the mid 1950s. After the poor election showing of 1954, when they lost nine seats primarily because eight independent TDs joined or rejoined parties in the 1951–54 period, independents recovered somewhat in 1957 to win nine seats, but this redemption proved only temporary and they fell into decline in the 1960s. This marks the beginning of the second electoral phase for independents, when it appeared as if their time in Dáil politics had come to an end. Writing in the late 1950s, Chubb foresaw the decline of independents as elections got more expensive and constituency revisions did not work in their favour. He said 'the established independent finds it difficult enough; the newcomer will rarely succeed. Their numbers are, therefore, likely to be small except in unusual circumstances' (1957, 141). Twenty years later it seemed as if Chubb was correct, as Carty (1981, 58–61) was writing on the demise of independents and to where their support had disappeared. No new independent TDs were elected in the 1965 and 1969 elections and only two in the 1970s (Neil Blaney in 1973 and Mick Lipper in 1977), both the product of internal party conflict.

Figure 3.4 indicates how the mean first-preference vote per independent declined radically over this period, from over 4,200 in 1951 to 1,300 in 1965. It never really recovered from this fall, although this is in part due to the increased number of fringe independent candidacies with limited electoral prospects. This kept the mean vote low, even though the total vote rose. To control for the effect of such outliers, the median, or middle score, is also included in Figure 3.4, but this indicates pretty much the same pattern.

The 1960s and 1970s was the era of the two-and-a-half-party system in Ireland, as Fianna Fáil, Fine Gael and Labour consolidated their dominance of political life to such an extent that they won all Dáil seats bar three in the 1965 general election, bar one in 1969, bar two in 1973 and bar four in 1977. With the retirement or death of the civil war generation of independents, no new wave emerged. Aspiring politicians saw little value in the independent brand, and as few as twenty independent candidates contested the 1965 election, winning an average of 619 first preferences. Nationally, support for independents declined in this period to an all-time low of between 2 and 3 per cent. In an interview before the 1973 election, Joe Sheridan, the sole independent elected in 1969, acknowledged that 'the glory days of independent deputies are fast fading into memory ... the going is getting more difficult all the time for independents' (*Irish Independent*, 12 February 1973).

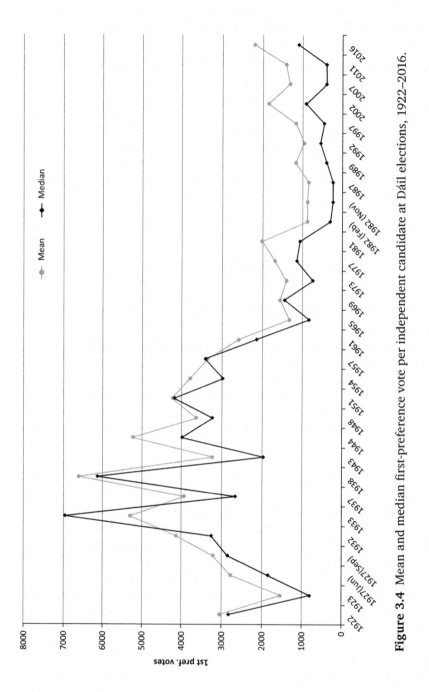

Figure 3.4 Mean and median first-preference vote per independent candidate at Dáil elections, 1922–2016.

Manning (1972, 86) claims that this was due to the evolution of Fianna Fáil and Fine Gael as catch-all parties, and the renewed shift of Labour to the left to capture a far-left vote, which was sometimes a source of support for independents.

Another factor was the electoral rule changes in the 1950s and 1960s (Garvin 1972, 369). Large-seat constituencies disappeared, as three-seaters became ever more commonplace. This raised the mean electoral quota, making it more difficult for independents to win a seat. As discussed in Chapter 2, this is one of the reasons given for the disappearance of independent unionists in the border constituencies (Sacks 1976, 535–6). While it may well account for the decline in the number of independent TDs, it does not explain why their vote fell, and both Carty (1981, 60) and Gallagher (1975, 506) doubt the direct influence of constituency revisions.

Other reasons expounded to explain the fall of independents in this period include the increasing expense of election campaigns, the inclusion of party labels on the ballot paper and the change in the media – where the decline in the number of local newspapers, and the increasing importance of television, made it difficult for independents to have a 'competitive presence' (Carty 1981, 61). The latter argument overestimates the impact of television on Irish elections. The continued importance of premodern campaigning meant that local mediums that independents could access, particularly newspapers and radio stations, were still crucial channels of communication for candidates.

1980s–2000s

The second electoral phase for independents did not prove to be their last, as they made an unexpected comeback in the 1980s. This was a rather slow re-emergence, however, as the numbers of independent TDs remained a handful and, nationally, support for independents did not rise above 4 per cent until 1992. This third phase of independents is primarily about the rise of the independent candidate, as much greater numbers contested elections under this brand. While the average number of independent candidates at Dáil elections between 1922 and 1977 was twenty-six, this immediately doubled to fifty-two in 1977, and since 1997 the mean figure has doubled once again, to more than one hundred. It is not surprising that this produced a larger national vote for independents, but it does not explain why gradually more of them were elected. There is no clear answer as to what caused this rise in independent activity. In terms of eligibility to run, there was no major easing of restrictions (which were not severe in the first place), although the required deposit remained fixed at £100 – meaning it actually declined in real terms. The deposit was trebled in 1997 to £300, but concurrently was made easier for candidates to retain, requiring just one-quarter of the electoral quota (calculated as the number of valid votes divided by the number of seats plus one, with one added to this figure). Following a court case in 2001 by a prospective candidate who claimed that the deposit restricted his ability to run as an independent, the deposit was deemed unconstitutional and was replaced by the requirement of thirty signatures, which has to be verified by public officials, and which was claimed to be a more expensive and time-consuming process than the £300 deposit (Gallagher 2003, 88–9). This may explain why the number of independent candidates did not increase radically in 2002 as had been predicted (*Sunday Tribune*, 17 March 2002), but actually fell from its 1997 figure. These rules were again amended for the 2007 election, when independents had the option of supplying thirty signatures of registered constituency voters, or paying a €500 deposit.

A premise that the public simply became more politically active and were more willing to contest elections as independents does not stand up in light of the declining membership rates for political parties and interest groups. Another reason might be that the type of independent changed and a new-style candidate emerged. This was the community independent, often the nominee of local community-based and residents' organisations. They first emerged at the 1974 local elections, when community independents – including Seán Dublin Bay Rockall Loftus and Carmencita Hederman – won six of forty-five seats to the Dublin Corporation. This group was joined in 1979 by Tony Gregory, and community independents experienced electoral success at the national level in the 1980s, with Loftus elected in 1981 and Gregory the following year. It was perhaps the election of Gregory in 1982 that marks the real beginning of this phase. Holding the balance of power following the February 1982 election, Gregory was able to negotiate a range of provisions for his constituency from the government in return for his vote in parliament. The 'Gregory Deal' (see Chapters 4 and 7 for more details) demonstrated what an independent could achieve, and it validated the idea of voting for an independent to achieve something for the local constituency, rather than having to necessarily vote for a party that could form a government. Voters in other constituencies envied the Gregory Deal, and wanted similar arrangements for their localities. Consequently, whenever one or a combination of parties lacked the numbers to form a majority government, Gregory-type deals were struck with independent TDs holding the balance of power. This happened after the 1989, 1997 and 2007 (and perhaps 2016, although it was not wholly clear) elections and indicated that independents were not in the Dáil to simply make up the numbers. The electorate recognised this, and rather than support for independents being an irrational, wasted form of behaviour, there emerged an element of rationality to the independent vote. For example, in 2002 the number of independents elected more than doubled (from six to thirteen), because the concessions four independents (Healy-Rae, Blaney, Fox and Gildea) had extracted from the outgoing government convinced some voters that they should have an independent TD in their own constituency. Indeed, many of the nine new independents elected in 2002 had campaigned on their ability to procure such an arrangement. However, the outgoing government won a majority in 2002, meaning that the independents elected to secure a Gregory-type deal were in many ways redundant. Consequently, at the following election in 2007, the number of independent TDs fell to five as voters switched back to parties. Ironically, though, independents were back in a position of influence as Bertie Ahern needed their votes to form a government. With independents once more to prominence, in 2011 their ranks swelled again, to fifteen, the largest number elected since 1948 (although there were other factors at play, in particular the ongoing economic crisis).

Increasing numbers of independent voters and independent TDs in the 2000s, and particularly the 2010s, suggest a fourth electoral phase for independents, when they became a not insignificant political force. Although some might argue this is only since the 2011 election, it began earlier. At the ten Dáil elections between 1961 and 1997, eight new independents were elected. At the four elections between 2002 and 2016, thirty new independents were elected, including five in 1997, nine in 2002, nine in 2011 and seven in 2016. As shown in Figure 3.1 the vote for independents in 2011 was the highest ever at a national parliamentary election in a mainstream democracy since 1950. This did not constitute a peak, as support for independents continued to rise in the opinion polls in the months that followed, until they became the largest political grouping in 2014, with support ranging between 20 and 30 per cent. This figure included support for some small parties; but even when these were excluded, independents' popularity was at record levels. This was evident in the local and European elections of 2014 which, although of a mid-term second-order nature, still saw independents achieve an unprecedented number of votes and seats. At the local elections almost one in four voted for an independent candidate, and they won more than 20 per cent of seats. One in five voters at the European elections voted for independents, who won three of the available eleven seats. Such electoral feats were repeated at the 2016

Dáil election, when one in six cast a first preference for an independent candidate, twenty-three of whom were elected to a Dáil of 158 seats. This was contrary to the predictions of many pundits, who had assumed that support for independents would decline during a general election campaign once voters focused on national issues, such as the question of their preferred government. Support for 'independents and others' in fact remained pretty constant in the run-up to the election at between 25 and 30 per cent. The only substantial change was that some of the independents became 'others' as they formed new parties, such as Renua and the Social Democrats in 2015. Consequently, the more accurate figure for independents' support levels was closer to 17 per cent, a figure repeated on polling day in February 2016. Some constituencies proved particularly conducive to independents, as two of them were elected in the five-seat constituencies of Galway West (Noel Grealish and Catherine Connolly), Kerry (Danny and Michael Healy-Rae) and Dublin Bay North (Tommy Broughan and Finian McGrath), and in the three-seat constituency of Roscommon–Galway (Michael Fitzmaurice and Denis Naughten), where a majority of voters supported independent candidates. For the first time ever, three independents were returned from a single constituency,[2] as Séamus Healy, Michael Lowry and Mattie McGrath all held their seats in the new five-seat constituency of Tipperary (Weeks 2016).

The source of this new wave of support for independents was a much discussed topic both before and after the 2016 Dáil election. One possible explanation is that independents' resurgence is part of a wider comparative phenomenon of the rise of populism. While in other countries electorally this has taken the form of parties, it could be that independents are one Irish variant of populism. Certainly, independents tap into the anti-party sentiment that has fuelled support for populist parties such as the Five Star Movement in Italy and Podemos in Spain, and for populist candidates such as Donald Trump and Bernie Sanders in the United States, who contested the Republican and Democratic primaries for the presidency in 2016. When asked in May 2015 why they would vote for an independent, 26 per cent said it was because they do not trust or like the parties and 16 per cent said it was because such candidates were independent of parties (*Irish Times*/IPSOS MRBI 2015). While Sinn Féin and other left-wing parties have also been accused of espousing populist politics, for many voters for whom a vote for one of these parties is a non-runner, independents constitute the primary populist option.

Stemming in part from their populist streak, the role of independents in a modern parliamentary democracy was a theme of discussion around the 2016 election. Both commentators and political parties pondered the stability that could ensue from a parliament with a large grouping of independents, particularly if they held the balance of power (this is discussed in more detail in Chapter 9) (Collins 2014). There was an express fear that it could be very difficult to form a government if there were too many independents in the Dáil; and if one was formed dependent on their support, it might be a weak administration unable to impose its will. At a time when the national economy was recovering from a recession, the fear was that a weak, unstable government would not be good for Ireland. Some independents sought to counter these fears by developing strategies and tactical alliances. For some this comprised full-blown parties, in the form of Renua and the Social Democrats. A different initiative was an Independent Alliance of five independent TDs (Michael Fitzmaurice, Tom Fleming,[3] John Halligan, Finian McGrath and Shane Ross) and two senators (Fergal Quinn and Gerard Craughwell), which launched in 2015. Keen from the outset to emphasise that it was not a party, the Independent Alliance nevertheless pledged united support to a government on financial legislation and confidence issues, provided its ten key demands, as outlined in a 'charter for change', were met. Another, less high-profile and primarily left-wing, group of independents was Independents 4 Change. This included four TDs – Mick Wallace in Wexford, Clare Daly in Dublin Fingal, Joan Collins in Dublin South-Central and former Labour TD Tommy Broughan in Dublin Bay North. Although all members of the group maintained independence of each other, as mentioned in Chapter 2, the group was officially registered as a political party. A 'rural alliance' of five independent TDs also formed after the 2016 election, which sought to maximise its leverage in the government formation process. One particular demand of this group was the creation of a new cabinet post of minister for rural affairs. Altogether, this formation of alliances is one indicator of the emergence of a new phase for independents. It suggests a more strategic approach by independents to maximise their newfound position of strength.

This surge in support for independents also brought a sea change in the attitude of the parties towards them. Where previously independents were castigated as being irresponsible and mere parish-pump politicians, the political parties realised that with one in six voters preferring independents, they were not a fringe group and were voicing valid concerns. Consequently, independents of various shades were included in the negotiations with both Fianna Fáil and Fine Gael to form a government following the February 2016 election. Ultimately, independents, and particularly the Independent Alliance, proved the kingmakers, as their votes were crucial in electing a minority Fine Gael government in May 2016. As is discussed in more detail in Chapter 7, independents were granted unprecedented levels of influence in return for their votes, as three – Shane Ross, Denis Naughten and Katherine Zappone – were appointed to cabinet, Finian McGrath was appointed a super junior minister and Seán Canney and John Halligan were both appointed ministers of state. These appointments were not just compensation to independents for their parliamentary support. The new government was a self-styled partnership arrangement, and Fine Gael wanted to include independent voices. It was tacit recognition that independents had arrived as a political force. One other feature of this new era of independents is that they wanted to steer clear of the localistic, parish-pump politics that had been a feature of previous minority government arrangements with independents. Consequently, both the rural group and the Independent Alliance insisted in their discussions with Fianna Fáil and Fine Gael that local deals were not the price of their support. No such concessions were included in the resultant programme for government produced in May 2016, but there were still claims that projects in the constituencies of the independents supporting the government would be prioritised (Leahy 2016).

Finally (at least for this section), although this study is primarily about independents' performance at national elections, it is also worth considering how they fare at other levels in Ireland. To this extent, Table 3.4 outlines their performance at second-order elections, including those to local councils, the European Parliament, presidential and by-elections. Taking into account the support for independents at Dáil elections that was outlined in Tables 3.1 and 3.4, it is quite apparent that they fare much better at these lower-level elections. This is neither unexpected nor an unusual comparative phenomenon. While independents are primarily absent from most national parliaments, this is not the case for local assemblies, where they are far more prevalent and in some cases the dominant form of representation. Support for independents at local elections in Ireland is pretty solid, never falling below 10 per cent since the 1970s. This may be the core independent vote, which drifts to parties at Dáil elections, or it may be due to their oppositional nature, with party voters drifting to independents to protest at mid-term elections. Whatever the source, this independent vote increased again at elections to town councils (which were abolished in 2014). The outlier performance of independents at European Parliament elections in Ireland has already been discussed, but what is apparent is that it is pretty consistent, averaging 12 per cent, until the 2014 set when it soared to 27 per cent. While independents historically did not contest by-elections, given their perceived limited opportunities

Table 3.4 *Independents' performance at local, European Parliament, presidential and by-elections in Ireland*

Year	County & city S	V	Borough & UDC S	V	European Parliament S	V	Town council S	V	Decade	By-elections S	V	Presidential Year	V
1974	10.1	11.8	23.3	24.9			17.4	18.6	1920s	0	2.2	1945	19.6
1979	7.8	11.2	21.9	22.3	13.3	14.6	22.2	22.9	1930s*	11.1	2.9	1990	38.9
1984					6.7	10.1			1940s	0	1.7	1997	25.5
1985	8.5	10.3	23.3	26.3			23.1	23.8	1950s	20.0	7.9	2011	40.3
1989					13.3	11.9			1960s	0	1.6		
1991	9.6	12.0							1970s	0	7.8		
1994			22.7	25.2	13.3	22.2	22.8		1980s	0	2.5		
1999	8.0	12.3			13.3	12.6			1990s	9.1	11.5		
2004	9.7	12.3	19.7	21.0	15.4	14.6	13.4	21.0	2000s	50.0	20.6		
2009									2010s	14.2	13.8		
2014	23.3	20.3	–	–	19.8	27.3							

Note: There are no official returns for local elections prior to 1974. UDC denotes Urban District Council. S denotes percentage of seats, and V percentage of first preference votes.

* In 1933 Robert Rowlette was elected unopposed to one of the Dublin University seats.

Author's figures calculated from Weeks and Quinlivan (2009); www.electionsireland.org.

to win a seat, this has changed in recent decades. By-elections are now seen as a classic second-order protest vote, and independents won four of thirteen by-elections held between 2000 and 2015. Independents occupying the presidency is not a rare occurrence internationally, particularly since the post is non-partisan in most countries. Independent candidates have performed particularly well at presidential elections in Ireland, with one elected (Mary Robinson, albeit with the backing of the Labour Party) in 1990 and, between them, four winning 40 per cent of the first-preference vote in 2011.

Geography of the independent vote

The previous sections in this chapter analysed the evolution of independent support from a national perspective. This may not be the most appropriate means of doing so for the reasons outlined in Chapter 2: that 'independent' is a residual brand, a collective label for all those outside of the party fold. In addition, the national patterns mask the far more interesting variation that is taking place at the local level. This section focuses, therefore, on the geography of independent support. Using aggregate-level data back to 1922, it examines the evolution of the independent vote across elections, per county and constituency. Are there particular areas that are hotbeds of support for independents, and are there no-go regions for prospective independents where such a candidacy is doomed to failure?

For reliable analysis the smallest working unit of aggregate data available is the county. In some cases, such as Cavan–Monaghan and Carlow–Kilkenny, the units comprise two counties, while in one other, Longford–Roscommon–Westmeath, it comprises three counties. In the case of Dublin, although there has been a considerable level of alteration in the city's constituency boundaries across the decades, it is still possible to identify three consistent groups of constituencies: those in the north of the city, those in the south (both separated by the river Liffey) and those in the suburbs of Dublin, stretching from north county to south county. This leaves twenty-five working units, which are: Carlow–Kilkenny, Cavan–Monaghan, Clare, Cork East, Cork Mid, Cork South-West, Cork City, Donegal, Dublin North, Dublin South, Dublin County, Galway, Kerry, Kildare, Laois–Offaly, Limerick, Longford–Westmeath–Roscommon, Louth, Mayo, Meath, Sligo–Leitrim, Tipperary, Waterford, Wexford and Wicklow.

With these units in mind, Table 3.5 indicates the mean vote for independents for each of the three electoral phases of their support. Rolling averages were also calculated, but are not included because there was

Table 3.5 *Mean level of support (%) for independents per constituency at Dáil elections, 1923–2016*

Constituency	1923–61	1965–77	1981–2016
Cavan–Monaghan	26.3	4.0	6.8
Dublin North (C, N, NE, NC, NW)	22.0	4.1	8.5
Donegal	13.0	11.3	16.7
Cork City	10.3	4.5	5.4
Dublin County (S+SW+W+MW)	9.6	3.6	5.5
Wicklow	8.7	2.1	9.0
Cork South-West	8.7	0.0	5.8
Sligo–N. Leitrim	8.7	3.2	8.4
Longford–Westmeath–Roscommon	8.4	9.4	9.6
Laois–Offaly	7.7	2.8	4.1
Cork Mid	7.3	1.0	2.4
Cork East	7.3	2.7	1.7
Dublin South (SC+SE+DL)	6.7	2.5	4.3
Clare	5.9	1.7	8.8
Waterford	5.5	1.1	6.0
Kerry	5.3	5.0	11.0
Louth	4.4	2.1	8.3
Limerick	3.6	4.0	5.9
Carlow–Kilkenny	3.3	0.4	1.4
Tipperary	3.0	0.5	15.8
Galway	2.2	2.5	7.4
Mayo	1.9	0.5	6.0
Meath	1.5	2.4	4.9
Wexford	1.4	1.1	5.5
Kildare	1.0	1.4	3.4

Author's figures calculated from various issues of Election results and transfer of votes for Dáil and bye-elections. Dublin: Stationery Office; Gallagher (1993).

Note: C denotes Central, DL denotes Dun Laoghaire, N North, NE North-East, NC North-Central, NW North-West, S South, SW South-West, W West, MW Mid-West

little difference between these and the overall mean. The prominence of independents in the border constituencies is quite apparent in the first column, as is their decline in the second phase. Donegal proves something of an exception, as independent support has been pretty consistent in the county across all three electoral phases. Indeed, an independent has been elected in Donegal at twenty-four of the twenty-nine general elections between 1923 and 2016. Their diversity – ranging from independent unionists, to independent republicans, to independent farmers – suggests there is something of an independent vote in this region that is itself independent of the nature of the candidacy.

Apart from this Donegal exceptionalism, the decline in the independent vote in most counties in the 1960s and 1970s is pretty stark. It is only in Longford–Westmeath, Joe Sheridan's (independent TD, 1961–81) home constituency that it averaged more than 5 per cent during this period. Examining the three phases as a whole, support for independents across Dublin and Cork in general declined, falling by more than half in Dublin County and Dublin North, by half in Cork City and Dublin South and to almost negligible levels in Cork Mid and Cork East. Apart from the dramatic increase in Tipperary, there are no other counties that saw considerable increases in independent support between the electoral periods. It is difficult to discern other clear patterns. While independents have fared poorly in some Leinster counties (Carlow–Kilkenny, Kildare, Meath and Wexford), this has not been the case in Wicklow or Longford and Westmeath. Likewise, while they have struggled in Mayo and Galway, this has not always been the case in the other counties of Connaught.

A separate analysis, comprising electoral constituencies rather than counties, since the 1981 election is permissible as there have been more or less the same constituencies in the eleven elections over this period. Although not shown here, it indicates the same patterns as the last column in Table 3.5. It also found that the constituencies of Carlow–Kilkenny, Cork East and Cork North-West are not very amenable to independents, despite their rising levels of support nationally. Not only was no independent elected in these three constituencies at any Dáil election since 1981, their electoral performance has been pretty negligible. No independent candidate ran at seven of the Dáil elections in Cork North-West (2016 was the first time independents ran in this constituency since 1997), and on only one occasion before 2016 when one did was support greater than 1 per cent. Showing that few regions were immune to the rise of independents in 2016, five candidates between them won an aggregate 0.80 of a first-preference quota at the Dáil election, with Cork county mayor John Paul O'Shea losing out by less than 250 votes on the third and final seat. The two other constituencies that historically were not happy hunting grounds for independents saw no change in their fortunes in 2016. In Carlow–Kilkenny, half of the general elections in the 1981–2016 period did not feature an independent and in the six that did the mean independent vote was just over 2 per cent, the same average over this period in Cork East – where independents have not contested four of the last eleven Dáil elections. These three constituencies are possibly the worst for any ambitious independent. Cork as a whole is not very favourable towards independents, and Michael

Collins in Cork South-West in 2016 was the first independent elected from any of the constituencies in the region since Florence Wycherley in Cork West in 1957.

Traditionally, voting patterns in Irish elections are examined per province. This is repeated in Figure 3.5, which indicates the mean support for independents for each of the four provinces, with Dublin separated from Leinster. There is not a great deal to read from the graph. Support for independents has been greatest in Ulster, confirming previous findings. It has never been especially prolific in Connaught and Leinster, where it has only recently risen above 10 per cent for the first time.

To what extent are these voting figures an indication of some areas being more receptive to independents, or an indication of where more prominent and better independent candidates ran (or where intra-party conflict is more likely to spill over into the emergence of dissident independents)? This conundrum highlights the difficulty in interpreting the independent vote because of its candidate-specific nature. For example, the constituency of Tipperary North had little history of support for independents until Michael Lowry resigned from Fine Gael and ran as an independent in 1997, since when the mean independent vote has been more than 20 per cent in the constituency (until its merger with Tipperary South to form a new constituency in 2016). However, rather than this suggesting that the independent vote in such cases is simply a misplaced party vote, it indicates that all politicians attract an independent vote, which is linked to their personality and is independent of their party label. The strength of this independent vote varies according to the personal attractiveness of the candidate and explains why the likes of Lowry or Neil Blaney retain their vote as an independent, whereas others, such as Paudge Brennan, fail. Brennan, a Fianna Fáil parliamentary secretary, was expelled from the party in 1971 and ran as an independent in 1973. His constituency vote in Wicklow fell from 29 per cent to 8 per cent. Brennan did not regain his seat until he rejoined the party, subsequently being elected again in 1981.

While Table 3.5 details the vote for independents per region, to what extent is this a consistent vote? This can be assessed by a simple correlation of the distribution of votes across the counties for each election year. The figures, or coefficients, vary between −1 and +1: the closer to 0, the weaker the relationship. Figures close to +1 indicate a very similar spread of support for those particular election years. Table 3.6 is a correlational analysis for the years 1923 to 1948 and Table 3.7 analyses the years 1948 to 2016. This division was chosen because of the change in constituency boundaries under the 1947 Electoral Act.

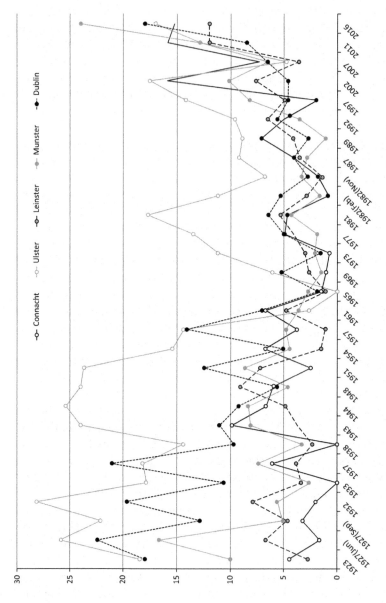

Figure 3.5 Percentage vote for independents per province, 1923–2016.

Table 3.6 *Correlation of independent vote per county, 1923–48*

	1948	1944	1943	1938	1937	1933	1932	1927s	1927j
1944	0.71								
1943	0.57	0.75							
1938	0.50	0.61	0.55						
1937	0.45	0.49	0.62	0.83					
1933	0.27	0.41	0.46	0.52	0.43				
1932	0.25	0.35	0.44	0.65	0.55	0.82			
1927s	0.35	0.41	0.49	0.58	0.61	0.47	0.71		
1927j	0.20	0.25	0.42	0.36	0.49	0.41	0.42	0.62	
1923	0.12	0.44	0.41	0.41	0.40	0.46	0.49	0.56	0.45

Author's figures calculated from Gallagher (1993), 1927s denotes September 1927; 1927j
June 1927.

The higher correlation coefficients in Table 3.6 suggest a more consistent independent vote in the early decades of the state, but some of the
extremely low coefficients (as well as the negative signs) in Table 3.7
suggest a weaker relationship in the independent vote in recent decades.
This is in line with a point raised earlier in the chapter about the homogeneity of the early wave of independents. Being of a similar ideological
ilk they were more likely to experience similar electoral fortunes than
if they were a diverse group, as was the case in later decades. The consistency between elections persisted for longer in earlier times, which
is reflected in higher coefficients. Aside from the early independents'
homogeneity, this may also be a product of the fewer independents
who ran for office then, as well as their comprising many of the same
candidates, making a stronger correlation more likely. Larger numbers
in more recent years can result in a greater fluctuation in the independent vote since it is so dependent on candidate frequency.

The consistency of the independent vote is far lower than the equivalent figures for political parties. A potential independent vote can exist
in every constituency, but it primarily depends on the presence of a
capable independent candidate to flesh this out. Overall, the geography
of the independent vote seems to suggest that this is a slight misnomer
as it is more a vote for independents; that is, it is difficult to speak of
a core independent vote. It is a sum of votes for many local independents. This finding indicates that the term 'independents' does not refer
to a unitary, or even a collective, being, supporting the evidence from
Chapter 2. Most of the support attracted by independent candidates
comes from the force of their personality, not their brand. Independents
are not one, but many.

Table 3.7 *Correlation of independent vote per county, 1948–2016*

	2016	2011	2007	2002	1997	1992	1989	1987	1982n	1982f	1981	1977	1973	1969	1965	1961	1957	1954	1951
2011	0.47																		
2007	0.38	0.57																	
2002	0.43	0.57	0.55																
1997	0.46	0.51	0.43	0.38															
1992	0.09	0.25	0.28	0.35	0.65														
1989	0.15	0.05	0.13	0.35	0.25	0.60													
1987	0.30	0.41	0.21	0.57	0.56	0.53	0.51												
1982n	0.12	−0.03	−0.28	0.22	0.32	0.25	0.26	0.46											
1982f	−0.02	−0.09	−0.21	0.18	0.29	0.32	0.28	0.67	0.61										
1981	0.21	0.04	−0.07	0.33	0.28	0.33	0.55	0.59	0.54	0.73									
1977	0.04	0.01	−0.29	0.08	0.32	0.37	0.59	0.65	0.56	0.65	0.57								
1973	0.19	0.06	0.04	0.28	0.47	0.70	0.52	0.60	0.28	0.42	0.45	0.48							
1969	0.19	−0.01	0.06	−0.08	0.14	0.19	0.33	0.32	−0.01	0.30	0.34	0.24	0.44						
1965	0.50	−0.05	0.03	−0.07	0.18	0.15	0.12	−0.04	−0.17	−0.07	0.06	0.34	0.19	0.34					
1961	0.23	−0.30	−0.08	0.13	−0.07	0.21	0.22	−0.05	0.10	0.17	0.18	0.06	−0.07	0.19	0.45				
1957	0.34	−0.22	−0.13	0.07	0.13	0.02	0.24	0.13	0.34	0.26	0.42	0.25	0.16	0.44	0.20	0.32			
1954	0.15	−0.33	−0.24	0.20	−0.14	0.01	0.38	0.07	0.22	0.11	0.30	0.25	0.17	0.02	0.04	0.24	0.63		
1951	0.31	−0.02	−0.01	0.08	0.02	0.11	0.06	−0.08	−0.10	−0.02	0.18	0.07	0.28	0.18	0.14	0.09	0.53	0.55	
1948	0.00	0.17	−0.07	0.23	0.03	0.23	0.20	0.21	−0.01	0.15	0.24	0.37	0.36	0.15	0.05	−0.05	0.19	0.39	0.75

Author's figures calculated from various issues of *Election results and transfer of votes for Dáil and bye-elections*. Dublin: Stationery Office, 1982f denotes February 1982; 1982n, November 1982.

Conclusion

The significance of independents in Irish party democracy is detailed in this chapter. It is shown that the only two other established democracies where independents have a regular presence are Australia and Japan, but even then this does not match the Irish experience. Much of independents' electoral success in Australia takes place at the state and territorial level, while the independence of the Japanese variety is questionable, given their affiliation to parties. This accentuates the exceptionalism of their presence in Ireland.

Maintaining the claims of the previous chapter, it is evident that the party system is an important factor affecting independents. In most party democracies it acts to suppress independents, in terms of the nature of party competition, but also by the actions of the parties themselves to cement their dominance. Although some rules have negatively affected independents in Ireland, such as the introduction of party names and logos on the ballots, and the lowering of the district magnitude, generally speaking Ireland is one of the least cartelised liberal democracies. In a comparative analysis of ballot access, Abedi (2004, 93–4) ranked countries by their ease of access for potential candidates, which considered the electoral deposit, the number of petitioned electors required for a nomination and the proportion of votes needed for a deposit refund. Ireland was ranked second after Luxembourg, making it one of the least cartelised systems, which means it is easier for independents to run in Ireland than most other political systems.

Returning to the nature of the party system, this has affected independents, as the consolidation of the two-and-a-half-party system acted to suppress them, whereas the openness of the formative early decades and the dealignment of more recent decades has been a permissive factor. This indicates that there is a rational evolution to independents' electoral fortunes, as they respond in a strategic fashion to elements of the party system. This in turn lends credence to the first core argument of this study about independents' significance, that it is related to developments in the party system. The tradition of electoral success outlined in this chapter provides evidence to support this study's second premise, as it shows that independents are an established norm. This has been particularly evident in recent years as voters turned to independents rather than new parties (Weeks 2012), the latter of which is the pattern across Europe. Given their previous record of success and their influence vis-à-vis minority governments, independents were perceived as a credible and rational choice.

Finally, two health warnings about independents' electoral support need to be issued here. There are many other factors that influence the variation in support for independents which were not discussed in this chapter. These vary from socio-economic to institutional factors and are the focus of separate analyses in Chapters 5, 6 and 8. Second, the rather large size of the aggregate units means we should be wary of reading too much into these figures, since they can mask many local variations. Analysis of individual-level data from surveys permits a much deeper understanding and a greater number of factors can be controlled for. This is the topic of Chapter 5.

Notes

1 Details of all the elected independent TDs are in the appendix to this book.
2 Excluding the Dublin University constituency, whose three seats were always occupied by independents up until the removal of university representation from the Dáil in 1937.
3 Tom Fleming later decided not to contest the election.

4

Independent parliamentarians

The first three chapters have focused on establishing the presence of independents in the Irish political system. Before the reasons for this presence are examined in the next four chapters, we need to consider the experience of those who run on an independent platform. This chapter comprises seven separate contributions from independents who have been elected at various levels in Ireland, from local councils, to the Seanad, the Dáil and the European Parliament. Although this study is primarily on independents in the Dáil, it is nevertheless useful to consider all these levels as it demonstrates the role and function of independents across the Irish political system. For example, as discussed in Chapter 3, independents won almost one-quarter of seats at the local elections in 2014. On the same day they also won three seats to the European Parliament, more than the combined number elected across the other twenty-seven member states.

The independent contributors provide an insider's account of life as an outsider within the Irish political system. With their years of experience on the political frontline, they speak with clarity and insight on the failings of the system, and in particular the lack of transparency and accountability. They suggest a number of reforms that would allow both parliament and the people to wrest back true political power. Each of the contributions provides a unique perspective. Finian McGrath and Maureen O'Sullivan detail their involvement in deals negotiated with Taoisigh leading minority governments. Seán D. Loftus recalls his time in the Dáil when his vote was likewise needed, but no deal was forthcoming. Catherine Murphy, with a history of involvement in political parties, both past and present, is able to provide an insightful comparison of life in a party and outside it. Kathy Sinnott, as a complete outsider, recalls her experience of narrowly missing out on a Dáil and Seanad seat, before eventually being elected to the European Parliament in 2004. Along with Marian Harkin, they were the only independents in a parliament of 732 in Brussels. The first and last contributions are by two independent senators elected from the separate university panels. Although not directly elected, independent university senators have made significant contributions to Irish parliamentary life, which is recalled by John A. Murphy and Seán D. Barrett.

John A. Murphy

Professor John A. Murphy represented the National University of Ireland constituency as an independent member of Seanad Éireann from 1977 to 1982 and from 1987 to 1992. He was Professor of Irish History at University College Cork (UCC) from 1971 until his retirement in 1990. His book Ireland in the Twentieth Century *was one of the first surveys of contemporary Irish history.*

Whatever reservations people have about the need for a second house of the Oireachtas, there is a general agreement that independent members have made an impressive contribution to the work of Seanad Éireann and to the public discourse. Properly speaking, there is no provision in the Seanad articles in the constitution for independent members, only for university senators who may or may not be independents.

University representation in parliament seems increasingly anomalous and elitist in an age of ever-expanding popular education. Yet the concept has a long history. British universities (including the University of Dublin up to 1920!) historically sent members to the House of Commons until the practice was abolished by an egalitarian Labour government in 1948. Under the British-influenced Constitution of the Irish Free State in 1922, there were to be two seats in the Senate for the National University of Ireland (NUI) and two for the University of Dublin, which effectively meant Trinity College Dublin (TCD). Provision was also made for the representation of Queen's University Belfast, if the six counties of Northern Ireland stayed in the Irish Free State: in the event, Queen's was represented in the 'old Stormont' parliament until the O'Neill reforms of 1969. Meanwhile the Free State Dáil, sitting as a constituent assembly in 1922, generously transferred university representation from Senate to Dáil where there now would be two three-seat university constituencies for NUI and TCD respectively, from 1922 down to their abolition in 1936. It should be noted that electors (i.e. graduates) in the Dáil university constituencies could not exercise another vote in the 'geographical' constituencies.

A new constitution (Bunreacht na hÉireann), enacted in 1937, provided for the two universities to be represented in Seanad Éireann (Art.

18.4.1, i and ii). Thus, representation was transferred to the second house. Presumably it was also felt that in a chamber organised along vocational and cultural lines (theoretically!) it was appropriate to give higher education a particular place. It was recognised on all sides that the graduate body of NUI electors (41,000 on my first outing in 1977) was a multiple of the TCD electorate (8,000) and that equal representation of seats could be seen as unfair and anomalous. But the situation was accepted, nay planned, in the interest of a perceived greater value, that is, the need to give a minority, protestant and ex-unionist ethos a special place in the life of the nation.

A further quirk in respect of the universities, which is still the case today, should be noted. Though the electors are required to be registered graduates, no such restriction applies to the candidates. In fact, a university senator need have no particular identification with the institution he or she is elected to represent.

Moreover, NUI and TCD still have a duopoly of university seats in Seanad Éireann despite the plethora of third-level institutions now in the State, including the creation of Dublin City University and the University of Limerick in 1989. A constitutional amendment (Art. 18.4.2) approved by referendum in 1979 provided for Seanad representation for 'any other institutions of higher education in the State'. This seemed to recognise the shape of things to come, as well as dealing with what then appeared to be the imminent demise of the NUI. I well remember the Minister for Education, the late John Wilson, telling us in the Seanad that the necessary legislation would implement the constitutional change within four months. But the NUI rallied on its deathbed and, thirty-four years after the 1979 amendment, the 1937 position still obtains in respect of university representation, much to the resentment of the graduates of the new universities and third-level colleges. This state of affairs is partly due to sheer political inertia, but it also suits the interests of the current university representatives, despite their periodic clamour for Seanad reform. The late John Kelly, constitutional authority and public man, regarded university representation as unacceptably elitist and imitative, 'paddy copycatting his late colonial master'. But the idea of an unreformed elite unwilling to broaden its ranks would have further inflamed his indignation.

In my experience, university senators, by and large, made independent contributions to Seanad proceedings. But their commitment to being independents – that is, unattached to party – varied greatly over the years and across the spectrum. Some were 'closet' party members who 'came out' in the course of their Seanad career, some were formally attached to a political party from the outset and others remained staunchly independent throughout. At times, a university senator would be assiduously courted by a party, particularly if he or she had attained a high public profile.

In 1979, in the period leading up to the first directly elected European Parliament, the Fine Gael organisation carried out a private opinion poll among a sample of voters in the Munster constituency. Party activists were listed on the 'ballot paper' which also, unknown to me, included my name among the possible candidates. It appears that I performed very well in this 'trial' election. The party leader, Garret FitzGerald, invited me to meet him to discuss the possibility of my joining the party and standing for Europe. He suggested my contribution to Irish politics as an independent had been completed and that, in my own interest and that of the party, it was time to move on. I was flattered by the invitation, especially because I admired the man and (much of) his political philosophy, but it didn't take me long to make a polite refusal.

In the first place, orientating my life and my career to a European Parliament held no attraction for me. It would be an understatement to say that in 1979 I did not share Garret's enthusiasm for things European. However, my principal reason for turning down the invitation was that my whole political raison d'être was independence. Joining a party would have totally contradicted my 'mission' of contributing to, and helping form public opinion on, national issues according to my own views.

If a politician is serious about getting attention for his views, he must court and secure popularity. This would seem to be a more difficult task for the independent than the party member who enjoys organisational support and facilities. Before I develop this point, let us remember that Seanad Éireann, during my membership from the late 1970 to the early 1990s, was very well served by media, especially newspaper coverage. The four broadsheets (the now defunct *Irish Press* included) carried generous daily reports of Seanad proceedings under the bylines of interested reporters who occasionally wrote distinctive colour pieces. In contrast, only one daily now reports on Seanad meetings, extending to no more than ten paragraphs or so. One consequence is public indifference, if not hostility, to the second house.

In my day, the independent senator got far more attention and coverage from journalists than did his political party colleagues, frequently to the latters' chagrin. The independent had more interesting and unpredictable things to say, outside as well as within the chamber. He made good copy. He was a newsworthy phenomenon in that he provoked speculation about his 'real' inner convictions, about what party he might join and whether he might eventually stand for the Dáil. I counted myself fortunate in that I became friendly with a number of journalists who gave me welcome and generous publicity, crucially so during election campaigns. Aengus Fanning (later editor of the *Sunday Independent* where I was to become a frequent columnist) was an *Irish Independent* reporter when I was a senator, and I recall his occasional visits with a portable typewriter to my (shared) Seanad office to pick up on some views I had recently expressed and to draft a feature story about them there and then.

A secure university post offered me the opportunity (with impunity!) to express totally independent views on public issues. In fact, I had been doing so from the late 1960s, thus achieving a fairly high profile. I was encouraged (not that I needed much encouragement!) to stand for the NUI constituency in Seanad Éireann in 1977, especially to take advantage of the retirement from the constituency of Professor Patrick M. Quinlan of UCC. Quinlan had comfortably held a Seanad seat for many years, in general following a catholic conservative line. (When I was elected in due course, he congratulated me with the injunction to 'keep the flag flying'. 'Yes, Paddy,' I rejoined, 'but it won't be the same flag!')

University senators were regarded as secure academic gentlemen, uniquely positioned to speak their minds boldly. TCD senators were perceived as espousing more liberal, critical views than their 'National' colleagues, traditionally representing the conservative values of the catholic majority. All university senators, unlike their party political colleagues aspiring to win or recover Dáil seats, were largely exempt from the mundane obligations of clinics and clientelism. They were not expected to concern themselves about 'looking after' their graduate voters, but rather to concentrate on high matters of state. During my time in the Seanad I was approached now and then by worthy interest groups whose cause I championed, but only twice in eleven years was I asked by individuals to make 'representations' on their behalf, in one case to expedite planning permission for a house site, in the other to recommend a temporary third-level teacher to the relevant minister for permanent appointments. In both cases, somewhat to my astonishment, my intervention seemed to produce immediate results!

UCC was pleased to have a staff member representing the institution in Seanad Éireann – as they saw it. NUI graduates living in Cork are of a similar mind. Of course, there was no provision in the constitution or in the law for regional representation in the university constituencies. But there was always a strong sense locally that 'Cork' (UCC) was entitled to one of the NUI seats and that 'Dublin' (UCD) must not be allowed to monopolise the constituency. The media commonly referred to me as 'the UCC senator'. I must say that the 'Cork' expectation was powerfully advantageous to me and I readily exploited it at election times. However, electoral advantage apart, I promoted regional issues whenever possible and I constantly challenged condescending metropolitan assumptions.

There were drawbacks to being an independent (in either house), more so thirty years ago than today. Telephone use was limited, accommodation and secretarial facilities had to be shared and the lack of group organisational support was a price to be paid. Membership of significant Oireachtas committees was beyond reach, and only once in my eleven years did I get to enjoy what the public would regard as a parliamentary junket. In 1978, I was included on the Irish delegation to the Interparliamentary Conference at Bonn, and this was made possible only through a little rule bending on the part of friendly officialdom. Also, an independent had no knowledge of likely forthcoming Seanad business, unlike the party politicians.

Of course, an independent senator did not function in total isolation. Though I pointed out every so often that a true independent was independent of all other independents, in practice there was a fair degree of consultation between the university senators – for example, on procedural matters such as the order of speakers, or the choice of a spokesperson on ritual or formal occasions. But the university senators were not given, nor did they seek, group recognition by the Cathaoirleach (chairperson). In maximising speaking and procedural opportunities, it was man and woman for themselves.

I can't recall any instance of being frustrated by the machinations of party politicians (generally, Fianna Fáil in government) or being crowded out by them. Naturally there were tensions on particular issues; I usually took stances against the party in power and it's fair to say I was regarded as troublesome. Party politicians tended to be suspicious of university senators ('bah! Intellectuals!'), but on the whole there was a good deal of mutual respect. More than once in the house, I acknowledged that independents were a kind of democratic luxury made possible only because political parties facilitate the workings of the mundane machinery of government.

The majority of party senators were not primarily committed to the house itself or to preserving and enhancing its status in the Oireachtas (parliament). For many members the Seanad was an ante-chamber where they marked time and used its facilities for 'elevation' to the Dáil in due course. Defeated Dáil candidates waited to return to the house where, they believed, the real action lay. A session in the Seanad also maintained their parliamentary continuity for pension purposes and the like. For those who, like myself, held the Seanad in primary esteem, it was galling and demeaning to hear the Cathaoirleach, prior to each Dáil campaign, wishing good luck to those senators about to enter the Dáil election fray.

Other party stalwarts sailing into the serene waters of retirement were rewarded for services rendered with a Seanad seat, with no serious expectation of any real contribution to the business of the House. For such privileged elders, the Seanad was a comfortable retirement home.

In this connection, I recall hosting a friend on her first visit to Leinster House. 'Hmmm,' she observed as I led her along the corridors of power, 'smells like a nursing home,' but then, fearing I might be offended, she hastily added 'a *good* nursing home'. Indeed, one of the residents who had befriended me during my early months often kindly asked me from his perch in the bar how I was getting on 'upstairs'. I was astonished after a considerable time to see him turning up in the chamber voting on a critically tight division. He was not, as I had assumed all along, a retired official but a venerable senator whose party needed his vote in an emergency with apologies no doubt for rudely disturbing his retired tranquillity.

But there were also senators from all the parties who commanded respect because of their qualities and commitments, and I was fortunate to enjoy their friendship. It should also be mentioned that the Taoiseach's eleven nominees (article 18.3) included some distinguished and able public figures who were by no means beholden to their patron and who exercised a quite independent and even critical role. Such a pre-eminence was Dr T. K. Whitaker who was also chancellor of the NUI when I served on its senate.

The fixed membership of Seanad Éireann (60) is less than half that of the Dáil. Arithmetically, this enhances the independent's chances of recognition. Physically, the Seanad has a far less confrontational character. This is facilitated by a companionable seating arrangement, a semi-circular grouping around the chair. The Seanad is housed in a particularly beautiful chamber, which is conducive to a sense of dignity, tranquillity and intimacy. This benign atmosphere favours the independent senator in a way difficult to define. Unlike the Dáil, the chair seems to be in physical proximity even with the backbenches.

Whatever arguments I might have had with the chair from time to time, I have to say I always got *cothrom na féinne* (fair play) from successive Cathaoirligh (chairpersons). As an individual independent rather than a member of a group, I was never denied a speaking opportunity. Apart from contributing to debates on legislation, the independent can get publicity by commenting on the order of business announced at the beginning of each sitting. From time to time, the independent can introduce a private member's motion, outlining his or her case in an opening speech and summing up in conclusion. He or she can, of course, also contribute to motions introduced by other members. When appropriate, and if selected by the Cathaoirleach, a specific topical matter can be raised 'on the adjournment'; that is, at the conclusion of proceedings on any given day. The 'raiser' of the topic is the sole speaker and, most importantly, a government minister has to come to the house to reply. One of the most interesting matters I remember raising under this rubric was 'the presence of the army at religious ceremonies'.

Basil Chubb defines an independent as 'an elected representative who campaigns without the backing of any party organisation, who refuses to take the party whip and who is answerable only to his constituents' (1957, 131). He might well have added: 'and whose campaign expenses are independently funded'. During my first campaign in 1977, I was in part indebted to the financial generosity of individuals; thereafter my Seanad salary provided for my election expenses. I might add that the early 1980s was a time of unprecedented parliamentary instability, involving three Dáil (and Seanad!) elections within eighteen months. During my entire Seanad career of approximately eleven years, I fought a total of six elections which worked out at an average parliamentary service of less than two years per election.

Enthusiastic voluntary support is absolutely essential for the independent candidate. Who were my supporters, what was their input and what motivated them? Family and friends rallied to me in the first instance, as did my UCC colleagues who did not want to see 'their' seat lost after Quinlan's retirement. Secondary school teachers, particularly history teachers, were staunch supporters. I had been a secondary teacher myself from 1950 to 1960 and still strongly identified with the profession. By 1977 my university students of previous years were now graduates and potential voters. Beyond all of these, the general body of NUI graduates across the professions were familiar with my views which had been given wide coverage on the media over the previous decade.

Whatever support was forthcoming on the basis of my views, I think the integrity of my independence was generally acknowledged and remained my enduring political strength. Fianna Fáil had been returned to power with a huge majority in the summer of 1977 and to those who cared about such things, it was felt that the overwhelming party tentacles should not be allowed spread into the university constituencies of Seanad Éireann. Even those who had voted the party ticket in the Dáil election shared this view. It was to my benefit then that I should be seen as an independent (Cork) David taking on the party (Dublin) Goliath. On the night of my election, topping the poll of twenty-four candidates, some of them party political, I was reported as claiming the result was a vindication of the independence of the university seats. 'My greatest joy was the political party candidates in this election were told in no uncertain terms that they were not wanted in this oasis of independence.' But this was not always to be so. Some years down the line, in 1983, the Labour Party, in the person of Michael D. Higgins, took a seat in the NUI constituency at my expense.

The foot soldiers/spear carriers of my campaign army comprised all sorts of people, young and old. The children, teenagers and younger, of my friends and supporters were recruited for such basic but vital tasks as filling envelopes with my election leaflets. It is a well-known aspect of political psychology, going back to the time of Daniel O'Connell, that those who help with an election campaign thereby identify themselves with the struggle. The supportive ardour is all the greater where the candidate is an independent – at least that was so in my case. (My comments here apply to all my six campaigns, but I have particularly warm memories of the 1977 struggle, it being my 'glad confident morning'.)

Many of my supporters were non-graduates, for every true political soul loves an election. Their most valuable contribution was to garner the votes of the graduates in the family, to make sure they got on the register (alarmingly large numbers of graduates never registered), to coax them to vote for me and post their votes in time. I remember with particular affection a grandmother who had been a Sinn Féin activist with my own parents in the revolutionary years and who now busied herself with reaping for me the rich harvest of her graduate grandchildren's votes. My family grocer, who had never gone to college, successfully worked on his graduate siblings while bitterly complaining he had no franchise himself. I could understand his democratic and anti-elitist feelings.

While my many supporters contacted graduate friends and acquaintances through telephone calls and letters, I did as much personal canvassing as possible. This was obviously a hit-and-miss approach in a nationwide constituency of 40,000 graduates. One could only attempt sample meetings with this vast number, but it was important to 'show the face' in as many places as possible. Since it was a fair assumption that the bulk of my support geographically lay in Munster, it was decided to visit places in the province (Cork city and county foremost) where clusters of graduates might be encountered, notably school common rooms but also local authority buildings (engineering and commerce graduates) and hospitals (medical graduates). And, of course, convents! At a time when nuns were to be met with in sizeable numbers, it was more than worthwhile to renew acquaintance with former reverend students of mine. Nuns were conscientiously minded to get out and vote. Besides, as they recalled, I had always been 'nice' to them as students!

A small and zealous committee orchestrated my campaigns, led by my (entirely voluntary) director of elections, the charismatic and effervescent John V. Lennon. On my canvassing expeditions I was always accompanied by a committee member, Lennon more often than not. Despite the early risings, hard work and breakneck schedules, I found the canvassing circuit an enormously enjoyable and genuinely educational experience.

What had I, as an independent candidate, to offer to the graduates whose votes I solicited? First of all, a public voice unattached to any faction, contributing conscientiously to the legislative process. But I also promised I would use Seanad Éireann as a platform to express my views and thereby hope to influence and change public opinion on crucial matters of national concerns.

But what *were* my views? Though their impetus changed in response to the course of events, I like to think that throughout my Seanad career I acted in accordance with a consistent and coherent political philosophy. I was taken aback by a commentator's description of me in the 1980s as 'an old-fashioned nationalist' and was equally startled quite recently by being called 'the prominent voice of Southern nationalism' in the 1970s. I had thought of myself as quite a sophisticated, if not cosmopolitan, political animal, and a social radical rather than a nationalist. On reflection, however, the commentators were not far off the mark.

I stood, first and foremost, for things native and close to home, for the use of our natural resources in the people's interest; for the protection and promotion of native culture – language, music and games; for equality of opportunity in education, particularly at third level (in the 1970s class and privilege were still dominant). In foreign policy, I was for neutrality in its positive and constructive sense, a United Nations man rather than a European, Aikenite rather than FitzGeraldian, believing we should stay clear of Cold War blocs, playing the independent role of a small nation in sympathy with the emerging ex-colonial states, and contributing to the policing of trouble spots worldwide. This last activity has been our greatest success. All that was, and is, my reading of Emmett's vision, 'taking our place among the nations of the earth'.

I was a twenty-six county nationalist rather than a United Irelander, and I came to oppose passionately the 'armed struggle' of the Provisional IRA, and the subservient politics of its mouthpiece, Sinn Féin. As I wrote in my 1982 election leaflet, 'we cannot tolerate sectarian terrorism perpetrated in our name and contrary to the best principles of Irish republicanism'. I also argued for 'a transcendent Irishness which will encompass conflicting traditions'. We could no longer tolerate the take-it-or-leave-it catholic, Gaelic nationalist package which had been laid down for the majority tradition. Various individual strands in that heritage were valuable, but they must be disentangled: church from state, faith from fatherland, language and culture from nationalism, nationalism from physical force.

The Seanad Éireann parliamentary debates, 1977–83, 1987–92, record my contributions on a wide range of issues reflecting the views I have just outlined. I spoke on educational, cultural and environmental matters, Northern Ireland, church–state relations, constitutional reform (especially reform of the Seanad itself), Anglo-Irish relations and extradition. I tried, whenever possible, to put contemporary issues in a historical context, thereby, I would like to think, providing the enlightenment which only history can give.

Throughout my Seanad career, and in my election literature, I emphasised my independent role, first and last. Standing for the first time in 1977, I said:

> I intend to uphold the admirable tradition of the independent university voice. I will neither accept party whips nor yield to pressure groups. My independence will be limited only by my representative status as an NUI senator and by my responsible concern for the national interest.

When I retired from the Senate in 1992, I could safely claim that I had kept my 'independent' promises. And though I conceded (1987 leaflet) that 'it is pretentious for individual Seanad candidates to talk about implementing social and economic policies', my independent membership of Seanad Éireann helped me to make a substantial contribution to moulding public opinion, I would hope for the better. In any case, it was a great privilege to serve in the national parliament, as a true independent.

We all have to acknowledge the truth of Edmund Burke's observation on the primacy of party politics: 'party divisions ... are things inseparable from the government'. But equally forceful is the comment of Sir Harold Nicolson, British diplomat and politician: 'We must have independent members of exceeding virtue and therefore very few' (1946).

I claim no virtue whatsoever but I am proud to have been among the few.

Seán Dublin Bay Loftus

Seán Dublin Bay Loftus was an independent member of Dublin City Council for twenty-five years, and served as Lord Mayor of Dublin from 1995 to 1996. A founder of the Christian Democrat Movement in Ireland, he changed his name by deed poll several times to promote his political platforms. He was ultimately elected to the Dáil in 1981, a term that was to prove short lived, as his vote contributed to the fall of the government seven months later. He contested all thirteen general elections between 1961 and 1997.

(Note: this section is based on an interview with Seán Dublin Bay Loftus, 27 May 2008.)

My father was a doctor with the Electricity Supply Board. I was the eldest of seven, so I did what was expected of me, which was to go off and study medicine. I spent three and a half years at University College Dublin (Earlsfort Terrace) in the late 1940s, not really studying, trying to get the feel of the place, going to the Literary and Historical (L & H) debating society and the likes. One day someone came in from Fianna Fáil, inviting us to come down to Mount Street, the party headquarters, as they were interested in hearing our views. I went down to see what it was all about, but I discovered all they wanted was hands to help out with the church-gate collections. They showed no interest whatsoever in our views about the state of the nation or anything else like that. So that finished me with party politics.

However, I remained interested in politics. There was a lot of disillusionment in the immediate post-war years, and so in the winter of 1947, in Charles Stewart Parnell's old house in Avondale, I organised a forum to discuss national issues as they affected people in their lives. We had weekly meetings, with an average attendance of about eighty or so. People attended from all kinds of organisations; they included those who felt their voice was not being heard, and also those who wanted to hear the voice of others. I chaired the meetings. We had seventeen consecutive meetings over the winter and spring. I then could have led a campaign against the political system, but lacked the resources to do anything about it.

I moved to the US in the late 1950s, and in Washington in 1960 I was introduced to the President of the Christian Democratic Party (then the largest party) of Chile, Dr Frei Montalva. He had come to Washington to get a blank cheque from President Kennedy to defeat the combined left in a presidential election. He asked me why I did not come into the field of Christian Democracy. He told me that Christian Democracy came from the ideas of the founders of St Vincent de Paul, which said that ideology had failed and that democracy needed to be christianised. So I decided on my departure from the US after three years to set up the Christian Democratic Movement of Ireland. I wanted to move away from party politics, which was so divisive, and create a movement of people, rather than a political party. The aim was to set up an organic movement that grew from the grass roots. I held a press conference in the US announcing this decision in 1961 and then I came home.

A friend of mine, John O'Halloran, held a meeting at the same time in Dublin, setting up a Christian Democracy movement in Ireland. On my return, I set about plans to register the movement as a legal political party with the electoral authorities. This was a new requirement under the 1963 Electoral Act, because up to that time there was no official register of parties. Any group could call itself a party, but it made little legal difference as there was no state financial support for parties as is the case today, and party labels were not stated on the ballot. Voters were expected to know the party affiliation of their candidates, which created a few problems when candidates of the same or similar name ran in the same constituency!

The party register was set up because the established parties were annoyed by Sinn Féin's electoral victories at the 1957 Dáil election (when it won four seats), in particular that a party which refused to recognise the state still had people elected. As a consequence, they came up with the solution that any group that wished to contest elections would have to apply for recognition from the registrar, thereby a de facto acknowledgement of the state's existence. Although there were guidelines in place to qualify as a party, the decision remained an arbitrary power of the registrar. Anyway, we applied to register the Christian Democratic Movement of Ireland as a party in 1963. At this time we had all the requisite material: a constitution, a public image, trustees, a bank account and several hundred members, but our application was rejected.

At the time I was friends with Sean MacBride (founder of Clann na Poblachta and an eminent senior counsel) and Thomas Connolly (the top lawyer in Ireland at the time), and they were livid at this rejection. MacBride encouraged me to appeal the decision in the High Court. This involved getting into a witness box before Justice Kenny to defend the movement. In court, the judge asked me how I planned to fund the movement. I said I knew individuals who would provide me with financial help at election time, but I was not prepared to divulge their names without their consent. The judge accepted my answer, but said I would need to come back again. MacBride was furious with this. While he didn't agree with my views, he felt that you are entitled to be registered in a democracy and to have your beliefs heard.

Another leading counsel and politician, T. F. O'Higgins, then jumped on board my campaign. He and Thomas Connolly signed a statement of claim to my constitutional challenge to this decision that it was in opposition to freedom of association. Usually these appeals are quickly dealt with in the courts, but for one reason or another my case did not come up until 1969. Unfortunately, it was fixed for the same day as Charlie Haughey's trial in the Supreme Court over the importation of arms. Because Connolly was representing Haughey, he had to withdraw his services, which left me scrambling for counsel.

By this stage, on advice from the Registrar of Parties, I had changed the name of the group to the Christian Democratic Party of Ireland, albeit reluctantly. To no avail. The same Justice Kenny dismissed my appeal after a day and a half because of the costs of the case. Basically, he wanted it out, as he deemed it a nuisance.

I further appealed this to the Supreme Court, but the case was thrown out in 1972. With this decision, I gave up my campaign to register the party. Instead, I opted for a cheaper and easier method of promoting the party by changing my name by deed poll. So, in February 1973, I changed my name to Sean D. Christian Democrat Dublin Bay Loftus, something which no judge could reject! I included Dublin Bay to reflect my interest in campaigning for the preservation of Dublin Bay, against several plans to build oil refineries and further industries in the area.

Unfortunately, my name change made little electoral impact. At the 1973 election, my vote increased by only a few hundred on my 1969 showing, to 578 first preferences. Daniel MacCarron, the honorary secretary of our Christian Democracy movement, also ran in Donegal North-East, but he fared little better, winning barely more than 200 votes. With these results, I felt there was little point maintaining the party. I simply hadn't got the resources. There was a lot of apathy towards parties, and I saw little point being part of a lot who received such negative attention. I thought then that was the end of my political career.

A phone call from the deputy editor of the *Irish Independent* in 1974 changed matters. He mentioned to me that as Carmencita Hederman was running as an independent on behalf of a residents' association in the south of the city, I should stand on the north side of the city. I was not convinced at the time, as I was not really interested in local government; national government was my preference, as I believed reform of the political structure needed to take place at the national level. However, as was pointed out to me, you have to start somewhere. The same journalist said that if I managed to get elected I would get more recognition from the media, and that my issues would attract more publicity.

My position was, though, that I would not stand unless invited to do so by the people. By this time, another independent, Vincent Manning (who was secretary of ACRA, the Association of Combined Residents' Associations), had been nominated to run in Dublin electoral area no. 1, where I lived. At a meeting of residents' associations to support Manning's nomination, it was suggested that I should also stand. I was persuaded by Manning's organisation, somewhat reluctantly, to run, but the chairman warned me to stick to local issues and not to air my opinions on national issues, particularly on Northern Ireland, about which I was in favour of a federal solution. The two main issues I stood for then were on planning law and Dublin Bay.

I soon realised that the purpose of my nomination was to attract additional votes that would transfer to Manning and see him elected. We had agreed to split the constituency in two for canvassing purposes, but one morning after mass in Killester, which was in my bailiwick, I found leaflets on all car windows that said 'Vote 1 Manning'. I knew I was on my own after that. As things turned out, both of us were elected, with Manning the first candidate home. It was unusual to have two independents elected in the same ward, but there was a strong disillusionment about the party system at the local level. That year, six independents got elected to Dublin Corporation, including Brendan Lynch from the Liberties and Kevin Byrne from the East Wall. As community independents we agreed to work in a kind of alliance, to come together to get agreement on some primary issues and ways and means of solving them in a free vote in the corporation. We did not impose a formal whip, as we realised the importance of working as a team of independents, with independent thoughts. We only acted together when we were all agreed on an issue; there was no coercion involved.

My election to local office had a positive effect on the support I received at Dáil elections, which I had been contesting since 1961. Where my vote in 1973 amounted to 578 first preferences, by 1977 it increased sixfold to over 3,000. Further, at the first European Parliament elections in 1979, I managed to win almost 22,000 votes in Dublin – over 7 per cent of the total poll. It was obvious then that local office gave me a platform to air my views on issues, both local and national. Without the backing and resources of a party, this is a vital advantage for any independent, and I know of very few who have been elected to the Dáil without first holding office at the local level.

1981 was my sixth Dáil election. Although I was ultimately elected, my vote was actually down by over two percentage points on the 1977 election. However, the vote in Dublin North-East, outside of Fianna Fáil's Michael Woods' showing (he got one-third of first preferences), was quite fragmented. There were six candidates with between a third and a quarter of the quota battling it out for two seats. In such situations, being an independent can be advantageous as we have the ability to pick up transfers from all candidates. In particular, my stance on environmental issues helped get me over the line. I was as surprised as anyone that I won a seat. In all my political life I never canvassed the constituency or held political clinics. I did leaflet drops, but never knocked on doors.

On my first day in the Dáil the Fine Gael leader Garret FitzGerald said to me: 'Welcome to the club Seán. We have unwritten rules and conventions in this club. We will let you know what they are as we go along. If you follow our advice, you could be here for life.' I knew then that the parties controlled parliamentary matters, and that I was to be a marginalised force.

This was highlighted to me by one particular episode a few months into my Dáil career. The parties, in conjunction with the Ceann Comhairle, controlled speaking times. The then Ceann Comhairle, John O'Connell, had granted me a few minutes' speaking time. However, when my turn came to say a few words, I was interrupted by John Boland, the Minister for Education, who questioned my right to speak because my name was absent from the list of speakers. O'Connell then sided with Boland and asked me to resume my seat, even though I was only standing because he had called on me to speak in the first place! A few cross words were exchanged, but rather than seek cheap publicity and be thrown out of the Dáil, I sat down. In the transcript of the Dáil debates, this argument was edited out, which for me was against all the rules and regulations. I naturally complained, but a fat lot of good it did. The parliamentary correspondents also did not mention the incident in their coverage of the day's proceedings. You really were on your own as an independent.

The outcome of the 1981 election was unclear. With eighty-four seats needed for a majority, Fianna Fail won seventy-eight, Fine Gael sixty-five and Labour fifteen. While the election of two abstentionist H-Block candidates reduced the required majority down to eighty-two, it still left the few independents holding the balance of power. With the greater numbers, FitzGerald clearly had the upper hand on Haughey, but he never sought my support (probably because he knew he would never get it), instead relying on the two independent socialists, Noël Browne and Jim Kemmy. One of the big issues in Irish politics at the time was FitzGerald's 'constitutional crusade', to which I was strongly opposed. As a committed christian I didn't want to secularise the country.

Holding fewer aces, Charlie Haughey had me driven out to Kinsealy to canvass for my vote. On arrival I was led into a grand room at his Abbeville mansion, where Haughey sat at the back in the dark like the Delphi Oracle while a beam of light shone down the centre of the room. I told Haughey that even if I supported him, the numbers did not stack up. His reply was, 'I respect your independence.' That was my one and only encounter with Charles J. Haughey.

FitzGerald was elected Taoiseach a week later, but it was a short-lived administration. Seven months later the government fell after it failed to get its budget passed in the Dáil. Not for the first time in Irish politics, independents played a significant role, and this time it was in bringing down the government. The week before the crucial budget vote of January 1982, Jim Kemmy wrote an article in the *Sunday Independent*, with five or six demands for the budget that no government could accept. I presumed from this that Kemmy planned to vote against the government. This made me realise how crucial my vote was to the coalition, so I wrote to Garret FitzGerald saying I would support the government on basic conditions – if taxation for the low waged was reasonably fair in the upcoming budget, and if the proposed VAT was not introduced. I received no response and no one in the Fine Gael party asked me how I was going to vote. Although I was opposed to FitzGerald's constitutional crusade, for me the budget was a different matter. It was to do with politics and I was prepared to come to a compromise.

On the day of the budget, I met an economist in Leinster House who told me that 20,000 jobs would be lost if the VAT went ahead. As a result, when I met Jim Mitchell, the Fine Gael whip, I told him I would not be supporting the budget unless there was a modification to the VAT rate. This was the first time anyone in government had asked me my voting intentions. I was left waiting in the Fine Gael committee room for two hours for a response from the party that never came. The division bells went and I almost missed the budget vote. The door to the chamber was being locked and I had to crash through it. Contrary to popular legend, it was then my vote, not Jim Kemmy's, that brought down the government. When Kemmy voted no, despite FitzGerald's pleadings from the floor, this left the division at eighty-one votes each. When the Fianna Fáil deputies in the gallery saw this, Albert Reynolds rushed back into the chamber and attempted to push me through the níl (no) corridor. Brian Fleming, a Fine Gael TD, tried to prevent this, and there was a literal tug of war over my support, with me as the rope!

After I voted to defeat the budget, FitzGerald was obliged to go to Áras an Uactharáin to resign as Taoiseach and seek a dissolution of the Dáil. All this was unnecessary as I was willing to work with Fine Gael if they would only meet with me. I rang the President's aide-de-camp to pass on this message, but I was never connected and so sent on a telegram instead. My efforts did not come to fruition, as I did not receive any response, no doubt due to Fianna Fáil pressure put on President Hillery (he was a former Fianna Fáil TD and minister). No explanation was ever given by Fine Gael nor any deal sought. I was ignored. In such political dealings, FitzGerald was an amateur, although in part I blame his advisors. His unwillingness to work with me proved particularly ironic because at the subsequent election the following month, another independent, Tony Gregory, held the balance of power. This time FitzGerald did not ignore the independent benches, and both he and Haughey engaged in a financial bidding war over Gregory's vote.

My role in the downfall and attempted saving of FitzGerald's government was unknown at the time, but the story was reported by Mark Hennessey in the *Irish Examiner* on 7 November 1990, the day after the presidential election. The RTÉ television chat-show *Nighthawks* contacted me to appear on the programme to discuss the story. I was naturally delighted as it was my opportunity to tell my side of events, but at the last moment RTÉ phoned me to say they had to pull the story, with no clear reason given for their actions, although I had my suspicions. I subsequently lost my seat at the February 1982 election, and never won it back, despite a further six attempts. I never spoke to FitzGerald again, and when he devoted a line in his autobiography to describe me as 'a conservative catholic' I wrote to the publishers threatening to sue. As a result they had to print a new edition.

In 1995, near the end of my political career, I was elected Lord Mayor of Dublin. For me it was a vindication of my independence. An independent is a person who has strong beliefs and promotes them, to direct his beliefs to whatever parties are in power, to try and accommodate those beliefs. I opted for this individualistic path because I could not go along with the idea of a party whip. I am a strong believer in a firm conscience. I always had that belief. For me, the parties had had their day. They're all the same.

Postscript: On a point of clarification, I believe my name changes have attracted some attention amongst the political science community as evidence of alphabetic voting – in other words, people voting in an alphabetical fashion down the voting paper. This phenomenon implies that the higher up the ballot paper, the more votes you are likely to attract, all things being equal. This explains why the Dáil is overpopulated with surnames beginning with letters closer to the start of the alphabet. (Editor: 53 (34 per cent) of the 158 TDs elected in 2016 had surnames beginning with the letter A, B, C or D.)

Certainly, I was aware of this phenomenon when I changed my name by deed poll three times, but this was also done to highlight the political issues that I was most interested in. So, I first changed my name in 1973 to Christian Democrat Loftus to promote my political movement; then to Dublin Bay Loftus to highlight my concerns about the preservation of Dublin Bay; and finally to Dublin Bay-Rockall Loftus to reflect my interests in the outcrop of Rockall, over which there was an Irish–British dispute due to oil and mineral rights.

However, despite political folklore, I never changed my name to Alderman Dublin Bay-Rockall Loftus to secure election in 1981 (which would have put me at the top of the ballot paper). Alderman was not mentioned on the ballot, and as I mentioned earlier in the chapter, I actually lost votes at that election. It was only on the Dáil register that I signed my name as Alderman, which explains why it has been recorded as such.

Finian McGrath

Finian McGrath was elected as an independent to Dublin City Council in 1999. He was elected to the Dáil in 2002 in Dublin North-Central, and was re-elected in 2007 and 2011. In 2007 he negotiated a deal with first Bertie Ahern, and later Brian Cowen, in return for his parliamentary support. This was withdrawn in October 2008. From 2011 to 2012 he was chairman of the Technical Group in the Dáil. In 2015 he helped establish the Independent Alliance, which supported a Fine Gael minority government after the February 2016 Dáil election. In May 2016 he was appointed a 'super-junior' minister of state, with responsibility for disability issues.

I was born and grew up in Tuam, County Galway. My father was the local postman and my mother was a nurse. Growing up in a small town like Tuam meant that, while you lived in the town, you were also very close to rural life and there was always a good mix of people in and around the town. As a result of this I've never really gone with this urban and rural division and my political philosophy was always on the side of small farmers and ordinary working people in urban areas. I did not realise it of course, as a child, but those influences were playing a part from an early age.

My mother and father were classic examples of what we today call community activists. They were involved in a lot of voluntary work like the St Vincent de Paul and the Order of Malta, and my father was involved in the Gaelic Athletic Association with the Tuam Stars, so there was a strong community and volunteer aspect to our household. Newspapers and politics were always discussed in the house, political history was like an open forum and I suppose it was in my gene pool to be politically aware and to want to participate in these discussions. My mother had emigrated to England at the age of sixteen and worked there during the war and she was the classic returned emigrant, with a strong work ethic and a desire to see her children get on and do well. My father had left school at thirteen and therefore they were both determined that their children would get a better education.

My parents also had a strong sense of patriotism and there was an ethic passed down that you had to work and do something for your country as well as doing something for yourself. When I was a teenager I was already heavily involved in volunteer work in the junior St Vincent de Paul and the local youth group. Of course, these years coincided in 1966 with the anniversary of 1916 and there was a big debate at the time about what had been achieved and about the leaders. I suppose it was at about that time that I found myself moving away from de Valera and more towards Connolly in terms of heroes. That was the kind of debate going on in my head as a teenager, trying to assess Pearse, de Valera, Collins and Connolly.

By the time I was eighteen I had come to the conclusion that I was a total maverick. I could not agree with any one side completely and therefore I could not join a political party; I knew then I was an independent. I liked being a maverick; I had very definite political philosophies that were just part of me. I was always a great admirer of Wolfe Tone; I loved his idea of 'catholic, protestant and dissenter'. My mother and father were always very catholic; I had neighbours down the road who were protestant, but I felt like the dissenter. As a result I felt Wolfe Tone was the only guy I could truly identify with as he acknowledged this idea of a dissenter. So I guess I built my own philosophy around that and that was something that stayed with me throughout my life.

I just did not like Fine Gael because they projected a sense of intolerance. There was definitely a strong sympathy for Labour but I felt that they were not representing the poor in all sections of society. Studying statistics, I felt Fianna Fáil was doing more for the poor nationally and that was another conflict. There was that constant debate going on in my brain. This perhaps explains partially why I could only ever opt to be an independent.

After I qualified as a teacher I went to work for the Simon Community in Cork and that alerted me to why politics mattered. At the time the grant to run the Simon Community centre in Cork for the homeless was less than the grant given to run the cats and dogs home, and I really felt that people did not give a damn about the homeless or services for them. So issues like that began to increase my activism.

I went on to focus on teaching and, working in inner city Dublin, I found it a great privilege. However, I never stopped being active and trying to do things in the community where I lived and worked. After many years I became principal of the school, and I really enjoyed that because it was then that I could start to implement certain policies and beliefs about education and how to deliver it. However, I remember the day I was made principal I went out to celebrate with my father that evening and have a pint. For him this was huge news that his son had become a school principal, and I remember him saying to me, 'Now Finian, will you do me one favour? Will you forget about that auld politics stuff because you have a great job now!' We laughed about it because he was a political animal himself and he knew the draw politics could be.

During that time I had met Tony Gregory, who was then a young councillor working in the inner city. A lot of the issues I was dealing with working in education, including disadvantage, unemployment and the drugs epidemic, were all issues Tony was involved with. This was the late 1970s and early 1980s and a lot of good kids were slipping through the system. I was a young teacher who saw it as my job to try keeping them in it and helping them. Tony Gregory, Fergus McCabe and Mick Rafferty were all trying to do the same. So as I got involved in more and more of these local activities, I came to know Tony Gregory well. It was shortly before the general election when he rang me and asked me would I lend a hand dropping some leaflets for him and it was from there on, when I started going around with Tony, that I began to take politics seriously.

Tony got elected in 1982, and of course that changed everything because for us as a group of foot soldiers, getting Tony elected was like winning the All-Ireland. Everyone now knows about the famous Gregory deal, but for us it was very simple, the whole idea was about supporting people in the most disadvantaged area of the country. It was an essential deal, and although some elements of the establishment complained about it, it was still the right thing to do.

I was married and living in Marino, I loved my job and had two daughters, but I continued to help Tony and work for him in a voluntary capacity, dropping leaflets and canvassing. Then quite out of the blue one day Tony said to me, 'McGrath why don't you try it where you are living?' I thought about it a lot and discussed it with my late wife Ann, and we decided ok, let's do it. We knew it would not be easy in Dublin North-Central, but there was some history of independents as Seán Dublin Bay Loftus had operated in the constituency before. We made a clear strategy and decided we would have to build a base over a number of years. A lot of friends said to me at this point that it would just be easier if I aligned myself with a party. The base would already be there; even my own family was doubtful about me making the break-through as an independent. I just knew I would not have the discipline to stay in a mainstream party. At different stages every party in the Dáil approached me to run for them. I finally got my big break in 1999 when I was elected to Dublin City Council as an independent.

The following general election was 2002. Having just won a council seat we did not really expect to take a Dáil seat; we were aiming for the election after that to have a realistic prospect. It was a strange election in 2002; there was a sense of confidence and even arrogance among some sections of the community that I was very uneasy with. But no matter how good things seemed, there was always a section of society that was left behind and serving them was my agenda. I often got frustrated by a cocky attitude among some, especially what might be called the 'gated community' within our society, quite literally areas where you could not even canvass because they were gated off and if you rang the buzzer you were told 'No, we don't want politicians.' The funny thing is that as soon as the downturn happened they were among the first to start ringing my office. Now, by the same token, there are wealthy people who vote for me, usually because they have a social conscience and they impress me through that and their desire to help others. It's certainly not true to say I only get my vote in disadvantaged areas, even though those areas are my priority.

On the day of the count I arrived into the Royal Dublin Society (RDS) and saw we had received 3,800 votes, we were very happy with that as it was a great showing, but we did not think I would be elected on it. However, as the count went on I started picking up transfers from all sides and directions and suddenly I was up to about 6,500 votes and I managed to take the last seat. We hadn't expected to win it so it really took us by surprise, but it was an amazing feeling. It was such an honour and I will never forget walking through the Dáil gates with my family, and in particular my mother.

After that election we had the numbers as independents to form a technical group. That idea, of course, came from Tony and from his experience of the Dáil, but it gave us speaking rights which was a very positive step. It was the first time this had been done and we repeated this in the following Dáil (2007–11). There were some within the group who might have wished to move towards something more formal in terms of an embryonic political party, but for others it was strictly a technical arrangement to derive speaking rights. I get a lot of requests from the public asking independents to form a new political grouping, but personally I'm not in favour of starting or joining any new political party. I still see myself as very much an independent. For all the diversity that existed within the technical group and the number of different views, we were in some ways stronger for it. The same is true of the Independent Alliance I helped form in 2015. Within the group everyone has their own view and agenda but they respect the others' position. The only thing that upsets people is when someone lets down the brand of independents, because whether we like it or not we all feel it reflects on us. There is no doubt we were very annoyed by the issues surrounding Mick Wallace and the non-payment of tax, for example. There was a great sense of disappointment because a lot of us were elected on new politics, integrity, and then that happened and it showed the opposite.

From my earliest days in politics I have always tried to communicate a vision, a broader national message, but there is no doubt that the reason I got elected was because I was active locally. While my views might be based on something locally it always has a national dimension. I remember during the good times suggesting that a tax increase might be necessary to fund the kind of projects we needed and to make them sustainable, but that was because I could see what was needed on the ground. I would feel that my time is divided 50 per cent on national issues and 50 per cent on local issues. I am fully in favour of political reforms, in areas like the Seanad in particular, although I do not agree with its abolition. There is a mood that suggests constituency work is a bad thing and I don't agree with that at all. I meet MPs from the UK and representatives from the US and they don't have a link with their constituency at all. In Ireland the PR-STV electoral system is very inclusive and I think Irish politicians across parties and independents are very close to their public, and through their offices they face the effects of the decisions they make and I think that is a good thing. I would be very much against the idea of going down the road of the UK or America, where it's all television advertisements and media campaigns without ever really having to get out among the public and facing people.

I think you learn more from meeting people in constituency offices or on doorsteps than you do from anything else in politics. When you go into someone's home, particularly someone with a disability, and see for yourself the challenges they face and the services they depend on, it is a real eye opener. I think it is important to be in touch with real people as well as sitting in the Dáil being a legislator; one role informs the other. There is a need for procedural reform and more speaking time and things like that.

From 2002 to 2007 I felt the government did not take independents seriously, but I will say that if you came up with a good idea or a strong proposal, individual ministers were very willing to listen and work with you. My personality always led me to want to talk to people and mingle with them, and I was no different towards members of the government, so I became friendly with a number of ministers who were open to listening, people like Mary Hanafin in Education and Dermot Ahem in Justice. I always got on well with Micheál Martin and to be fair there was lots of connection with Bertie Ahem because he was a northside TD and he was familiar with a lot of the issues I faced. So you can build those relationships and use them when you have a worthwhile policy to advance. The idea that an independent TD in opposition has no power is simply not true. They have as much influence and as many contacts as any other ordinary TD. My approach has always been based on the belief that I was elected to try and achieve things and make a difference and I work towards that every day.

In 2007 all the experts wrote off my chances of retaining my seat as the constituency was reduced from four seats to three. We went into the campaign under major pressure, but we fought all the way and in the end Ivor Callely lost his seat and I retained mine, something nobody predicted. I had put in huge work in the constituency and people recognised that; they were also more aware of me now and what I was about. I got a bit of luck as well which you need when competing with the big party machines, and doing the charity 'You're a Star' programme on television was a help as it boosted my profile in a way that independent TDs don't often get to do.

After the 2007 election, Phil Hogan approached me about an effort to form a Fine Gael government, but Fine Gael was divided on the inclusion of Sinn Fein. Bertie Ahern also approached me and Fianna Fáil was in a strong position to form the government. I saw these negotiations strictly as business; I knew the issues I wanted to get over the line. I had Tony Gregory and Joe O'Toole helping me out from my side in terms of reviewing drafts. I had objectives such as the National Centre for Cystic Fibrosis – that was a promise I had made to parents – and then there were also local issues such as funding for groups, education and the disabled within the community. I always felt I had a moral obligation to deliver those issues given the position I was in.

In 2008 Bertie Ahern resigned, but it didn't cause me any problems because I got on well with his replacement, Brian Cowen, and I knew he would uphold the deal we had made. I knew him on a personal level and behind closed doors I saw the respect he showed to people and the massive compassion he had on the disability issue. I saw a sincere and warm side that the public never saw.

The problems mounted for the government and one crisis just followed another. As the cuts began to bite though I felt a red light go on. I understood the economic difficulties but I felt we were shifting away from some key issues for me. I made alternative proposals and we discussed things at length, but there were certain policies I could not stand over. I felt we had to tackle waste and services for people like ourselves in the Dáil before you cut services to disabled people. It was a difficult and traumatic time; I didn't want to blow the agreements I had secured from the government but there came a point when I couldn't support it any more. I was getting a lot of calls from people who felt they had crossed the line and I began to feel the same.

The transfer to being on the opposition benches was a big change, like going into a completely different zone. I got a lot of abuse for it but I found I was trying to have a balanced view. I understood what the government was trying to do and when they did something good I supported it; I opposed them on other issues but I was definitely not in opposition for opposition's sake. Luckily I found the electorate very understanding and my voters saw where I was coming from and appreciated what I was trying to do. The 2011 election was a very difficult one; I had never experienced anything like the anger and annoyance on the doorsteps. For a lot of people it didn't matter what side you were on, all politicians were to blame. It was certainly a brutal election and I was glad to come through it and thankfully retain my seat.

I joined a technical group of independents again after the election, and became its chairperson. After this experience, as well as working with independent councillors around the country, I decided to get involved in the Independent Alliance. It was a radical and positive experience. I also wanted to send out a strong signal that I can work with people who have very different views and come from diverse backgrounds. This is my national vision, particularly in 2016. Our 'Charter for Change' showed clearly that independents can work together in the interests of our citizens. The cynics and hurlers on the ditch predicted failure. But we had six members elected to the Dáil in 2016 and I am very proud of that result. Of course it was a tough general election and I had to fight hard for my seat, but I got there in the end. I am very proud of that win, particularly as it is now four in a row. The public want independents to work together and deal with the real issues. I will continue to do that and build a more democratic and inclusive Ireland. The Independent Alliance is now leading the reform agenda and the major political parties are moving in our direction. It is up to all of us now to act and get on with the job.

Politicians provide a vital link in society and too many people like to give out about the work we do at a constituency level. You can make a contribution at national level and at the same time serve your constituency. A good TD can easily balance that. The system itself does not react to individual citizens; big organisations like the Heath Service Executive or government departments just do not give answers. Getting information can prove an impossible task, whereas a TD can usually obtain an answer a lot quicker, or perhaps people sit up and take notice when a TD enquires in a way they don't when it's just an ordinary person. TDs might not want to be doing this work, but you are not going to turn someone away who needs help. The system is not trained or managed well enough to actually deliver efficiently for the public.

My role is to serve those who elected me. That means I carry their views through on national policy and legislation; I try to ensure their voice is heard when legislation is being put in place. I also serve them in any other way I can that makes a difference to their lives. Whether that's seeking information or debating a local issue, it's still part of my job as their representative, and that mix is a good thing. As an independent I am open to listening to anybody and to working with them for a solution. I'm a maverick, I will always be a maverick, but the dissenter is needed today as much as ever in the past.

Catherine Murphy

Catherine Murphy was first elected in 1988 as a town councillor for the Workers' Party and then again in 1991 as a Kildare county councillor. When the party split a year later, she joined the breakaway Democratic Left. Following the merger of Democratic Left and Labour in 1999 she contested, and held, her council seat at that year's local elections as a Labour candidate. She resigned from Labour in 2003 and was elected to the Dáil as an independent at a by-election in 2005. She lost her seat in 2007, but regained it in 2011, following which she became whip of the technical group of the 31st Dáil. During the course of the 31st Dáil, Catherine joined with fellow Independent TDs Róisín Shortall and Stephen Donnelly to form the Social Democrats, for whom she was returned to the 32nd Dáil in 2016 as co-leader of the new party.

Roots of my political involvement

I often describe myself as an accidental politician. I was first introduced to electoral politics when I joined the Workers' Party in 1983,
the motivation for which was that there was a lot about Irish life that I
wanted changed and, for me, the only way to influence and drive that
change was to become directly involved in the process of governance.
Looking back, I always had an interest in how decisions were made and
in whose interest they were made, and my involvement in politics was
a natural extension of that. Although, much like many women at the
time and perhaps even now, my initial approach was to volunteer in
a behind the scenes capacity, I was naturally drawn to activities such
as campaign management, and held no particular ambition towards
becoming a candidate in my own right. But that all changed when I was
talked into contesting the 1988 local election for the newly established
Leixlip Town Commission. After that ended successfully, the path of my
involvement in politics took a turn I hadn't expected, but ran with, and
have continued to follow since.

Running in 1988 was a decision I didn't take lightly. Politics is a
way of life that for some might cause conflict in their personal life, but
thankfully this was not the case for me because of the shared political outlook at home. I gave a lot of consideration to the fact that my
views would become public property; there would be an impact on my
children and husband, and that I was unsure of what I might be able to
achieve, but ultimately I felt it was worth the risk. It turned out that this
was the right call, as I have made some great friends through politics
and the political activity that goes with it, and I have had a long and
rewarding career.

The decision to take the plunge resulted from a combination of
factors, not least of which was the encouragement of a strong support
group of family and friends. A couple of key events I had experienced
decades previously also, however, left a deep impression on me and
eventually led me onto this path; one was a strike my late father was
involved in and the other was the horror of poverty I witnessed while
in school in Goldenbridge.

My father had been a carpenter and general foreman, and was
involved in a three-month long general strike of building workers in the
mid 1960s. The strike was centred on working conditions, which were
deplorable at the time, yet the newspaper headlines screamed 'greedy
building workers'. Despite the harsh times that came along with his
being out of work for such a long period of time, my father engaged
in the strike rather resolutely in order to help achieve better working
conditions for construction workers. At the same time my mother took

117

in sewing for a major department store, work that was organised on a piece-work basis and for which she was hugely exploited. I found it ironic that there were no corresponding 'greedy bosses' headlines in any of the newspapers. Feeding the nine of us, paying the mortgage and other bills, meant there was little choice but to put up with this exploitation. The major lesson I learned was that we are not all in this together; there are always sides in such struggles, even if they are not always obvious, and all too often the injustices and inequities experienced in our society are glossed over or unseen by those in charge.

The second big event I witnessed during childhood that helped to ignite my fascination with decision-making and the corresponding desire to become involved in driving change came about after I changed schools between fifth and sixth classes. For sixth class I attended Goldenbridge Primary School in Inchicore, Dublin, which was located beside Keogh Square – a former British army barracks known as Richmond Barracks which had come to be used to house people, many of whom were moved there when they could not afford to pay council rents and were forced out. My family was not well-off by any stretch of the imagination, but attending school with the girls from Keogh Square showed me what real poverty was like up close. I caught a glimpse of just how harrowing and hopeless it was for those who endured it, and the experience has never left me.

The irony of the time and location was not lost on me, even at such a young age. It was around this time that the triumphalist fiftieth anniversary of the Easter Rising was taking place. In school we read the 1916 Proclamation, which talked about cherishing all the children of the state equally, yet there were children in my class who were hungry, cold, and neglected. The other irony of the situation was that the place in which they lived, Keogh Square, was the barracks to which my grandfather and the other insurgents who had taken part in the Easter Rising were marched prior to being dispatched to gaols in England and subsequently the squalor of Frongoch internment camp in Wales.

Initial party involvement

Having spent almost two decades in parties before becoming independent, I had a solid knowledge of how parties organise and fund elections, and this was enormously helpful to me when striking out alone as an independent. It would also prove invaluable in helping me to make the decision to re-enter party politics in 2015 with the Social Democrats. Back in the 1980s, I was one of those protestors looking for a voice, and eventually I found it by joining the Workers' Party. This first came in the form of participation in a small number of major tax marches in the late 1970s and early 1980s, the aim of which was to achieve a rebalancing of what we felt was an unfair distribution of the burden of taxation on ordinary PAYE workers. When water and bin charges were imposed in 1983, this was the final catalyst for my decision to join the Workers' Party. I wanted to do something more than attend the odd protest march, and joining a campaigning party such as the Workers' Party seemed like a good place to start. The organisational structure of the party provided members the opportunity to participate actively, and was also geared towards encouraging non-members to become more active in an effort to change things. I saw involvement as an opportunity for ordinary people to challenge the decisions being made about their lives, and to force a situation whereby those decisions would favour ordinary people as opposed to the elites in society.

I remained with the Workers' Party until it split in 1992, went on to become a founding member of Democratic Left, and was still a member at the time of the party's merger with the Labour Party six years later. I decided to remain with the newly merged entity that was simply known as the Labour Party despite my misgivings about the merger; my decision to do so came only in the eleventh hour. My particular concern was that the two parties had different political cultures and I did not believe it would make for an easy mix. I felt Labour was basically a collection of personal fiefdoms, while Democratic Left – and before that the Workers' Party – was a campaigning party. To make a long story short, the experience of the merger in Kildare for me was generally unhappy and unrewarding, and, come 2003, I threw off the shackles to become an independent.

Although the first chapter of my career as a party politician did not end as I would have liked it to at the time, life is a learning experience and having the combined experience of practising politics both as an independent and within a party structure was invaluable in the years that followed. I very much enjoyed the collaborative approach to policy development and the sense of achievement that came with the more inclusive campaigning model of politics; in many ways, I was sorry to leave those aspects of party politics behind when I first became independent. But, for me, those qualities fell away after the merger with Labour, and all that was left was a rather cumbersome set of internal governing structures that hindered rather than helped the sort of politics I was interested in practising.

Becoming independent

The merger provided me with a host of very valuable lessons, not least of which was the revelation that the political culture of a party is key to determining the experience of members. This is something I have been acutely aware of in my role as a co-founder and co-leader of the Social Democrats. Having had a range of rather different experiences when it came to party culture, I am always conscious of the responsibility and the opportunity I have to develop a member- and policy-centred culture within the Social Democrats. Although it was a blow at the time, I have benefited in the long run from the issues I encountered and the decisions I made during this time. My experience of party politics in a wider sense also provided me with a solid frame of reference for my years as an independent, which, despite the general perception, is not nearly as isolating as it is perceived. For example, there is a perception that even small political parties have big electoral machines, but in my experience this is a bit of a myth. The occasions I had the most offers of support and assistance were for elections I contested as an independent; if I were to hazard a guess, I think this could be because many of those who wished to assist did not want to become labelled as partisans and were happier to assist in a personal capacity.

The first election I faced as an independent was a local election to both authorities in 2004, and less than a year later I was elected to the Dáil following a by-election to replace Charlie McCreevy. So, it's safe to say that my first few years as an independent were both a rollercoaster and a highly exciting time in my political career. But what goes up must come down, and the general election of 2007 saw a reversal of fortunes for many independents, including me. The economic horizon was looking uncertain, and Fianna Fáil offered themselves as the party with the relevant experience to keep the so-called good times going. The election choice was narrowed by the media to one of a Fianna Fáil-led government or a Fine Gael one, and it was a disastrous election for independents and smaller parties. I was one of the many independents not returned to the Dáil. Soon after the new Fianna Fáil/Green Party/Progressive Democrat coalition was formed (ironically with the support of some independents), the economy began to unravel with catastrophic consequences.

The same things that had drawn me into politics in the first place rekindled my interest in returning to the political arena in 2008 when I was co-opted back to Kildare county council to retake the seat I vacated in 2005. The issue of proper planning and sustainable development had consistently dominated my time in politics. Our approach to developing our cities, towns and villages was crazy; everything was done backwards. The development-led approach resulted in a mismatch, where one housing estate after the other was built with little thought for those who would eventually live there. The delivery of schools, public transport, leisure facilities and so on were an afterthought rather than planned and resourced in parallel with developments. The construction sector was at the forefront in terms of 'planning laws'; those who purchased a home often found they were at the mercy of the developer to complete the estate, while the level of oversight by local authorities was wholly inadequate. The re-zoning of land had made some landowners and speculators very wealthy as a result of the enormous increases in the price of purchasing a home. I, and a handful of others, had been to the forefront of curbing the worst of the excesses in Kildare over the years and had instead forced a more strategic approach to the issue of development. This had been achieved by providing information and support to communities when development plans were being prepared. Consequently, St Catherine's Park, within the Liffey Valley at Lucan Demesne, is a public park today because the community resisted proposals to build houses there. So too, Castletown House in Celbridge remains within its natural landscape, and the proposed 'town centre' extension, composed mainly of multi-storey apartment blocks, was rejected by the planning appeals board.

The type of clientelist politics generally practised in this country was a huge part of the problem. The politician acted as a broker for securing entitlements, a type of politics that had been hugely successful for Fianna Fáil. They were a populist centrist party that followed rather than led change. During a time of plenty, when major reforms of our political and public service institutions should have, and could have, been undertaken, the opportunity was squandered. The opportunity to reform and redesign our civil and public services in a way that simplified the interface with the citizen in order for them to get what they were entitled to, without political assistance, was ignored.

The lack of reform of our institutions was outrageous during times of plenty. What masqueraded as reform was a public/civil service 'decentralisation' decision that distributed public servants throughout the country to constituencies where Fianna Fáil had a minister. There was little thought given to how that would impact on the delivery of public services, and it disgracefully paid no attention to a recently adopted National Spatial Strategy. The Health Service Executive (HSE) was established under the guise of reform, yet all that occurred was that a new administrative tier was added on top of the old health boards, complicating an already complicated system and removing direct responsibility for health services from the health minister – this included removing their role in accounting to the Dáil on matters of healthcare delivery. It also added to the cost of running the service at the expense of front-line services. The mistakes made in the boom both drove and exacerbated the crash and, despite having lost my seat in the Dáil, I couldn't let that go. My family often tease me in referring to my involvement in politics as my political habit, and unfortunately I have to agree; I was compelled to keep on going after what was a particularly devastating blow.

While I would describe myself as an optimistic but realistic person, I never cease to feel frustrated by just how long it takes to make even small changes. Our political institutions require radical rather than piecemeal reform. It is not enough to cut costs; we must rebuild both our political and public service institutions. That is not easy given that we have little heritage of building good institutional architecture. I try to imagine the benefits if we were to take the values that are so evident at community level and build them into our governance. Values such as trust, volunteerism, solidarity and generosity; they have been the values that have driven the creation of tidy towns and credit union movements, of 'meals on wheels', not to mention the raft of sporting, cultural and leisure organisations. If, for example, our local government system could be reformed in a way that unleashed the particular genius that is so evident in our communities, we might begin to build the foundation of something different with values of which we might feel very proud. The focus of political reform at national level is way too narrow. What is needed is a holistic governance approach beginning from the bottom up.

The resurgence of independents at the 2011 election was a reflection of the lack of real political choices and the will for a real change in how we do things. While independents come in all shades of political opinion, one thing they all have in common is that they must think for themselves. The absence of anonymous party political handlers is a major asset, in that the citizen can better judge exactly who and what they are electing. This is a quality that resonated strongly with people in the Dáil elections of 2011 and 2016, and I think it is a part of why independents have enjoyed such strong levels of support during these years. All we need do is look at the conduct during election campaigns – where promises are made, particularly by the parties that are expected to form a government, and then not delivered upon – to see what has likely contributed to the breakdown of trust in the political system. This, combined with the over-application of the party whip system, which turns government backbenchers into voting fodder and heavily disadvantages them when they go against the party line, has added to the cynicism surrounding party politics. I believe it is this culture that the Irish voting public is trying to break free of, and our political system allows them to express that by voting for independents and newly emerging parties like the Social Democrats. It is also clear that parties are aware of the threat independents pose to the status quo given their attempts to publicly minimise the role of independents during elections; although this does not stop them from seeking out the support of independents and new parties when forming governments.

From both a personal and political perspective, my own experience of working as an independent was very empowering and, maybe ironically, it taught me a lot about working collaboratively with party politicians. For example, in my early years as an independent local representative I focused on seeking out commonality rather than political differences, as this was the best way to get things done. It was not about party labels and allegiances, but was more about finding ways to make things happen by engaging with a broad range of colleagues. This may well have been aided by my natural tendency to take an evidence-based approach to my work, which makes me inclined to consult others, particularly those who have experience or expertise on a specific topic. It did, however, also involve learning to realise the value of my own sense of judgement. As an independent, that is of critical importance as there is no party headquarters or spokesperson to go to for guidance. You are on your own in many ways, and while there is great freedom in that, it also leaves you very exposed.

Focus on reform for the future

Having been elected at town council, county council and Dáil levels, I have had the benefit of experiencing the Irish political system from a variety of angles – this has been particularly useful during my time in the Dáil. Leixlip Town Commission – later to become Leixlip Town Council – was the first authority to which I was elected, and, not only was I one of the first members elected to it, but I was also heavily involved in campaigning for its establishment. This was no mean feat, as only four towns have been granted the establishment of such a local authority since the foundation of the state. While its powers were limited, the nine of us elected in that first year were full of ideas and enthusiasm that ensured the Commission punched well above its weight. Being elected to the county council in 1991 was a bit of a culture shock, as my background was exclusively urban, but the focus of the council was heavily weighted towards rural and agricultural affairs. I remember the culture shock that hit during my first council meeting which involved a long and detailed discussion about sheep dipping; I nearly lost my reason! I had showed up with the expectation that I was going to immediately immerse myself in a debate about how we were going to address the large-scale residential development that had occurred in the county without any thought having been given to the provision of key services. Instead, I found an over-bureaucratic, complicated local government system that delayed and frustrated decision-making. Unlike the town council experience, which was inclusive and outward-focused, the county council system was dominated by process and had an inward focus. I had to find my way of working within that system while at the same time never forgetting that I was not part of it but was there on behalf of my community. My time in the council served me well though, as it forced me to develop ways of working within the government system and with people I would not necessarily have gravitated towards otherwise. For my part, I like to think I developed a reputation for being an effective member of both authorities, as I was returned to both authorities on every subsequent election I contested.

Ultimately, my experience of local government led me to the conclusion that, while there were some really good people working within the county council system, the system itself was, and continues to be, the problem, and it needs radical reform. This should be tied in with Oireachtas reform. We need to remove the excessive localism that is evident at national level, and to do so we need to disperse responsibility for those services that are best delivered locally to local authorities. This would change the entire focus of the Dáil by empowering local representatives to take ownership of local administration, while allowing national representatives, and the national legislature itself, to concentrate on the national agenda. I cannot emphasise enough that this will only happen if the system of local government is radically reformed.

Oireachtas reform is also badly needed. While the first several months of the 32nd Dáil elected in 2016 have been encouraging in this regard, it remains to be seen if the reforms will be meaningful and long-term. One aspect of Dáil business that stands out for me as being in particular need of fixing is that of the involvement of members in the legislative process. In previous Dála, it was not unusual for a bill to be published less than a week before being scheduled for debate in the Dáil, and for that debate to be subject to a guillotine at all stages. Key pieces of complex and often controversial legislation were also deliberately scheduled for debate late at night to minimise the glare of the media. It is an appalling way to make laws, and is reflective of the dysfunctional relationship between the legislature and the executive in the Irish system, whereby it is the latter that determines the entire agenda. For someone like myself, who is passionate about the need for reform, the lack of reform in the 31st Dáil was hugely frustrating; an excellent opportunity for reform was squandered by a government that introduced only superficial changes when there was a demand, an understanding and an appetite for substantial parliamentary and governmental reform. Despite all the talk of 'doing politics differently' in the lead up to the general election in 2011, very little changed throughout the course of the 31st Dáil.

From independent to the Social Democrats

It is this focus on reform that ultimately drove me back into the party system and away from being an independent. Empowering and liberating as it was, it became clear to me as the term of the 31st Dáil progressed that working as an independent involved accepting a number of limitations. Although, for example, I was fortunate enough to be involved in a technical group in both the 29th and 31st Dála, and could contribute fully as a legislator, it was very obvious that the institutions of government and of parliament were built to favour parties. I began to see that belonging to a party would give me greater scope to impact decision-making. Ironically, this decision came about at a time when my political profile had never been higher and my sense of accomplishment in affecting change at national political level had never been stronger. In many ways, it would have been a lot easier to have remained independent as I could have continued to practise the sort of politics I enjoyed and was good at, unfettered and without the substantial additional workload that comes with forming and organising a party. But I felt an obligation to be a part of something bigger than myself. I believe a social democratic future for Ireland will respect the fact that we are a small country that needs to trade with others while also recognising that the entire purpose of our economy should be to create the fabric of a healthy, functioning and sustainable society that facilitates equality in every sense of the word.

Resistance to water charges was at fever pitch, and large contingents of Irish people were demonstrating loudly that they were wide awake and determined to bring about political change. I felt that as a member of the Oireachtas it was my job to hear those calls and respond in kind, and the best way I knew to do that was to provide an option for a different type of politics. Joining a party was not really something I could do, as the options simply were not there. Whether by virtue of ideology, policy approach or political culture, none of the existing parties would have been a good fit for me, so I began giving serious consideration to party formation. Two other independent TDs (Róisín Shortall and Stephen Donnelly) and myself somehow came together to discuss the idea, and we made a very conscious choice to take our time so that we were sure that our policy approaches, priorities and goals were aligned. The whole process took around nine months, but by July 2015 we were ready, and the Social Democrats was launched.

It is still early days for the party, but we contested – or should I say survived – our first general election. We ran fourteen candidates across the country, and although no gains were made, Róisín, Stephen and myself each topped the poll in our respective constituencies with notable surpluses. Our focus is now on building a new party that can promote a new kind of transparent, accountable and open politics. We as a nation have become too entrenched in our view of what politics is and how it should be practised, and in forming the Social Democrats I hope to help change that view by showing there is another way. We have an opportunity to look outward towards different models of political engagement that are being implemented in various political systems around the world and draw from the lessons learned. This includes drawing on fields such as deliberative democracy and co-responsibility models of engagement. Ultimately, I want to see the development of a politics that resonates with people's lives, as I strongly believe in the need for a system with direct relativity to the citizen. My time as an independent showed me just how important it is to be open to different types of political actors, and I hope to draw on the positive experiences I had in building the party into the future.

Maureen O'Sullivan

Maureen O'Sullivan worked on Tony Gregory's thirteen election campaigns from the 1970s up to his death in 2009. First elected in 1982, Gregory achieved national prominence when he held the balance of power in the Dáil after the same election. Gregory agreed to back Charlie Haughey's nomination for Taoiseach, in return for which he negotiated the famous 'Gregory Deal', a multi-million-pound package of investments for his constituency of Dublin Central. Gregory was continuously re-elected at the next seven general elections, serving the final twenty-seven years of his life in Dáil Éireann. Maureen O'Sullivan won the by-election to fill Gregory's seat in June 2009, the same day she was elected to Dublin City Council for a seat she was co-opted onto in 2008. She was subsequently re-elected to the Dáil in 2011 and 2016.

I do not believe any history of independent public representation can be written without looking at the work of the late Tony Gregory, the second-longest serving independent TD. The question is how did that happen, how did he keep his independent seat for Dublin Central for twenty-seven years until his death in January 2009?

I met Tony Gregory in the 1970s when both of us were involved in voluntary work in our respective communities. In my case it was youth

126

work, primarily in the East Wall where I was born and living, but also involving youth in other inner city areas; in Tony's case it was with community groups where he lived in Ballybough. It's interesting to note that Ballybough in Irish is Baile Bocht, town of the poor. The issues he addressed, fought for and promoted had a general common theme of the poor, those who had been marginalised for many generations.

In those early years, before winning a seat, the issues were housing, employment, community services and facilities, education, and later would include animal welfare, the environment and planning, drugs, street traders, crime, prisoners' issues and causes like Shell to Sea, Cuban Five, Anglo-Irish Bank and the Docklands, republican issues, the Dublin/Monaghan bombings, Palestine and opposition to the Iraq War. These are issues that Tony worked on, campaigned on, and they were the issues that kept him to the fore with the public, ensuring his continued electoral success.

He was a voice for the community, for people whose voices had never been heard, and then – having been with them in giving them the confidence to speak out on their issues – he was a voice with them, until he died. He believed change would only come for the people of the inner city, economic and social changes, when the local people pushed for those changes. So while he, with other activists, was a voice for them in the early years, many community groups acknowledged that because he was confident in them, they became confident in themselves. Consequently the north inner city was a significant innovator in community development.

So my initial answer to the question I posed – how and why did he hold an independent seat for twenty-seven years? The answer is in community.

Tony was born in Ballybough and lived there all his life: he went to school locally; he had first-hand knowledge of the area and of the lives of the people living there. His family shared some of the difficulties faced by inner city people.

His parents had difficulties accessing local authority housing – his mother, in her forties with two sons, was told by the local authority to come back when she had more children. Obviously that didn't happen, but by dint of hard work and sacrifice his parents managed to start the process to buy the house in Sackville Gardens, where Tony would be buried years later.

Housing conditions in parts of the inner city in the 1970s, particularly along Summerhill and Seán MacDermott Street, were the same as the tenements that were the settings for the Dublin plays of Sean O'Casey from the 1920s. There was little progression into second-level education and practically none into third-level. There was neglect and dereliction. Of the 311 derelict sites in the city in 1978, most were within the north inner city. With changes in Dublin Port there was high unemployment, further exacerbated by the moving of a number of factories from inner city locations to the suburbs. Community facilities, if they could be called that, were the local pubs.

These were the issues that brought Tony Gregory into politics. He began in community politics and I think that is a significant reason why he kept that seat. I do acknowledge his point that in the last two elections before he died, 2002 and 2007, his vote had been declining. I think that contributed to my success in the by-election in June 2009, as I believe there were people voting for me because they were sorry they had stopped voting for Tony and this was their way to apologise.

While Tony was local in these concerns he was not parochial, as his biographer Robbie Gilligan pointed out, and a quote from Tony underlines this: 'It is important to state that Dublin's inner city holds no monopoly on poverty and injustice. The inner city possibly suffers its most acute levels but that inequality and injustice are mirrored throughout Irish society.'

His success came from working with local people and his first group was the Sackville Gardens Residents' Association, then the North Central Community Council, which would be a type of coordinating body for the various community and tenant groups that were emerging in the different flat complexes and parishes in the north inner city. Once again, while 'big' issues were on the agenda, such as the proposed motorway and unemployment, Tony made sure the 'smaller' issues never lost out in the priorities for the groups.

One of those 'smaller' issues, but not smaller to me as my main interest was youth, was the lack of facilities. A group of us had formed and we took over a premises, a former boarding school in Cavan. It became a holiday venue, education and training centre, primarily for the people of the north inner city, and continues today with a policy of active discrimination in favour of marginalised and vulnerable communities. In time, Tony became the chairman of the Cavan Centre Management Committee, a position he held until his death. I was the secretary and still continue today in that voluntary work.

Once again, involvement in the centre showed a Tony who was practical, who did the painting and decorating, who drove the young people up there for weekends and holidays, who supported the fund-raising – such as the annual sponsored cycle from Dublin; there is a great photo of Taoiseach Charles Haughey starting the cycle from the Five Lamps and Tony on his bike ready to cycle the sixty-odd miles.

Tony was very well known to his constituents and did not just appear at election time. He had a slogan on some of the leaflets that he was around when no one else was. This was another contributing factor to his continued success.

I think he also had an ability to work with people of varying political views and that was obvious in his relationship with the team who negotiated the famous Gregory deal of 1982. Two of them did not share Tony's republican views, while he did not share the pro-European views of another. For Tony, European integration would mean an erosion of our national sovereignty. The principles they did share, and which have always been my guiding principles, were broadly socialist, based on equality, fairness and social justice.

After a number of years building up the community groups, Tony decided to stand for election to the city council in 1979, feeling he could do much better than the existing elected councillors; as far as Tony was concerned they were completely out of touch with what was going on in the north inner city. He was convinced that he could be elected. I don't think he would have stood if he had any doubt at all.

I remember that first campaign very well. We were all novices when it came to electioneering and campaigning, apart from Tony who had experience with the late Seamus Costello. I remember knocking on doors that were not inner city and of course the question was, 'Who is he, who is this Tony Gregory?' That certainly did not happen on later campaigns, after the Gregory deal.

For Tony, elections were about knocking on doors, going back to those that had not answered. The street traders gave him breadboards for his posters; at times there was a limited supply of leaflets. The professional in Tony secured a really good photo from Derek Spiers for the poster. We also had a good attendance at the polling stations on the day of the vote and then the new experience of attending the tally and the count.

Tony won comfortably – enough first preferences with a healthy supply of transfers – and that was the combination that would continue over the following twelve campaigns. There were thirteen campaigns in all, local and national; Tony won all except his first attempt at a Dáil seat.

I do wonder, at times, if Tony had not been in that balance of power situation in the general election he won in 1982 how would he have fared in politics, because there is no doubt that the Gregory deal brought him a prominence he would not have had otherwise. I think he would have retained his seat, such was the community support, such was his community involvement, but holding that balance of power was a pivotal moment for him.

Yes, he used it to address those issues which had brought him into politics in the first place, but he made no apology as it was the first time that those issues were addressed in the political arena. He supported Charles Haughey because Tony believed he would not go back on what they had agreed in the deal.

Tony did dislike the word 'deal'; as far as he was concerned it was a programme. What was in that programme? He obviously addressed housing. There was agreement on a specific number of houses that would be built in the following years, and specific areas of high neglect were named in the agreement – Seville Place/Oriel Street, Mountjoy Street, Portland Row, Rutland Street and Russell Street. There would be a compulsory purchase order on Oriel Street as part of the development plan for Sheriff Street. A special fund would be set up to acquire land for long-term housing purposes and a budget for the maintenance of houses and flats. Tony did not forget his promise to the women of the flats who did not have bathrooms or showers – there would be a works programme, starting in Liberty House, to fit out those flats with bathrooms and showers.

Regarding employment, Dublin Corporation would take on additional craftsmen for the maintenance service, a new job creation initiative for the inner city that would create more than 3,500 new jobs and a budget to employ 500 on environmental work for the benefit of the local communities. On education, the north inner city would be declared an educational priority area, where positive discrimination would be exercised with special measures involving suspending normal Department of Education rules. Much of this had to do with pupil/teacher ratios, provision for early education and initiatives to keep young people in school, increases in the number of remedial teachers, psychological services and family liaison officers and for a new community school to be built with increased facilities. There were special plans for the Port and Docks Site, which would include sport and recreational facilities. I think those provisions meant Tony Gregory would not be forgotten in subsequent elections, especially by those most directly affected by the provisions of the deal.

Of course, when he read it into the Dáil a voice called out 'What about Cork?' So do we accuse Tony of clientelism? No, his answer would be that his was a rights-based approach; the rights of people in the north inner city communities had either been forgotten or abused in previous years. He got the opportunity to do something and he seized it. Not for personal gain – no mention of a job for him or a car or any perks. It was for the communities.

I think another aspect that brought him to national prominence was the fact that there were national aspects to the deal: the development of our natural resources; tax on derelict sites; tax on banks and financial institutions; free medical cards for all social welfare pensioners and other pensioners in need; regular and rigorous inspection of all institutions caring for children, the disabled, the mentally ill, the elderly; the cost of drugs would be controlled by the Health Service; a tax holding period of a few years for new industries; a National Council for Children with a children's bill; abolition of illegitimacy; review of the adoption system; a major review of social welfare; capital gains tax on profits accruing to sales of land and buildings with a higher tax where planning permission has been granted for change from a lower to a higher value use.

Tony struck a chord with the public, particularly the public of the north inner city communities but also with the general public. He was in the national arena, in print media, radio and television. He was a national figure; other areas outside the constituency would make the point that they would like a Tony Gregory too. He maintained that high profile throughout the following years with a number of other issues he worked on; two in particular were very well covered in the media and brought him great praise in the inner city and nationally. Those issues were the street traders and drugs; the former meant he ended up in Mountjoy Jail. He was furious that the gardaí would arrive in force and bundle women and prams into paddy wagons and off to the cells in Store Street garda station while at the same time, as far as the community were concerned, the gardaí were ignoring the heroin pushers.

When he was arrested on the street trading protest, he was subsequently sent to prison because he would not sign a bond to keep the peace; he felt if he signed it would prevent him from highlighting the rights and needs of his constituents. We had protests outside the prison, and again it was well covered in the media with an iconic photo of Tony on his release. He had served two weeks and on his release he continued with this support, eventually seeing results for his efforts. The street traders were special to him, he was a regular shopper on Moore Street and is still fondly remembered there today. One of his last public appearances was in the documentary, directed by Joe Lee, on the story of the street traders – 'Bananas on the Breadboards'.

The drugs issue became a major part of Tony's political work and this also continued until his death. Today it is a major issue for me. While teaching, I chaired the North Inner City Drugs Task Force; now I am there as a public representative and chair the Prevention and Education sub-group. Tony's work in this area led to the establishments of the Drugs Task Forces. He himself chaired the Supply Control sub-group of the North Inner City, but later was a member of the Finglas/Cabra Task Force.

Drugs were, and are, an absolute scourge. In those early days, officialdom was happy to ignore this. Tony accused them of 'ignorance, complacency, denial'. The sheer scale of the problem was both frightening and alarming. The physical and psychological dependence on drugs brought further crime, people getting into debt, intimidation. Tony was relentless in pursuing this issue, organising community meetings and demanding action from the various authorities. He took every opportunity to raise the issue. He risked his own personal safety on numerous occasions, notably when he named a significant drug pusher in the Dáil and also on the marches to the homes of known pushers. It was through his work that a special sub-committee on drugs was set up in the Dáil. He made the point 'follow the money', which would eventually lead to the setting up of the Criminal Assets Bureau – though it took a while for officialdom to acknowledge Tony's role. He pursued other issues like animal welfare; a great regret of his was that in his time in the Dáil more was not done on banning blood sports.

We as a group, the loosely styled Gregory Group, had a decision to make after his death as to what to do politically. My view, shared by a few, was that it was over, because no one could replace Tony; others took the view that we had all given so much to him and to the independent role in politics that we couldn't just let it go – at the very least we had to defend the seat.

Some months previously, our independent councillor Mick Rafferty (Tony had combined both roles as councillor and TD until the dual mandate change came in 2004) decided to step down in the last year (2008) of that term. We discussed his replacement and it fell to me to go on the council. My decision to do so was very influenced by Tony's illness at the time, and I knew he did not need additional stress and worry regarding the council seat. I have to admit that I had no real interest in it. I could have stood in 2004 but declined it then; my only reason for agreeing in 2008 was to assist Tony at such a difficult time in his life.

We worked together from September 2008 until he died on 2 January 2009. I continued on the council and our next decision was the upcoming local elections in June 2009. The group decided I would contest the seat in the local election, but then some time later the government decided to hold the by-election on the same day. I stood in both and was successful in both. I successfully held the Dáil seat in the 2011 general election. Both Tony and me (me in a very limited way, time wise) experienced life in the Dáil both being part of a technical group, and on our own. The latter is extremely frustrating due to lack of opportunities for speaking time, initiating private members' bills, having priority questions and the like.

Tony was very proud of the technical group in the 2002 Dáil when he was the whip of the group. He said it showed how people of varying and diverse views could cooperate, work together in order to have speaking time, priority questions and so forth, and I too can see that. The technical group in the 31st Dáil worked well in spite of the efforts of the media to treat us as a political party and get us to react to situations/issues/individual difficulties of members as if we were a political party. It is very sad that Tony is not here today to be part of that technical group.

He appealed to a wide range of people and interests, but was always guided by the principles of fairness, equality, social justice. He was re-elected time after time because of his phenomenal work rate, his passion, commitment and integrity. He was always available – right up until two days before he died. People came out to vote for him who had never voted before in their lives. He had an amazing political mind; his speeches were always well planned, to the point. There was no rambling, no waffle. He never made false promises – if he felt something could not be done he told the person honestly and directly which I believe also contributed to his re-elections.

When I spoke, at his request, at his funeral, I said that he sought solutions based on rights, that he abhorred the way politicians put the interests of the party first and not the interests and needs of the communities who elected them. Regardless of whether you agreed with him or not, no one doubted that dedication which was also acknowledged by his critics after his death.

The independent seat has been held in Dublin Central for thirty-five years now. There is a part of me that will always see it as Tony Gregory's seat – he did so much to get it and hold it. I believe the independent movement would not have the respect and integrity it has today, despite the detractors, were it not, to a large degree, for the work of Tony Gregory. I am proud that my involvement in politics was with Tony Gregory, proud of his independent voice which I have been trying to continue to keep that independent seat in Dublin Central and see more independents in both local authorities and the Dáil.

Kathy Sinnott

Kathy Sinnott is a disability rights campaigner and founder of the Hope Project. She represented the South constituency in Ireland as an independent in the European Parliament from 2004 to 2009. She had previously contested the 2002 general election as an independent, losing out on a seat in Cork South-Central by six votes after two recounts. She subsequently stood at the 2002 Seanad election, again narrowly losing out on a seat, this time by three votes. She was elected to the European Parliament in 2004, winning over 89,000 votes. In Brussels she served as a co-chair of the European Parliament's Independence/Democracy group. She was also a member and Vice-President of the EU Democrats – Alliance for a Europe of Democracies.

As a young mother in the 1970s I was blissfully ignorant of the politics and politicians around me. The only issue I remember taking an interest in was the accession/annexation of Ireland into the EU. I am not even sure if I always knew who was Taoiseach; I certainly didn't know the names of any of my TDs or MEPs. That whole world was just not part of my life of husband and small children.

It was only after fruitless attempts to get help for my third child, Jamie, whose health had been destroyed and development derailed by his first vaccination, and finding out that this was the experience of many others, that I formed my first disability group and contacted my first politican. Coming from this starting point, I wasted years thinking that if we just explained the needs of children with disabilities and our needs as their carers and how to meet those needs, then the right thing would happen. When I think about it now I realise how naive I was. 'Maybe they didn't get our letter.' 'They promised to ring back but maybe I gave them the wrong number?' To me, if someone said they would do something they would do it. Politicians taught me that wasn't true.

What was especially confusing to me was the roller coaster. Politicans who were not in government were always friendly, encouraging, sympathetic and indignant at the way that government was treating children with disabilities. But once in government the same politicians reacted to the same issues completely differently. Because some of the politicians seemed to be really decent people, it took me a long time to face the reality that it didn't matter how ardent the politican proclaimed him- or herself to be about our disability issues, what mattered at the end of the day was what their political party wanted. Out of government, the political party wanted in, and of course that takes votes, so agree and sympathise with voters, even make promises, but once in power stick with the party agenda. This is why it is important to ignore what politicians say and study the fine print in their political party manifestos.

The realisation that politicians behave this way had two effects. It turned me very firmly independent. I became committedly independent in my voting – choosing candidates not by party but in the order that I agreed with what they said they stood for and their freedom to stand by what they said. The second effect was that I became determined to never be a politician.

So when my campaign for people with disabilities – which had seen me start groups, lobby, write endless letters, establish a helpline, fundraise, host summer camps, learn to read legislation and finally go to court – seemed to lead me to running for election on the basis that 'if you want something done, do it yourself', I not only ran as an independent but made it clear that I was running as a potential 'public representative', not a politican. This gave me the freedom to put myself forward on a take it or leave it basis.

Once elected, my experience inside the world of politics did nothing to change my determination to stay independent; rather, I gained an added appreciation of the freedom it afforded, and wondered why anyone would bother staying attached to a political party. For example, even when I was looking for support from other MEPs on a disability amendment that was commonsense and not at all controversial, I was met with the usual answer from party members: 'Sounds okay but I have to ask.' I just thanked God I was an independent and didn't have to ask anyone if I could do the right thing.

In fact it is misleading for politicians to say that they are public representatives if they are first loyal party members, which most seem to be. One cancels the other. By voting the party's position they are again and again having to ignore the citizens they are representing, and sometimes their own conscience.

When I was first elected, like most new MEPs who were not committed to joining a particular grouping already, I was approached by a number of parliamentary groups. I was given a tome of policy papers by a representative from the European People's Party. I flipped it to the page on education, an important issue for me and my constituents, and made my decision immediately that I would not find a home in that group. Fortunately I found one that allowed me the advantages of a group – extra committee places, lots of speaking time and so on – and yet didn't tamper with my independence.

In Brussels, I learned quickly that MEPs are restricted in the area of legislation because what the European Council and Commission want, they get. Take for example the issue of EU funding of embryo destructive research. Before we even went into the vote on what was called advanced medical therapies, we, the rapporteur and the shadows rapporteurs, that is the core committee of MEPs representing every group working on the legislation, were told by the panel from the European Commission and the European Council that EU funding was going ahead. To be very clear, I asked, 'Are you telling us now that it doesn't matter how the parliament votes next week, funding of embryo destructive research is going ahead?' The answer was yes.

This is how the EU operates. So although I can point to some of my amendments that made it into legislation and some resolutions that I helped to achieve, because I was often in the way of the EU juggernaut, my work on legislation and that of others like me was more that of voicing the concern of our constituents and getting opposition on record. If you want MEPs that can proudly say they supported successful legislation, then just keep voting for party candidates who are happy to give away our rights and resources to Europe, because in Brussels they are on the winning side, though their constituents aren't.

Illusion is another part of the party dynamic. Once I realised how little democracy there was in the EU system, I no longer had illusions about my role. Instead I focused on getting things of a much more practical nature done for my constituents and their issues. But in political parties the MEPs seemed to consider themselves as part of something much bigger and more important, a force to further the party agenda (which just happens to further the EU agenda!). So just being there, occupying the seat, casting the vote dictated by the groups' voting list booklet that was on their bench when they arrived in the voting chamber, was somehow fulfilling for them. More than once I heard an MEP heading to lunch after an extensive voting session in Strasbourg saying that they hadn't a clue what they just voted on. For them it didn't matter, it was the strength of their European political party that mattered.

I was grateful for the opportunities I was given to serve constituents. I was able to inform the Commission that there was an autism epidemic and get a Europe-wide project going on the study of its prevalence. I got ordinary Irish fishermen into the Commission to inform the people writing policy. I brought over experts on the dangers of water fluoridation and seemed to make progress. I brought the Tara struggle and many local social and environmental battles to the Petitions Committee and I defended life.

There is a funny thing about service; I came to love my constituents and got to know many of them. They taught me about so many issues that were challenging them. I hope I was a good student. I developed a great network of contacts so that I could reach and be reached by my constituents on issues. I had an informal but effective 'phone a friend' system through which I could call on real, if unrecognised, experts like Caitlin Hayes and Brian Polly on fishing, John McCarthy, Mary Maddock and Martin Hynes on mental health, Robert Popcock on fluoride, John Crowley, Con Cremin and many others on farming. The same applied to every issue that I was asked to look at. The people I worked with are too many to name, but all of them are real experts who lived with the issue and knew what was at stake. I was free to not just listen, but to act on their advice and to bring them directly into the Commission and the parliament to meet the people dealing with their issue.

Looking back now the effort we put in was worth it! All the pundits said that my election was a fluke and that I wouldn't be re-elected. I knew this was probably true, so I just saw every day as an opportunity to work and tried to make the most of them. We worked on farming, fishing, quarries and forests, homeschooling, Tara, illegal tolling, lack of services for children with disabilities, lack of rest stops for truck drivers, struggling businesses and threatened jobs, support for children and families and much more. We had major projects in the Commision on emergency response to people with disabilities, mental health, fluoride, protection of the human embryo and protection of the vulnerable from euthanasia, carers and a Europe-wide autism prevalence strategy running to 2020 which previously only had funding until 2010. I tried to make people aware of the problems for Ireland in the European Constitution, which later became known as the Lisbon treaty. As a result of taking a hands on approach, I had some real accomplishments but I was painfully conscious that so many of our constituent campaigns were left unfinished when term ended and time ran out.

Reflecting on these experiences in Brussels now as an ordinary citizen-voter I feel even more strongly that we have something precious in Ireland – our sovereignty, battered and greatly diminished though it may be, we must preserve and nourish. Essential to this is our election and referendum system. But these are the very underpinnings that are most at threat. I don't think people realise how much Brussels hates our referendum system and how much they would like to see it just disappear. If the divorce, Nice and Lisbon referendum repeats were not warning enough, the childrens' rights referendum, which resulted in the McCrystal judgment, should really wake us up. Our constitution is the statement of our rights, it is meant to limit government, not give it more power. Only we the people can change it with a referendum. Unfortunately, referenda have become a frequent tool of government and the EU in eroding our rights. Governments have even developed a sense of entitlement such that they illegally use our money in referenda to take our rights away. To add insult to injury, when they fail to get their way they force us to vote again until we give the right answer. I remember a leading light in the European Parliament's Constitutional Affairs Committee saying that there was no question of the EU accepting a negative answer on the Lisbon treaty from Ireland, rather the question was how many times would the referendum have to be held until we accepted Lisbon.

I learned a lot on this particular committee about the 'European dream'. To summarise what seems to be envisioned in Brussels, the EU, now twenty-eight countries, will eventually expand to encompass the forty-eight country Council of Europe in a federal power block. Politically it would be a bi-party system, revolving around the European People's Party and the Socialist Party, with smaller parties like the Liberal Democrats and Greens gradually being absorbed or diminished. A number of things will help to progress this long-term vision. First, a system of pan-European voting in European Parliamentary elections. This of course requires that the last three hold-outs – Ireland, Cyprus and Malta – embrace a list system of voting, so that European-wide lists can be created and the power of the main European political parties solidified. Second, national parliaments must be downsized and streamlined to reflect their dimished role as they become more like county councils, implementing centralised policy rather than the legislating bodies of sovereign nations that they once were. Third, dropping the age of voting to sixteen years is seen as important so that a person's first vote is made while in secondary school where 'guidance' will be available within a curriculum that includes a standardised EU citizenship programme.

What Irish voters are maybe not very aware of is that our leading politicians are no longer representing their Irish political party, but the European political party to which the Irish political party belongs. I myself did not realise this until I went to Brussels. It was not just that MEPs would say and vote for things in parliament that they would never openly admit in their constituency, but that the policies that the party's TDs supported in the Dáil are coming straight from the European People's Party (Fine Gael), the European Socialists and Democrats (Labour), or the Alliance of Liberals and Democrats (Fianna Fáil). In the past, we could have some reliance on an election promise. Now, the gap between what the Irish people want and therefore what the candidate and their political party promise in an election, and their European political party policy for our future, is so vast that blatant election lying is the norm among politicians who know that after the election they will do whatever their European party tells them.

In many countries the presence of a list system, in which people vote for the party directly or through a lead candidate rather than casting a personal vote as we do in Ireland, makes the election of an independent impossible or very difficult depending on the type of list. Also the election funding system, voting age and other specifics can affect the chances of an independent candidate. If in Ireland we go with this agenda and we give up our type of personal voting it will mean much less choice than we enjoy now. Instead we will face the rigidity of party lists with the elimination of small parties and independents and the dynamic of hope and flexibility they add to the political landscape.

When our politicians suggest getting rid of the Seanad, dropping the voting age or throwing out most of our constitution, remember they didn't just think it up, they are following the game plan. So what can we do to hold the line on our legitimate sovereignty – to arrest its decline? How can we help it to grow? Keep your TDs on a short rope. Elect them as your public representatives, not as someone that negotiated your medical card – where is the credit in that? If the revenue knows enough about us to send us an uninvited tax bill, it knows enough to send a medical card or the children's allowance without being asked.

I feel strongly about the value of independent public representatives. It seems to me politics, and especially party politics, are part of the crisis in democracy we face in Ireland because much of the time it seems politicians take a seat not to serve the people but to serve the party. Holding an elected position should be a means of serving the people. I remember meeting a Labour Party member in 2002, a couple of months after I had won and lost a Dáil seat on a recount. I said that I didn't feel bad about losing because my candidacy wasn't about the seat. He looked at me and said sternly, 'Kathy, it's always about the seat!'

But it isn't about the seat. It is about service, representatives serving the constituents through just priniciples they have clearly enuciated in their election campaigns. Parties serve themselves. If we the people want to be represented then we should carefully select people who share our values, keep them close to us and replace them when they forget they are there to serve us.

An added problem is lack of leadership. Past their first bloom, political parties seem to have fewer and fewer leaders. In fact, given the nature of ageing political parties, what are called 'leaders' are just the most obedient followers. To rise in a party that has passed its use-by date, they must have set aside themselves and anything they once believed in or dreamed of in favour of the party. They must have carried out any task that the party required unflinchingly to gain the trust necessary to rise to the top. And since the top is now the headquarters in Brussels, not Dublin, we have perfectly obedient European functionaries 'leading' our parties and unfortunately our government and opposition. I would go so far as to say, don't elect someone who desires political office or political advancement, because they clearly do not understand the responsibility of the job. Rather, vote for someone who seeks to serve and who is willing to serve even if that should be in the war zone of politics.

Seán D. Barrett

Seán D. Barrett served one term in the Seanad (2011–16) for the University of Dublin (Trinity College) constituency. He was formerly an Associate Professor in Trinity College Dublin's Economics Department. He is one of the foremost economists in Ireland, particularly in the areas of transport and social policy. He is one of the original founders of the annual Kenmare Conference, an important yearly economic summit. He was a member of the Oireachtas Committee of Inquiry into the Banking Crisis.

Dublin University has a tradition of parliamentary representation dating back to 1603. Seventy members of parliament representing the constituency sat successively in the Irish Parliament in College Green, Westminster, the Dáil and, since 1937, in the Seanad. I was elected the seventy-first parliamentary representative in that proud tradition in 2011.

In the Seanad, the constituency has typically returned independents. I strongly support the role of the independent university senator and retention of the links between the universities and parliament. There are some sixty-four academic departments in TCD, and I sought to bring that body of knowledge to the Oireachtas and allow for the maximum amount of evidence to be incorporated into the policymaking process. I also know first-hand the challenges and pressures that young people in Ireland face; as a long serving junior dean at TCD, I had constant contact with students from right across Trinity College.

My first parliamentary year in the Seanad convinced me that the role of independents in the house is a valuable one. The five independent university senators and the Taoiseach's eleven nominees formed an independent bloc comprising 27 per cent of the membership of the house. The Taoiseach's nominees were remarkable in their independence and added much to the house.

The speaking rights of independents are protected by the Cathaoirleach and his deputies. The design of the debating chamber facilitates genuine dialogue and compromise rather than the bear-pit atmosphere of some tiered debating chambers. The success of the Seanad is seen in its role in providing scrutiny of government and checks and balances to an executive with a Dáil majority and a tradition of rigid application of the party whip system.

The independent bloc in the Seanad, aided by the nonpartisan conduct of business by the chairpersons, assists government ministers in improving legislation. Most ministers commend the house for its constructive debates on legislation and policy. This continues a tradition going back to the foundation of the state with Minister Patrick Hogan praising the Senate as early as 1923, ministers Seán Lemass and Dr James Ryan in the 1930s, and Tánaiste Michael McDowell in recent times. In the bicameral system, the role of independents in the upper house is crucial. The differences in the composition of the Dáil and Seanad are vital to the latter's scrutiny role. A Seanad identical to the Dáil would be a pointless body.

In his definitive work on the Free State Senate, O'Sullivan writes that 'it is unfortunate, but inevitable, that the immensely valuable work of revision performed by an efficient second chamber attracts little attention whereas its occasional clashes with the government and the other house provoke wide public controversy' (1940, 349). With one exception, the print media do not cover the Seanad debates. Printed volumes of Seanad debates are no longer published. Social media may be the future of access by citizens to the work of the Seanad.

Background as an independent

My decision in 2010 to run was based on the economic disasters of the two previous years in particular. The decision to rescue the banks in September 2008 appalled me. My election video included footage outside Anglo Irish Bank on St Stephen's Green. I did not believe that this bank was of systemic importance to the Irish economy. I also believed that the repeated turning of a blind eye to Allied Irish Banks since the Insurance Corporation of Ireland affair in the 1980s had created a moral hazard problem in Irish banking. I was concerned that regulatory capture of Irish governance by pressure groups including the social partners had undermined parliamentary democracy and the economy. I opposed a series of expensive public spending programmes such as Transport 21 and the 'Bertie Bowl'. I was also concerned about the sheer lack of economic expertise in the public service and the capture of governments by the construction industry.

I was a founder member of the annual Kenmare Economic Policy conference with fellow economists Brendan Dowling and Paddy Geary. The objective of the conference was to bring together, in a location well away from Dublin, economists, senior civil servants, the media, politicians and others interested in bridging the gap between economic theory and how policies are made and implemented. I was also influenced by the strong tradition of public service in Irish economics.

Professor Louden Ryan, my first head of department at Trinity, led by example in public service. He was a key figure in the reforms of Irish economic policy pursued by Dr Ken Whitaker.

My first economic/political campaign was against the 1985 Air Transport Act which sought to imprison, fine and withdraw the travel agent's licence for persons charging less than the minister decreed under a 'sign here, Minister' relationship with Aer Lingus. This campaign was supported by the so-called 'Doheny and Nesbitt's School' of economists. The campaign against the Air Transport Bill was a huge success in turning all-party agreement to protect Aer Lingus into all-party agreement to promote competition. Ireland was the first country to expose its national airline to full scale competition on its major routes. Ryanair had the benefit of first mover advantage as an airline based on competition rather than the old European airline cartel of colluding national airlines. It is today the largest airline in Europe with some 85 million passengers, with an annual profit of over half a billion euros in a sector with a tradition of loss-making and taxpayer bailouts. In combining economic theory with better policymaking I hoped that the airline deregulation example would be followed throughout the Irish and European economies.

I also opposed in a parliamentary petition the Trinity College Dublin Private Bill which sought to change the composition of the university governing authority in order to comply with government pressures arising from the 1997 Universities Act. I believed strongly that Ireland should ensure university autonomy and this posed a threat to such autonomy. Irish universities have been damaged by the 1997 decision to treat universities as state bodies. The rise of external and internal university bureaucracy has created a new managerial class which has added nothing to Irish education, while substantially increasing the costs and burdens of managerialism and bureaucracy.

Election and parliamentary experience

I knew from lecturing to large classes at TCD over the years that there were many graduates who were dissatisfied with governance in Ireland long before the problems of 2008–10 made change imperative. My fear after my first few years in the Seanad was that the government was too conservative, and that the senior civil service retained control. Parliament must seek greater control over the executive, and increased checks and balances on the operation of a powerful bureaucracy. Bankers, builders and bureaucrats all caused the collapse of the Irish economy, and none of them should be exempt from the consequences of their inefficiency. I fear at this stage that the government has been largely unwilling and unable to reform the civil and public service and come up with new and radical ideas about how to better govern Ireland.

A minority of ministers appear not to be in control of their departments. The spectre of Sir Humphrey haunts the Seanad when a coterie of civil servants sit behind the minister and pass notes dealing with issues raised by senators. I find this disconcerting in a parliamentary democracy.

A further problem in our parliamentary democracy is the rigid whip system in our main parties. Rigid whipping promotes clientelism, public relations and placemanship, rather than the radical ideas required to deal with Ireland's unemployment and debt problems. In the 24th Seanad I held the post of whip of the independent university senators, an obvious oxymoron. I believe that the whip system in the Seanad should be phased out by gradually increasing the number of no whip days for members of the main parties.

Life as an elected independent

I was elected to continue the Trinity tradition of both independence and of relating to both main traditions on this island. I was also elected because of the economic crisis. The voters wished me to connect the work of the university directly to the parliament as the 1937 constitution intended.

In the Seanad, I spoke on the order of business on most days. The Cathaoirleach was scrupulous in allocating speaking time, favouring brevity in order to facilitate a wider range of views. I frequently proposed amendments to government bills and had several accepted. I also proposed six private member's bills: the National Mortgage and Housing Corporation Bill and the Universities (Development and Innovation) (Amendment) Bill in 2015; the Seanad Electoral (Panel Members) (Amendment) Bill and the Higher Education and Research (Consolidation and Improvement) Bill in 2014; the Financial Stability and Reform Bill in 2013; the Mortgage-Credit (Loans and Bonds) Bill in 2012; and the Fiscal Responsibility (Statement) Bill in 2011. My main interests were in the economic sphere, ranging from the need to improve competitiveness in sectors such as energy, to competition policy, to public expenditure appraisal, to the elimination of tax expenditures and shelters. I strongly defended university autonomy and raised issues such as Ireland's poor performances in mathematics and foreign languages. I also raised the cost problems of health insurance and local issues, such as retaining the Fry Model Railway at Malahide, protecting the views of Dublin Bay from Clontarf and excluding trucks from Slane. I supported Senator John Crown on smoking in cars and

Senator Fergal Quinn on genetically modified foods and nuclear power.

Life as an independent senator is definitely not frustrating. There is a very good spirit in the house, thanks to the party leaders and the Cathaoirleach. The debates are open and frank. I would find it very frustrating to be told by a party whip how to vote or to be denied speaking time in the house.

I sat on the Oireachtas committees on Finance, Public Expenditure and Reform and Transport and Communications and I was also part of the Banking Inquiry. The chairmen of both committees discharged their functions with fairness and courtesy. Party political differences rarely surfaced and independent members were at no disadvantage.

As a senator, I found Leinster House a very friendly place across the various political divides. Occasional rows in the chamber are rewarded with media coverage. There seems to be a greater media interest in parliamentary Punch and Judy shows than in parliamentary scrutiny of the government. In addition to friendliness, the other contrast with the public image is that the members of the Oireachtas work far harder than a cynical public generally believes. The media has generally little interest in the Seanad. I regret that, but sought to communicate with constituents through social media.

Overview

Independents are needed in political life in Ireland to bring new ideas and perspectives to a system dominated by the executive and by military-style discipline in the political parties. The large number of independents in Ireland compared to other countries reflects support for greater diversity than the traditional parties generate. A role model for independents might be Henry Grattan, who according to McDowell:

> seems to have regarded himself as destined to be a permanent independent, a constant, alert observer of the administration, delivering commendation and censure as circumstances demanded ... there would still be the corrupting pleasure of power, and a strongly principled man who wished to bring an unfettered mind to bear on public issues would be wise to remain an independent member. (2001, 31–2)

I believe that the tradition that university senators do not join political parties is a good one and should be maintained. My constituents would not have wished me to join a political party. I am very happy to have chosen the independent path. I found no disadvantages in being an independent in the Seanad, and maintained good relations with all the parties in the house.

While governments have sought the support of independents in order to secure a working majority, my inclination was not to give such support but to approach each issue on its merits. Two Dublin University MPs at Westminster, David Plunkett and John Ball, voted against Gladstone's proposals to reduce the autonomy of TCD on 12 March 1873. The government was defeated by three votes and the votes of the TCD members were crucial. The Webb and McDowell history of Trinity College records that 'the College was thus saved from the gravest threat to its future since the Jacobite occupation of 1690. But Gladstone was never to be forgiven' (1982, 252).

In the 1990s the university senators held the balance of power in the Seanad. They supported the government. This support included voting against an opposition motion to defend the autonomy of TCD in particular and Irish universities in general. I was appalled by this vote on 30 November 1995. It paved the way for much of the loss of autonomy of Irish universities in the 1997 Universities Act and led to many of the current problems of Irish universities. I will never support any proposals by governments to undermine university autonomy.

My voting record for and against the government depended on the issue. For example, I opposed the abolition of the seventeen elected members from Irish speaking areas to serve on Údarás na Gaeltachta and their replacement by nominees from September 2012. I could not envisage ever supporting any weakening of democracy at the behest of the government, whether they depended on my vote or not.

Ireland has imported much democratic deficit from the European Union. Large chunks of EU directives are nodded through the Oireachtas without scrutiny. Much of Ireland's banking debacle was caused by the Central Bank and the Department of Finance sleepwalking into economic and monetary union without sufficient scrutiny of the currency's design faults. These included lack of bank regulation, lack of an exit mechanism, abolition of the exchange rate as an instrument of economic policy, the 'one size fits all' interest rate policy, the lack of protection for small countries from tsunami movements of capital from large countries and inadequate fiscal transfers. Irish policy on Europe inordinately emphasises free money from Brussels in public relations hyperbole. Successive failed summits on the euro currency are hardly a surprise given the design faults of the currency. Little has been done to fully achieve the needed banking union to operate the single currency and the democratic deficit has only worsened over time, as seen in the case of recent political events in Greece and Portugal.

Ireland's problem of governance is a lack of the same accountability in the bodies which caused the economic collapse over the period

2006–10 and their success in avoiding the consequences of their incompetence. Accountability of the bankers, regulators and senior bureaucrats for their role in the destruction of so much of the Irish economy is the major task facing Irish political life, as it tackles the long-run economic, social and political costs of the bank bailout. This is part of what I tried to highlight at the Banking Inquiry. The economic disasters of 2008–10 require more scrutiny and accountability in public life. This entails strengthening both houses of the Oireachtas with many members independent in mind and spirit.

5

The independent voter

Introduction

Given the control parties wield in modern parliamentary democracy, it might be expected that support for independent candidates is an irrational, wasted vote. Because independents in most countries have very little chance of being elected, and even if they do get into parliament have very limited opportunities for influence, voting for such a candidate might not seem the optimum means of maximising a voter's utility or, more informally, getting the most bang for one's buck. It might therefore be expected that an analysis of voting patterns for independents is likely to reveal a high degree of randomness, with little to no structure or rationale.

However, as was discussed in the overview of independents' electoral performance in Ireland in Chapter 3 – and is the underlying theme of this study – such an expectation of irrationality would be misplaced. It was already suggested in Chapter 3 that support for independents is positively related to the influence they can wield over governments (which is discussed in greater detail in Chapter 7), and the aim here is to further explore the motivations of those voting for independent candidates. Although it is not possible to directly tell if such voters are maximising their utility, the key argument is that there is a logical structure to the behaviour of voters, and that where suitable conditions and factors arise, support for independents is greater.

Bearing this in mind, the overall aim of this chapter is to provide an insight into the make-up of the independent voter. In Chapter 2 it was shown that there are different types of independent candidates, but to what extent does this carry over to independent voters? Are there general incentives to explain support for independents, or are the factors unique to every candidate? Understanding the presence of independents requires an understanding of the nature of the incentives that motivate support for these candidates. Who is the archetypal independent voter? From a historical perspective, an image of a typical party voter can be readily drawn for most party families. For example, the typical social democrat was a blue-collar worker, the typical liberal was a member of the petit bourgeoisie, while, in more recent times, green voters are drawn from the urban, university-educated, middle-class. Such stereotyping, however, does not always extend to independent voters, in particular because the level of knowledge about them is quite limited. In addition, the nature of support for independents often depends upon the contextual nature of the individual candidacies. For example, pro-establishment conservative independents in the 1920s and 1930s naturally attracted a conservative centre-right vote. In more recent years, the anti-establishment nature of many independents has seen the independent vote become more left wing.

Four features of the independent vote are examined in this chapter, all of which stem from the previous analysis and are usually cited to explain support for independents (Ehin and Solvak 2012, 16). The first concerns the socio-economic basis to the independent vote, with the expectation that there are few social bases, given its heterogeneity as discussed in Chapter 2. The second feature examined is the extent to which support for independents is a personalistic and localistic vote. The third concerns the importance of voters' detachment from parties, since independents are non-party candidates; and the fourth feature examined is the protest nature of the independent vote, because such candidates lie outside the establishment and tend to be oppositional. These features feed back to the central thesis of this study that there are factors at play in Ireland that are permissive of independents. One of these is the norms and values of the Irish political system – while in other jurisdictions there may be a party-centred political culture that militates against independents, this is not the case in Ireland. There exists candidate-centred political competition where personality and locality are to the fore. This creates an environment in which independents are at less of a disadvantage caused by their lacking a party brand. They can compete on a more even keel, and in recent years have been able to tap into increasing levels of dealignment from parties. Each of these four features of the independent vote is examined in detail, before their collective influence is assessed using survey data from Dáil elections between 2002 and 2016. As a prelude to such analysis, the evidence concerning support for independents from the academic literature is discussed, both from an Irish and a comparative perspective.

Why vote independent?

Although the bulk of research on independents primarily comprises case studies, there are a number of themes common to independent voters across these political systems. Two factors repeatedly re-iterated are the importance of localism and personalism. Localism in the electoral context can be defined as when voters evaluate the issues, parties and candidates in relation to their own locality; while personalism involves voters supporting candidates based on the latter's personal attributes. This is important for independents as most of them lack a national profile and are almost entirely dependent on their local persona to deliver a vote. This is because 'people won't vote for an independent they don't know' (Ted Mack, former independent MP in Australia; *The National Interest*, Radio National, 12 September 2004). Anckar's study of small island states with no parties claimed that their absence was due to the strength of personalism in small islands (2000, 262) and because 'island voters are occupied with local things' (2000, 263). Similarly, in Australia, Sharman stated that successful independents 'must have a strong engagement with a local community and a high local profile' (2002, 64), a theme also emphasised by Costar and Curtin, who referred to the focus of successful independents on local policies (2004, 9, 18). In a survey conducted for the latter authors of supporters of an independent MP (Peter Andren) in Australia, local representation was found to be primary reason to vote for him. The importance of this was emphasised by the concurrent finding that a majority of Andren's supporters disagreed with his stance on a major national issue concerning asylum seekers (Costar and Curtin 2004, 53); for such voters, it was local policies that mattered.

Two of the four reasons offered by Singleton (1996, 67–8) to explain why independents attract votes in Australia were because of a prominent standing in the local community, and due to a strong personal following built up while a party politician (the other reasons were as a protest against the party establishment, and as a representative of one or more issues). Gallo (2004) put the success of independents in some parts of Russia down to their ability to exploit a centre–regional conflict by appealing to local interests. The relationship between these cultural features and independents was extrapolated by Chubb (1957, 132). He noted that a politician does not have to be a party man to satisfy localistic and party demands; in an environment where such features of political culture are exceptionally strong, an independent who panders to these demands has a reasonable chance of electoral success.

Anti-party sentiment is another oft-cited incentive. In the US, the convergence of the parties towards the median, or middle-of-the-road, voter, and the perceived decline in parties' efficacy, has been associated with the rise in independent and third party voters (Allen and Brox 2005; Owen and Dennis 1996). The influence of anti-party sentiment is not surprising because a vote for an independent is in effect a rejection of political parties. It was also found to be a significant factor in Australia, Britain and Canada (Bélanger 2004), but not so in Estonia (Ehin and Solvak 2012). It is this decline in party–voter linkages that explains why voters drift to independents; increasing levels of party detachment and disaffection with party offerings have all been found to have an effect on support for independents (Bélanger 2004; Copus et al. 2009). In Estonia, support for independents is explained by it being a mild protest by voters who usually support the government parties. It is much easier for them to protest by voting for an independent than by going all the way over to the opposition. Voting for an independent is 'a low-cost alternative' (Ehin and Solvak 2012, 17).

It is important to note here that the independent voter in this study implies someone voting for an independent candidate. This is distinct from the use of the term to describe someone not identifying with a political party. This is particularly prevalent in the US, where studies refer to the rise of the independent voter as attachment to the Democrat and Republican parties is in decline. However, almost all these independent voters vote for parties, not independent candidates – hence the so-called 'myth of the independent voter' (Keith et al. 1992). These voters call themselves independents because partisan feeling does not sway their vote – they vote for whom they deem to be the best candidate. Perhaps ironically it is rare to see the term independent voter used to describe those who ultimately do vote for an independent candidate. One particular reason for this, which is explored later in the chapter, is the lack of partisanship and attachment associated with voting for an independent – few voters are necessarily drawn to the independent brand.

Institutional rules are frequently referred to, particularly the electoral system, and this was the focus of a large comparative study by Brancati (2008). Being minor actors, independents are especially affected by electoral rules, which Weeks (2014) found in Australia – although not always in the predicted manner. While electoral systems can have a direct, mechanical effect on independents, of often greater impact are the psychological effects, which can result in voters rejecting independents for fear of wasting their vote. Because there is a great deal to say on the nature of this relationship, this is the preserve of the entirety of Chapter 6.

The texts on general voting patterns in Ireland usually include a few sentences on independents, with three factors repeatedly re-iterated: personalism, localism and brokerage or clientelism. The latter feature refers to the importance of politicians being able to deliver services for their local constituents, with the difference between brokerage and clientelism simplistically being voters getting what they are entitled to (brokerage) or not (clientelism). The reasoning is that in a culture where politicians are valued for what they can provide for a constituency, competition becomes quite individualistic and independents have an opportunity to compete with party politicians, provided they can deliver on this score. A related feature of these factors is the 'friends-and-neighbours effect', whereby voters prefer a candidate who resides in close proximity to them. The consequences of this are that 'a local man running for office has a strong claim on his village's vote, regardless of his party or religion' (Sacks 1976, 146), which implies that independents, regardless of their merits as a candidate, can expect to attract support from such localistic voters. Gallagher (1999, 676–8) found evidence of this in 1992 in the constituency of Laois–Offaly, where an independent candidate, who won just 0.2 per cent of the overall constituency vote, received almost 17 per cent of the vote in his home base, a similar finding to King (2000, 283) in his analysis of voting patterns in the constituency of Clare in 1997.

In the early years of the state, Mansergh noted that the electoral appeal of independents tended to be largely of a personal nature (1934: 290), a theme echoed by Carty, with his emphasis on the importance of 'local loyalties and personal ties' (1981, 58), and Busteed (1990, 41). In more recent times, Gallagher noted that the vast majority of the successful independent candidates in 2002 were 'local promoters' (2003, 102), while FitzGerald (2003, 67) and Murphy (2010, 328, 346) identify the importance for independents of a capacity to deliver pork-barrel benefits for their respective constituencies. The evidence concerning the influence of anti-party sentiment is mixed. It was found not to matter in the 2002-based study of the Irish voter (Marsh et al. 2008, 177–8), but this is contrary to what was found in 1997 (Marsh and Sinnott 1999, 174). As with the comparative literature, there are frequent references to the causal effects of the electoral system. In particular, it is argued that the candidate-centred nature of STV helps foster and sustain a political culture conducive to independents.

The main shortcoming of the literature on independent voters is that very few studies are able to rely on individual-level data because of the low numbers of independent voters surveyed. Research by Ehin and Solvak (2012) on Estonia, and by Ehin and others on the European

Union (2013), are notable exceptions. However, even then, of the 820 independent voters in the latter's study, 718 were from Ireland. To have almost 90 per cent of data from a country with less than 1 per cent of the population (in the EU) poses a number of problems concerning validity. What it does indicate is that for an in-depth study of the independent voter, Ireland is the case par excellence. The remainder of this chapter is devoted to an analysis of these voters, primarily using data from the Irish National Election Study (INES) (2002–11).[1] This was an extensive five-wave panel survey of the Irish electorate, carried out over the 2002–7 period, as well as an additional survey after the 2011 election. In total, the INES dataset comprises over 7,000 respondents. There was no comparable election study in 2016, but a much shorter version was conducted in the form of an exit poll, with a sample of approximately 1,500 voters.[2] Some international data is also accessed for comparative purposes. This comes from the Comparative Study of Electoral Systems (CSES) project, a collaborative programme involving similar election studies from around the world.[3]

Features of the independent vote

From this survey of the literature, there are four general features of the independent vote to examine. The first concerns its socio-economic nature – are particular groups in society drawn to independents? The second feature is the extent to which support for independents is a product of a personalistic and localistic political culture, whereby voters are oriented towards the candidate and their locality, sometimes over and above party and ideology. The third feature concerns the importance of party detachment given the nonpartisan status of independent candidates; while the final feature to examine is the extent to which support for independents is a protest vote. This section compares the evidence from Ireland with that of the international experience, to assess if the features that are claimed to help independents in Ireland are necessarily unique features of the Irish political system. Although it has been shown in Chapter 2 that there are different categories of independent candidates, independent voters are here treated as a unitary actor. This is to examine if there are any general and universal factors explaining support for independents irrespective of the nature of the candidacy. In addition, a subdivision of independent voters might lack generalisation beyond Irish shores, limiting the relevance and implications of the findings of this study. From a logistical point of view, it would also reduce the sample sizes for analysis to numbers that were too small.

'Politics without social bases'

Paraphrasing Whyte's (1974) description of classless politics in Ireland, the first feature to examine is the social base to the independent vote. The expectation here is that support for independents is pretty much the same across different social groups. The primary reason for this is that independent candidates are such a heterogeneous category, with policy and ideological preferences ranging across the political spectrum. Support for these candidates is very candidate specific. For example, as detailed in Chapter 2, independent unionist candidates attracted the support of the protestant community, who retained an affinity to the UK. Independent republicans, on the other hand, attracted support from the other side of the political spectrum, those who wanted to end this affinity. As such, the national vote for independents is simply the aggregate of a vote for a fragmented group of candidates with perhaps nothing in common bar the lack of a party label. It would be unusual for social structures to matter for candidates not held together by any national brand, policy platform or unitary organisation.

To test such expectations, a range of socio-economic variables in the INES are examined, with support for independents per each particular social group detailed in Table 5.1. As the results indicate, there are very few differences that cannot be ruled out as the product of sampling error. These range from social class, to occupational status, to education qualification, to level of religiosity, to gender. The few socio-economic indicators that are significant are that young people are more likely to vote for independents than older generations (13 per cent of eighteen to twenty-four year olds versus 7 per cent of pensioners), as are countryfolk compared to their city brethren (9 per cent versus 5 per cent). The first finding could be a product of the weak partisanship levels of young voters. Because they are less likely to be attached to parties, and because they are more likely to express a protest vote, there should be an increased likelihood of their voting independent (for reasons that are later discussed). The difference between city and country voters could reflect the higher levels of personalism and localism in rural areas, something that is explored in later sections. Overall though, independents tend to attract pretty heterogeneous levels of support. The rise in support for independents after 2011 saw some social differences emerge, as evident in the survey results from 2016 in Table 5.1. Independents had less support from AB white-collar workers, with twice as much support among the semi- and unskilled manual workers and farmers. However, among the other social groups, most of the differences in independent support were relatively small and not statistically significant (this means that we cannot rule out

Table 5.1. *Support for independents (%) by socio-economic status*

	2002–11	2016
Class		
White collar	10.4	8.5*
Petty bourgeoisie	10.9	14.5
Skilled manual	7.7	13.3
Semi/unskilled manual	11.1	20.9*
Farmers	8.1	24.1*
Work status		
Full-time	9.0	12.8
Part-time	11.9	22.3*
Unemployed	7.4	11.4
Retired	7.3	12.9
Student	12.9	12.8
Age		
18–24	13.0*	10.6
25–34	10.0	12.7
35–44	12.0	17.0
45–54	8.7	14.3
55–64	8.5	15.7
65+	7.2*	13.5
Gender		
Male	8.8	14.4
Female	8.9	17.4
Education		
University degree	10.3	11.7
Diploma/Certificate	10.3	–
Leaving Certificate	8.9	17.6
Junior Certificate	7.3	–
None or primary only	10.5	13.5
Religiosity		
Regular attender[†]	8.2	16.1
Not regular attender[††]	7.7	17.2
Region		
Open Country	9.0	17.0
City	5.6*	13.1
Total	8.1	15.8
N	6,523	1,436

Source: Author's figures calculated from INES 2002–11 and a 2016 exit poll conducted by Behaviour and Attitudes for RTÉ in partnership with the School of Politics and International Relations in UCD, the Department of Government in UCC, the School of Politics, International Studies and Philosophy in Queen's University Belfast, and Trinity College Dublin; figures succeeded by an asterisk(s) are where the proportion with a characteristic has a voting preference significantly different from that of those without that characteristic (*p < .05).
[†] This category ranges from those attending a religious service at least once a week to those attending several times a week.
[††] This ranges from those attending a religious service at the most once every few months to those who never attend.

the possibility that such differences are because this data came from a sample, not the entire population).

Political culture

The second feature of support for independents to consider concerns the importance of personalism and localism in Irish political culture. The expectation is that those who base their voting decision on the personal characteristics of the candidate and what they can achieve for the locality are more likely to vote for independents. The rationale is that in a community where a premium is placed on the personality of politicians and their attachment to the locality, the structure of political competition is such that independents are at less of a disadvantage than in a more national and policy-oriented system.

Personalism and localism tend to work in tandem to produce a culture where 'choosing a candidate to look after the needs of the constituency' has regularly been cited as the most important voting incentive for the Irish electorate. Politicians respond to this demand by undertaking a large amount of constituency work and canvassing for votes for themselves, sometimes with little mention of their party affiliation. This personalistic appeal is further reinforced by the presence of multi-member constituencies that produce intra-party rivalry, impelling candidates to canvass for votes on a personal and local, rather than a party, basis. All this is relevant for independents because it means their nonpartisan status does not give them a major electoral disadvantage. It is not automatically implied that the cultural features of personalism and constituency service should necessarily positively impact on independents; what is crucial is that the latter need to be able to feed this demand and look after the interests of their constituency. In many countries this may not be possible because parties tend to control how patronage is distributed. Being on the outside, independents have little to no influence and so few vote for them. Malta is a typical example of this. Despite possessing many similar cultural and institutional features to Ireland that are conducive to independents – such as a high level of personalism, brokerage and the STV electoral system – independents have a negligible electoral impact because the two main parties control the purse strings.

The importance of these features can be tested by examining if those partaking in such a culture are more likely to vote for an independent. A measure of personalism that can be gleaned from the 2002–11 INES concerns whether party or candidate is more important in deciding how to vote and whether respondents would still vote for the same candidate if they switched party. Those who said yes to the first question, and also said candidate is more important than party, are considered 'pure' candidate-centred voters. Of this group, 8 per cent voted for an independent. Of those who said party is more important and would not vote for the candidate if they switched party, only 0.5 per cent voted independent. Slightly different questions were asked separately of independent and party voters in 2016, making comparison a bit more difficult. While 43 per cent of party voters said they would not have voted for their preferred candidate if he or she had been running for another party, only half this proportion (24 per cent) of independent voters echoed similar sentiment. Likewise, while 53 per cent of party voters said candidate was more important than party in deciding their first preference, 69 per cent of independent voters said candidate was more important than the fact that their preferred candidate was independent.

In terms of localism, a number of indicators can be gleaned from the INES. These are: the nature of incentives listed to vote for a candidate, whether the first preferred candidate was deemed to be good at working for the local area, and voters' perception of the performance of the local economy during the lifetime of the outgoing government. First, of those who cited localism as their primary voting incentive, 15 per cent voted independent, compared to 7 per cent of those citing a non-local factor. Second, those giving their first preferred candidate the maximum score on a ten-point scale in terms of their ability to work for the local area were almost three times as likely to vote for independents (12.7 per cent) as those giving the candidate a low ranking of between 0 and 5 on the same scale (4.2 per cent). Third, those who felt the local economy was performing worse than the rest of the country were almost twice as likely to vote for an independent (13 per cent) than those who felt it was doing better (6.7 per cent). Few of these questions were asked in the 2016 study, but voters were asked to state the most important incentive to them in making up their mind to vote. While just 10 per cent of those citing more national incentives – such as choosing a Taoiseach or between party policies – cast a first preference for an independent, 24 per cent of those who said 'choosing a candidate to look after the needs of the constituency' voted for an independent. Similarly, 26 per cent of those who cited a local issue in their constituency as the main influence on their vote cast a first preference for an independent, whereas less than 8 per cent of those citing a more national incentive – such as stable government – voted for an independent.

While personalism and localism seem to be influential factors, from a comparative perspective we would expect there to be a greater prevalence of these cultural features in Ireland than in other countries where independents are absent. One means of determining this is from the CSES dataset, in which there were questions concerning the degree of face-to-face contact between candidates and voters at elections. In a polity where personalism and localism are to the fore, there should be greater levels of contact between local candidates and voters. Forty-four per cent of voters in Ireland reported such levels of contact during the 2011 general election campaign (this question was not asked in 2016), the highest proportion of all countries in the CSES dataset, amongst whom the average was just 10 per cent. The comparable figures in 2007 were 55 per cent, 72 per cent in 2004 and 56 per cent in 2002 (comparative data on personal contact in these years is not available). Such high levels of contact should help independents because this is an activity in which independents can partake, particularly in the relatively small constituencies of Ireland. Indeed, those who reported such contact in the INES were more than twice as likely to vote for independents (12 per cent) than those who had no such contact (5 per cent). The differences were even greater for those who reported contact from independents (40 per cent voted independent) against those who had no such contact (7 per cent voted independent). It is important to note that other forms of contact, such as by mail, email and text message, had no significant effect on the independent vote; it is the personal nature of the contact that seems to be the decisive factor.

Party detachment

The third element of the independent vote to examine concerns the extent to which it is motivated by a detachment or dealignment from parties. With parties declining in esteem, is this a motivation to vote for independents? More specifically, is support for independents motivated by anti-party sentiment? One common factor used to explain voting behaviour is partisanship, whereby someone votes for a party which he or she feels attached to or identifies with. Transferring this theory of party identification to independents can be a difficult task for a number of reasons. First, is it possible to speak of individuals voting for non-partisan candidates for partisan reasons? Second, the concept of party identification involves the establishment of loyalty to a party label, often inherited from parents, an allegiance that usually holds constant as the electoral representative of the party (the local candidate) changes. This implies that it may be difficult to speak of an independent label akin to a party brand, as it would be most unlikely for voters to identify with independents at an early age, and to stick with them as the nature and type of independent candidate in their local constituency varies across elections.

Looking at the INES, voters casting a first preference for an independent in 2011 were three times more likely to state that the calibre of the candidate was more important (70 per cent) than the fact that they were independent (23 per cent). The respective proportions in 2016 were 69 and 27 per cent. It is difficult to know if we should expect higher proportions, but it is not wholly valid to compare these to attractions to a party brand as they are completely different in meaning. Some might call independent almost a non-brand, in light of which one in four independent voters being attracted to the label is a significant figure and instead suggests that independence may have some brand appeal. In addition, 62 per cent of those who recalled voting independent in 1997 and 2007 continued to vote independent at successive elections. Similarly, in 2016, 51 per cent of those casting a first preference for an independent recalled doing so in 2011. These proportions are lower than party voter loyalty, but it does suggest that independent candidates can retain their support, contrary to expectation.

One other problem that the party identification model causes for independents is that voters often identify with parties as a rational information-economising device. This time-saving method cannot be applied to independents, who do not have a central organisation determining their policies. As such, their respective platforms can vary radically from one independent candidate to the next, with the implication that the policy positions of each independent at every election have to be studied. This task is made additionally difficult because of the limited media coverage afforded to independents and the limited resources such candidates have to promote their policies.

Despite these difficulties over the validity of the party identification model, it can be applied using a reverse logic. It is a reasonable assumption to make that in political systems where significant proportions of the electorate do not identify with a party, independents have a greater chance of receiving more votes. Examining the comparative data in Figure 5.1, Ireland has consistently had one of the lowest levels of party attachment, which may explain why it experiences the highest level of support for independents. From an initial level of 37 per cent in 1978, as many as 79 per cent in 2011 said they did not feel close to any particular party, a level unmatched in any other Western democracy. The comparative results that year were 40 per cent in France, 13 per cent in Australia, 45 per cent in New Zealand, 53 per cent in Germany and 39 per cent in the US. This detachment fell back slightly in Ireland in 2016 to 73 per cent, but it cannot be a direct cause of independents' presence, because although detachment is increasing in most countries, the vote for independents at the national parliamentary level in the

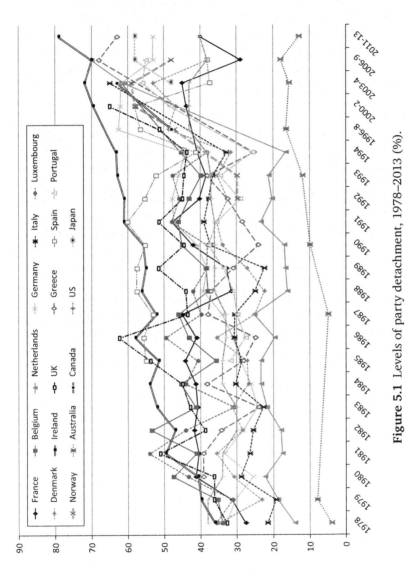

Figure 5.1 Levels of party detachment, 1978–2013 (%).

Note: Percentages given are those who said they do not feel close to a party.

latter remains minuscule. Nevertheless, the presence of a large proportion of non-identifiers is an important point. It means that independent candidates in Ireland are fishing in a large well-stocked pool, compared with independents in most of the other countries for which we have data. As well as providing an explanation of the vote for independents, this could also act as an inducement to mobilise potential candidates. Indeed, a simple correlation over the 1978–2016 period between the independent vote and the level of detachment in Ireland produces a rather high coefficient of +0.75, which suggests the higher the detachment the higher the independent vote. The INES also has evidence of such a relationship. Those who said they were not close to a party are almost three times as likely to vote for independents (10 per cent) than those who are close (3.7 per cent). A similar ratio was repeated in 2016, with 19 per cent of those not close to a party voting for an independent, compared to 6 per cent of support among party identifiers. Independent voters had higher levels of detachment (85 per cent) than voters for any of the parties (whose mean was 62 per cent).

A step on from party detachment, which could just imply a disinterest in parties, is anti-party sentiment, implying open hostility. It was shown earlier in the chapter that a relationship between anti-party sentiment and support for independents has been established in the academic literature. This is hardly surprising: the non-party status of independents makes it quite reasonable to expect that someone voting for such a candidate is manifesting some kind of negative expression about parties. Testing this on a comparative level can be difficult because of the cross-national variations in what constitutes anti-party sentiment. One, admittedly not perfect, measure from the CSES is whether voters think it makes a difference whichever party is in power. For many, disagreeing with this statement can imply a disillusionment with the political parties and their offerings (P. Webb 1996). Alternatively, if there are few policy differences between the parties, it might simply indicate an astute observer of the political scene. In any case, in 2002 the proportions agreeing with this statement (49 per cent) were far higher in Ireland than the other countries in the dataset. It fell to 39 per cent in 2007 (the question was not asked in 2011 and 2016), when there were equally high levels in Greece and Japan, but Ireland remained one of the highest-ranking countries expressing such sentiment towards parties. The equivalent figures in the US were 13 per cent, Canada 7 per cent, France 19 per cent, Spain 12 per cent, Australia 12 per cent and New Zealand 13 per cent.

In terms of whether this motivates support for independents, the evidence from the INES points in a positive direction. In both 2002 and

2007 those who agreed that it does not matter which party is in power were almost twice as likely to vote for independents (2002: 11 per cent; 2007: 8.2 per cent), compared to those who disagreed (2002: 6 per cent; 2007: 4.7 per cent). Those who strongly agreed were almost three times more likely vote for an independent (18 per cent) than those who strongly disagreed (6.7 per cent). Another measure of anti-party sentiment from the INES is the 'feeling thermometer' scores given to parties. Voters were asked to indicate whether they had warm or cold feelings towards parties, with a score of between 0 and 50 implying the latter and 50 and 100 the former. The mean score given for each of the parties was compared between independent and party voters, but there were very few significant differences. On a similar level, voters were also asked their likelihood of voting for parties. There were no substantial differences between independent and party voters in terms of their probability of voting for particular parties. To summarise, these different sets of variables seem to indicate that general anti-party sentiment is more influential on the independent vote than sentiment directed towards specific parties.

Protest vote

The final feature of the independent vote to examine concerns the extent to which it is a protest vote. Because independents are outside of the political establishment and almost permanently in opposition, the expectation is that voting for such candidates must be a protest vote, an expression of dissatisfaction with the existing political system. Comparative indicators of this from the CSES include questions on satisfaction with democracy and whether voting makes a difference. In 2007, 66 per cent expressed their satisfaction with democracy in Ireland, above the CSES average of 50 per cent. Only voters in the US, New Zealand, Norway and Netherlands expressed higher rates of satisfaction. Likewise, just 9 per cent agreed that who people vote for does not make a difference, below the CSES average of 13 per cent. Again, it was only lower in the same set of countries. What this indicates is that Irish voters are quite satisfied with the workings of the political system, so it is not that independent candidates have an exceptionally large pool of disgruntled voters to attract, comparatively speaking.

Looking at the INES data, there is little evidence that support for independents is motivated by a political protest vote. Those who are not satisfied with the way democracy works are no less likely to vote independent than those satisfied. Similarly, those who believe who people vote for does not make a difference are no more likely to vote for an independent than those who believe it does. On a related theme, voting for an outsider might be an expression of alienation from the political system, a theme already explored for independents in Australia (Costar and Curtin 2004, 33) and in the US (Keith et al. 1992, 171) (and also for third party candidates in the US, see Allen and Brox 2005, 631–3). A number of questions in the INES measured the alienation of the electorate, which asked for levels of agreement on a range of statements from whether politics is too complicated, to whether the ordinary person has any influence, to whether they feel better informed, to whether the government can influence what happens. On all these measures, there were no differences in the level of agreement between party and independent voters, suggesting the latter are no more or less alienated than the rest of the electorate.

Another means of assessing a protest element is voting behaviour at referendums. At referendums in Ireland there appears to be a core group of no voters, who use their franchise to register a protest against the government, regardless of the issue at stake. INES respondents were asked how they voted at previous referendums, and those who voted no to the proposals on abortion (in 2002), citizenship (in 2004) and the Nice treaty (in 2001 and 2002) are all no more likely to vote for an independent than those who supported the referendums. These findings seem to suggest that independent voters are not general protest voters, by which it is meant the type who want to protest regardless of the issue or circumstances.

It may be the case that independent voters are instead protesting about specific, rather than general and political, issues. The five key issues cited by voters at the three elections over the 2002–11 period were crime, the economy, health, housing and unemployment. It was only on health and unemployment, but surprisingly not on the economy, that those who felt these issues had become worse over the lifetime of the government were more likely to vote for an independent (by a ratio of almost two to one on both issues) than those not sharing this sentiment. In general, with these types of issues, while there are clear differences between those voting for independents and those for the government parties, such differences are not as significant between independent and opposition party voters. The two latter groups are more likely to be motivated by a protest vote, in contrast to supporters of government parties who prefer to defend the latters' record in office.

These differences were evident again in 2016, except this time independent voters were much more likely to air economic grievances than at past elections. Those who felt the economy was worse off than in 2015 were twice as likely to vote for an independent (20 per cent) than those who felt it had improved (9.4 per cent). Similarly, those who felt their own personal financial situation had deteriorated in the past year were twice as likely to vote for an independent (17 per cent) as those who felt it had got better (8.4 per cent). In terms of the differences between independents and party voters, just 27 per cent of those voting for independents said the economy was better off than in 2015, compared to over 66 per cent of government party voters – but 37 per cent of those voting for one of the opposition parties. Likewise, while 28 per cent of independent voters said the economy was worse off than in 2015, this was compared to 5 per cent of government party voters, but 26 per cent of opposition party voters. In terms of their personal financial circumstances, 13 per cent of independent voters felt better off than in 2015, compared to 40 per cent of government party voters, but 34 per cent of those voting for opposition parties. On these issues, independents are different to government party voters, but not always so different to those supporting the opposition.

What explains the independent vote?

The analysis thus far in this chapter has comprised simple bivariate analysis that, while suggesting some interesting findings, could be masking other effects. What may appear to influence the independent vote might really be the product of its correlation with something else. To control for these effects, and to determine the collective influence of all the discussed factors, they are analysed in a single model using the 2002–11 INES dataset. This facilitates the determination of what really explains the independent vote.

Two measures of support for independents are utilised: those casting a first-preference vote for an independent (1/0), and voters' probability of ever casting a first preference for an independent (on a scale of 1 to 10). The advantage of the latter measure is that there are far more values involved and that it may account for individuals who intend to vote for an independent but, for a variety of reasons, fail to do so. In addition, some, such as Tillie (1995), have argued that this is a far more reliable measure of voters' preferences than voting returns, because it can measure the utility individuals give to a potential vote for each party. To examine what affects the variation in the values for these measures (i.e. the support for independents), the factors to include in the models are those discussed in the previous section. They include a range of socio-economic factors, position on the left–right spectrum, personalism, localism, contact by candidates, party detachment, anti-party sentiment (both general and specific) and attitudes that measure the level of protest. Two additional factors to include are the number of seats in the constituency and the number of independent candidates running, in the expectation that the higher these two are, the larger the independent vote. Measures of these variables are taken from INES 2002–11, further details of which are in the appendix to this chapter.

The results of the analysis are indicated in Table 5.2, which summarises the factors found to affect the two measures of the independent vote in terms of whether they have a negative or positive influence. Those factors with no corresponding sign indicate that no significant effect was found in the models; that is, we cannot say that they influence support for independents. A more detailed version of these models, containing the full statistical results, is in the appendix to this chapter. In the first model the factors that we can say matter include being candidate-oriented, not being close to parties, negative sentiment towards Fianna Fáil, but positive feelings for the Greens. Considerably more variables were found to matter in the second model examining the likelihood of voting for an independent. Again, party detachment, negative sentiment towards Fianna Fáil and positive sentiment for the Greens were all found to matter. While general anti-party sentiment does not have a significant effect, when it is directed towards specific parties (in particular Fianna Fáil and Fine Gael, as evident from the negative coefficients in Table 5.3) it does increase the tendency to vote for an independent. It is noticeable that independent voters have a more positive sentiment towards the new parties that have emerged since the 1980s, with the exception of the PDs, who were in government for most of the period under study (see Table 5.3). A sense of alienation has a negative influence on the independent vote, in that those who are less disaffected are more likely to vote for an independent. This suggests a sense of empowerment to independent voters. That grievance over the state of the health service was an important factor is not surprising in light of (a) this being an important issue at elections over this period, and (b) the numbers of independents running on this platform, particularly in 2002. Of the socio-economic variables, age held its importance from the bivariate analysis with younger voters more likely to favour independents. Finally, the number of independent candidates running per constituency had no significant effect, while district magnitude, confirming earlier suggestions that independents fare better in smaller constituencies, had a strong negative effect.

In relation to the four features of the independent vote that have been the focus of this chapter, some of our expectations were met. The independent vote is pretty heterogeneous with few social bases; personalism and localism seem to matter but not as much as expected, as

Table 5.2 *Models of independent vote*

	Voted independent	Probability of voting independent
Contact by candidate		
Localism		
Local economy doing worse than rest of country		
Candidate is good at working for local area		+
Personalism		
Candidate-centred	+	
Party identification		
Not close to party	+	+
Anti-party sentiment		
Anti-party general		
Anti-party specific		
Fianna Fáil	–	–
Fine Gael		
Labour		
PD		
Greens	+	+
Sinn Féin		
Protest – alienation		
Satisfaction with democracy		+
Vote makes no difference to who is in government		–
Protest – issues		
Economy		
Health		+
Socio-economic		
Age		–
Rural		
Female		
Education		
Employment		
Left-wing		
Right-wing		
District magnitude		–
Number of ind. candidates		

Author's figures calculated from INES 2002–11.

does party detachment; and there is a slight element of a protest vote, but it is not borne out of alienation – it is rather directed towards the main political parties. Overall, though, the two models are not very powerful. For example, as is shown in the appendix, the coefficient of determination (r-squared) for the second model is a lowly 0.15, which implies that 85 per cent of the variation in the independent vote is dictated by factors outside those examined. In some ways this confirms the notion that it is difficult to speak of a collective independent vote. There is a vote for independent candidates, but given the chalk and cheese difference between them that Frank Sherwin referred to in Chapter 2, many independents attract a different type of vote. Consequently, the discovery of any general factors explaining the vote for such a diverse range of candidates is an important finding.

It was not possible to carry out a full repeat model for the 2016 election as many of the questions from the INES of 2002–11 were not repeated. This was unfortunate, particularly considering it was the most significant electoral performance by independents anywhere since 1950. Nevertheless, it was possible to carry out some exploratory analysis. A similar model examining vote choice found that party detachment, voting for independents in 2011, an orientation towards one's constituency and economic grievances were the significant variables affecting the independent vote. Socio-economic characteristics, such as class, age, residence and gender, had no effect; neither did ideological placement nor policy preferences. Although the specific reasons for the independent vote were not explored in survey questions in greater detail, this was done in opinion polls a year previously. In December 2014 and May 2015, those willing to vote for an independent were pressed on the reasons for their preference.[4] The two most popular reasons given were because they did not trust the parties (36 per cent in December and 26 per cent in May), and because the independent candidate focused on local issues (27 and 31 per cent). Other reasons given included: because the voters agreed with the independent's policies (19 per cent in December and 14 per cent in May), because the candidate was known to them personally (10 and 14 per cent) and because they advocate political reform (10 and 13 per cent). Party voters were not asked similar questions, making comparison difficult. However, one common question asked of all voters in March 2015 was the importance of a range of issues in affecting their vote. While there were no significant differences between independent and party voters on most issues, the former were more likely (13 per cent) to state a desire to reform the way Ireland does politics than supporters of the main parties (7 per cent) (March 2015 ISPOS MRBI). This reform agenda was an issue promoted by many independent candidates during the 2016 election campaign, in particular by the Independent Alliance.

Conclusion

Writing in the 1970s on what determines electoral success in Ireland, Ayearst stated that 'the ideal candidate is one who is well known, well liked and, if he has had previous service in elected office, has proven to be accessible and useful to his constituents – all of which characteristics are non-partisan' (1971, 185). This explains why independents in Ireland have a greater chance of electoral success than in other countries; a candidate does not have to be a party person to possess such attributes. In other words, there exists a political culture and system permissive of independence, supporting the central thesis of this study.

This chapter has examined the source of independents' support, and has tested the various propositions put forward in the literature concerning such support. In particular, the importance of nonpartisan voting incentives was stressed. It was shown that an independent candidate who panders to local concerns, makes him or herself accessible to constituents and who protests about a key local issue (preferably reproaching a few parties in the process) will receive a positive return on his or her investment at election day. Independents' nonpartisan status is therefore an important factor behind their electoral success. Candidates new to the electoral field not only have to attract votes, but also have to try and persuade voters to abandon the party they supported at the last election in favour of a different one. Ceteris paribus, independents are therefore at an advantage, since they are not asking voters to jump from one party to another, but rather just to leave their preferred party, a less demanding leap.

An important finding is that a vote for independents is not a completely irrational, aberrant vote. The presence of some consistent features suggests there is a logical structure to the independent vote. Under certain permissive conditions, such as a localistic and personalistic political culture, and a declining attachment to political parties, support for independents is greater. In other polities, voters are more oriented towards parties, which results in few independent candidates running, let alone winning a seat. A key strategic institution that was not examined, apart from district magnitude, is the electoral system. This might be the underlying condition that binds these factors together, as has been suggested in some of the literature. This is the focus of the next chapter.

Appendix to Chapter 5

Analysis of survey-level data

The details for the statistical models used for analysis of the individual-level data in the section 'What explains the independent vote?' are as follows.

The two dependent variables are:

- Cast a first preference for an independent (1/0).
- Probability of voting for an independent (1–10, where 1 is not very probable and 10 very probable).

The independent variables for inclusion in the models examined in Tables 5.2 and 5.3 are:

Personalism

- Candidate-centred vote: vote for candidate rather than party, and would still vote for candidate if they changed party (1/0).

Localism

- Local candidate: how good candidate is at working for local area (0–10).
- Local area: performance of local vis-à-vis national economy (1–3: better, same, worse).

Contact

- Candidate called to home (1/0).

Party detachment

- Not close to a party (1/0).

Anti-party sentiment

- Anti-party sentiment (general): (7-point scale: strongly disagree/ strongly agree).

- Anti-party sentiment (specific): probability of casting a first preference for a party (1–10).

Protest

- Protest at alienation: level of agreement on two statements measuring alienation:
  (a) Are you satisfied with the way democracy is working in Ireland? (1–4 scale of agreement).
  (b) So many people vote, my vote does not make much difference to who is in government (1–7 scale of agreement).
- Attitude over two key issues (health, economy,) since previous election: (1–5 scale, where 1 is 'got a lot better' and 5 is 'got a lot worse').

Socio-economic factors

- Nature of residency, rural or urban (1/0).
- Level of education (1–6).
- Female (1/0).
- Age (year of birth).
- Nature of employment (from full-time to retired, 1–8).

Ideology

- Self-placement on the left of the spectrum (0–4, on a scale of 0 to 10).
- Self-placement on the right of the spectrum (6–10).

Two additional factors that may affect the variation in the independent vote are included. These are:

- The number of independent candidates running in a constituency (1–14).
- The district magnitude of each constituency (3–5).

The results of the analysis are in Table 5.3. Given the dichotomous nature of the dependent variable (voted independent or not) in the first model, a binomial logistic regression is the favoured method of analysis. The coefficients for this model indicate the effect on the predicted odds ratio of voting for an independent caused by a unit change in the independent variable. The asterisks after some coefficients in the two models indicate which variables have an effect that cannot be due to random sampling error; that is, because it is based on a survey of voters. In other words, we can be pretty confident that these effects are present among the wider electorate. All other coefficients seem to have

Table 5.3 *Models of independent vote*

	Binomial logit	PTV ind
Contact	−0.15 (0.18)	0.04 (0.07)
Localism		
Local economy	−0.02(0.02)	−0.02(0.01)
TD good for local area	0.01(0.01)	0.01(0.00)**
Personalism		
Candidate-centred	0.91(0.13)***	−0.02(0.04)
Party identification		
Not close to party	0.75(0.24)***	0.20(0.14)
Anti-party sentiment		
Anti-party general	0.12(0.05)	0.01(0.02)
Anti-party specific		
Fianna Fáil	−0.01(0.00)***	−0.01(0.002)***
Fine Gael	−0.001(0.00)	−0.01(0.00)
Labour	−0.02(0.01)	0.001(0.00)
PD	−0.005(0.00)	−0.01(0.01)
Greens	0.02(0.00)*	0.02(0.03)***
Sinn Féin	0.004(0.00)	0.005(0.00)
Protest – alienation		
Satisfaction with democracy	−0.30(0.18)	0.21(0.13)*
Vote makes no difference to who is in government	0.04(0.07)	−0.12(0.11)**
Protest – issues		
Economy	0.09(0.06)	−0.01(0.004)
Health	0.14(0.11)	0.13(0.11)**
Socio-economic		
Age	−0.01(0.01)	−0.02(0.01)**
Rural	0.28(0.20)	−0.13(0.12)
Female	−0.31(0.18)	0.24(0.17)
Education	0.05(0.05)	0.14(0.13)
Employment	−0.03(0.02)	−0.02(0.01)
Right-wing	−0.10(0.17)	−0.01(0.03)
Left-wing	0.07(0.28)	0.09(0.11)
District magnitude	−0.13(0.12)	−0.29(0.09)**
Number of ind. candidates	0.12(0.07)	0.06(0.05)
R^2		0.15

Note: Standard errors are in parentheses. Significance levels: *$p < 0.05$, **$p < 0.01$, *** $p < 0.001$. PTV denotes probability to vote.
Binomial logit model: Pseudo-R^2=.17; Log likelihood = −377.
Only those constituencies where an independent ran are examined.
Author's figures calculated from INES 2002–11 (N=7,532).

non-significant effects, which suggests that what is evident in the table may simply be because the results are based on a sample, not the entire population. Because the other measure of support for independents is an interval-level variable, the chosen method of analysis is an ordinary least squares regression. The figures, or coefficients, for this model indicate the effect on the probability of voting for an independent for each unit change in the respective independent variable.

Notes

1 See www.tcd.ie/ines.
2 The exit poll was conducted by Behaviour and Attitudes for RTÉ in partnership with the School of Politics and International Relations in UCD, the Department of Government in UCC, the School of Politics, International Studies and Philosophy in Queen's University Belfast, and Trinity College Dublin.
3 See www.cses.org.
4 These polls were conducted by ISPOS-MRBI for the *Irish Times*, and published on 4 December 2014, 25 March 2015, and 14 May 2015. See www.irishtimes.com/news/politics/poll.

6

Independents and the electoral system

Introduction

One factor frequently cited to explain the rare and unusual presence of independents in Ireland is the use of a rare and unusual electoral system, PR-STV. Strom (1990, 103) says that 'to a large extent the survival of these independents is a function of the Irish PR-STV electoral system'; Carty that 'the single transferable vote can lead to the proliferation of independent candidates' (1981, 23); Coakley that 'the most distinctive consequence of Ireland's version of proportional representation is the presence in parliament of a large number of independent or non-aligned deputies' (1987, 164); and Chubb that 'the independent member in Dáil Éireann owes his existence to the operation of proportional representation' (1957, 132). Such claims focus on, among other things, the primacy STV places on candidate over party, and its operation in multi-member constituencies, which lowers the threshold necessary to be elected. In a country with a small population, such as Ireland, this means that an individual standing on his or her own, who can hope to attract 5,000 or 6,000 votes, can have a reasonable chance of winning a seat. Such significance placed on STV stresses the importance of institutionalism when understanding the presence of independents. The core premise of this alleged relationship is that the electoral rules facilitate independents because they are permissive of them, unlike other voting systems. The previous chapter indicated the presence of a candidate-centred political culture, and the Irish electoral system – because of its candidate-centred nature – works in tandem with these norms to produce an environment that fosters an independent presence. The importance of the institutional setting indicates the rational nature to independents' emergence in Irish party democracy. Because there is a particular set of rules in place, it caters for the expression of a political culture that is conducive to independents. The aim of this chapter is to examine this interaction of institutional features of the voting system and independents' electoral performance, not only in

Ireland, but also on a comparative level. This dimension is necessary because there is not enough variation in the Irish case to control and isolate particular effects. Just because few other countries use STV, and few others have independents, does not imply a significant relationship; a valid empirical test is required to consider the experience outside of Ireland.

The primary arguments given in terms of STV's causal effects relate to its candidate-centred nature. The election of independents is seen as an almost logical outcome because of the emphasis on personalistic competition fostered and facilitated by this electoral system. However, in the two other national directly elected parliaments using STV – the Maltese Chamber of Deputies and the Australian Commonwealth Senate – independents have experienced very little electoral success. No independent has been elected in Malta since 1950, and only a handful of independents have been elected to the Australian Senate since it adopted STV in 1948. What does the experience of these two countries say about the nature of the relationship between STV and independents? Is the latter's election really an inevitable effect of STV? No study of independents in Ireland could be complete without an analysis of this institutional dimension.

The structure of this chapter is as follows. The four primary reasons for how STV can help independents are outlined, before it is detailed how they impact on independents in Ireland. There follows a comparative approach, using data from Australia, where STV is used to elect seven parliaments. The relationship between STV and independents is examined via a three-step method. First, the experience of independents under STV in Australia is compared to how they perform under the Alternative Vote (AV), the other main voting system of choice in Australia. Second, there is a focus on why the factors that help independents in Ireland are not so conducive in Australia. Third, using a unique dataset of constituency-level data from STV elections in both countries, the effect of institutional variables on the independent vote is analysed in a quantitative model. Ultimately, it is shown that STV matters, but not wholly in the expected manner.

Independents and electoral systems

The literature on the consequences of electoral systems for minor political actors is generally in agreement that electoral features, such as ballot access requirements, candidate expenditure regulations and constituency size all affect such actors' electoral success rates. However, only a few studies have considered the effects of electoral systems on independents (Brancati (2008) being a notable exception), and even then the latter are usually grouped together with minor parties (Abramson et al. 1995; Hansen 2010; Rosenstone, Behr and Lazarus 1996; Sharman 1999). These studies tend to focus on the failure of minor parties, assuming the same effects apply for independents. In addition, most are single-case studies, which makes it difficult to tease out the importance of the effects of national institutions, such as the electoral system. This can also result in contradictory claims, which are often quite contextual and thus extremely difficult to generalise to other countries. For example, Chubb (1957) sees a positive rela-tionship between the introduction of STV and the emergence of inde-pendents in Ireland, while Sharman (2002) cites the early adoption of STV in Tasmania as a reason for the lack of independents in its House of Assembly. Brancati (2008) is one of the few to examine the direct effects of electoral systems on independents, finding that majority and plurality systems (such as the British first-past-the-post or the French double-ballot system), with their candidate-centred nature and small constituency size, help independents. She also finds that increasing district magnitude has converse effects on independents, strengthening them in majority and plurality systems, but weakening them under PR.

Before analysing the relationship between STV and independents, a brief explanation of the workings of STV is necessary to appreciate how it can affect voting behaviour. Voters indicate their first choice on the ballot paper by writing the number 1 next to a candidate's name. This is sufficient to cast a valid vote, but voters can also express their lower choices by writing 2, 3, 4 and so on beside their next pre-ferred candidates' names. The counting of votes revolves around the Droop quota, the minimum number of votes that guarantees election (although it is not always necessary to reach this number to be elected). It is calculated by dividing the total number of valid votes cast by one more than the number of seats to be filled, and adding one, disregard-ing any fraction. Except in the highly unlikely event that the requisite number of candidates filled all of the seats by reaching the quota on the basis of their first preferences alone, the counting process comprises a series of counts or stages, each involving the distribution of the surplus votes (those over and above the quota) of a candidate whose total exceeds the quota or, if no one has reached the quota, the elimination of the lowest-placed candidate, all of whose votes are re-distributed. If a voter does not express a further preference, his or her vote is discarded, with only transferable votes being examined. Counting continues until all the seats have been filled. This occurs when a sufficient number of candidates have reached the quota, or if the number of candidates left is one greater than the number of seats to be filled and there are no further surpluses to distribute, at which stage all bar the candidate with the fewest votes are deemed elected. These are the general STV rules, although there are slight variations in each of the jurisdictions using this method.

How does STV help independents? The reasons given generally revolve around four factors (Gallagher 2005, 522; Sinnott 2010; Weeks 2010a): the presence of multi-member constituencies, STV's ordinal structure, its candidate-centred nature, and how it can foster independent-minded behaviour. Multi-seat constituencies can help independents in a number of ways. The first is that their operation in a small population such as Ireland ensures a relatively low electoral threshold to win a seat. An increasing district magnitude also brings with it a rise in the importance of personal reputation, as candidates focus on their own characteristics to distinguish themselves from a larger pool (Carey and Shugart 1995, 418). This aids independents, who have little other than reputation on which to campaign. Some dispute the direction of this relationship, as it might be that smaller magnitude is more likely to produce candidate-centred politics (Ehin et al. 2013, 39). The multi-member constituency also engenders a strong element of intra-party competition, forcing candidates to develop a personal vote and devote excessive attention to localistic and particularistic concerns, features which it was shown in the last chapter encourage a vote for independents. While few doubt the link between localism and independents, the link between the culture and STV has been open to dispute (Farrell, Mackerras and McAllister 1996; Gallagher 2005).

The second reason given why STV helps independents is its ordinal and preferential nature; that is, the ability to rank candidates. Most industrial democracies use an electoral system that does not allow voters to rank candidates, or where they do, the option to cross lists and include independents in this ranking is rare or non-effectual. So STV (in Ireland) is unusual in that voters must express a preference for a candidate for him or her to receive a vote; there are no pre-ordained lists determining the destination of transfers should voters cast just one preference; there are no pre-ordained rankings of candidates that independents must overcome to win a seat. This ordinal and preferential nature can put independents at an advantage, as their non-partisan nature can result in party voters preferring them to candidates from opposite parties when it comes to casting their lower preferences; in other words, STV rewards 'transfer-friendly' candidates such as independents. At the same time, the lack of running mates could also put independents at a disadvantage compared to party candidates who receive large numbers of transfers from their fellow party candidates. This was the rationale behind the decision of independents in Tasmania to come together and form party groupings when STV (or Hare–Clark as it is known there) was introduced in 1910 (Sharman 2002, 62).

Preferential electoral systems should also encourage sincere voting; that is, voting for one's most preferred candidate, rather than voting strategically against a least preferred candidate. The latter is a frequent occurrence in single-member plurality systems, and is one of the reasons why so few independents have been elected in the UK and the US. Strategic voting should be relatively non-existent under STV, because of both the complexity of the system (Bartholdi and Orlin 1991), and the fact that the transferable vote enables voters to cast preferences for all candidates. However, this comes with a slight health warning. The low district magnitude in Ireland means that some voters may be discouraged from casting a preference for independents, because not all may understand the rationale of the system and the median number of preferences cast on a ballot is four (Laver 2004, 522). This has the consequence that some are unlikely to favour listing a large number of preferences to facilitate a sincere vote. Their rationale may be that where they believe an independent to have little chance of winning a seat, there is not much point giving them a preference. One way of testing this hypothesis is to look at the difference in the proportions between those who favoured a particular candidate and who actually voted for the same candidate. This data is available from the INES (2002–11) by comparing declared probabilities of voting for particular candidates (on a scale of 1 to 10) to actual voting patterns. Of those who separately said there was a high probability (a score of 9 or 10) of their voting for Fianna Fáil and Fine Gael, two-thirds ultimately voted for these parties. In contrast, the comparative figures for those giving a high probability of voting for independent candidates is just 26 per cent. This means that three out of four voters who state they will very probably vote for an independent fail to do so come election time. The sincere voting that should be a product of STV does not seem to materialise for independents.

The third reason why STV might help independents is its candidate-centred nature, which puts independents at far less of a disadvantage than a party-centred ballot. Indeed, Farrell and McAllister (2006, 154) ranked Irish STV as the most candidate-centred electoral system in the CSES dataset of twenty-nine democracies. The impact of this candidate-centred design is reinforced by the ordinal nature of the ballot (Rae 1967, 17), which distinguishes STV from other candidate-centred systems such as single-member plurality or the French double ballot. When an electoral system is both ordinal and candidate-centred, it encourages politicians to cultivate personal support (Farrell and McAllister 2006, 11), creating a form of political competition conducive to independents.

The fourth factor is that STV is believed to favour independent-minded behaviour, primarily because of its candidate-centred nature. This in part stems from its origin as a product of Victorian liberalism, with the aim of maximising individual choice (Bogdanor 1984, 77). As such, under STV, voters are given a choice between candidates, with the intention of minimising the role of parties in the electoral process (Mackenzie 1957, 62). Indeed, one of the aims of its originators in the nineteenth century, Thomas Hare and John Stuart Mill, was for 'a scheme devised partly with the aim of weakening the power of parties and increasing the independence of MPs both in and out of parliament' (Hart 1992, 97). Both viewed STV as a means of securing the election of independents (Hart 1992, 267). It is for this reason that STV is some-times seen as an anachronistic system, more suited to a nineteenth-century era of small government and independent parliamentarians primarily focused on personal representation. To this extent, a Royal Commission in 1908 in the UK described STV as 'a system of personal representation' designed 'to secure the return of men as men, not as party units, a purpose which it is well calculated to serve' (cited in Meredith 1913, 57). Hare also liked to call STV 'personal representa-tion' rather than proportional representation (Knight and Baxter-Moore 1972). This promotion of independent-minded behaviour under STV might encourage fractionalism within parties, increasing the likelihood of party dissidents running as independents.

Singularly, each of these features is not unique to STV; however, as a combination they distinguish STV from most other electoral systems (Farrell and McAllister 2006, 3), in that STV is candidate-centred, ordinal, parties have no control over the ballot and it operates in multi-member constituencies.

Independents and STV in Ireland

Bearing these features in mind, has STV helped independents in Ireland? To understand the relationship between the two it is necessary to appre-ciate why STV was adopted in Ireland in the first place. One of the very reasons given at the time was that it might help to secure the represen-tation of protestant minorities (Weeks 2010a, 109), many of whom, as is highlighted in Chapter 2, ran as independents, given the lack of a party suitable for their interests. The first direct elections held under STV were successful in these aims. In Sligo corporation in January 1919, four independents and five protestant members of the loosely-affiliated Sligo Ratepayers' Association were elected to the twenty-four member council. This experience was undoubtedly a factor in the introduction of STV for local elections in 1920 and Dáil elections in 1921.

STV was therefore adopted with a particular aim in mind (on the part of the British authorities it was to lessen the influence of Sinn Féin, the majority party at the time). This indicates that there may be an element of endogeneity in examining the effects of STV on independents – in other words, it may not be that independents are solely a product of STV, but rather that STV was adopted with the aim of lessening the power of parties. This needs to be borne in mind when the psychological, or indirect, effects of electoral systems are considered. These are consequential effects stemming from the perceived mechanical, or direct, effects of the electoral system. Such psychological effects should have been a factor in helping independents when STV was first introduced, because if it was believed that STV was advantageous for them, more independents might have been expected to run. However, as described in Chapter 3, there was not a glut of independents contesting Dáil elections in the 1920s. This was not an experience unusual to Ireland; there was no increase in independent candidacies in Canada in the same time period when STV was introduced in Alberta and Manitoba (Jensen 1998, 90). Nor did it result in an increase in independent candidacies when STV was adopted for elections in Australia or Scotland (see below). The nature of these effects can be examined in greater detail, and in the following section the influence of two of the prime causal factors of STV – district magnitude and preferential voting – are assessed.

District magnitude

As already discussed, district magnitude should affect independents in that the larger the district, the more independents are expected to run. Figure 6.1 details the average number of independent candidates per constituency size at Dáil elections since 1923. Initially, it appeared that large constituencies helped independents, as the largest numbers running were in seven-, eight-, and nine-seat constituencies. However, this effect quickly dissipated, as the main pattern appears to be that fewer independents run in three-seat constituencies (eight- and nine-seaters were phased out in 1933, followed by seven-seaters in 1944). It could be argued that we might expect more independents to run in larger constituencies, simply because they have larger populations. To control for this factor, the mean number of independent candidates per seat from 1923 to 2016 can be considered, which was 0.3 for three-seaters, 0.5 for four-seaters, and 0.4 for five-seaters. The comparative mean figures for seven-seaters is 0.2, 0.4 for eight-seaters and 0.2 for nine-seat constituencies. This lessens the value of the initial findings from Figure 6.1, as it suggests that district magnitude has less of an effect on the emergence of independent candidates. It supports the assertion in the previous section that the psychological effect of STV on independents is not as considerable as some might believe.

What is the direct effect of district magnitude on independents' electoral success? As hypothesised earlier in this chapter, there should be more independents elected the larger the district magnitude, as this lowers the electoral threshold. Looking at the overall trend in Figure 6.2 since 1923, independents have won 5 per cent of the seats in three-seat constituencies, 6 per cent in four-seaters, and 4 per cent in five-seaters. They won just 2 per cent of seats in seven- and nine-seat constituencies, with the one anomaly being their winning 19 per cent of seats across the three eight-seat constituencies. Apart from this latter figure, district magnitude appears to have little effect on independents' electoral performance.

The influence of multi-member constituencies can be further tested by examining whether proportionality increases in line with an increase in district magnitude. This tends to be a general law in studies of electoral systems (Taagepera and Shugart 1989, 120), resulting in the recognition of district magnitude as 'the decisive factor', since it determines much of the relationship between seats, votes and parties (Taagepera and Shugart 1989, 124). The validity of this 'law' can be determined by calculating the 'advantage ratio' (A), which is the ratio of the percentage of seats won to the percentage of votes (first preferences) won (Taagepera and Shugart 1989, 68). If A is therefore greater than 1, independents are receiving a bonus of seats over votes; if A is less than 1, they are receiving fewer seats than what their vote might otherwise entitle them to in a world of perfect proportionality.

In general, 'allocation rules' (the number of seats in an electoral district) tend to penalise small parties (Taagepera and Shugart 1989, xiii). Dealing with national figures first, this appears to also hold for independents as, to borrow a phrase from Taagepera and Shugart, they are 'underpaid' for their vote (*ibid.*). Independents have been 'penalised' at every general election held between 1923 and 2016, as their national percentage of seats won has always been less than their percentage of votes won (although the relevance of this may be validly questioned since independents do not run collectively on a national ticket). There are some deviations per constituency size, however, as is indicated in Figure 6.3. In particular, independents

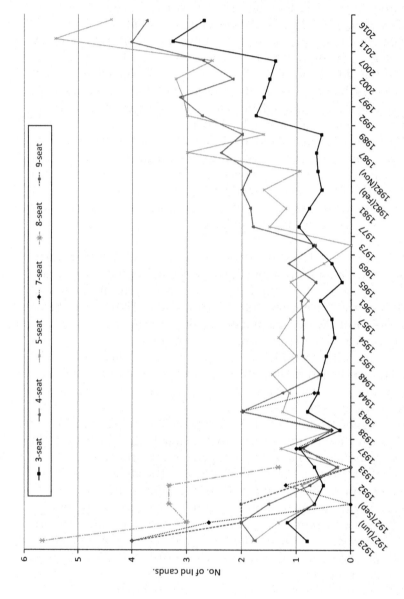

Figure 6.1 Number of independent candidates per constituency at Dáil elections in Ireland, 1923–2016.

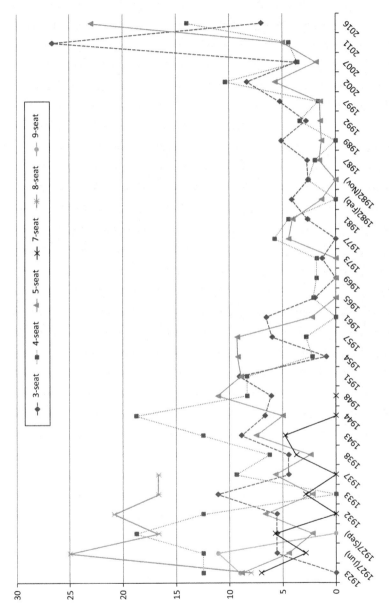

Figure 6.2 Percentage of seats won by independents at Dáil elections in Ireland, 1923–2016.

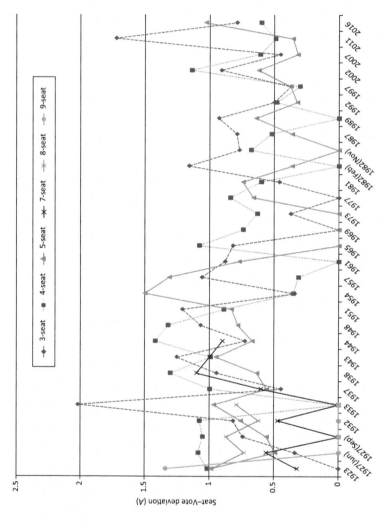

Figure 6.3 Seat–vote deviation by district magnitude at Dáil elections in Ireland, 1923–2016.

regularly achieved a mean A of greater than 1 in three-, four- and five-seat constituencies up until the 1950s. Since then, their decline in support and the limited range of magnitude made it more difficult for independents to win seats. A has exceeded 1 on only five occasions since the 1950s, and in general has been smallest in five-seat constituencies. In theory, if district magnitude has a positive effect on independents' seat return, then A should increase in line with district magnitude. However, this does not prove to be the case, as A has an inverse relationship with district magnitude. The mean A in a three-seater was 0.75, in a four-seater 0.71 and 0.60 in a five-seater, while the overall correlation between district magnitude and A is –0.20, suggesting a (albeit weak) negative relationship between the variables, contrary to expectation. From this evidence, it seems to be the case that the lower the district magnitude, the greater return of seats for independents from a given vote. It could be hypothesised that this is because more 'no-hope' independents run in five-seaters. However, an analysis confined to independents winning more than 5 per cent of the first-preference vote repeats the same findings, with an average A of 0.83 in three-seat constituencies, 0.69 in four-seat constituencies and 0.66 in five-seat constituencies.

These results come with a slight health warning. The percentage of seats won is not just due to the percentage of first preferences received, but also the number of lower preferences. Thus, the determination of proportionality as the ratio of seats to first preferences has to be taken with a grain of salt, as it produces an 'artifactual scatter' (Taagepera and Shugart 1989, 227), because the role played by lower preferences is not taken into account. Data from the INES and constituencies using electronic voting in 2002 indicate that independents receive a greater proportion of votes the lower the preference (Weeks 2008b), which suggests that including such preferences in the calculation of the index of proportionality would simply give A a lower value. However, it cannot be deduced if this would be a uniform decline across constituencies of differing district magnitude.

Preferential voting

Does the transferable nature of STV make a difference to independents' electoral performance? This is only likely to be the case if most of the preferences of each voter are taken into account, something that rarely, if ever, happens at Irish election counts. In addition, at the counts when most transfers are distributed, many independents are already eliminated. Another problem with transfers for independents is that there are very low rates of transfer solidarity between independent candidates. Gallagher's analysis of transfer patterns between 1922 and 1977 found that only 24 per cent of independents' votes transfer to fellow independents. In contrast, the comparative figure for Fianna Fáil was 82 per cent (1978, 3). While intra-party transfer rates have declined considerably since the 1970s, they have remained pretty stable for independents, with the solidarity rate at 23 per cent in 2011 – an election with the most independents ever available to receive transfers. Independents can make up for this lack of team solidarity, however, by their nonpartisan status, which puts them in a position to receive votes from all quarters. The impact of transfers can be tested by comparing independents' position in the electoral contest after the first count to their position when they leave the electoral contest; that is, when they have been either elected or eliminated. This is done in Figure 6.4, which provides details of the number of places all independent candidates moved in total during their respective election counts. For example, for the last observation in 2016, independents jumped an aggregate of 23 places because of transfers, and fell 11 places. Looking at independents' overall performance, there was not as much movement during the counts as might be expected. Of the 1,317 independent candidates who ran between 1948 and 2016, just 142 had their position in the count altered by transfers. Of these 142 independents, 68 jumped an aggregate total of 86 places, while 74 dropped 88 places, which seems to indicate that transfers have a greater negative impact on independents' electoral performance. However, the effect of transfers is limited, since the vast majority of these candidates either drop or jump just one place. As a result, only a small number of the 1,317 independents either won seats (twenty-one candidates) or lost (seven) them due to transferred votes. As detailed in Figure 6.4, the overall effect of transfers seems to vary across elections, and it can be reasonably hypothesised that the more votes independents receive, the longer they remain in the contest and, by implication, the odds of transfers affecting their final position increases. A strong positive correlation coefficient of +0.86 between the independent first-preference vote and the total number of places changed at each election lends evidence to the nature of this relationship.

This section has shown that the institutional effects of STV on independents in Ireland are not as significant as might be expected. This does not necessarily mean that STV does not matter. Rather, it may be the product of the limitations of the case study approach. For example, the narrow range of district magnitude might be preventing the realisation of the effect this could have on independents. What is required is a greater comparative approach to determine the nature of the

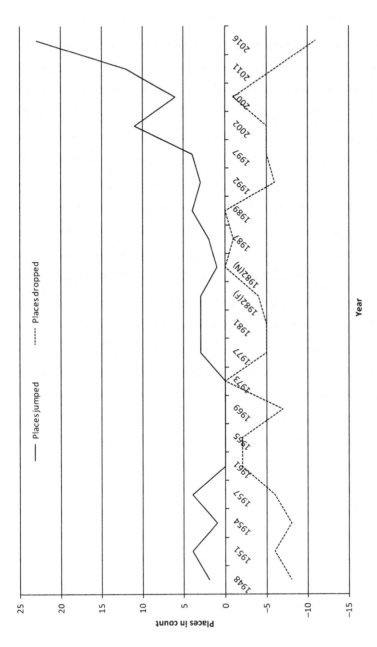

Figure 6.4 Effect of transfers on independents' performance at Dáil elections in Ireland, 1948–2016.

Note: This denotes the total number of places jumped and dropped during the election count by independent candidates at each election.

relationship between STV and independents, which is the focus of the remainder of this chapter.

STV in other countries

STV has been used in a number of democracies (most of which are former British colonies), but the difficulty for comparison is that many of these experiences were in the past and at the regional level. They include Australia, Burma, Canada, Estonia, Gibraltar, India, the Isle of Man, Malta, New Zealand, Pakistan, South Africa, the UK and the US. So while independents were elected under STV in these systems, this may have been a product of the regional nature of these elections (where independents tend to have greater success than at national elections), and of a previous age when independents were more prevalent. In more recent times, STV has been adopted for local elections in New Zealand and Scotland. It has also been used for elections to the Northern Ireland Assembly since its establishment in 1998.[1] While independents have won seats in all these jurisdictions, this is not an unusual feature of second-order, regional elections, particularly at the level of local government. Along with Ireland, Australia and Malta are the only two other countries to have used STV on a continuous national basis, which makes them ideal for comparison. However, in Malta, an independent candidacy has been described as 'a virtual invitation to electoral defeat' (Hirczy de Mino and Lane 2000, 190). No independent has been elected to parliament there since 1950, and the mean number of votes won by an independent at a typical Maltese general election, such as in 2013 – when only one independent candidate ran in the entire country, is less than one tenth of 1 per cent (generally less than one hundred votes). The Maltese voter is very partisan, with almost everyone turning out to vote and almost everyone voting for one of the two main parties: the Nationalists and the Labour Party. One example of the high level of partisanship in Malta is that 99 per cent of ballots are non-transferable when no candidate of the same party is left in the count to receive transfers (Hirczy de Mino and Lane 2000, 192–3); in other words, 99 per cent of voters cast all their preferences for just one party. The consequence of this dominance of the Maltese political system by two parties is that it is extremely difficult for anyone else to be elected, and consequently very few cast a vote for another party, let alone an independent. The negligibility of the independent vote in Malta means that it cannot be used for comparative analysis, simply because it barely exists. Instead, Australia is a far more suitable test case for comparison of the relationship between STV and independents.

Not only have independents achieved some levels of electoral success there, but STV is also in operation at the state and territorial level, along with another electoral system (AV), which increases the cases for comparison.

STV in Australia

The widespread use of STV in Australia makes it an ideal case for an analysis of the effects of the electoral system, as it has been used across local, state, territorial and federal elections (see Weeks (2013) and Farrell and McAllister (2006, 21–46) for a discussion of its introduction). In 1896, STV was first trialled in Tasmania, and in 1909 its lower house became the first parliament in the world to be elected by STV. In 1948, STV was introduced for elections to the Commonwealth Senate, a practice that has since been replicated by state upper houses in New South Wales (in 1978), South Australia (in 1985), Victoria (in 2003) and Western Australia (in 1987). Since 1993 STV has also been used for elections to the unicameral legislature in the Australian Capital Territory. All other parliaments in Australia are elected by AV, which is essentially STV in single-seat constituencies.

Based on the theorised advantages STV affords independents, it might be expected that they fare better at elections under this system in Australia than under AV, which is a plurality system that does not favour minor political actors such as independents. In addition, because elections to upper houses are generally deemed of the second-order variety, compared to the more important first-order elections to the lower house, independents should further prosper at this level (with the exception of Tasmania, which uses these systems in reverse order; that is, STV for the lower house, and AV for its upper chamber).

None of these expectations are met, however, as is detailed in Table 6.1 and Figure 6.5. As is apparent, independents have won far more seats at lower-house elections, despite the extensive use of STV at the upper-house level. Since 1950, independents have won 256 seats at the combined commonwealth, state and territory lower-house level. The equivalent figure across the six upper houses is 178, but 158 of these victories were in the Tasmanian Legislative Council, which uses AV. As was discussed in Chapter 3, this chamber is something of an anomaly, one of the few democratic parliaments in the Western world that has always been dominated by independents. In total in Australia 47 independents have been elected under STV, 385 under AV and 2 under a hybrid list system (in the Australian Capital Territory (ACT) in 1992). The level of independent representation in upper houses elected by STV is quite sparse. None have been elected in New South

Table 6.1 *Independent seats won at upper and lower house elections in Australia, 1950–2015*

Region	Lower house	Upper house
Commonwealth	24	14*
New South Wales	66	0*
Tasmania	20*	158
Victoria	20	1*
Western Australia	25	1*
South Australia	40	4*
Northern Territory	15	–
Queensland	39	–
ACT	7*	–

Note: Figures are the total numbers of seats won by independents at elections.
* denotes use of STV for elections, as of 2015; the remainder use AV.
Author's figures calculated from Australian Politics and Elections Database accessed at www.elections.uwa.edu.au; Rodrigues and Brenton (2010).

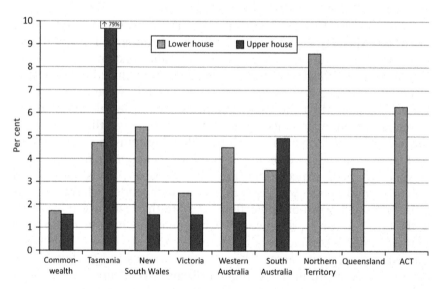

Figure 6.5 Mean vote for independents at lower- and upper-house elections in Australia, 1950–2015.

Note: The ACT, Northern Territory and Queensland legislatures are all unicameral.

Wales, one in both Western Australia and Victoria and three in South Australia. Figure 6.3 compares the mean independent vote across the same chambers, and the same pattern is repeated: independents are more successful under AV than STV elections (with the recent exception of South Australia).

Not only can the influence of STV for independents be assessed by comparing their performance at AV elections, it is also possible to consider how independents fared before the adoption of STV and after the adoption of STV ticket voting (a de facto form of list voting, which theoretically penalises independents and is discussed later in the chapter). As Table 6.2 indicates, the adoption of STV had little effect on the independent vote. There was no significant increase in the Commonwealth Senate, the Australian Capital Territory or Western Australia. In Victoria, support for independents has decreased since the switch from AV to STV in 2003. It is only in South Australia that STV is associated with an increased independent vote, and even then this took a number of elections to materialise, when it was largely a single-candidate phenomenon. The failure of STV to boost the independent vote is not just confined to Australia. STV did little for independents in Scotland when it was first used at local elections in 2007. The introduction of PR meant that many areas of previously unchallenged independent dominance faced competition, resulting in an overall decline in support for independents (Clark and Bennie 2008; Denver, Clark

Table 6.2 *Mean vote for independents before and after the introduction of STV and STV ticket voting, 1950–2013*

Jurisdiction	Independent vote before STV	Independent vote under STV	Independent vote under ticket STV
Commonwealth Senate	1.5	3.2	1.9
ACT	7.2	7.3	–
New South Wales	–	0.9	1.1
South Australia	1.7	–	5.5
Victoria	1.5	–	0.5
Western Australia	2.3	–	2.3

Note: Both the NSW Legislative Council and Tasmanian House of Assembly have always used STV for direct elections in the specified period.
Pre-STV eras included: Commonwealth Senate: 1919–46; South Australia: 1975–82; Western Australia: 1960–86; Victoria 1988–2002.
Ticket STV eras: New South Wales 1978–88; Commonwealth Senate: 1983–2013; South Australia 1983–2013; Western Australia 1987–2013; Victoria 2003–2013.
All figures are percentages.
Author's figures calculated from Australian Politics and Elections Database accessed at www.elections.uwa.edu.au.

and Bennie 2009). In a reverse manner (but still with the same causal relationship), independents' support doubled from 11 to 20 per cent when Northern Ireland switched from STV back to first-past-the-post in 1926 for its parliamentary elections, increasing further to 29 per cent in 1933 (Knight and Baxter-Moore 1972). However, the adoption of STV for elections to the new Stormont assembly in 1998 did not result in a raft of independents, with an average of just one independent MLA returned at every election since to the 108-seat chamber. Independents are more successful at local elections in Northern Ireland, where an average of approximately 5 per cent of councillors since the re-organisation of local government in the 1970s have been independent. As already noted, this prevalence of independents in local councils is a feature of many democracies, regardless of the electoral system in operation.

Why STV does not help independents in Australia
It is apparent from this analysis that STV has not helped independents in Australia. What are the implications of this for the assumed relationship in Ireland? Does this mean that the findings from the initial analysis of independents' performance in Ireland are correct in their suggestion that STV is not the independent-friendly system we are led to believe? To answer this question it is necessary to examine in greater detail the causal influence in Australia of the four factors originally cited that explain independents' success in Ireland. They are: multi-member constituencies, ordinal and preferential voting, a candidate-centred ballot and the promotion of independent action. In terms of the first factor, multi-member constituencies result in electoral quotas as low as 5 per cent in New South Wales and just over 8 per cent in South Australia. This should theoretically make it easier for independents to be elected, but this does not materialise because the necessarily large geographical size of these constituencies is a major handicap for independents, it being very difficult for independents to canvass the entire region and to cultivate a personal vote. The personal vote might also be less important in such large constituencies, where electoral competition takes a more party-centred alignment (Ehin et al. 2013, 39). Standing out in a race that is likely to attract a significant number of competitors is a particular challenge for independents, especially those lacking 'brand recognition'. Although AV uses single-member districts, this is counteracted by the smaller size of these constituencies, which improves independents' electoral prospects. They can make contact with a greater proportion of the electorate, and the smaller constituencies gives those with a concentrated area of support an increased possibility of election

(J. Curtin 2005, 1–2; Rodrigues and Brenton 2010). Costar and Curtin (2004, 49) cite the example of Peter Andren in the federal constituency of Calare in New South Wales in 2001. He was elected to the lower house with a vote of 40,786, but he would have needed an additional half a million votes to win a Senate seat in the same state.

In terms of the third and fourth factors that help independents, the ballot design of STV in Australia differs from Irish practice. There are two types of STV ballot in Australia, which is best illustrated by visual means. Farrell and McAllister (2006) identified the first type as 'party-controlled'; this is shown in Figure 6.6, which is a sample ballot for elections to the Commonwealth Senate. The ballots in New South Wales, South Australia and Victoria employ a very similar design. There is a slight variation in Western Australia, where the parties are listed in the first column and candidates in rows to the right of a vertical line.

The upper-house STV ballot resembles that used for party-list elections; parties are listed in the top row and candidates in columns underneath a line. Known as the group-ticket vote, a single preference is enough to cast a formal vote (for a party), with the parties then directing the flow of preferences. All ungrouped candidates (i.e. unregistered parties and independents) are placed below the line, on the right-hand extremity of the ballot, what Orr (2010, 284) decries as the 'lumping of independents in an undistinguished mass, tucked away at the end

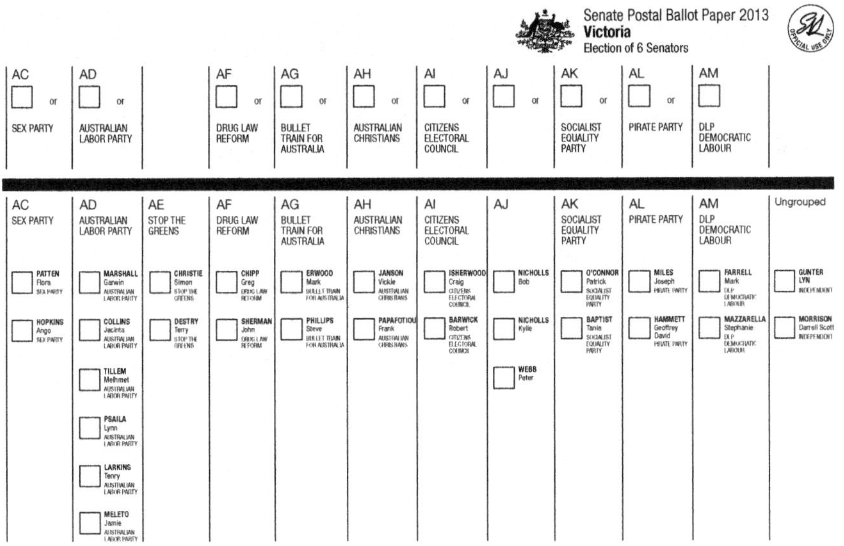

Figure 6.6 Commonwealth Senate STV ballot paper.

of the ballot'. To cast a formal vote below the line, a preference for every candidate (bar one) is required.[2] This means that casting a first, or a relatively high ranking, preference for an independent (unless an incumbent, who can be placed above the line) requires a good deal of effort when there is a large number of candidates on the ballot, as is frequently the case under STV in Australia. This is a considerable challenge for independents because over 90 per cent of voters eschew this effort and vote above the line. Independents' only escape clause is to form a group, which need not necessarily imply a party, but still lessens the value of their independence. Concern has been expressed about this treatment of independents, as it makes voting for them 'a more arduous task' (Farrell and McAllister 2006, 171) and 'more time-consuming' (Orr 2010, 184). Since independents are below the line, they are also denied control over the flow of their preferences. This lessens independents' bargaining power for preference arrangements (Sawer 2004), a handicap not shared by minor parties who typically negotiate such deals to get their candidates elected (Orr 2010, 184). Because most voters treat this ticket version of STV as a party-list ballot, it is not surprising that the mean vote for independents at elections since 1950 under the traditional non-ticket version of STV in Ireland and Australia (almost 6 per cent) is almost three times that under ticket-style STV (2 per cent). In addition, 151 independents have been elected under the former method, and as few as 8 under the latter. If the two cases that used both the ticket and non-ticket versions of STV are compared (New South Wales and the Senate), there has been a 40 per cent reduction in support for independents at the federal level since the introduction of ticket voting. The impact in New South Wales, where the vote increased marginally from 0.9 to 1.1 per cent, is not so clear because independents have always had a weak presence in its Legislative Council. Overall, these findings imply that ballot design matters: it ensures that three of the four reasons why STV helps independents in Ireland do not apply to this form of Australian STV. It is not candidate-centred, does not promote independent-minded behaviour and independents do not profit from transfers because parties control the flow of preferences.

The non-ticket type of STV ballot in Australia, generally known as Hare–Clark, is used in the ACT and for lower-house elections in Tasmania (a non-ticket version was also used for the federal Senate prior to the 1983 reforms and in the New South Wales Legislative Council between 1978 and 1988). Depicted in Figure 6.7, it has been called voter oriented (Farrell and McAllister 2006) because there is no 'line' and voters can rank candidates in any order they wish, with the requisite number of preferences for formality limited to the

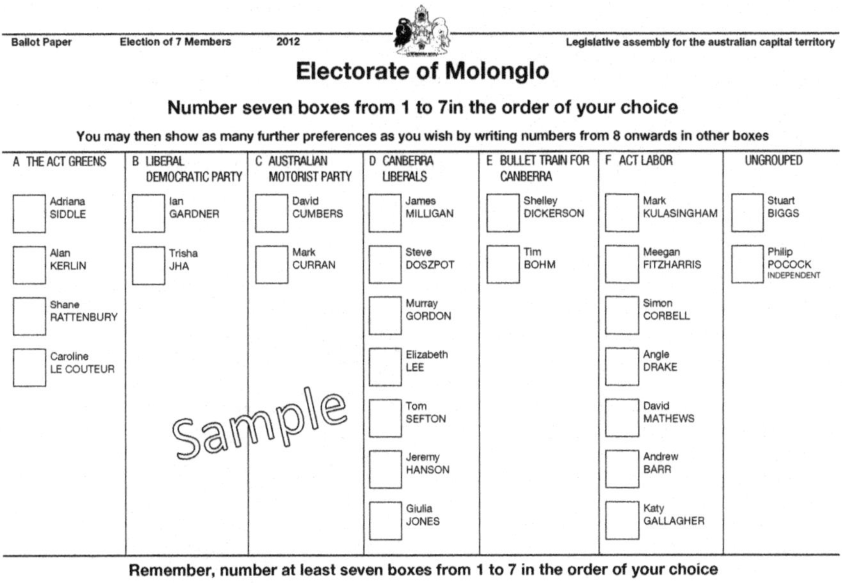

Figure 6.7 ACT STV ballot paper.

number of seats available (five in Tasmania and seven in the ACT). The order of candidates is also rotated, thus preventing the use of 'how to vote' cards by the parties, the presence of which can disadvantage independents.

As a consequence, independents receive higher levels of support at STV elections under this ballot than under Senate-type STV. That said, this lower-house form of STV is not entirely candidate-centred. Although it acts like a preferential system, unlike the ticket version of STV, it still gives the impression of the voting act being a party-centred decision. Candidates are grouped by party and the distinctiveness of independents' candidacy is removed by their forced grouping. This was also the case in the Senate before the introduction of STV, where although party labels were not stated on the ballot (parties were identified by letters), candidates were still grouped in this format. So two of the factors (a candidate-centred ballot, which also promotes independence) that help independents at lower-house STV elections in Ireland are not present under Australian lower-house STV.

The Irish STV ballot is shown in Figure 6.8. Of all the cases analysed in this chapter, it is the only STV ballot that does not group candidates by party; instead they are sorted alphabetically by surname.[3] Independents can thus compete on a more even keel with party

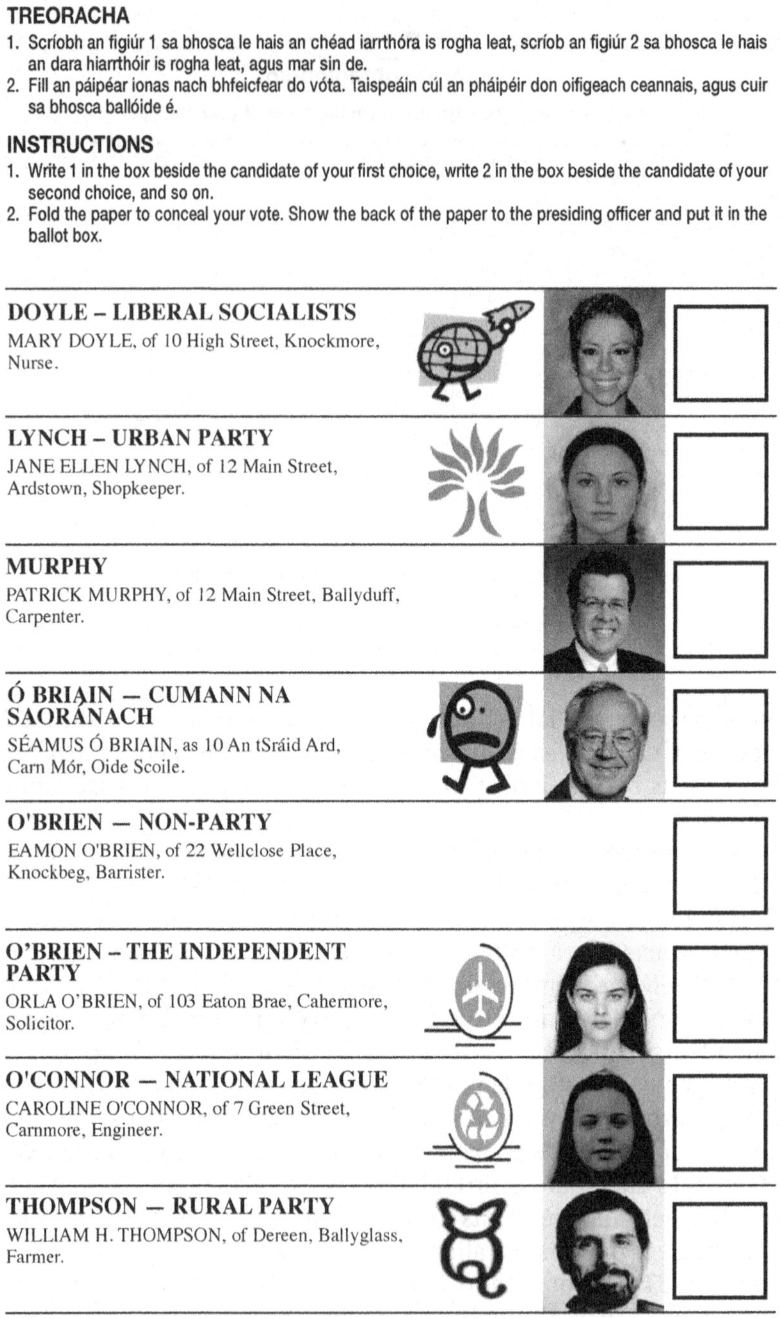

TREORACHA

1. Scríobh an figiúr 1 sa bhosca le hais an chéad iarrthóra is rogha leat, scríob an figiúr 2 sa bhosca le hais an dara hiarrthóir is rogha leat, agus mar sin de.
2. Fill an páipéar ionas nach bhfeicfear do vóta. Taispeáin cúl an pháipéir don oifigeach ceannais, agus cuir sa bhosca ballóide é.

INSTRUCTIONS

1. Write 1 in the box beside the candidate of your first choice, write 2 in the box beside the candidate of your second choice, and so on.
2. Fold the paper to conceal your vote. Show the back of the paper to the presiding officer and put it in the ballot box.

DOYLE – LIBERAL SOCIALISTS

MARY DOYLE, of 10 High Street, Knockmore, Nurse.

LYNCH – URBAN PARTY

JANE ELLEN LYNCH, of 12 Main Street, Ardstown, Shopkeeper.

MURPHY

PATRICK MURPHY, of 12 Main Street, Ballyduff, Carpenter.

Ó BRIAIN — CUMANN NA SAORÁNACH

SÉAMUS Ó BRIAIN, as 10 An tSráid Ard, Carn Mór, Oide Scoile.

O'BRIEN — NON-PARTY

EAMON O'BRIEN, of 22 Wellclose Place, Knockbeg, Barrister.

O'BRIEN – THE INDEPENDENT PARTY

ORLA O'BRIEN, of 103 Eaton Brae, Cahermore, Solicitor.

O'CONNOR — NATIONAL LEAGUE

CAROLINE O'CONNOR, of 7 Green Street, Carnmore, Engineer.

THOMPSON — RURAL PARTY

WILLIAM H. THOMPSON, of Dereen, Ballyglass, Farmer.

Figure 6.8 Irish STV ballot paper.

candidates. Independents are not consigned to the extremity of the ballot, they are not forced into groups, and voters are not required to cast a preference for all candidates to formalise a vote for independents. It is no wonder that independents fare better in Ireland. Comparing mean support for independents across the three variants of STV since 1940, the party-controlled upper-house Australian version is the least friendly to independents and records the lowest independent vote (1 per cent). The voter-oriented Australian lower-house variant attracts a higher independent vote (3.4 per cent), as it is less antipathetic than its upper-house counterpart. The candidate-centred Irish version attracts the highest independent vote (6.2 per cent), as parties are not afforded any advantage in the ballot design (apart from the possible inclusion of party logos; independents cannot use any logo or indeed use the label 'independent'). This pattern is generally consistent across the decades and supports the core thesis of this study that there is a strategic element to the presence of independents. Because Irish STV is more permissive than the Australian format, it explains why independents are more successful at elections in Ireland. This is also a contributory factor in explaining why independents are not facilitated by STV in Malta. It was stated at the beginning of this chapter that one advantage of STV for independents is its primacy of candidate over party. However, in both Malta and Australia, the political parties have tweaked STV to afford a greater emphasis on party than intended by the originators of STV. In Malta, candidates are grouped by party affiliation, and also, since the 1980s, the key determinant of who wins a parliamentary election is the number of national first preferences won by a party. The evidence from the Maltese and Australian cases indicates just why STV does not help independents in these respective jurisdictions – because the electoral rules and regulations have been tweaked by parties to their own advantage, and to make them less candidate-centred. With the exception of the introduction of party logos on the ballot and perhaps the minimal constituency size, no such interference has happened in Ireland. This is one clear factor why STV facilitates independents in its political system.

All this suggests a clear institutional link between features of STV electoral systems and independent performance. Holding other factors equal – such as a facilitative political culture and a propensity to vote for independents – support for independents varies in a rational manner with electoral rules. The fewer the disadvantages against independents, the more votes they receive. To test this claim in a more valid manner and to take into account the other possible factors influencing an independent vote, their performance can be assessed in a multivariate model using data from both Ireland and Australia.

Constituency-level analysis

To fully extrapolate the nature of the relationship between STV and independents, it is necessary to consider the piecemeal effects of the electoral system. It is preferable to look at the constituency level because national and state/territory averages can mask the presence of significant variation. For the reasons already discussed in this chapter, it is not enough to look at just Ireland because of the lack of variation in ballot structure, assembly size, signature and candidate requirements, and the generally limited district magnitude. To understand if STV is a causal factor in the presence of independents in Ireland, the more cases for inclusion the more valid the findings. The data of interest is from each of the eight jurisdictions using STV in Australia and Ireland since 1945, descriptive summaries of which (for the numerical data) are provided in Table 6.3. The mean independent vote per constituency is highest in the Australian Capital Territory, at just over 8 per cent, followed by South Australia (7 per cent), Ireland (6.1 per cent) and Tasmania (5.5 per cent). The number of independent candidates running per constituency is highest in South Australia (14) and New South Wales (13), both of which are single state-wide constituencies. In terms of geography, the three smallest jurisdictions (the ACT, Tasmania, and Ireland) have the first, third and fourth highest levels of support for independents. Indeed, these three have the lowest electoral quotas, which has been cited as a factor behind independent success (Costar and Curtin 2004, 51; Gallagher 1989a, 32). The last three columns in Table 6.3 detail the number of valid votes per constituency, the number of constituencies analysed for each jurisdiction and the number of elections.

To assess the influence of these variables on support for independents, a statistical model is devised using the constituency data summarised in Table 6.3, which comprises 1,205 cases. This was primarily sourced from official election reports, electoral commissions and online archives – such as the Australian Politics and Elections Database (elections.uwa.edu.au) and Adam Carr's election archive (psephos.adamcarr.net). It is necessary to look at Australia and Ireland in separate models because the numbers in the Irish data far outweigh the individual Australian cases, and would mask the effects of STV in the latter. The size of constituencies was calculated from electoral maps provided by electoral commissions and, in the case of Ireland, Brian Mercer Walker's *Parliamentary Election Results in Ireland, 1918–92* (1992). With the constituency vote for independents the dependent variable that the models sought to explain, the independent variables,

Table 6.3 *Performance of independents at STV elections, 1945–2016*

Region	Vote	Candidates	DM	Mean km^2	Quota	Mean vv	N	Ne
National								
Australian Senate	2.5	7.8	5.9	993,243	157,130	1,120,787	180	24
Ireland	6.1	1.5	3.8	1,745	8,091	39,364	817	20
State/Territory								
ACT	8.1	6.2	5.7	786	9,740	63,487	18	6
New South Wales	0.9	13.0	21.0	809,444	178,317	3,425,352	11	11
South Australia	7.0	14.4	11.0	982,779	76,085	913,023	8	8
Tasmania	5.5	2.8	6.4	13,860	6,495	46,091	105	21
Victoria	0.4	2.0	5.0	28,460	66,751	403,238	24	3
Western Australia	2.2	3.0	5.7	420,353	25,474	172,215	42	7

Vote denotes first preference support for independents as a percentage; vv denotes total valid votes for independents.
Candidates denotes mean number of independent candidates; DM denotes mean district magnitude.
N denotes number of constituencies; Ne denotes number of elections. Quota denotes electoral quota. Mean km^2 denotes size of constituency.
Author's figures calculated from Australian Politics and Elections Database accessed at www.elections.uwa.edu.au; various issues of *Election results and transfer of votes for Dáil and bye-elections*. Dublin: Stationery Office; Gallagher (1993).

or factors, for inclusion are (all per constituency level): the number of independent candidates, the district magnitude, the geographical size of constituencies, the number of valid votes, assembly size and ballot design. In the case of Australia, an additional variable to measure the use of ticket voting is included. Another variable related to the ballot measures if party labels are stated on STV ballots. The electoral quota is excluded because it measures a similar phenomenon to the number of valid votes (there is an extremely high correlation of 0.98 between the two variables). In any case, valid votes is a more suitable variable because independents are focused on attracting as many votes as possible; achieving just a quota, which is sometimes the aim of party candidates (to assist with vote management) is the least of their concerns. Assembly size is included in the analysis because it could be easier for independents to gain representation in larger parliaments, where a fraction of the total vote is required for representation. To control for the effect of an already established independent vote, usually confined to one individual, a measure is taken of the independent vote in the same constituency at the preceding election. Two additional variables related to ballot access are the electoral deposit and the number of signatures required to nominate an independent. Replicating Brancati's (2008) analysis, the former is expressed as a proportion of Gross Domestic Product (GDP) per capita per region, and the latter a proportion of the total votes cast in a district. The lack of data on regional breakdown of GDP in Ireland necessitates the use of national figures. GDP and Gross State Product (GSP) per capita for Australia was obtained from the Australian National Accounts (www.abs.gov.au/AUSSTATS) and Cashin (1995). The Central Statistics Office (www.cso.ie) provided the Irish data. The results of the analysis are summarised in Table 6.4, which indicates the factors found to affect the two measures of the independent vote, in terms of whether they have a negative or positive influence. The factors with no sign indicate that no significant effect was found; we cannot say that they influence support for independents. A more detailed version of these models, containing the full statistical results, is in the appendix to this chapter in Table 6.5.

Overall, there is not a huge number of significant variables in the two models; that is, a lot of the discussed factors do not seem to have an important effect on the independent vote. Nevertheless, there are still some interesting findings. Beginning with Australia (the four state upper houses, the Commonwealth Senate, the ACT assembly and the Tasmanian lower house), it is clear in the first column of Table 6.4 that an independent presence is an important influence on the independent vote; both the numbers of independent candidates and their previous

Table 6.4 *OLS (Ordinary Least Squares) regression of independent vote on STV, Australia and Ireland, 1945–2016*

	Australia	**Ireland**
Candidates	+	+
DM		−
Assembly		
Sq. km (log)		
Valid votes (log)	−	
Ticket		
Deposit		
Signatures	−	
Previous ind. vote	+	+
Party label		−

Author's figures calculated from Australian Politics and Elections Database accessed at www.elections.uwa.edu.au; various issues of *Election results and transfer of votes for Dáil and bye-elections*. Dublin: Stationery Office; Gallagher (1993).

vote have significant positive effects. The effect of district magnitude is negligible but not surprising for Australia, the size of the electorate (measured by valid votes) has a negative effect, in that the larger the constituency, the fewer votes attracted by independents. This may also reflect the heterogeneous nature of large STV constituencies, it being difficult for independents to appeal to a wide variety of groups. Independents are likely to fare better in more homogeneous constituencies (in particular rural and regional areas (Curtin 2005)), where they can appeal to the dominant group without being hampered by the need to develop catch-all policies. Somewhat surprisingly, ballot design does not have a significant effect, and the same is true for electoral deposit and signatures. This supports findings from similar studies, which found that such ballot requirements do not affect either independents (Brancati 2008) or minor parties (Hug 2001).

The results for Ireland vary slightly. The ticket variable is dropped here because this model involves a candidate-centred ballot. The number of candidates and previous independent vote are still highly significant variables (they have the strongest effect by far). District magnitude also matters, but not in the direction some might expect, as support for independents increases the smaller the constituency. A factor in this variation from the Australian model is possibly the low range of district magnitude in Ireland (between three and five), and the small size of the country, certainly relative to Australia. Signatures do not have a significant effect, but because they have only been required since 2002, for now we have fewer cases to test their significance. Unlike the Australian case, party label has a significant negative effect. This suggests that independents are penalised by their inability to describe themselves as such on the ballot. It also explains why Independents 4 Change registered their movement for the 2016 election, and why the Independent Alliance also considered this option. The independent label is valuable, but to what extent cannot be determined from this test. This last finding indicates that the influence of STV on independents is not uniform. The significance of party labels in Ireland, but not in Australia, could be because independents can use this label on Australian ballots, but in Ireland they can only opt for the label 'non-party' or have a blank ticket. In terms of the wider implications of this, it means that the features of STV interact with other factors to have an effect – district magnitude with geographical size, for example. To understand the effects of STV on independents, it is therefore necessary to comprehend the context in which it operates. For example, STV does not have a positive effect for independents in Malta because of the country's party-dominated political culture.

Overall, the relationship between STV and independents is complicated. Thought to be a primary contributory factor to their presence in Ireland, the comparative analysis in this chapter indicates that it is not as clear-cut as once imagined. Some of the findings challenge preconceptions over the interaction of institutional effects and minor political actors. Contrary to the expectation that multi-member constituencies should help independents, this is not the case in Ireland (nor is it significant in Australia). Small constituencies in almost all respects are necessary, but not sufficient (of which the negligible presence of independents in Malta is confirmation) for independents to get elected. It appears, however, that the size that really matters for independents is territory, not necessarily district magnitude. While increasing the latter does lower the quota and theoretically make it easier for independents to get elected, this is countered by a necessarily larger constituency, which is more difficult for independents to cover in their campaigns. This explains why independents are more successful under AV than STV in Australia. It also supports the comparative findings of Ehin et al. (2013, 39) that independents do better the smaller the district magnitude. They found no cases of independents winning seats in constituencies of six seats or greater.

Ballot access requirements have an effect on the independent vote, but perhaps not wholly in the manner predicted. Increasing signature requirements is likely to lower support for independents, although raising the deposit has no such effect; in fact, quite the opposite in Australia. Of additional importance to STV realising its perceived consequences is ballot design. Including party labels on voting papers disadvantages independents, perhaps testament to the importance of brand recognition. In particular, upper-house STV elections in Australia have been structured in such a way to make it almost impossible for an independent standing on his or her own (i.e. ungrouped) to be elected. This shows that apparently minor electoral rule changes can have major effects, removing their defining feature(s), in this case turning STV into a party-centred system. This tampering with ballot design has made the upper-house version of STV in Australia as unfriendly to non-party candidates as any party-list system. It is no coincidence that independents receive greater levels of support in STV elections where there is no ticket voting. This explains why the independent vote did not collapse when STV was introduced in Scotland and Northern Ireland in recent years: their ballot design was a replication of the Irish method. The importance of ballot design also lends credence to the hypothesis that the introduction of party labels in Ireland in the 1960s disadvantaged independents (as is discussed in Chapter 3), and may well have been a contributory factor in their decline in that decade. Political parties recognise this, and their opposition to use of the independent label on the ballot is testimony to the strategic importance of ballot design.

Conclusion

This chapter has analysed the interactive relationship between STV and independents. Institutional features of the electoral system matter, and independent candidates and voters respond in a strategic manner to the interaction of STV and other related variables. However, the effects of STV in Ireland may not be as great as initially imagined. Certainly it works in a manner to support independents, but this is in part due to the presence of other factors, such as a conducive political culture and relatively small constituencies – both in terms of geography and voters. This explains why STV is not necessarily the magic formula for independents in Australia. At the same time, there are different variations of STV, and it is undoubtedly the case that the Irish version is far more candidate-friendly than STV as practised in other jurisdictions. This is one clear way in which the voting system facilitates independents in Ireland. Having perhaps the most candidate-centred system acts to incentivise independents in a way that could not occur under party-centred voting systems as used across Europe.

It is generally believed that it is the multi-seat constituency aspect of STV that helps independents, but the results here indicate that this is not necessarily the case, as they tend to fare better the lower the district magnitude. Admittedly this could be due to the limited range of magnitude, thus masking the real effects of constituency size. However, the evidence from Australia and the experience of previously larger constituencies in Ireland does not support this premise. The finding that district magnitude does not have an effect in the manner expected does not mean that independents are not strategic in their emergence. Rather there is a different element of strategy, as more seats mean larger geographical constituencies, which are far more difficult for independents to cover in their campaigns. This explains why independents are more successful in single-seat constituencies in Australia, which is a possible factor in their success at by-elections in Ireland.

Overall, these findings do not mean that independents are a product of STV. After all, the adoption of this system in New Zealand, Northern Ireland and Scotland did not result in a raft of independents. Nor, as has been pointed out, are there any independents in Malta. Certainly STV can help independents, but only in an environment that is already conducive to their presence. This includes a facilitative political culture and a political arena in which they can have an influence and be seen as a credible, rational choice. This is the focus of the next chapter.

Appendix to Chapter 6

Analysis of constituency-level data

Because the variables are interval-level data and a linear relationship is assumed throughout, an ordinary least squares regression is the preferred methodology for the analysis in the section 'Constituency-level analysis'. The figures, or coefficients, for these models indicate the effect on the percentage vote for independents caused by a unit change in the respective independent variables. Natural logarithms of the sq km. and valid votes variables are taken because they include a few cases with very large values. The asterisks indicate which effects are likely not to be the product of random sampling error. The extremely large coefficient for signatures is because this is expressed as a proportion of the total votes cast. Overall, the adjusted *r*-squared figures indicate that the

Table 6.5 *OLS regression of independent vote on STV, Australia and Ireland, 1945–2016*

	Australia	Ireland
Candidates	0.15(0.05)***	2.30(0.16)***
DM	0.02(0.03)*	–1.17(0.55)*
Assembly	–0.04(0.02)	–0.05(0.03)
Sq. km. (log)	–0.07(0.06)	0.14(0.12)
Valid votes (log)	–0.99(0.28)***	0.28(0.65)
Ticket	–0.04(0.25)	
Deposit	0.77(0.98)	–2.98(3.12)
Signatures	–5583.35(2040.54)***	–5.29(10.51)
Previous ind. vote	0.38(0.05)***	0.40(0.03)***
Party label	–0.11(0.86)	–3.41(1.37)***
Ireland: *N*: 817; Adj. R^2: 0.41		
Australia: N: 387; Adj. R2: 0.32		

Note: *** significant at .001; * significant at .01.
Author's figures calculated from Australian Politics and Elections Database accessed at www.elections.uwa.edu.au; various issues of *Election results and transfer of votes for Dáil and bye-elections*. Dublin: Stationery Office; Gallagher (1993).

Australian and Irish models explain between 20 and 40 per cent of the variation in the independent vote.

Notes

1 STV is also used for local and European Parliament elections in Northern Ireland.
2 The number of required preferences varies per jurisdiction, and has been changing in recent years. For the 2016 Commonwealth Senate Election, twelve preferences below the line were required to formalise a vote
3 Candidates are also listed alphabetically on the ballot for local elections in New Zealand and Scotland, and for all STV elections in Northern Ireland.

7

Independents and government

Introduction

In almost all democracies, parliamentary government is party government. This is also the case in Ireland, but it comes with a slight twist in that historically many of these party governments have relied on parliamentarians outside of parties – that is, independent TDs – who frequently hold the balance of power in the Dáil. This gives independents what Sartori (2005) defines as 'relevance', whether of the coalition (that is, they are needed to form a government) or blackmail (they can prevent government formation) variety. This makes independents important political actors. Such influence was neatly captured by a front-page story in a national Sunday newspaper following the 2007 Dáil election, which ran with the headline 'the kingmakers', accompanied by portraits of the five elected independents, and details of the cost of their support (Rafter and Coleman 2007). Such coverage is not unusual in the Irish context, and it is this role that enhances independents' significance, particularly vis-à-vis party backbenchers, given the usually very weak position of the ordinary (outside of cabinet) parliamentarian in the Dáil (Gallagher and Komito 2010, 238).

This chapter examines the role of independents in parliament, specifically in terms of their contribution to the formation and maintenance of governments, because this is where their influence is most obviously exhibited. What follows is a thick-descriptive account of each of the minority administrations that needed the votes of independents, in terms of the leverage wielded by the latter, and the consequences for the former, with a focus on their longevity and stability. Parliamentary roll-call data is used to measure the participation levels of the independents, to what extent they worked collectively as a team and what level of support was offered to individual minority administrations. Of particular interest is the nature of the relationship between independents and such governments, since independents fall outside the whip system, the latter of which is claimed to be necessary for executive stability. It is generally believed that reliance by party governments on independents contributes to instability, because the threat of the whip cannot be used to guarantee their support, and their influence can also generate unrest in the government backbenches, especially among those who resent the attention afforded to the independent kingmakers. The analysis of the dynamics between independents and minority governments indicates that there is no one-size-fits-all model to describe such relationships. Instead, there have been four different types of arrangements, each of which are described at length in this chapter. In general, the stronger the working relationship between independents and the parties, the higher the level of support received from independents and the more stable the government. This indicates that independents respond in a rational manner to the strategies of parties.

In terms of the central theme of this work, independents are not always suppressed in parliament. Far from being ostracised backbenchers, they are frequently looked to by the political parties to support them in power. This is the fifth premise of this study concerning independents' significance. The process of government formation is permissive of independents and gives them a real relevance, which can have an effect on potential candidates and voters alike. Disillusioned party backbenchers might be more inclined to run as an independent, and aspirant candidates might also be more willing to don these colours given the clout an independent can wield. In other political systems, where party discipline is high and backbenchers have very little impact on policy, the incentive to run as an independent is almost negligible because of the non-influence such a position brings. This also has an impact on voters because, as discussed in Chapter 3, in an arena where independents have influence, it is logical to expect greater levels of support for independents. Hence the pattern of recent years when increasing numbers are elected following a minority government reliant on independents, only to lose these seats when they are not in such a position of influence. The next sections lay out the framework for this chapter, before the role of independents in the formation of every minority government back to the 1920s is discussed in detail. The chapter concludes with an assessment of this participation for the governments and the independents themselves.

Independents and governments

Minority governments are not that unusual, but the comparative lack of independent parliamentarians explains why it is a very rare occurrence that such administrations look to independents for support. When it does happen, such as in Canada in the early 2000s, the independents the governments look to tend to be rogue party MPs who have left a party while in parliament. Such individuals are not the concern of this study, which is rather about those elected as independents and with an independent mandate. This also means that technocrats, experts from outside of politics brought into government, are not considered. While such individuals are examples of independents in government, and have been particularly prevalent in Mediterranean and former communist countries in central and eastern Europe (McDonnell and Valbruzzi 2014), because these technocrats are unelected, they are outside the scope of this study. Australia is the one other established democracy outside of Ireland where independent parliamentarians have had a role to play in the government formation process, perhaps not surprising given that it is one of the few other polities to have had a regular presence of independent MPs. It is also due to the historically dualistic structure of the party system in Australia. Whenever one of Labor or the Liberal–National coalition fails to win a majority, they are usually left with little choice but to look to independent MPs for support, a situation that has changed slightly with the entry of the Greens into the political market. Since 1989, there have been examples of minority governments formed with the support of independents in every state and territory, and from 2010 to 2013 also at the federal level. Two distinctive costs of independent support in Australia include charters of reform and cabinet seats. The former are statements of principles drawn up collectively by independents as a precondition of their supporting a government on finance bills and confidence motions, while maintaining a free vote on all other legislation. The latter feature involves cabinets being expanded to include independents and the establishment of new conventions whereby the independent ministers have to abide by collective cabinet solidarity only in cases affecting their portfolio and budgetary legislation (Griffith 2010).

Determining the impact of independents' support for minority governments requires a deep understanding of the nature of the arrangements between independents and parties, as well as the attitude of the parties. The remainder of this chapter examines this in an in-depth fashion in Ireland, with the ultimate aim to indicate the function and the level of influence independents can have in the Irish political system. Parties courting their vote and independents supporting parties are rational outcomes for both sets of actors. For independents, it allows them to demonstrate their relevance and to achieve some of their policy goals, while for parties it means the ability to form a government without needing to rely on an additional party – which would lessen their share of the national pie.

Independents and minority governments in Ireland

There have been varying types of support arrangements between independents and party governments in Ireland. These range from simple external parliamentary support, to formal agreements that are not far removed from contract parliamentarianism (a concept that relates to an explicit institutionalised relationship between a minority government and its support parties that is so institutionalised it is akin to a de facto majority government (Bale and Bergman 2006)).

In Ireland, 40 per cent of governments have been minority administrations, and in almost all cases independents have had a role to play in their formation and maintenance. This has become a more frequent occurrence in recent decades. Of the eleven governments formed after elections between 1980 and 2016, seven ultimately relied on independents, while in another two cases (2002 and 2011) independents had some bargaining power and were considered an option for a single-party minority government. Symptomatic of the accepted role independents now have to play in this process, some independent TDs were sounded out by the parties in the run-up to the 2016 election about the potential support they could offer should their vote be needed in the new parliament (Hennessy 2015). Table 7.1 provides an historical overview of all the minority governments that have relied on independents. There are only a couple of cases where such

Table 7.1 *Minority governments needing the support of independents in Ireland, 1922–2016*

Parties in government	Years in office
Cumann na nGaedheal	1927
Cumann na nGaedheal	1927–32
Fianna Fáil	1943–44
Fine Gael/Labour/National Labour/ Clann na Poblachta/Clann na Talmhan	1948–51
Fianna Fáil	1951–54
Fianna Fáil	1961–65
Fine Gael/Labour	1981–82
Fianna Fáil	1982
Fianna Fáil	1987–89
Fianna Fáil/Progressive Democrats	1989–92
Fianna Fáil/Progressive Democrats	1997–2002
Fianna Fáil/Progressive Democrats/Greens	2007–11
Fine Gael	2016–

administrations looked to parties for support, which indicates the role independents have carved out for themselves in this area. It is sometimes forgotten that the only reason independents are included in this process is because of the willingness of parties to do so. Indeed, it is primarily the attitude of the parties that determines the nature of the arrangement and the relationship between the government and independents. Following on from a model developed by P. Mitchell (2001), there are four broad types of relationships between independents and these minority governments.

1. Ad hoc management: when there are no agreements between government and the independents, who are instead managed on a case-by-case basis.
2. In government: when independents hold seats in cabinet.
3. Vote for investiture: when independents agree to support the formation of a government, but no commitment is given beyond this.
4. Negotiated deals: when independents commit to support a government from the outside for its lifetime, provided it meets certain goals.

This categorisation is based on the type of support independents provide such governments and the nature of the working arrangement between them, and is described in further detail in the next section. As already discussed in Chapter 1 – and is broached again in Chapter 9 – one of the criticisms of the influence independents wield over minority government is the effect this can have on distributive policy. However, there is some ambiguity concerning the level of influence independents have over government spending plans. As is outlined in this chapter, while independents like to claims hundreds of millions of euros worth of projects for their constituencies, parties in government prefer to deny the existence of such influence, arguing that the projects which independents claim to deliver would have happened with or without their support. To be more specific, how the process works is that when an independent's vote is courted by a government-in-waiting, the independent meets with his or her local council to see what projects are forthcoming in the constituency. The independent can then ask the government to place a priority on particular projects, but at best they can generally only speed things up. For example, in the negotiations Bertie Ahern as Fianna Fáil leader had with independent TDs in 1997 and 2007, Ahern maintains that there were never specific costings done on the independents' proposals. At least 90 per cent of what the latter sought was already on the council estimates (Ahern, interview 2015). However, the government tends to provide early news to independents on major jobs announcements or infrastructural investments in their constituencies, so that they can use this information to their advantage.

The difficulty in establishing the nature of independents' influence is that their agreements with governments are often not publicly released, particularly if they concern significant elements of patronage. For example, it was reported in 2011 that in return for supporting the previous Fianna Fáil-led administration, independent TDs Jackie Healy-Rae and Michael Lowry had both procured three appointments for their supporters on state boards, a deal which was not even known to the cabinet (F. Kelly 2011). Two of Healy-Rae's nominees were his children, and when the story was leaked, Healy-Rae claimed to have forgotten the contents of the deal. When independents make public the levels of their influence, the government tends to deny this, with the nature of the making-public process being such that it is impossible to discern the truth. But the decisive issue is that the exact nature of independents' influence is a moot point. What is key is that it is believed to exist, an image enhanced by the signing of deals and the consistent support independents involved in these arrangements provide to governments. It is difficult to believe that independents would not get some compensation for their parliamentary vote, particularly if they are supporting unpopular policies and administrations. At the same time, the independents understand it is necessary for government parties to deny the existence of such deals to lessen criticism from the media and their backbenchers. Bearing this in mind, the aim of this chapter is not to determine the exact nature of the patronage delivered by independents, but rather the influence they are seen to deliver. This is probably more important given the significance attached to image and perception in politics. The following sections describe the thirteen cases from Table 7.1 in which independents had a role to play in the formation and maintenance of governments in Ireland. The other administrations not involving independents are not covered, because non-participation of independents means there is little to say. There were only four other cases of government formation where independents could have played a role. In 1932 Fianna Fáil was five seats short of a majority, but its leader, Éamon de Valera, chose to look to the votes of the Labour Party rather than some of the fourteen independents, since most of the latter were anti-Fianna Fáil. In 1992, a rainbow government could have been formed two years earlier than it ultimately did in 1994 had it looked to some of the five independents elected. In 2002, Bertie Ahern could have formed a single-party minority government with the backing of independents, which is discussed later in this chapter; while in 2011, Enda Kenny could have done likewise for Fine Gael. He would have needed the support of eight of the fourteen independents, and some of them were approached with the offer of speaking rights in the Dáil and to find out their issues of interest. However, the Fine Gael leadership maintained that this was never a realistic option, and that coalition with Labour was their preferred option (O'Malley 2011, 267–9). Some of the independents were likely to have excessive demands, while others had ideological differences with Fine Gael. The stability of such an arrangement was unclear, with the likelihood being that the discussions were simply a tactic to indicate the presence of an alternative arrangement prior to coalition negotiations with Labour.

The fourteen governments that have looked to independents demonstrate the role and relevance that independents have in the Irish political system. This support can be categorised into four general types of arrangements, each of which is described below. The data for this chapter comes from contemporary newspapers, secondary literature and interviews with political actors for the more recent governments. In addition, the voting records of independents in the Dáil between 1937 and 2014 stems from an original dataset compiled by Hansen (2010; 2009).

It might be expected that in the absence of a whip and given their heterogeneity, as discussed in Chapter 2, independents have pretty different voting patterns in parliament, which is one of the reasons advanced why governments should not rely on their support. However, the independents elected to the Dáil tend to be more homogenous than the overall collection of independent candidates. This is indicated in Figure 7.1, which features the unity rates for independents per Dáil since 1937. More formally known as the Rice index of cohesion, these are calculated as the mean difference between the proportions voting yes and no on a motion.[1] For example, if 80 per cent of independent TDs vote yes and 20 per cent vote no, the unity score is sixty. Consequently, higher scores imply higher levels of unity among independents. Undoubtedly this is not a perfect measure, because it neither weights issues by importance nor takes into account abstentions. In addition, Dáil votes are just one means of measuring whether independents sing from the same hymn sheet. Nevertheless, it is a comparative measure of cohesion within parties and is a useful tool for examining independents' behaviour. Contrary to expectation, Figure 7.1 indicates surprisingly high levels of cohesion amongst independents in the Dáil. This mean score has certainly fluctuated over time, but the average is a high seventy-six (excluding the Dála from 1965–77, when there were only between one and two independents). This means that the average voting split between independents was eighty-eight to

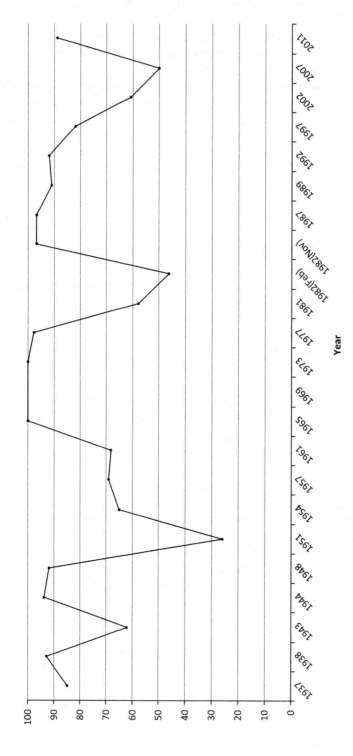

Figure 7.1 Cohesion rates of independents in Dáil, 1937–2015.

Note: the figures given are the average Rice cohesion index score for independents per Dáil.

twelve, hardly evidence of a divided grouping. While we might expect this to be inversely related to the numbers of independent TDs, in the 2011–16 Dáil – with fifteen independents – it was quite high, at 89 per cent. Such figures suggest an element of unity amongst independents, which might explain why they have been able to work with parties in minority governments.

Cases of independent influence

There have been four different types of arrangement between independents and minority government. These have ranged from independents being ignored and their bluff being called in parliament, with the expectation that they would not vote for an early election, to their being included as a full partner at the cabinet table. These varying levels of influence have depended on a number of factors and have had varying consequences, which are detailed in the following sections. The first cases treated are those where the government dealt with independents in an ad hoc fashion with no formal agreement.

Ad hoc management

Ad hoc management describes where the parties in minority government have no formal arrangement with independents, who are instead managed on a case-by-case basis. This tends to involve discussions with independents when their votes are needed in parliament, and their being ignored otherwise. Although independents possess the absolute power of being able to form and bring down a government, this does not necessarily translate into significant influence. The parties assume that independents are not willing to bring about a collapse in government and a subsequently early poll.

June–September 1927

This was the first de facto minority government in independent Ireland. Although Cumann na nGaedheal won a minority of seats in 1923, the abstention of the anti-treaty Republicans from the Dáil had given the party a comfortable majority. After the June 1927 election, even excluding the new Fianna Fáil party that initially did not take its forty-four seats, Cumann naGaedheal's forty-seven seats still left it in a minority against the other sixty-five TDs. To continue in government, leader William T. Cosgrave had to rely on the support of the eleven Farmers' Party TDs and some of the sixteen independents (O'Leary 1979, 23). He did not, however, form any arrangements with independents during the lifetime of this Dáil. On his re-nomination as President of the

Executive Council, Cosgrave stated 'I do not seek office, and that I shall accept office only if the opposition parties are unable, or unwilling, to do so, and then upon very definite understandings' (Dáil debates 20: 13, 23 June 1927). He would not be beholden on anyone:

> If I am to accept and continue in office it will be only on the very clearest understanding that I shall receive sufficient support in this House to carry out my programme ... Nor do I intend to allow myself to be placed in the position of endeavouring to carry out the policies of others should a majority here agree to disagree with me in any matter of vital importance. I would not stultify myself or my colleagues or my supporters by taking office under such conditions (Dáil debates 20: 14, 23 June 1927).

There was no other nomination for the presidency, and only the Labour Party opposed Cosgrave. So he became president simply because there was no alternative. Subsequently, the future of this government was quite uncertain; it seemed likely to be defeated once Fianna Fáil crossed the Rubicon and entered the Dáil. It did so in August 1927, when it seemed as if a coalition of Labour (twenty-two) and the National League (eight), with external support from Fianna Fáil, would have enough votes to defeat Cumann na nGaedheal and form their own government. However 'the real power brokers' (Meehan 2010, 104) were the sixteen independents who held the balance of power. The voting records of some independents in the Dáil might have led the opposition to expect them to back the motion – Alfie Byrne had never voted with the government, Michael Brennan just once and Gilbert Hewson on six occasions out of thirty-five. In addition, some other independents were offered seats at the cabinet table, including Bryan Cooper (in Fisheries), Jasper Travers Wolfe (Justice) (Ungoed-Thomas 2008, 202) and John F. O'Hanlon. However, when it came to the decisive vote on 16 August, not one independent voted against the government. The reasons given varied from O'Hanlon and Wolfe not wanting a government headed by an Englishman (Thomas Johnson, Labour's leader) (Meehan 2010, 105), to John Daly bearing a grudge against Johnson for denying him a Labour candidacy four years previously, to Michael Brennan not wanting a coalition supported by a party outside of government (Mitchell 1974, 265–6). The strongest reason, however, was that almost all the independents were hostile to Fianna Fáil. The vast majority of them were conservative constitutionalists (independent unionists, independent business TDs and former IPP MPs) who preferred to keep Cumann na nGaedheal in power. A desire to avoid an election so soon after the last was also a factor weighing on independents' minds, since few of them had the resources to match their electoral achievements of June. Another potential factor is that Labour claimed that it did not 'make any promises or offer any inducements, or compromises ... in any way in order to obtain support for the motion' (Mitchell 1974, 260), whereas the government had sought to appease some wayward independents, including Alfie Byrne, with promises to alleviate unemployment in Dublin in return for his support (Mitchell 1974, 260).

Even with all the independents voting for the government, it looked as if it might be defeated by a solitary vote in the Dáil, so political legend has it that independent Bryan Cooper had a role to play in John Jinks, a National League TD, missing the confidence vote, which was consequently tied. The Ceann Comhairle voted with the government, defeating the motion. Whether Jinks was voluntarily absent because Cooper told him that the ex-servicemen of Sligo had not elected Jinks to put Cosgrave out and de Valera in (O'Sullivan 1940, 220), or because Cooper had plied Jinks with alcohol and put him on a train back to his constituency (see Mitchell (1974, 264) for different theories), it seems likely that an independent had a considerable role to play in the survival of the government.

1927–32

After the government survived the confidence motion, Cosgrave adjourned the Dáil until October. Just over a week later, Cumann na nGaedheal won two crucial by-elections, immediately after which Cosgrave requested a dissolution of parliament for another general election. With so many independents in the Dáil, and the gap between government and opposition so narrow, Cosgrave knew another confidence motion was most likely imminent, and there was a strong possibility that Cumann na nGaedheal could be ousted from office without an election. Calling an early election was designed to prevent this and to capitalise on the momentum of the by-election victories. Although no party won a majority at the September 1927 election, Cumann na nGaedheal won an extra fifteen seats and Cosgrave formed a minority administration with the support of the Farmers' Party. With a combined total of sixty-eight seats, they were still six short of a majority, but the support of the independents was assumed and he was elected President by seventy-six votes to seventy. Eleven of the thirteen independents supported Cosgrave, and not one opposed. Again, no deal was struck because most of the independents were from a constitutional, conservative stock and feared the instability that would ensue from Fianna Fáil in office. In spite of this, the government's minority status gave it the feel of a lame-duck administration (O'Leary 1979, 25), and it was a dangerous game taking independent support for granted, as an editorial in the *Irish Times* warned:

> The independent group, which keeps the government in office, has been reduced to a dangerous state of mind. It still desires to keep Mr. Cosgrave's government in power, but consistent contempt of its wishes and interests has imbued it with a spirit of apathy. It has fallen into the category of those who, as the saying is, are not good companions on a tiger hunt. A stage has been reached, indeed, when the independent members, though still lacking courage to oppose the government, are losing the habit of support ... the government must recognise its debt to the party that keeps it in office. If it continues to ignore that debt, the independent members must begin to realise their duty to their constituents. They must school themselves to use bravely the only weapon that all governments fear ('Morals of Defeat', *Irish Times*, 29 March 1930).

This came to a head when the government was defeated sixty-four to sixty-six on a private members' bill on old age pensions, when the only independents to support it were those from the unionist ranks. Cosgrave resigned rather than accept the legislation, which would have added £250,000 to the bill, but resumed his post because no one else was willing to form a government. Following this a period of stability ensued, because having boosted its numbers by three with five by-election victories, the government focused on internal security and foreign policy issues, while Fianna Fáil concentrated on building up its extra-parliamentary organisation (Collins 1996, 51).

1943–44

At the 1943 election, Fianna Fáil lost its majority, winning sixty-seven out of 138 seats. However, de Valera was comfortably re-elected Taoiseach by sixty-seven votes to thirty-seven (Labour and Clann na Talmhan abstained). One independent, Ben Maguire (a former Fianna Fáil TD from Sligo-Leitrim) voted for de Valera, while four (James Dillon, Richard Anthony, Patrick Burke and John Cole) of the ten others voted against his nomination.

There was some uncertainty after the election (Girvin 2006, 248), but never enough to undermine the government. In office, Fianna Fáil continuously complained about minority government, and about the perils of having their fate dependent on independents, particularly in the middle of World War II. The underlying factor was that there remained a tradition of opposition to Fianna Fáil among the independents. Outside of Maguire, independents voted with the government on average just 10 per cent of the time during this Dáil.

With a better organisation than the other parties, who along with the independents were ill-prepared for another poll, Fianna Fáil's policy was to prepare the ground for a snap election, as de Valera had done twice in the previous decade. Consequently, the Taoiseach was not too distraught when in May 1944 the government was defeated on a motion by one vote, with nine of the eleven independents casting a no vote. The motion simply sought to delay the implementation of a transport bill, but de Valera used it as an opportunity to call a snap election rather than allow the opposition to form a new government (Manning 1999, 193). As in 1933 and 1938, this tactic was again to prove successful, as Fianna Fáil won an overall majority of seventy-six seats.

1961–65

Fianna Fáil won seventy seats against a combined total of sixty-eight for the opposition parties, with six independents holding the balance of power. With the support of two independents (Jim Carroll and Frank Sherwin), Seán Lemass of Fianna Fáil was re-elected Taoiseach by seventy-two votes to sixty-eight (three independents – Joe Leneghan, Joe Sheridan and Patrick Finucane – abstained). Despite the government's minority status, Lemass was determined to rule as if he was in a majoritarian position. Lee describes how he 'quickly dared the independents to do their worst' (1989, 366) when defeating a Fine Gael motion to help out wheat farmers. With none of the independents that long in the Dáil, they were particularly anxious to avoid an early election, but made it clear they were not supporting the government for partisan reasons. On the nomination of Lemass, for example, Sherwin said 'I am not voting for Fianna Fáil – I am voting for a government' (Dáil debates 192: 26, 11 October 1961).

Not having any arrangements with the independents, whether formal or informal, the government went through a number of moments of instability and crisis. Sherwin cycled home from the Dáil for his tea every evening, and Fianna Fáil always feared a vote being called in his absence (Faulkner 2005, 43–4). One significant episode was the introduction of an unpopular turnover tax (VAT) in 1963. This led to the government facing a motion of no confidence. Despite much pressure from the opposition and demands for an election on the tax, four of the six independents supported the government and Lemass survived the division by seventy-three votes to sixty-nine. At the time there was much rumour and speculation that the independents had been bought, with Oliver J. Flanagan (having joined Fine Gael from the independent benches) using the term the 'Sherwin government' (Dáil debates 204(8): 1288, 17 July 1963) in derision. The *Irish Times* repeated

Flanagan's assertion that Sherwin had been bribed with a retrospective IRA pension to support the government (Sherwin 2007, 112), but Sherwin sued the newspaper for libel, a case he won on appeal in the Supreme Court. In his memoirs, Sherwin wrote 'during all of the time that I was a member of the Dáil, I never had any discussions with the Taoiseach or any other minister regarding my vote for the government' (2007, 90). He did say that James Carroll told him that he (Carroll) and Joe Sheridan were given assurances by Lemass that in return for their support of the turnover tax there would be no election for two years (Sherwin 2007, 128). Sheridan, however, claimed never to have been in the Taoiseach's room in his life – 'that is reserved for only choice people' (*Irish Times*, 7 October 2000). Leneghan claimed that he and Sherwin had been offered £5,000 each by someone in Fine Gael to defeat the bill (Dáil debates 204(8): 1301, 17 July 1963).

It was never wholly clear what influence the independents brought to bear on this administration. Although it seemed that Lemass was not prepared to be held to ransom by the independents, it would be quite unusual – given his pragmatic nature – if he (or one of his representatives) had not at least discussed the government's fortunes with them. It is likely that the independents had greater access to the channels of government than usually afforded them (Farrell 1987a, 140), and the high rates of support for the government from some of them lends credence to this (99 per cent in the case of Joe Leneghan and 94 per cent from Sherwin, who participated in 70 per cent of votes). Leneghan, known as 'turnover Joe' for supporting the unpopular tax, cemented his relationship with Fianna Fáil by joining the party after the turnover vote. Joe Sheridan, despite having contested the previous three Dáil elections for Fine Gael, was rumoured to have the ear of the Taoiseach. Notwithstanding his protestations to the contrary, Sheridan apparently met Lemass six times in one week before a crucial Dáil vote, enhancing his reputation in his home constituency as a man with influence in Dublin. Evidence of this came in the form of guarantees for a heifer scheme to help farmers, and another to increase housing grants. Sheridan was friendly with Paddy Smith, the Minister for Agriculture, and his questions in parliament were not ignored (*Irish Times*, 7 October 2000). Collins (1991) claims that in a manner similar to future arrangements between Jackie Healy-Rae and Bertie Ahern in 1997 and 2007, Sheridan procured, or at least got early wind and took credit for, projects for Longford–Westmeath. He managed to do so without becoming too attached to the government, participating in fewer than 20 per cent of Dáil votes, and even then backing the government less than half of the time. This might explain why Sheridan managed to increase his vote and held his seat at the next election, whereas the three other independents who backed Lemass all lost theirs (Leneghan on a Fianna Fáil ticket).

1981–82

Fianna Fáil won seventy-eight seats to Fine Gael and Labour's combined total of eighty. With the abstentionist H-Block campaign having two of its political prisoners elected, this reduced the numbers necessary for a Dáil majority. Four independents and the solitary representatives of Sinn Féin the Workers' Party (Joe Sherlock) and the Socialist Labour Party (Noël Browne) held the balance of power. Nominating the independent John O'Connell as Ceann Comhairle to reduce the size of the opposition, Garret FitzGerald of Fine Gael was elected Taoiseach by eighty-one votes to seventy-eight. Jim Kemmy was the only independent to vote for FitzGerald, although he said his support would be 'conditional, qualified, and critical'. He intended to use his position not in a reckless way, but responsibly to pursue some of his objectives: 'It has been said that the independent members can play the role of king-makers ... sometimes king-makers do not last as long as kings. I am very conscious of that and I do not intend to let this fleeting moment of notoriety go to my head' (Dáil debates 329: 23, 30 June 1981). Being elected with a majority of three while four TDs abstained might suggest that FitzGerald was living on borrowed time, but two of the abstainers were left-leaning and opposed to a Haughey-led Fianna Fáil alternative (Mitchell 2001, 201). Consequently, with a bit of management, the minority coalition need not have been as unstable as materialised.

From the start the government acted in a majoritarian manner, barely consulting the independents on any issues. To adopt such a strategy at a time when the country was on the on the verge of an economic crisis and required drastic cutbacks and tax hikes was reckless. The semi-permanent 'air of crisis' (O'Byrnes 1986, 123) that hung over the government was consequently more a product of its failure to consult the independents than the actual economic situation.

Having passed a supplementary budget in July 1981 by eighty-two votes to seventy-nine with the support of Kemmy and Seán Dublin Bay Loftus, the government took the independents for granted. Loftus supported the government 57 per cent of the time in the 55 per cent of votes in which he participated. There were just thirty-eight divisions in the short-lived Dáil, but Loftus' vote was not decisive in any in which he abstained. Kemmy backed the government in 97 per cent of the 87 per cent of votes in which he took part (this contrasts with the other independent, Neil Blaney, who voted against the government on every issue). Given the support Kemmy offered, the government's compla-cency angered him, particularly since they offered little recognition of this:

> I had taken all the flak that went with my backing for the coalition in those votes. I believed that I had a certain responsibility for government decisions since my vote was keeping them in power ... They had got it entirely wrong if they felt that I was simply a broken lap-dog willing to do their bidding in order to retain my Dáil seat ... I believed in taking a broad national approach and I saw myself not just as a Jim-will-fix-it type of politician but one who had to concern himself with what was best for the nation (R. Smith 1985, 63–4).

This all came to a head with the January 1982 budget, on which the sur-vival of the government was dependent. Although FitzGerald met with Loftus, Browne and Kemmy, no agreement was struck, with FitzGerald assuming that the merits of his proposals would win out. The naivety of this approach was highlighted on budget day: when realising that Kemmy intended to vote against the government, FitzGerald gave him four pages of handwritten notes of tables and figures to demonstrate the impact of the budget on various sectors of the economy. Kemmy could not support the proposed reduction in food subsidies and VAT increases that would hit his working class constituents particularly hard.

While it was expected that Browne would support the budget because of his agreement with FitzGerald on some social issues (such as capital punishment and divorce), the government acted in a compla-cent manner towards Loftus (see Chapter 4 for his version of events). Having just been elected at the seventh attempt and not of social-ist stock, Fine Gael assumed he would not vote for an early election because of proposed tax increases. Even on the day of the budget when Loftus told FitzGerald he could not support the proposed VAT hike, Fine Gael did little to persuade him to the contrary. Loftus was even left waiting in a Dáil committee room in the middle of the budget debate for a response from FitzGerald that never came.

The irrationality of the government's tactics was realised right at the end when the Taoiseach, literally on his knees, forlornly sought to change Kemmy's mind on the floor of the chamber. This became the first, and only, government in Ireland to have its budget defeated, but it was a classic case of legislative mismanagement because it resulted in an election that no one wanted. Had the independents been consulted, some kind of compromise could have been reached and Loftus himself, on whom the deciding vote rested, seemed confused as to what was happening as he cast the decisive vote (Smith 1985, 62).

Looking back, Kemmy said of the government: 'They approached it with total naivety and dealt with my response and that of other independents to the budget in a ham-fisted way. They did not get down to brass-tacks, to the nitty-gritty of why I was voting against the budget and others like me' (R. Smith 1985, 68). Instead, FitzGerald believed the 'logic' of his proposals would win out, and that the independents would do what was in the interests of the nation: 'we might, I suppose, have minimised or even perhaps eliminated the risk of losing their support by proposing a somewhat less ambitious reform programme ... Logically, I felt, these two socialist independents must when the crunch came support such a redistributive budget' (FitzGerald 1991, 395).

That FitzGerald expected logic, rather than compromise, to win out is symptomatic of the government's majoritarian attitude. He assumed independents saw reason, without double-checking and ensuring that they were on side. As Kemmy recalled:

The machinery for dealing with the independents that evening was all wrong. I am convinced that the responsibility should never have fallen on Garret FitzGerald's shoulders to deal with us. He had too much on his plate as it was. The toughest members of the cabinet ... should have been charged with the task of working out some kind of compromise ... In my case, there was a take it or leave it attitude at the crucial moment. I got the impression that they thought I was only bluffing, that I would back down at the last second and cast my vote with the government as I had done on every key division (Smith 1985, 68–9).

There was an almost fatalistic air about this government, as if it was prepared to die on FitzGerald's logic, and in his memoirs FitzGerald talks of a relief that they were going to the country on the issue of the budget: 'I experienced a moment of total exhilaration: *this was it*' (FitzGerald 1991, 397). Even after the division on excise duties was lost, the situation could still have been rescued. Loftus attempted to phone the president (who has a constitutional role to play when the government has lost the confidence of the Dáil) to pass on a message to FitzGerald that there was no need for an early election, and that the budget could be rescued with his support (see Chapter 4). Whether FitzGerald ever got this message is unclear, but given his failure to listen to independents over the past year, he was unlikely to do so at that stage.

1987–89

The 1987 election produced another stalemate. Fianna Fáil had eighty-one seats, Fine Gael fifty-one, Labour twelve and the newly formed PDs fourteen. There were four Workers' Party TDs, three independents, and Jim Kemmy now representing his Democratic Socialist Party (DSP). When the Dáil first met on 10 March it was not clear if Haughey would be elected Taoiseach. He nominated one of the independents, Seán Treacy, as Ceann Comhairle, but Haughey still needed the support of Neil Blaney and Tony Gregory, as the Workers' Party refused to back either him or FitzGerald. Unlike 1982, Haughey refused to negotiate deals with any of the independents and said it was a Fianna Fáil minority government or nothing. Haughey had slightly more bargaining power in 1987 because there was no alternative government for the independents to play off against. It was Haughey or no one.

The night before the Dáil met, Blaney visited Haughey, offering his support if he promised to end the Anglo-Irish Agreement of 1985, scrap an extradition bill and make changes to the Supreme Court (Kenny and Keane 1987, 59). Haughey repeated his line that there would be no deals. The day of the vote, Gregory told four Fine Gael TDs of his intention to vote against Haughey, which would have led to the latter's defeat. FitzGerald interpreted this as an attempt to shift the pressure onto Fine Gael to get them to abstain so that the responsibility would not lie with Gregory (FitzGerald 1991, 644), but he was having none of it.

Just when it seemed as if Gregory was set to vote against Haughey and cause another election, victory was snatched from the jaws of defeat. Far from revelling in his role as kingmaker, Gregory preferred to form an alliance of the left with the Workers' Party, the DSP and Labour, which could have had a greater influence on a Fianna Fáil government. When this failed to materialise, as in 1982 he did not want the potential government to be defeated on his vote (see p. 233), so he abstained. As one columnist quipped, 'it was eyeball to eyeball and Gregory blinked' (Farrell 1987b, 144). With Blaney voting for Haughey, this produced a tie at eighty-two votes to eighty-two, and the Ceann Comhairle (speaker) cast his vote for Haughey to prevent a constitutional crisis. There was some criticism of Gregory's brinkmanship because of his earlier intimations that he was going to vote against Haughey. He said that this was just a warning to Fianna Fáil that it could not be expected to rely on his vote (Kenny and Keane 1987, 61). The instability of 1982 (see pp. 230–3) that might have been expected to materialise was not repeated because Haughey was subsequently able to attract external support from Fine Gael, which promised to back him so long as a responsible fiscal policy was pursued. This in effect froze out the independents and killed their bargaining power. No longer needed, the support rates of Gregory and Blaney fell to 12 and 21 per cent, respectively. Although the government was defeated six times during its two years in office (each time with the involvement of independents), when it came to decisive motions, such as on finance bills, it always had the support of Fine Gael (the so-called 'Tallaght Strategy').

Independents in government

This type of minority government arrangement involves independents having a seat at the cabinet table. There have been three cases of Irish governments including independent ministers – James Dillon in the 1948–51 coalition; Mary Harney in the Fianna Fáil–Green coalition from 2009 to 2011 following the termination of the PDs; and the Fine Gael minority government formed in 2016, which included three independents and one independent 'super junior' minister, who also sat at cabinet. The case of Mary Harney is not examined because it concerns a TD not elected as an independent, but who became one while in office when her party folded.

1948–51

At the 1948 election, Fianna Fáil won sixty-eight seats and the five opposition parties sixty-seven, leaving twelve independents holding the balance of power. When Fine Gael announced its intention to attempt to form a government, one of the most senior of the independents and former Fine Gael deputy leader, James Dillon, sought to organise 'an informal parliamentary group' (Manning 1999, 226) that could support such an administration. Five other independents joined this group, including Alfie Byrne Jr and Sr, Patrick Cogan and John Flynn, a former Fianna Fáil TD. Oliver J. Flanagan was secretary of the group and an informal whip.

Negotiations took place between the opposition parties and the independents, with the latter being treated as an equal government partner, recognised in their securing the important ministerial portfolio of agriculture for Dillon. De Valera's nomination as Taoiseach was defeated by seventy-five votes to seventy, with two independents supporting him (Ben Maguire, a former Fianna Fáil TD, and Tom Burke, a former Fianna Fáil councillor). Eight independents (the group of six plus William Sheldon and Patrick O'Reilly) voted for Fine Gael's John A. Costello as Taoiseach, who was duly elected by seventy-five votes to sixty-eight (Maguire and Burke abstained).

With the backing of his former Fine Gael colleagues, Dillon secured a number of policy concessions. These included the end of compulsory tillage, the negotiation of the Anglo-Irish trade agreement of 1948 (that improved the conditions for Irish farmers to export to the British market),and a land project to reclaim four million acres via a process of drainage and fertilisation, the cost of which was between 40 and 50 million pounds (McCullagh 1998, 58–9). Dillon's influence at cabinet did not imply that independents as a whole wielded greater power in this Dáil. Although he had organised the independent group, there was no sense that Dillon was either their head or a delegate for the other independents' views. One of the independents (Sheldon) wrote to Costello the day before the new Dáil first met, stating that he could not 'accept the position of having anyone "lead" or speak for me and therefore cannot consider myself represented in any way by Deputy Dillon' (McCullagh 2010, 173). At one of the early meetings of the independent group, in March 1948, Dillon told them 'each had been elected as an independent and each was entitled to maintain his independence' (Manning 1999, 234). His advice to them to appoint a whip was ignored, but Oliver Flanagan worked on an informal basis with the government chief whip, Liam Cosgrave. Dillon's biographer concludes that his approach to the independents was 'somewhat detached, offering them neither leadership nor intimacy' (Manning 1999, 235). While Dillon did not see it as his political responsibility to form the independents into a unitary organisation, it might have been more politically expedient to do so considering the troubles they were to ultimately cause him and the government in 1951. In any case, the members of the independent group generally voted along the same lines (that is, for the government 95 per cent of the time), with almost perfect correlations between the voting behaviour of the two Byrnes, Dillon and Flanagan.

An example of a non-agricultural policy on which independents flexed their parliamentary muscle was social security legislation in 1950. Many of the independents resented this perceived intrusion of the state into society, with one labelling it 'a slavish imitation of British Socialism' (McCullagh 1998, 194). They were also opposed to it practically, since the proposed scheme excluded casual workers and farmers, both of whom were a large source of support for independents. In an attempt to secure their support, the Minister for Health amended the bill to include measures that would appease the independents, which came at a cost of an extra £1.25 million, a sizeable amount when considering that the total annual spending on the new social welfare scheme was estimated to be £10 million (McCullagh 1998, 195).

It is generally, and wrongly, believed that the controversy over Minister for Health Noël Browne's proposal to introduce universal healthcare for all mothers, and children under sixteen, brought down Costello's government (Manning 1999). The reality was the government fell because it lost the support of independents. Going into 1951, things seemed pretty stable for the government and it looked as if it could serve a full five-year term. However, one by one, the independents withdrew their support, primarily over agricultural and local issues. Oliver Flanagan was growing increasingly uncomfortable with a number of issues, including the extravagance of some ministers, while Peadar Cowan published bizarre press advertisements to recruit a private army to invade Northern Ireland (Manning 1999, 265). William Sheldon, who had been a consistent supporter of Costello, withdrew his backing in December 1950 in protest at a number of the government's policies, including its withdrawal from the Commonwealth, an anti-partition campaign, a failure to join NATO, and a system of state socialism. In a letter to Costello, Sheldon wrote 'while it is true that there has been no compulsion on me to vote for anything of which I disapproved, I have felt that overt opposition from even a nominal supporter can savour too much of a stab in the back' (*Irish Times*, 2 December 1950). Sheldon was followed soon after by Patrick Cogan, whose support had been more unreliable, over an episode of blatant cronyism, what became known as the 'battle of Baltinglass' (Manning 1999, 265).

To an outside observer, it might seem unusual that divisions over agricultural policies (in particular prices paid to milk suppliers) cost the government independents' support, since an independent was Minister for Agriculture. However, as has been outlined, Dillon was rather distant from his fellow independents, and his cabinet colleagues made no attempt to negotiate with them, seeing Dillon as the independent representative. Eventually, this brought the government down, as Dillon refused to acquiesce to the independent farmer TDs' demands to increase the prices paid to milk suppliers, a move described by his biographer as 'astonishing given what was at stake ... it [the government] had the wherewithal to stay in office, at least in the short to medium term, had it so chosen' (Manning 1999, 273).

Facing a defeat in the Dáil, Costello called an election in April 1951 and let known his frustration at having to deal with independents. Unlike de Valera and Cosgrave before him, he had had to work at keeping them on board. In a letter to the British ambassador, Costello wrote he 'found it impossible to carry on in the face of [the] attitude of independents', and when announcing the election he accused the independents of having 'irresponsibly sought to embarrass the government by exploiting petty grievances' (McCullagh 2010, 253–4).

2016–
As has been detailed elsewhere in this book (see pp. 77–80), support for independents continued to grow after the 2011 election, reaching

its zenith in 2014 when they emerged as the largest political grouping, according to opinion polls. Consequently, there was much discussion in the lead up to the 2016 election about the role independents could have to play in the formation of the next government. As has also been discussed, this in part motivated the formation of groups or alliances of independents, and they were courted by the political parties in antici-pation that independents' support would be decisive after the election. In February 2015, the Minister for Finance, Michael Noonan, explicitly expressed his willingness to work with independents: 'I know that there are a number of centre-right independents who will support the government following the type of policies that we have been following ... independents don't want quick elections, independents stay with governments' (Hennessy 2015).

The result of the election in February 2016 seemed indecisive, as there was no clear winner, with the outgoing Fine Gael–Labour coalition winning half the number of seats it had claimed in 2011. Despite there being a record number of independents elected, it seemed as if this might not translate into more political influence for them, because the only obvious government arrangement seemed to be a coalition between Fianna Fáil and Fine Gael, which would have a solid majority and not need independents. Consequently, while groups of independents met separately with both parties in the weeks after the election, it looked as if this was mere shadow-boxing before the two main parties met. From the beginning of such talks, independents let it be known that any such agreement to form a government needed the support of both Fianna Fáil and Fine Gael. However, despite the Fine Gael leader, Enda Kenny, offering Fianna Fáil full partnership in a coalition government, the latter had from the outset ruled out this option. Fianna Fáil eventually agreed to facilitate a minority Fine Gael government by abstaining in a vote for Kenny as Taoiseach. One condition of their support, however, was that Kenny's nomination would be backed by an additional nine TDs outside of Fine Gael's cohort of fifty, one more than the bare majority Kenny needed if Fianna Fáil abstained.

With Labour, the Social Democrats and the far-left Anti-Austerity Alliance/People Before Profit Alliance deciding to remain in opposition, and the Greens having withdrawn from talks, Fine Gael consequently sought the nine votes from the ranks of the twenty-three independents. From a position where it had seemed as if they were no longer relevant to the process of government formation, independents were now very much back in the game. The four members of Independents 4 Change were opposed to a Fine Gael-led government, as were two other inde-pendents (Catherine Connolly and Thomas Pringle), who joined this group shortly after the government was elected. Michael Lowry, a former Fine Gael minister who had previously backed a Fianna Fáil-led administration, had from the beginning pledged to support Enda Kenny. Katherine Zappone had also played her cards early, voting for Kenny as Taoiseach in his first two unsuccessful nominations when most other independents abstained. The left-wing independent Séamus Healy was vocal in his opposition to Fine Gael's re-election, but the views of another left-wing independent, Maureen O'Sullivan, were not as certain. The two Healy-Rae brothers were divided, with Michael having been in negotiations with Enda Kenny, to whom Danny was opposed, a split which was rumoured to ultimately cost Michael a cabinet seat. Both the rural alliance and the Independent Alliance were also divided over support for Fine Gael, with the outcome uncertain even on the day of the vote on 6 May. What was certain was that if Kenny was not elected, he would immediately seek a dissolution of the Dáil, which put pressure on some independents, particularly the newcomers – such as Michael Harty – who would not have fancied another election. Ultimately, five of the six Independent Alliance TDs voted for Kenny, with Michael Fitzmaurice abstaining over the issue of turf-cutting rights (Fitzmaurice later left the Alliance to form a technical group in opposition). Two of the rural alliance, Harty and Denis Naughten, also backed Kenny, as did Zappone and Lowry. Noel Grealish, Michael Healy-Rae and Maureen O'Sullivan all abstained, while the other independents voted against Kenny's nomination, which was passed by fifty-nine votes to forty-nine. Rather than enticing independents with local patronage deals, as was the case in the past, independents were this time offered real positions of authority. Katherine Zappone was appointed Minister for Children and Youth Affairs, Denis Naughten Minister for Communications, Climate Change and Natural Resources, and Shane Ross Minister for Transport, Trade and Tourism. Finian McGrath was appointed a super junior minister in the Department of Health, with John Halligan appointed a minister of state. The two other members of the Independent Alliance, Seán Canney and Kevin 'Boxer' Moran, were to occupy another ministry of state in a rotating post.

During negotiations, the independents had all sought to stress that their focus was on national issues and that local deals would not be the price of their support. Indeed, the Independent Alliance had stressed from the outset that it was against the parish-pump style politics of the past. Nevertheless, all had not changed utterly, as following the formation of government, the independents maintained that – despite being ministers – they also remained local politicians. To this extent, they sought priority for particular projects in their constituencies. The specific concessions were not included in the programme for government, but the arrangement between Fine Gael and Fianna Fáil had specified that the government would 'publish all agreements with Independent Deputies and other political parties in full' (Fine Gael 2016). So, Finian McGrath got commitments on a hospital and cystic fibrosis unit in his constituency, Seán Canney on transport infrastructure, Katherine Zappone on childhood programmes in her area, Kevin 'Boxer' Moran on his local institute of technology, John Halligan on a local airport runway and regional hospital, and it was speculated that a previously closed police station in Shane Ross' constituency would be re-opened (F. Kelly 2016; Leahy 2016).

No announcements were made concerning the specifics of how cabinet would work with independent ministers, especially in relation to the principle of collective responsibility, which is constitutionally enshrined. It was assumed that independents would abide by this principle, unlike in Australia, where independent ministers were free to go rogue on matters outside of their portfolio and budgetary-related legislation. However, within days of the government's formation, two of the independent junior ministers said they would not pay the controversial water charges, with Finian McGrath, as a 'super-junior' member of cabinet, seeking advice from the attorney general on the matter. McGrath later changed his mind, but within days also called for an amendment to the ban on smoking in the workplace. Few could predict how this government would work because it was uncharted waters for the Irish political system to include so many independents at the executive level. Whatever the outcome, the extensive involvement of independents both in the process of formation and via particpation in government indicates their being a majorly relevant actor in the Irish political system.

Vote for investiture

Under these arrangements, independent TDs agree to support the nomination of a Taoiseach and the appointment of his cabinet, but no commitment is given beyond the formation stage. The main difference from the ad hoc style of management is that the initial support of independents is courted by the parties over explicit negotiations.

1951

Fianna Fáil won sixty-nine seats to the opposition parties' sixty-four, with the remaining fourteen seats won by independents. Dillon's independent group of five, as well as Patrick Lehane, Patrick Finucane and William Sheldon, pledged their votes to Costello, which left six independents with the balance of power: Michael Ffrench-O'Carroll, Noel Browne, Peadar Cowan, Patrick Cogan, Jack McQuillan and John Flynn. While it was initially expected that Costello would be returned to office, Fianna Fáil's deputy leader, Seán Lemass, was not happy at the influential position independents found themselves in: 'The position cannot be satisfactory no matter what happens ... another coalition, dependent on the support of nearly all these independent deputies, offers a very depressing prospect' (McCullagh 2010, 256). Despite this opposition to independents, Fianna Fáil drew up a shopping list to entice their support. Lemass, for example, had a secret meeting with Noël Browne, and although insisting 'there's no bargain, no deal', told him 'we'll try to give you a good health service' (N. Browne 1986, 210). Fine Gael also met a number of the independents, allegedly offering Cowan a ministry (Horgan 2000, 163). Fianna Fáil's main aim was simply to secure enough votes to elect de Valera as Taoiseach. It did not expect the independents to commit beyond this, and instead planned an ad hoc management policy to deal with issues as they arose. This plan succeeded, as five of the six undecided independents backed de Valera, who was elected by seventy-four votes to sixty-nine. Dillon was particularly angry at these independents, whom he described as 'Fianna Fáil's busted flush – four wild west diamonds and one bleeding heart' (Manning 1999, 281), and outgoing Taoiseach Costello said 'I have no doubt some of the independent deputies who voted against the inter-party government were voting against the very people who elected them to this Dáil' (McCullagh 2010, 258). This was a poor strategic move by the outgoing government, because Costello's nomination had been defeated by only two votes. Had they been more responsive to the independents, they need never have left office in 1951, or at the very least they could have used the independents to undermine the stability of de Valera's government (Manning 1999, 281).

Although de Valera had led minority administrations in the past, this was different because there was now a viable alternative opposition. This meant that he could not use the threat of a snap election to keep the independents in line, and that he had to be conscious of their policy positions. For example, a particularly harsh budget in April 1952 was introduced earlier in the year than any other previous budget, a tactic to ensure it was not rejected by the independents, whom de Valera calculated would not have favoured a swift return to the polls (Lee 1989, 324). It is also suggested that independent William Sheldon's appointment to the chair of the Public Affairs Committee was because of his new-found influence (Walker 2011).

The independents who had put Fianna Fáil back into power were not taken for granted by the party, in return for which they rarely voted against the government in the Dáil (the five independents who elected de Valera Taoiseach had a mean support rate of 97 per cent for the government for the duration of this Dáil). This continued even after a number of by-election defeats, although the leader of the opposition claimed this was a rational move on the part of the independents, 'whose political existence depends on their maintaining the present government in power' (McCullagh 2010, 271). De Valera even called a motion of confidence in July 1953 to put it to the independents to stand by him or face an election. Few were surprised when they chose the former. So successful was Fianna Fáil at wooing the independents that four of them (Browne, Cogan, Flynn and Ffrench-O'Carroll) joined the party in 1953. Unsuccessful negotiations also took place with Peadar Cowan and Jack McQuillan, the latter of whom was offered a post as parliamentary secretary (Horgan 2000, 176). Ultimately, it was not the independents who brought about the downfall of the government, but rather two more by-election defeats in early 1954, which led de Valera to call an early election.

1982

After the fiasco and mismanagement of the 1981–82 legislative arrangement between the Fine Gael–Labour coalition and independents, Fianna Fáil's leader, Charles Haughey, was determined to avoid a repeat scenario. The February 1982 election had resulted in another election stalemate, but the pendulum had swung slightly in Fianna Fáil's favour. It had eighty-one seats to Fine Gael and Labour's combined seventy-eight. There were three Sinn Féin the Workers' Party (SFWP) TDs and four independents. Initial attempts by newly elected independent TD Tony Gregory to form a left alliance between SFWP, himself and Jim Kemmy, which could act as a voting bloc to negotiate between the alternative Taoisigh, failed due to the opposition of the SFWP and because Kemmy could not countenance any arrangement with Fianna Fáil.

With one of the independents (Neil Blaney) likely to vote for Haughey, another to vote against (Kemmy) and another re-appointed as Ceann Comhairle (Haughey had initially offered this post to Kemmy, who he knew would definitely vote against him for Taoiseach; Kemmy declined, so independent John O'Connell remained in the chair), all the attention focused on Gregory. Having made an almost principled stand of refusing to negotiate with independents in the previous government, FitzGerald changed tack completely, as did Haughey, and met with Gregory to discuss the price of his support, offering him a forty-nine page deal of various patronage and policy concessions (Browne 1982). Although this was portrayed in the media as an independent holding the country to ransom, Gregory was adamant that he at no time approached any of the party leaders (Gregory 2000). Rather, they came to him, in the literal sense to his constituency office amid the tenements of inner-city Dublin, which put Gregory in a position he felt would be irresponsible not to maximise for the voters he represented.

FitzGerald (1991, 402) later claimed that such negotiations were against his own better judgement, but that he had been convinced by leading businessmen that a Haughey-led government reliant on a left-wing group would be detrimental to the economy. The Fine Gael leader asked his outgoing Minister for Finance to order a re-examination of the budget, which had defeated the previous administration, to alter aspects that would appease the socialist-minded independents. It begged the question why this had not been done in the first place.

When the new Dáil met on 8 March, there was still a great deal of uncertainty about the outcome of the vote to elect a Taoiseach. In his maiden speech, Gregory outlined the details of a deal he had struck with Haughey in return for his support. This comprised a thirty-page document signed by Haughey, Gregory and several other witnesses, and came to be known as 'the Gregory Deal'. It included a range of projects, such as the nationalisation of a large site in Dublin's docklands, the creation of thousands of new jobs, the building of 3,000 new houses, and an increase in both the number of remedial teachers and in the maintenance budget for local authority housing. The deal did not just concern largesse for Gregory's inner-city constituency, but sought to tackle a wide range of social and economic issues, primarily in the areas of education, employment, housing, healthcare and welfare. The total cost was unknown, but was speculated to range between £150 and £250 million, if everything was implemented (see Maureen O'Sullivan's description of these events in Chapter 4, and Gilligan (2012), chapter 4). Gregory was particularly adamant that it not be a secret arrangement and the document was published in full in the *Irish Times*: 'We called what we negotiated a programme for government, the media called it a deal ... I read it into the record of the Dáil, it was transparent, people knew I was voting for Haughey as Taoiseach and they knew why' (Brennock 1998). All Gregory promised in return was to vote for Haughey as Taoiseach, with his support thereafter being decided on an ad hoc issue-by-issue basis. He also told the government chief whip, Bertie Ahern, that his single vote would never bring down the government (Ahern 2009, 70).

Although the other independent, Neil Blaney, was of Fianna Fáil stock, Haughey did not take his support for granted. A six-man team from Blaney's Independent Fianna Fáil organisation met with Haughey, and wanted a tougher stance on Northern Ireland and a boost to the construction industry. Haughey agreed to these conditions, making reference to 'the northern question' in his acceptance speech as Taoiseach. He also appointed James Larkin, Blaney's director of elections, to the Seanad. In return, Blaney (now also an MEP) regularly flew back from Strasbourg to support Haughey in close Dáil votes, a situation he later regretted given Haughey's failure to fulfil his promises on the north and construction (Rafter 1993, 99).

Ultimately, the SFWP decided to support Haughey, who was elected by eighty-six votes to seventy-nine (Kemmy was the only independent to vote against Haughey). This meant that the support of the independents was theoretically not necessary, but the government's chief whip, Bertie Ahern, knew that the continuous support of the SFWP could not be relied on. The administration that followed was to be short lived, as it swung from one crisis to the next. Ahern described the government's term as 'among the most frenetic of my life' (2009, 60). This was not just due to its minority status, but was also a product of internal dissension within Fianna Fáil over Haughey's leadership. Indeed, Ahern said it was a lot easier to keep the independents on side than some of his own party's backbenchers.

The death of a Fianna Fáil TD in June meant Haughey had to rely on the SFWP to pass the Finance Bill. This plunged the government into further crisis, having to rely on the casting vote of the Ceann Comhairle on one occasion. This led to some criticism of Gregory, who had told Haughey he supported a particular SFWP amendment on the Finance Bill that would have defeated the government, but changed his mind in the chamber, tying the vote at eighty each. The opposition accused Gregory of having negotiated another deal, but the reality was he did not wish to see the premature fall of the government that would lead to the unravelling of the promises Haughey had made in March. On another issue later that month on which the future of the government was not at stake, Gregory combined with the SFWP to defeat a government motion. This sparked a vote of confidence in July, which the government won by eighty-four votes to seventy-nine with the left-wing TDs back on board (Joyce and Murtagh 1983, 179–83).

This situation was unlikely to hold, however, and in October the death of one Fianna Fáil backbencher and the hospitalisation of another severely shortened the government's life expectancy. The announcement of a package of more cuts in public spending led to the SFWP withdrawing its support and the calling of a vote of confidence. On 4 November the government was defeated by eighty votes to eighty-two, the first administration in the history of the state to lose such a motion. While SFWP cast the decisive votes, Gregory abstained. In his memoirs, Ahern states that it was much more difficult to keep SFWP on board than Gregory (2009, 60), and indeed Gregory was annoyed at the SFWP for bringing down the government. When the government had needed his vote he had always delivered. Gregory supported Haughey in 48 per cent of votes; even Blaney voted with Haughey only 58 per cent of the time, with the comparative figure for Kemmy of 3 per cent. While this short-lived government is often cited as an example of the instability that can ensue when independents hold the balance of power, it was not the independents that defeated the government, but rather political parties. It was not in Gregory's interest for the government to collapse, because with it went his deal.

1989–92

Falling seven seats short of a majority in 1989, Charles Haughey was unable to form another minority administration. The perceived drift to the right by Fianna Fáil meant Haughey could not look to the left-wing independents of Jim Kemmy and Tony Gregory for support, who both voted for Labour's Dick Spring as Taoiseach when the new Dáil met. Neil Blaney was no longer willing to support his former party colleague, so the only independent left for Haughey to look to was the newly elected Tom Foxe from Roscommon. In return for Foxe's vote for Haughey as Taoiseach and Seán Treacy as Ceann Comhairle, Haughey made an informal arrangement with Foxe that he would look after the health services in the independent's home constituency of Roscommon. Foxe was elected on behalf of the Roscommon Hospital Action Committee, and the three issues of concern to him were the planned downgrading of Roscommon hospital, and the closures of a psychiatric hospital and a state-run nursing home. The exact nature of the verbal agreement was not made known at the time, and Haughey denied the existence of such a deal, but Foxe was the only TD outside of Fianna Fáil to support Haughey's nomination on 30 June, which was defeated by seventy-eight votes to eighty-six.

Haughey ultimately formed a coalition with the PDs, with whom the government had the bare majority of one. Consequently, Foxe's vote remained important. This became more so when a Fianna Fáil backbencher lost the party whip in July 1989, leaving the government technically in a minority. When Foxe then began to exhibit more independent behaviour in the Dáil, and voted against the government out of anger that the health services in his constituency were not being looked after, Haughey sought to shore up Foxe's support with a Gregory-type deal. The specific issue that motivated this was a crucial motion of confidence in the Minister for Health, Rory O'Hanlon, in February 1990. Foxe complained to the local newspapers in his constituency that Haughey had broken the 'Kinsealy [Haughey's private residence] deal' struck the previous June, and he seemed set to bring down the government (*Connacht Tribune*, 2 February 1990). Consequently, a new deal was negotiated. In return for Foxe's vote on the motion, a £3 million agreement was struck in the chief whip's office between O'Hanlon and Foxe, which was sanctioned by Haughey. Extra beds and nurses were to be provided in Roscommon hospital, along with an anaesthetist, and Castlerea psychiatric hospital was to be upgraded. The existence of such a deal was denied by Fianna Fáil, and Foxe remained tight-lipped on the issue: 'I am not prepared to discuss this matter at all except to say that after consultations with a number of my constituents I am satisfied with the assurances given by the government' (O'Connor 1990). Akin to Gregory's arrangement eight years previously, no agreement was struck for Foxe to provide continuous support for the government, with the consequence that he supported Haughey in only 33 per cent of the votes in which he participated (still far in excess of Gregory's support rate of 2 per cent and that of Blaney, who voted with Haughey in just two of the eight votes that he turned up for in the lifetime of this administration).

This was the 'see no deal, hear no deal, speak no deal' policy adopted by Haughey throughout the lifetime of this administration. Because Foxe had won a key Fianna Fáil seat, Haughey could not be seen to kowtow to him, and for the same reason Foxe also could not crow about what he had achieved with his deal (although this did not stop the literal popping of champagne corks when a new wing of Roscommon hospital was opened in December 1991 (Casey 1991)). So, while on the outside it might have looked that Haughey was acting akin to FitzGerald's majoritarian style of 1981–82, the reality was it was a repeat of his own ad hoc handling of Gregory in 1982. It was not just a strategy on Haughey's part, but also reflective of his own style of leadership. Neither the cabinet nor his coalition partners were consulted about the deal, and he even denied its existence to his party's national executive. Similar to the manner in which he conducted much of his government business, including talks with trade unions, Haughey acted without consultation, but this may have worked with the independents, because it is unlikely his parliamentary party would have been so willing to compromise. For the remainder of Haughey's tenure, O'Hanlon continued to keep Foxe briefed on health issues pertaining to his constituency, while for his part Foxe maintained his support for the government on key issues, such as a vote of confidence in November 1991, until Haughey's resignation in 1992. As with most cases of governments reliant on the support of independents, it was not the latter that was to prove the downfall of the former, but rather the governing party's own internal conflicts. Haughey's replacement, Albert Reynolds, was not so generous to Foxe, whose support levels for the government consequently declined to 16 per cent.

Negotiated deals

Along with the agreements with independents in cabinet, these negotiated deals comprise the most solid of the type of arrangements between governments and independents, who agree to an explicit deal to support parties in power provided they meet particular pledges laid out at the beginning of the government's term. In some ways these agreements are similar to the programmes negotiated between parties in government, with the exception that those made with independents are often not made public.

1997–2002

After the 1997 election, the two opposing coalition pacts had both failed to win a majority, but the Fianna Fáil–Progressive Democrat alliance was much closer to the winning line with eighty-one seats than the outgoing rainbow government of Fine Gael, Labour and Democratic Left with seventy-five. The ten remaining seats comprised six independents, two Greens and one each from Sinn Féin and the Socialist Party. Although he talked with the Greens and some of the independents (even offering a cabinet ministry to Jackie Healy-Rae, one of the newly elected independents (Hickey 2015, 56–7)), Taoiseach John Bruton needed almost all ten votes to stay in power, an unrealistic option that left the Fianna Fáil leader, Bertie Ahern, with the upper hand.

Having been the party's chief whip during the early 1980s, and observed the manner in which both FitzGerald and Haughey worked with independents, Ahern had learned a lot about how not to run a government reliant upon their support. He was determined that any government formed be more than a short-term arrangement and so he spoke to most of the independents. Ahern wanted more than their vote for his nomination as Taoiseach. He wanted the independents on board for the long haul. In return they presented him with a shopping list of demands for their respective constituencies.

A deal with Michael Lowry in Tipperary was unlikely to materialise because of his Fine Gael background and the circumstances surrounding his resignation from ministerial office in 1995. Tom Gildea in

Donegal, elected on the single issue of a television deflector mast, was an unknown quantity, and the issue on which he ran was the subject of a court case, meaning that Ahern preferred to stay clear until any legal ambiguities about Gildea's campaign were resolved (when this was achieved a year later, Gildea came on board as one of the independents supporting Ahern's minority government). Tony Gregory was linked to the post of Ceann Comhairle, but he wanted a 'super junior' ministry and a place at the cabinet table in return for his support. Ahern says that Gregory 'overplayed his hand' (Ahern, interview 2015) and these talks failed to progress, which in part may also have been due to a prior history between the two TDs, both being from the same constituency.

This left the trio of Harry Blaney, Mildred Fox and Jackie Healy-Rae. All had some connection with Fianna Fáil – Blaney was a brother of Neil, who had supported minority Haughey governments in the 1980s; Healy-Rae was a long-standing Fianna Fáil activist and local council-lor who ran independent in 1997 because he failed to win a party nomination; Fox's father had been a Fianna Fáil councillor who first ran independent in 1992 when he too failed to get on the party ticket. Each of the three independents struck separate agreements with Ahern, but unlike the Gregory deal of 1982, none of them were published at the time. The deals were with Ahern as Fianna Fáil leader, rather than Taoiseach, to prevent their being released under Freedom of Information legislation (Rafter 2000). Their being kept private allowed both Ahern and the independents to save face with the public and with each other whenever conflict arose, since no one was the wiser as to the nature and details of each agreement.

The specifics of the individual agreements primarily concerned projects for the independents' local constituencies. Healy-Rae wanted a replacement industry for a recently closed factory, as well as extra resources for roads and piers. At the end of the government's term, Healy-Rae (in his election literature) stated that he had delivered £250 million worth of funding for his constituency of Kerry South. Amongst the projects that Mildred Fox claimed credit for was a new school, police station, additional hospital services and new council offices. Harry Blaney got a commitment to spending on Donegal's roads and infrastructure, best symbolised by a bridge across Mulroy Bay which, when opened in 2009 at a cost of €19 million, was named after the independent. In total, Blaney claimed to have secured €170 million of funding arising directly from his agreement with Bertie Ahern. When Gildea negotiated an agreement with Ahern in 1998, it too was unwrit-ten, and concerned primarily patronage for his constituency of Donegal South-West. This included the development of a harbour in a busy fishing port, new roads, a sewerage scheme and a school extension, all of which the total cost was estimated to be £31 million (A. O'Connor 2000b). Having lost two by-elections, Ahern was happy to bear the burden of the cost of an additional independent if it provided further stability. Gildea's motives were pretty clear: 'my supporters saw it as the practical way forward … I saw it as an opportunity to be able to derive more benefit for the constituency, because at the end of the day that is what it is all about' (*Ibid.*). Undoubtedly a factor that facilitated the handling of the arrangements with these four independents was the considerable economic growth of the time, which left a lot of surplus revenue in the state coffers, in stark contrast to the era of the Gregory deal. Blaney recalled: 'I remember that there was nothing we asked for that they didn't say was OK and I remember thinking that was a bit worrying' (A. O'Connor 2000a).

Not all politics were local for the independents, as two national issues of concern to them were abortion and Northern Ireland. Blaney continued the policy of his brother that the northern question be looked after (in particular that 'articles 2 and 3 of the constitution would not be amended until there was a fully agreed overall settlement of the national question' (O'Regan 1998a)). Blaney, Fox and Gildea wanted a referendum on abortion (to which they were opposed), and declared their support for the government conditional on one being called (Donohoe 2000); such a referendum was ultimately held in the last few months of the administration, in March 2002. The government also had to backtrack on proposals to tax credit union deposits, as well as on its position concerning legal funding for a residents' group taking a case against British Nuclear Fuels over the Sellafield nuclear reprocessing facility (O'Regan 1998b). One issue concerning all the independents was the initiative to ban the holding of multiple political offices, the so-called 'dual mandate'. So vociferous were the independents in their opposition that the legislation was delayed for the lifetime of the government. Healy-Rae also secured the chairmanship of the environmental committee and, as mentioned at the beginning of this chapter, managed to alter the government's regionalisation programme and achieve the maximum EU funding status for the counties of Kerry and Clare, although the latter was rejected by the European Commission. He claimed 'I think that happened because of the unwarranted publicity that was created. It looked to the fellows in Brussels that they were being dictated to by people like me' (O'Regan 2000).

The largesse agreed prior to the formation of the government was not the limit of the independents' influence. Together they met with the chief whip, Séamus Brennan, on a weekly basis, where they were briefed on legislation and other relevant government matters. A civil servant from the Department of the Taoiseach was also assigned to deal with their queries. Independents were free to bring up other demands along the way, and cabinet ministers were also made available to discuss legislation. Ahern was determined that the government would last a full term, and so he did not take the independents for granted. He wanted them to be treated seriously by his cabinet and parliamentary party, to the extent that a member of the opposition mischievously called Healy-Rae the real Taoiseach and Fox the real Tánaiste (O'Regan 1998b).

Although the independents had negotiated individual deals, they had first met together as a group before their discussions with Ahern. Together they drew up an informal written document that was more a pledge to be honest and open in their dealings with each other. During the lifetime of the government the independents maintained this team policy to maximise their influence. Fox stated: 'We operate better as a unit of four because we get on so well together and we want to make sure that we are taken seriously. When the three of us were negotiating at the beginning we agreed that we would back each other up' (A. O'Connor 2000c), while Gildea said 'it is a question of all for one and one for all' (A. O'Connor 2000b). The team modus operandi worked because the independents were all of a similar ilk, somewhat akin to a party. To quote Fox again: 'we are the same type of people with the same type of personalities, some more colourful than others. We get along pretty well' (A. O'Connor 2000c). Quite remarkably, Blaney, Fox and Healy-Rae voted the same way (for the government) on every single one of the 307 motions in which all three participated during the five years of the government, as did Gildea once he was on board in November 1998.

The agreement worked perfectly well for both the independents and the government, as barring the occasional hiccup (such as when Blaney opposed Ireland joining the NATO-sponsored Partnership for Peace programme, and threatened to withdraw support in 1998 because of proposed amendments to the aforementioned articles 2 and 3 of the constitution), they tended to support the government on almost all issues, and were happy to deliver their side of the bargain provided Ahern met his. In total, Fox and Blaney voted against the government on just three out of over 400 motions, while Gildea (once he had signed up to the arrangement) and Healy-Rae provided 100 per cent support. The consequence was that, contrary to initial media expectations, the government lasted a full term, being the then longest serving government in Irish peacetime history.

At the 2002 election, Fianna Fáil won eighty-one seats and the PDs eight. There were thirteen independents elected, the largest number since 1948, and primarily due to the influence the 'gang of four' had wielded in Ahern's previous administration. Local electorates wanted an independent to negotiate a Gregory or Healy-Rae type deal for their own constituency. Ahern could have formed a single-party minority government reliant on independents, since Fianna Fáil now had the same number of seats as it had combined with the PDs five years earlier. Ahern was also aware that Haughey formed such a single-party government with the same number of seats in more trying circumstances in the 1980s. In the immediate aftermath of the election, many of the independents made public their willingness to support such an arrangement. Paddy McHugh in Galway, a former Fianna Fáil councillor, said he would have 'no difficulty supporting a Fianna Fáil-led government provided there was a good return for my constituency'. Niall Blaney (Harry's son), made similar utterances, while Healy-Rae said 'I feel we worked well together, and I don't see why that can't continue' (Humphreys 2002). However, having a good working relationship with the leader of the PDs, Mary Harney, Ahern opted to continue with the coalition. But, ever the master strategist, he maintained regular dialogue with the same three independents (Gildea had not stood again) as the 1997–2002 arrangement during the lifetime of his second administration. Thus, Blaney, Fox and Healy-Rae supported the 2002–7 government in 93 per cent of votes, compared to a mean of 5 per cent from the ten other independent TDs. This gave Ahern more bargaining power against his coalition partner, and provided a safety net in case they parted ways. For their part, independents continued to make known their availability (Felle 2004).

2007–11

Bertie Ahern and Fianna Fáil had the upper hand after the 2007 election. Although the party's seat total had slipped back to seventy-eight, the only alternative to a Fianna Fáil-led government was if the five other elected parties came together in a diverse coalition. While this had happened in 1948, a repeat occurrence in 2007 was never a real possibility. Ahern ultimately formed a surplus majority government, including the six Green and two PD TDs. He also brought in the independents, both to provide a bulwark against future shifting seat numbers, and to lessen the bargaining power of the Greens in government. The arrangements and the management of the independents ran in the same manner as the 1997–2002 administration. Three of the independents (Finian McGrath, Healy-Rae and Michael Lowry) formed separate agreements with Ahern, with McGrath reading parts of his into the Dáil record à la Gregory in 1982 (see McGrath's description of these events in Chapter 4). Another independent, former Fianna Fáil TD Beverly Flynn, claimed to have a verbal agreement (Donohoe 2007), but this was denied by Ahern (Flynn was re-admitted to Fianna Fáil a year later in any case). Again, these deals primarily concerned constituency matters. They included a written pledge that twenty-six roads in Healy-Rae's constituency would be rebuilt, and a commitment on forty-one projects for Lowry – including a surgery of excellence and a public swimming pool. All told, these two deals were reported to be worth €71 million (McGee 2012). The weekly meetings with the independents in the whip's office continued in the same format as in the previous administrations. One aspect of these arrangements that Ahern was keen to stress, as he had done in 1997, was that they were with him as leader of Fianna Fáil, and not as Taoiseach (O'Malley 2008, 211). Consequently, it was not that the independents were holding the government to ransom, and it allowed Ahern to keep secret the details of the arrangements.[2] Within Fianna Fáil it was claimed that there were no deals, and that the independents were simply allowed to air their grievances and lend their names to projects that had already been signed off. From a strategic point of view this suited both Ahern and the independents. If he was dispensing largesse it might not look favourably on him, with both the electorate and members of his own backbench, if the details were made public. If he was not, and it was known, the independents would not be able to defend their support of him to their constituents. Ahern was happy to allow the independents make whatever claims they wanted concerning their influence and to issue threats in the media, just so long as they stayed on board. He knew what he had given the independents, and it is very unlikely that it would have been more than their positions warranted.

When Brian Cowen replaced Ahern as Fianna Fáil leader and Taoiseach in May 2008, he continued the same arrangements with the three independents. A government spokesman at the time said, 'He will want to keep the three independents on side, although he is likely to be more direct in his dealings with them.' Presciently, the spokesman also said, 'problems could emerge, however, if there is a significant downturn in the economy and money is scarce' (O'Regan 2008). A few months later this prediction was to prove correct, as government plans to remove the universal provision of medical cards for the over-70s led to Finian McGrath withdrawing his support.

A year later, the PDs formally disbanded, but its two TDs, Mary Harney and Noel Grealish – now independents – maintained support for the government (although Grealish withdrew his support in September 2010). Harney remained in her post as Minister for Health. As the economy nosedived, pressure grew on the government, and it led to resignations and internal dissension within Fianna Fáil. This increased the necessity for Cowen to retain the support of Healy-Rae and Lowry, which became especially apparent in November 2010, when the resignation of a government backbencher reduced the coalition's numbers to eighty seats against seventy-nine for the opposition. The votes of the two independents were now decisive for the future stability of the government. Communications were intensified with Healy-Rae and Lowry, with the latter acting for the pair of them when Healy-Rae's health deteriorated. With the support of these independents, the government was able to pass a crucial budget in December 2010 and a Dáil vote to accept a loan from the European Central Bank and International Monetary Fund (IMF) in the same month. In January 2011, with an election imminent, the Finance Bill needed to be passed to secure some of the loan payments from the IMF. Amid accusations that the two independents were holding the country to ransom (which lacked basis since some Fianna Fáil TDs had already walked, and the other independents and opposition parties all voted against the Finance Bill), Lowry and Healy-Rae wanted particular demands met in return for their vote. While Healy-Rae secured €1 million in funding for projects in his constituency, both he and Lowry sought the easing of some of the more punitive measures in the budget, concessions which they secured following meetings with the Taoiseach and Minister for Finance (Bréadún and Minihan 2011). In defence of the two independents, they needed to demonstrate to their constituents that they were not mere lobby fodder for very unpopular measures. Lowry had provided support for the two Fianna Fáil-led governments on 98 per cent of votes he attended since 2007, with the equivalent figure for Healy Rae of 99 per cent.

Minority governments and independents: an overview

From the analysis of these minority governments there are a number of clear patterns. The first is that they need not be a byword for instability. There are very few instances of independents bringing down governments, not necessarily because they put the interests of the country first, but because their limited resources mean that no independent wants an early election. Their fate at such polls is described in Chapter 3, where in almost all cases independents lost seats and votes. There is also the sense among independent TDs that they do not want to be the culprits for the fall of a government. Thus, even though some see Tony Gregory's influence in the 1980s as a symptom of the instability of that era, he let it be known that he would not bring down a government and was true to his word. The same applied to Lowry and Healy-Rae in the Cowen government of 2008–11. The key variable in the stability and longevity of most of these arrangements is rather the parties, not the independents. The parties are responsible for bringing independents into the process, and if they do not manage it adequately they are ultimately culpable. As is described, the inter-party government formed in 1948 need not have collapsed in 1951 if the parties had talked to the independents, and the same applies to the Fine Gael–Labour coalition that fell in January 1982.

Former Taoiseach Bertie Ahern, who was involved in a considerable number of negotiations to form governments, says that dealing with independents is not 'rocket science'. The key is to maintain communication, as is the case for dealing with any TDs in government: 'independents when treated properly are no worse than your own party' (Ahern, interview 2015). During his administrations of 1997–2002 and 2007–8 he gave independents the same access to ministers as he would any members of his parliamentary party (if not more, some argued). In nine out of ten instances this is all independents are looking for, according to Ahern, and in most cases they are prepared to accept that they cannot always get their way. For example, in 1998 Jackie Healy-Rae accepted Ahern's opposition to his proposal to extend Sunday opening hours for public houses by half an hour, because in the independent's own words: 'you couldn't have newspaper headlines about the government falling over pub-closing time on a Sunday night' (O'Regan 2014). It is also not the case that independents are apt to make excessive policy demands; most of their concerns, as with any backbench party TD, centre on their constituencies. For these reasons, independents need not necessarily imply instability; they can be very strong supporters of governments, provided they are not taken for granted. Just as when a government party ignoring its coalition partner results in instability, likewise it should not be any different when similar treatment is meted out to independents, especially when they lack a place in cabinet as an incentive not to rock the boat.

It should not be forgotten that the primary reason independents get involved in the government formation process is because parties look to them. The logic for parties is quite clear. If they brought an additional party into coalition, they would have to concede seats at the cabinet table and compromise on some of their policies. Neither has necessarily to happen with independents. The difference in influence between that of the four Progressive Democrat TDs who formed a coalition with Fianna Fáil in 1997, and the four independents whose support they needed, is evidence of why independents are preferable to an additional party in cabinet. While the influence of the independents in this administration has been detailed, it pales in comparison to that of the PDs, who had two junior and one senior ministry as well as considerable influence over budgetary policy. For parties, the downside of looking to independents is instability, as the expectation is that a majority government will last longer and be more stable. The evidence indicates that governments not reliant on independents last longer, but this does not tell the full story. As is evident in Table 7.2, such governments in Ireland on average last three years and five months, against a mean length of two years and eight months for those looking to independents. However, considering the four different types of arrangements outlined between governments and independents, there are some clear differences. Governments where independents are dealt with by an ad hoc arrangement are the shortest, lasting less than two years (732 days); those with negotiated investiture are slightly longer (831 days). Those with more formal arrangements last the longest – with an independent in government at 1,182 days, and those involving a formal arrangement for external support last 1,575 days. This indicates a significant institutional dimension to the stability of governments needing independents – the stronger the relationship between them, the longer the government lasts.

Length of government is not necessarily a proxy for stability, but another aspect that can be examined is the extent to which minority governments can rely on independents in parliament; that is, the extent to which they turn up to vote and how often they vote with the government. Some of these figures have already been mentioned in the analysis, and they are summarised in Figures 7.2 and 7.3 for every independent TD elected between 1937 and 2015. Dealing with Figure 7.2 first, which indicates the proportion of Dáil votes in which

Table 7.2 *Length of type of government (in days) in Ireland, 1922–2016*

Type of arrangement	Length of term
Government not reliant on independent support	1,275
Government reliant on independent support	961
Ad hoc arrangement	732
Negotiated investiture	831
Independent in government	1,182
Formal agreement with independent TDs	1,575

Author's figures calculated from Gallagher and Weeks (2010).

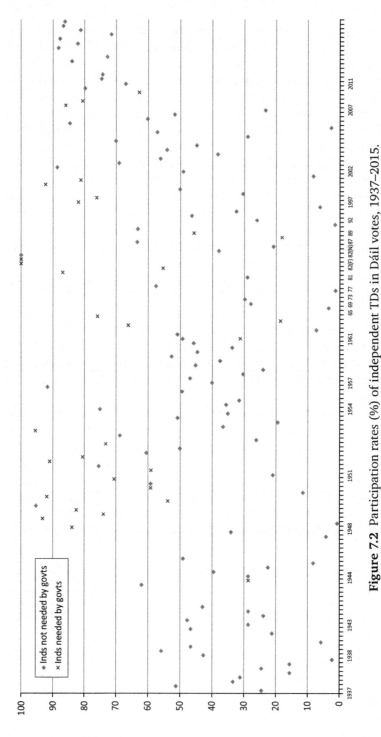

Figure 7.2 Participation rates (%) of independent TDs in Dáil votes, 1937–2015.

Note: Data points correspond to percentage of times independent TDs voted on motions for the lifetime of each Dáil. Crossed points are the independents who voted for the investiture of a minority government when their vote was needed. Diamond points are all other independent TDs.

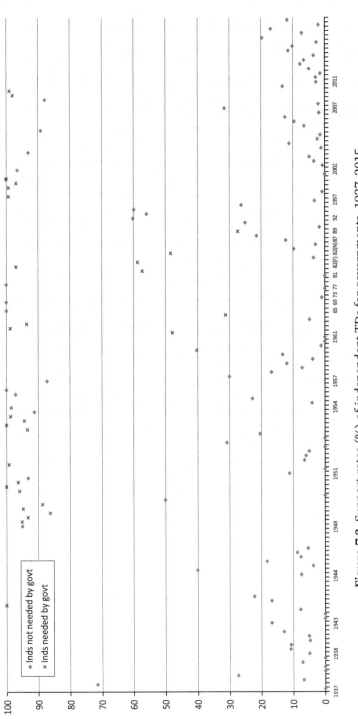

Figure 7.3 Support rates (%) of independent TDs for governments, 1937–2015.

Note: Data points correspond to percentage of times independent TDs voted with the government for the lifetime of each Dáil. Cross points are the independents who voted for the investiture of a minority government when their vote was needed. Diamond points are all other independent TDs.

independents participated, the less frequent set of data points (crosses) applies to independents who voted for the investiture of a minority government that needed their support, and the more frequent points (diamonds) for all other independents. It is quite evident that when their votes are needed, independents have higher rates of participation (74 per cent on average) than those instances where their support is not required (44 per cent participation).

Not only are independent TDs more likely to participate in parliamentary votes when their support is required, but they are also more likely to vote for the government, as is indicated in Figure 7.3. The mean proportion of times that an independent backing a government votes with the said administration is 86 per cent. The equivalent figure for independents whose votes are not needed is 23 per cent.[3] As Figure 7.3 demonstrates in more detail, these are remarkably high levels of support, with the mean lowered only by a number of deviant cases of independents whose support was not assiduously courted by the government (including James Carroll in 1961, Seán Loftus in 1981 and Tom Foxe (initially) in 1989). These two graphs indicate that independents can be relied on for their support when needed, and that such reliance need not necessarily be a recipe for instability, as is indicated by the variation in the length of governments being dependent on the arrangements with independents.

The support rates also vary in line with these different arrangements. For example, in 1948 when six independents formed an inter-parliamentary group and had an informal whip, their average level of support for the government was 95 per cent. This was not necessarily because these independents were simply pro-establishment and willing to support whoever happened to be in government. For example, when Fianna Fáil replaced the coalition at the next election of 1951, the agreement rates of Alfie Byrne dropped to 6 per cent, his son to 11 per cent, Dillon to 5 per cent and Flanagan to 0 per cent. In contrast, the mean support rate for the five independents who voted the Fianna Fáil government into office was 97 per cent. Likewise, when explicit deals are done with independents, as Bertie Ahern negotiated in 1997 and 2007, their support for the government is exceptionally high, close on 100 per cent. This is in contrast (for the 1997–2002 government) to support of 3 per cent from Gregory, 1 per cent from Healy and 0 per cent from Lowry. Likewise, in the 2007–11 Dáil, while Beverly Flynn, Healy-Rae and Lowry provided almost 100 per cent support, the equivalent rates were 2 per cent from Gregory and 13 per cent from O'Sullivan (who replaced Gregory in a by-election in 2009, following the latter's death).

Such arrangements are a greater means of ensuring the longevity and stability of a government than simply negotiating a vote for investiture. For example, despite all Gregory was promised in return for his supporting Haughey in 1982, he voted with the government only 48 per cent of the time (albeit still greater than the 37 per cent support rate of the Workers' Party, which ultimately brought down the government). Even then this is better than ignoring an independent and attempting to call his or her bluff. When Haughey refused to do a deal with Gregory in 1987 and 1989, even though he needed his vote, the latter backed Haughey's administration on only 12 per cent and 2 per cent of occasions, respectively.

Finally, in terms of the impact for independents, is it a rational decision for them to support minority governments? The disadvantage is that they lose some of their nonpartisanship and can be punished by their local electorates for compromising their independent position. This can be counteracted by the delivery of patronage (whether real or imaginary) for their respective constituencies, provided it is forthcoming from the parties. The advantage of this position from an independent viewpoint is that they need not be tarnished by the unpopular policies of such governments and can keep their distance, or even withdraw their support. Providing support for minority administrations could also be an act of self-interest to provide an element of stability and avoid an early election, which no independent wants. Examining the electoral fate of the forty-one TDs who ran as independents again (excluding the independent unionists from Trinity College who were elected unopposed) following a minority government that they had voted into office, thirty-one retained their seats, a re-election rate of 76 per cent, slightly below the average for all other independent TDs (80 per cent). Generally speaking, most independents hold onto their seats when seeking re-election, and this is no different for those who supported minority governments. Those with the closest forms of attachment to such administrations (independents supporting Fianna Fáil governments formed in 1997 and 2007, and the independent group of 1948–51) all held their seats. Only two particular crops of independents suffered from their support given to such governments: those who backed the 1961–65 Lemass government that introduced a very unpopular tax, and the 1951–54 group of five, of whom four joined Fianna Fáil in the lifetime of the Dáil. The fate of these independents can be compared to those who chose not to support such minority governments. They amount to thirty-two independent TDs, and of the twenty-seven of those who ran again following such a government, twenty-two held their seat, a re-election rate of 78 per cent.

This is in line with the aforementioned national mean for independents, so choosing not to back a government had little tangible effect.

In terms of the overall electoral impact of such arrangements on support for independents, the greatest increases followed the 1948–51, 1997–2002 and 2007–11 arrangements, with respective increases of 1.3 percentage points (two additional seats), 2.6 points (seven additional seats) and 5.6 percentage points (nine additional seats). While independents nationally may have profited from the exposure and prominence afforded their brand by such arrangements, ironically the gains were less for those specifically involved in them (although they all retained their seats). In 2002 Healy-Rae's vote declined three percentage points, Fox's increased one point and Niall Blaney (replacing his father) saw the IFF vote fall over four points. Likewise, in 2011 Michael Healy-Rae had a slightly lower vote than his father in 2007, while Michael Lowry had a minimal increase of 0.1 per cent. In 1992 Tom Foxe's vote fell almost in half, while Tony Gregory in 1982 was one of the few to substantially increase his vote after negotiating a deal, going from 10 to 14 per cent. Of the six independents in the 1948 group, three saw their vote increase in 1951 and three experienced a decline, with the aggregate change between them just over two percentage points. Overall, between 1922 and 2016 the mean vote for independents supporting a government was 18.2 per cent when it was elected and 17.5 per cent at the succeeding election. The comparable figures for those independents not supporting a minority government are 16.1 and 15 per cent. In addition, the mean national vote for independents after these arrangements increases by just 0.05 percentage points. At all other elections it increases by 0.5 points. There are a lot of figures here, but what they seem to suggest is that the stance of independents vis-à-vis minority governments has a minimal electoral effect. However, the relationship could be a little more complicated than this suggests. Perhaps the very fact that independents manage to avoid electoral decline is an achievement in itself, given the challenge they face from parties and their limited resources. It could be that supporting a government helps prevent a loss in support for independents, and that if they are not able to show relevance then independents as a whole may perform poorly at the succeeding election. In addition, independents at least manage to avoid the negative effect of supporting governments, in contrast to minor parties which tend to experience electoral setbacks from such an experience (albeit via participation, which may have a different effect) (O'Malley 2012). It could also be the case that the independents at the heart of such deals do not seem to receive significant electoral profit because the local party TDs are envious of such arrangements, and put up a greater than normal challenge to the independents to ensure they do not return to the Dáil. Overall, while this suggests that the direct consequences for independents of a role in forming and maintaining governments may seem marginal, this is only in relation to the immediate electoral effects. It does not detract from the relevance afforded to independents by this role. Were it not for their participation in the process, independents would most likely be legislative pariahs, with the consequence that they may not have been in the Dáil in the first place to wield such influence.

Conclusion

Independents have had a considerable role to play in the formation and maintenance of minority governments in Ireland, where they are not suppressed – unlike in other systems in which they can be ostracised. In the early decades of the Irish state most independents were anti-Fianna Fáil, and so they supported Cumann na nGaedheal and Fine Gael-led governments. Because the independents' motives were ideological, the government did not have to offer them anything for their vote. However this changed in the 1950s, both because of a change in the type of independents elected, and also due to the realisation that Fianna Fáil in power would not lead to the collapse of the state. In part motivated by a recurrent fear of early elections, most independents appear willing to support governments of any hue. Thus, Joe Sheridan and Joseph Leneghan, both former Fine Gael Dáil candidates, supported a Fianna Fáil Taoiseach in office in the 1960s. Likewise, Michael Lowry, a former Fine Gael minister, supported two Fianna Fáil Taoisigh. In addition, left-wing independents supported centre-right governments in the 1980s and in 2016. From the perspective of the parties, they may not always be as eager as the independents. In particular, parties tend to prefer community or vestigial independents (remnants of defunct parties) as they seem to be easier to rely on once patronage is provided for their respective constituencies. Such independents also have a relatively low profile in the Dáil and are cautious about rocking the boat, which suits governments to a tee. In contrast, relying on independents of a different ideological hue is not always a recipe for stability, as indicated by the example of the early 1980s, and the early months of the Cowen administration in 2008 when the left-wing independent Finian McGrath withdrew his support. These ideological independents tend to have a greater national profile than community independents, and are not willing to be seen as too close to any government. Despite the Gregory deal, for example, Gregory voted for the government on only

50 per cent of occasions in 1982, whereas the likes of Healy-Rae and Fox in more recent times provided close to 100 per cent support. This power wielded by independents is largely unrelated to their numbers in parliament and their support levels among the electorate. The key factor is the distribution of seats between the parties, and the presence of obvious majority coalitions. Thus, with just a handful of seats in the early 1980s, independents had considerable bargaining power. In contrast, despite achieving their highest seat return since 1948 in 2002, and since 1927 in 2011, independents had no such power as majority governments were elected.

The outside perception is that this influence afforded independents creates instability and is not a desirable outcome. For example, Farrell in a commissioned report for Davy stockbrokers on the Irish political landscape in 2015 outlined four possible scenarios after the next election, one of which was 'a minority and unstable government' (2015, 1) that would rely on independents. As has been outlined in this chapter, the assumption that minority status and instability go hand in hand is misplaced. It is correct that some minority governments have not even lasted one year, but it is also true that some have lasted five years. Some governments that struggled to run the economy have been minority administrations, but so too have governments that managed economic recovery and unprecedented economic prosperity also been of this ilk. On average, minority governments that have relied on independents have lasted almost three years, shorter than majority administrations, but still quite a reasonable length by any comparative measure. The behaviour of independents when their vote is needed in parliament, as graphically illustrated in Figures 7.2 and 7.3, can be quite supportive of minority governments. This indicates an element of rationality on the part of independents, because if they did not provide consistent support, they might become a byword for instability and be the target of negative attacks from their political opponents and the electorate. In addition, instability could bring about an early election, which independents do not favour, so it could be a rational act of self-preservation. If independents can provide solid and consistent support for governments, it portrays a public image of a reliable political actor, which means parties will court their support in the future, which then facilitates delivering more patronage for the independents' constituencies.

The instability that can ensue from some minority governments is not necessarily the direct product of unyielding independents. Rather, a contributory factor is also parties' mismanagement of the situation, whether with the independents or each other. Having swallowed their principle of nonpartisanship to support such administrations, it would not make sense for independents to desire an early end with an election – particularly since they could lose their position of influence at best, and their seat at worst. Indeed, there is a strong element of rationality concerning the entire process of minority governments reliant on independents. It suits the parties in power because they do not have to share the spoils. It is a lot easier to buy off an independent than a party. It is also a lot easier to put pressure on an independent than a party. No one wants to be the fall guy for the collapse of a government. Holding the balance of power also suits independents as it affords them leverage vis-à-vis the government, which they would otherwise not have. This also enables them to justify the rationality of a vote for them from their local electorates. Because the independents have coalition or blackmail potential, they have a clear role in the political process, which grants them relevance. This permissiveness of independents means they are not considered an irrationality, as they can wield tangible influence. This is a primary factor in explaining the significance of independents in the Irish political system.

Notes

1 Rice's Index of Cohesion was first outlined in Stuart A. Rice, 1924. *Farmers and Workers in American Politics*. New York: Columbia Univesity Studies in the Social Sciences (no. 253).
2 Ahern's agreement with Healy-Rae is published in full in Hickey (2015, 80–5).
3 These figures relate only to motions in which independents cast a vote. This is because an abstention could be interpreted in a number of ways: it could be support for the government if this is all the latter requires; an actual expression of non-support; the TD may simply have missed the vote and may have been paired with another TD; or the issue may have no relevance to the independent.

Introduction

The core thesis of this study is that independents are not an aberrant, irrational feature of the Irish political system. They have maintained a continuous presence in a stable party democracy because, unlike in other polities, the system is permissive of them. This permissiveness can occur via electoral rules, political norms, the structure of party competition and the attitude of political actors in terms of their willingness to incorporate independents into the political system. These factors all act to facilitate independents in Ireland, accounting for why it has an exceptional number in its national parliament.

These factors have been discussed in terms of a series of five premises throughout this study. The first was that the presence of independents is related to the openness of the party system; the second that it is due to a tradition of electoral success for independents; the third that there is a conducive political culture; the fourth that this is facilitated by a candidate-centred electoral system; while the fifth premise is that independents have relevance because of the decisive role they play in the formation of governments. So far in this study each of these explanations has been examined in a piecemeal fashion, using different datasets and engaging in some comparative analysis. The aim of this penultimate chapter is to bring together these factors, as well as a few others, to examine their collective influence on the presence of independents. Specifically, these other factors include the size of the country and parliament, and another aspect of the party system – the unstructured nature of party competition. The influence of both size and the party system on independents are discussed in more detail in the following section. Following this, and maintaining the theme of rationality, a number of hypotheses are constructed from the aforementioned five premises to determine what affects independents' significance. These are tested on the Irish case using an original dataset comprising three decades' worth of constituency-level material. The final section concludes with an evaluation of what explains the apparent paradox of a strong non-party presence in a stable party democracy.

Size and party system

What explains the significance of independents? Five contributory factors have so far been discussed, but there are two other relevant variables, both of which have been referred to indirectly. The first concerns size, of both the polity and the parliament, while the second is to do with the structure of party competition.

Beginning with size, in a jurisdiction with either a small population or territory, the levels of personal interaction are higher than in larger communities, and there is usually a greater premium placed on face-to-face contact (Anckar 2000). Such a culture, combined with a small-sized society, reduces the necessity of parties, which are not needed as heuristic cues or to mobilise voters. This in part explains the absence of parties in the pre-nineteenth century, when the limited suffrage meant that candidates had little need for party organisation to mobilise support. Instead it was assumed that the strength of a candidate's name was enough of a voting cue (Cox 1987). Small societies are also likely to be more homogeneous, with fewer social divisions, further reducing the need for political parties (Anckar and Anckar 2000). In general, therefore, we might expect independents to be more prevalent the smaller the society (below a particular threshold). The absence of parties in the small islands in the Pacific and the territorial governments cited in the introductory chapter lends credence to this hypothesis. For example, one study of thirty-one small island states indicates that eight of them lack political parties (Anckar 2000). The third means by which size can affect independents relates to parliament. In general, the smaller the assembly, the fewer the pay-offs arising from the formation of a party. In small arenas it might be easier and more beneficial for members to form temporary coalitions; this would allow them to reap both the benefits of collective action in parliament and non-partisanship in the electoral arena. Sharman (2013) cites the size of the Tasmanian Legislative Council (fifteen members) as a potential explanation for why independents have always been in the majority; a similar case could be made for all the aforementioned Pacific states and territorial governments. While there are many other small assemblies controlled by parties, all those with a dominant presence of independents are small.

Does size help independents in Ireland? Although the country's population and territory might classify it as 'large' compared to Pacific island states, it is still considered small from a comparative point of view. Twenty-two of the other thirty-six industrial democracies have a population that exceeds Ireland's 4.5 million inhabitants; twenty-five have a larger territory. The experience of independents in other small states in Europe, however, indicates that smallness is not a sufficient condition for electoral success. Luxembourg, Cyprus, Malta, Latvia, Estonia and Slovenia all have smaller populations and territories but no independents. They are also absent in Israel, Belgium, the Netherlands and Switzerland, all of which have smaller jurisdictions than Ireland. Although the Irish parliament is small (158 members) – only ten industrial democracies have a smaller lower house – it far exceeds the size of the Tasmanian Legislative Council or the Pacific assemblies, parliamentary chambers with a dominant independent presence. It is certainly too large for members interested in forming governments to consider an independent status as a rational option; assembling temporary coalitions of eighty independent members would be an unenviable and unlikely task. When assessing the comparative influence of size, it needs to be borne in mind that there are a number of intervening variables affecting the emergence of independents in many of the small states cited. These include the prohibition of independent candidacies, or some, such as Israel and the Netherlands, using extremely large constituencies (the whole country in these cases). Such factors negate the possible consequences of the countries' small size. In contrast, Ireland uses relatively small constituencies, and in the small, close-knit communities political competition is quite candidate-centred (Marsh et al. 2008), giving independents with an established profile and local reputation a reasonable chance of winning a seat. For example, the average number of first-preference votes for winning candidates at the 2016 Dáil election was 8,189, a figure not beyond the bounds of possibility for a candidate with a considerable local profile, whether party or independent.

The role of the party system has been discussed in Chapters 2 and 3 in relation to its openness. Where gaps in the electoral market appear, independents can rush in where parties fear to tread. However, there is another aspect to consider concerning the openness of the party system. This concerns the nature of party competition. In general, the weaker the parties and the social cleavages that bind the party system in place, the stronger the expected independent presence. This is because the weaker the premium placed on party affiliation, the greater the incentive to choose an independent status rather than form or join a party (Bolleyer and Weeks 2009). This is the case in some Pacific island states (Anckar and Anckar 2000), in some of the former Soviet republics, and is still particularly the case in Russia (Hale 2005). This argument can also be applied to party organisation. The more decentralised the party structure and the weaker the organisation in terms of its ability to offer loyalty-inducing incentives (in the form of patronage for example), the more likely we are to see politicians veer between party and independent status. Indeed, we can go one step further to argue that an independent presence is often the product of internal party dynamics; the more cohesive matters are within a party, the less likely we are to see party dissidents break away to run as independents. As was discussed in Chapter 3, this was particularly prevalent with the case of the Liberal Democratic Party in Japan, as significant numbers of 'Liberal Democrat Independents' have run when there was internal party strife.

The importance of social cleavages, such as a church–state or owner–worker divide, in structuring party competition has been well established (Lipset and Rokkan 1967). Parties compete on issues emanating from these cleavages, appealing to particular sides of a social conflict. In a system where the roots of such a conflict run deep and political competition is consequently polarised, loyalty to parties can be quite fixed, making it difficult for anyone outside the political system, such as independents, to gain an electoral foothold. Conversely, a party system not built on deep social cleavages is more fluid and open to the emergence of challengers. Of course, if there is a persistent electoral phenomenon such as independents, it might suggest that their continuance is not simply due to weak social cleavages, but that it is in fact the presence of a cleavage – or at least a social divide – that binds their support in place. It has been shown in the case of Russia, for example, that the success of some independents rests on their ability to exploit a centre–regional conflict by appealing to local interests (Gallo 2004).

The evidence from Ireland is not so clear cut. Indeed, this is what makes the case of an independent presence there all the more puzzling. Irish parties appear strong organisations, tightly disciplined and prone to increasingly centralised power structures (Weeks 2010b, 298). Although there are defections from parties, they quite often tolerate the existence of such independents because it rids them of volatile and disruptive members (and without losing a vote in parliament, since dissident parliamentarians often vote for their party of origin (Hansen 2010, 653–4)). That being said, the degree of strength of parties has been a source of some dispute, with some such as Katz (1980, 180) and Sacks (1976, 61) questioning how deep parties' roots run. The argument is that parties are superimposed onto 'parochial attachments'

(Sacks 1976, 61), and that they are essentially groupings of independents brought together for rational reasons. If this is the case, it implies that everyone is a virtual independent (Katz 1980, 108).

Although the Irish party system is not weak – in fact, it was remarkably stable up until the earthquake election of February 2011 – there are no obvious social cleavages structuring party competition. As noted in Chapter 5, Whyte (1974) famously describes it as 'politics without social bases'. For example, even at the height of the divisions in the early 1920s, when the issue of the recently ended civil war (the progenitor of the party system) was most to the fore, the mean level of support for the non-civil war options at the first three general elections in the new state (1922, 1923, 1927) was 40 per cent. The consequence of this is an open political system that caters for challengers such as independents.

As with the factors considered in the previous chapters, there is an element of rationality to the manner in which both the size and the structure of party system competition affect independents. The reason why parties are not present in small assemblies or polities is simply because they may not be needed. The problems that parties help to resolve, such as social choice or collective action, may not arise in small, homogeneous settings. In terms of the party system, if independents are more likely to emerge the weaker the social cleavages, it implies a form of strategic behaviour on their part. Maintaining the overarching theory concerning the importance of permissiveness, both size and a party system with strong social roots suppress the emergence of independents in most regimes. There is some evidence to suggest that this does not happen in Ireland, although the importance of size varies. Taking into account these two variables, plus political culture and electoral rules which have already been discussed in Chapters 5 and 6, the following section employs a more rigorous methodological test using constituency-level data.

Explaining the independent presence

A range of factors that affect the presence of independents in Ireland has been separately examined in this study, from the party system, to the electoral system, to the political culture, to independents' strong electoral tradition, to their influence in supporting governments. In this section, all these factors are considered collectively to assess their relative importance on the emergence of independents (the numbers of candidates running independent) and support for them. This is done in a systematic fashion using aggregate (constituency)-level data from Irish general elections between 1981 and 2011. As with the analysis in

Table 8.1 *Hypotheses on an independent presence*

Factor	Hypothesis
Size	H1: The smaller the constituency and electorate, the stronger the presence of independents.
Political culture	H2: The higher the level of personalism and localism and the lower the level of party attachment, the stronger the presence of independents.
Protest	H3: The lower the level of support for more ideological parties, the stronger the presence of independents.
Electoral rules	H4: The lower the electoral threshold the stronger the presence of independents.
Party system	H5: The lower the level of party system institutionalisation, the stronger the presence of independents.
	H6: The more open the electoral market the stronger the presence of independents.
	H7: The greater the centre–periphery divide the stronger the presence of independents.
Government influence	H8: Support for independents is greater after they have helped form a government.

Chapter 5 on individual-level data, independents are not subdivided into the categories suggested in Chapter 3 because this would reduce the number of cases to unmanageable levels and would lessen the generalisability of the findings. To test the influence of these factors, a number of hypotheses are constructed to determine the causes of an independent challenge to parties. These are detailed in Table 8.1 and build on the central premises of this study.

More specific details about the construction of these hypotheses are in the appendix to this chapter, but the logic and reasoning behind them is as follows.

Size: It was discussed in Chapter 6 on the electoral system and earlier in this chapter how small sizes should help independents. In particular, this variable measures the influence of the size of the constituency, both in terms of geography and electorate.

Political culture: It was shown in Chapter 5 and in this chapter how significant political culture is to the presence of independents, particularly in terms of the importance of personalism, localism and party detachment. This is measured here by the mean transfer rates between running-mates within the main political parties (Fianna Fáil, Fine Gael and Labour) at elections. It is a valid proxy for all three cultural features, because the higher the transfer rates, presumably the higher the levels of party attachment, whereas lower rates are driven by localistic and personalistic forces that run counter to party loyalism. Thus, higher intra-party solidarity means higher party attachment and lower levels of personalism and localism, which should be associated with lower support for independents.

Protest: The protest element to the independent vote was discussed in Chapter 5 in terms of disaffection and alienation. However, there is another aspect to consider, namely in terms of whether a vote for independents can be a conservative protest vote. From a comparative perspective, protest voters are usually drawn to more extreme parties on the right or left. In Ireland, such parties have not been very common; the more ideological anti-establishment parties that have made an electoral impact have generally been confined to the left. Irish voters wanting to make a protest with their ballot have therefore primarily two choices: a left-wing party or an independent. Given the stigma that has been attached to left-wing politics in a country that was up until recent decades dominated by a catholic, rural way of life, in many cases this reduced the protest option to independents. It can thus be hypothesised that the independent vote is a protest that voters are more likely to choose in regions where left-wing politics has little support. Where left-wing politics is more pervasive (measured by the mean support for left-wing parties – there being no openly far right parties in Ireland) we can expect to see a weaker independent vote due to the additional competition faced by the latter.

Electoral rules: Because this is a case study, there is little point including a measure of assembly size, ballot requirements or ballot design, all of which are constant across Irish constituencies. What can be used to measure the impact of electoral rules, which was the topic of Chapter 6, is the effective electoral threshold (Taagepera and Shugart 1989), which is the percentage of votes that will most likely secure representation. This is formally calculated as 75/(number of seats in constituency+1). Under STV in Ireland, the Droop quota for election is 100/(magnitude+1), but in many cases the winner of the last seat does not reach this quota.

Party system: This was discussed in a number of chapters, including Chapters 2 and 3. Three features of the party system are examined here, all of which relate back to the central hypotheses concerning the openness of the party system. The first relates to its degree of institutionalisation. The more institutionalised the party system, the more deep-rooted the social cleavages binding it in place, and the less likely independents are to attract support. To measure institutionalisation, the proxy used is electoral volatility at the previous election, replicating the methodology of Lago and Martinez (2011) in their analysis of new party emergence. Volatility is measured using the Pedersen index (1983), which is half the sum of individual party gains and losses of votes, which represents the net shift in vote changes. Lower levels of volatility indicate higher levels of party institutionalisation, as voters are less likely to switch between parties, which makes it more difficult for independents to make a breakthrough.

The second feature related to the party system is the capacity of the electoral market to cater for demand. Again replicating the methodology of Lago and Martinez (2011), it can be hypothesised that the larger the gap in the market, the more likely we are to see support for independents. This relates to the hypothesis discussed in Chapter 2 that independents occupy a space absented by parties. The market gap is measured by turnout, where lower turnout indicates a more open market, since it can be surmised that the greater the level of dissatisfaction with the electoral market, the less likely voters are to cast a ballot. Consequently, the lower the turnout, the greater the opportunity for independents.

The third feature, which was already discussed in this chapter, relates to the importance of social cleavages, which structure a party system. A continuous presence of independents can indicate something that binds them in place, a social divide perhaps. Similar to the already mentioned example of Russia, although it could not be called a conflict, a centre–periphery divide exists in Ireland. This is not geographic; rather, it refers to a socio-economic gap between the 'haves' and the 'have-nots'. Although this may not be a full-blown cleavage in the sense that it was defined by Lipset and Rokkan (1967), it is a divide that is very much evident in the rhetoric of voters and politicians from the peripheries. For example, when a new Dáil met following the 1997 election, in his opening speech one independent TD (Harry Blaney) stated that his county was 'marginalised more than any other ... it has the highest rate of unemployment in the country and the lowest income per head of population. One of the main reasons for this is the neglect of the county by all governments and state agencies' (Dáil debates 480: 48, 26 June 1997). Another (Tony Gregory) said that his constituency has 'some of the most disadvantaged communities, socially and economically, anywhere in the country' (Dáil debates 480: 36, 26 June 1997). As is evident from these examples, independents appeal to those on the peripheries, who feel neglected by the political parties and are frustrated at their disadvantaged status. It can therefore be hypothesised that the larger the centre–periphery divide, the greater the support for independents. A number of measures could be utilised for this divide, such as government spending per constituency, but such data are not readily available and, even if they were, evidence of this may not be clearly observ able to voters. More tangible and obvious measures include the unemployment rate, the numbers attending third-level education and the socio-economic occupational class divisions. Data on GDP per capita was included in preliminary analyses (where it was found to have a significant effect), but was excluded in the final analysis owing to its unavailability for the pre-1990 era.

Government influence: The final factor to consider stems from Chapter 7, which examined the influence independents can wield in the process of government formation. It was discussed that this gives independents a relevance which helps justify support for them. Consequently, the expectation here is that support for independents should be higher at an election immediately following a parliament in which they had helped sustain the government, although limited evidence for this was found in Chapter 7.

To test these eight hypotheses, data is drawn from the constituency level at ten national parliamentary elections in Ireland between 1981 and 2011. With just over forty constituencies per election, this produces 415 cases for analysis. Further details on the data are provided in the appendix. All the variables for inclusion relate to the hypotheses listed in Table 8.1. One additional factor that was not discussed, and was the subject of Chapter 3 is the tradition of support for independents. A strong independent vote may reflect an already established independent presence, so to cater for this effect, variables measuring the level of support for independents at the previous election and the mean number of independent candidates per constituency are included. Table 8.3, detailing summary statistics for each of these variables, is included in the appendix. These variables are used in two models to explain the independent presence in Ireland, where the latter is measured by support for independents and the numbers of independent candidates. This is the subject of the next section.

Results

To test the hypotheses and the significance of the various factors discussed in this book on the presence of independents, two models are considered here: one on their vote, and one on the number of independent candidates running at Dáil elections. These are similar to the models used to explain support for independents in Chapter 5 and the effects of the electoral system in Chapter 6. More details on the statistical methods and the results are in the appendix. The results and their implications for the hypotheses are summarised in Table 8.2. Beginning with independent voters, although territorial size has no significant effect, the size of the electorate is important and has a significant negative impact (H1), in line with our expectation: the more voters independent candidates have to canvass, the less support they attract, due to the logistics involved in campaigning in larger constituencies. Intra-party transfer solidarity has the predicted negative effect, confirming that decreasing levels of party attachment helps independents (H2). In other words, the lower the level of party-centred action, the more inclined people are to vote for independents. There also appears to be evidence supporting the hypothesis concerning the protest element of the independent vote for those with an anathema to left-wing parties (H3), which was evident in the 2016 Dáil election when protest voters oriented towards more left-wing parties in urban areas and independents in rural areas. It seems that the independent vote is partially a conservative protest action. The size of the electoral threshold needed to win a seat makes little difference to independent voters (H4), as support for them is independent of the required electoral quota. In terms of the importance of the party system, neither the electoral market (measured by turnout) (H5) nor the level of institutionalisation of the party system (measured by volatility) (H6) seem to matter. There is only mixed support for the importance of the centre–periphery divide (H7) in explaining the independent vote. Some socio-economic variables were found to have an effect on support for independents, but not all in the predicted direction. While higher levels of unemployment have a positive effect on support for independents, as does the proportion of unskilled workers, increased numbers of those with third-level education results in a higher independent vote, contrary to our expectations. In terms of the final hypothesis (H8), a role in government formation has a positive effect on support for independents.

Broadly similar results were found for independent emergence, with some slight, but notable, differences. Size again matters, both in terms

Table 8.2 *Summary of hypotheses*

	H1		H2	H3	H4	H5	H6	H7	H8		
Hypotheses	Size		Culture	Protest	Electoral system	Party system	Electoral market	Centre–periphery cleavage	Influence on government		
Variables	*Electorate*	*Area*	*Transfer solidarity*	*Left-wing vote*	*Threshold*	*Volatility*	*Turnout*	*Unemp- loyment*	*3rd level*	*ABC*	*D*
Voters	−	−	−	−				+	+	+	+
Candidates	−	−	−	−	−			+	+		

Note: − signifies a significant negative effect, + a significant positive effect.

of the electorate and the size of the constituency (H1). The effective threshold has a significant negative effect on the numbers of independents running (H4), implying that the more votes needed to win a seat, the fewer independents run. Support for left-wing candidates (H3) and turnout (H6) at the preceding election have no such effect. The former result indicates the lack of a protest element to the numbers running as independents, and likewise the institutionalisation of the party system (volatility) (H5) is not a significant factor. In terms of the socio-economic measures (H7), third-level education reverses its effect, with higher levels resulting in fewer independent candidates. Unemployment does not have a significant effect, but higher proportions of ABC professionals are associated with more independents. As with voters, an influence on minority governments has a positive effect for the emergence of independent candidates (H8).

What do all these results mean for the wider study? To reiterate the five premises that have been the focus of this study, an independent presence is said to be the product of an established voting tradition for them, of a conducive political culture, of an open party system, of favourable electoral rules, and of a relevance attained from their involvement in the formation of governments. Returning to Table 8.2, this facilitates an assessment of the contribution of all these factors by its conclusions regarding the various hypotheses tested. One factor that was not a key premise, but which was discussed in this chapter, concerns the importance of small size. There is reasonable evidence for this hypothesis; both smaller geography and electorate matter for candidates, but just the latter for voters. In terms of political culture, the proxy measure of higher levels of intra-party solidarity has a negative effect for independents, implying that personalism and party detachment do have a positive effect on independents' presence, repeating one of the key findings of Chapter 5 on the independent voter. In terms of the protest element to the latter, while support for independents is negatively correlated with a left-wing vote, it does not matter for candidates, which is not surprising since this hypothesis concerning the protest element centred on voters. This is different to the findings in Chapter 5 over the importance of protest, which found that alienation and disaffection are not significant. However, we are not dealing with protest motivations here, rather just a protest as a non-ideological conservative option statement. Independents' non-partisan status thus helps them to attract support from party voters who, although disaffected, prefer not to vote for a rival party.

The electoral system was the subject of Chapter 6, and here it was found that electoral rules matter for independent candidates, but not for voters, probably because the former have more at stake, but also because the strategic decision primarily rests with them, not voters. This is in line with Chapter 6, which although it explored this relationship in more detail, also had mixed results concerning the importance of the electoral system. Three other hypotheses related to the party system, which was discussed in Chapters 2 and 3, where it was found that its state of openness is a key factor. In this chapter, the evidence was not convincing, as the hypotheses tested cannot be accepted. Both factors of the institutionalisation of the party system (as measured by volatility) and the openness of the electoral market (as measured by turnout) by and large have insignificant effects. One other feature of the party system concerned whether the independent presence is structured on a social cleavage, specifically a centre–periphery divide. Of the four variables used to measure this in each of the two models, only three of the eight have a significant effect in the predicted direction. Obviously, four variables are not enough to measure the depth of a socio-economic division. It may be that the divide is not as important as imagined, or that it has not been captured accurately by these variables, or that independents do not profit from this divide. For now, we do not have enough evidence to determine if the independent presence is the product of a social conflict.

The final hypothesis concerned the importance of the influence independents wield over parties in the government formation process. As discussed in Chapter 7, it was argued that this gives independents a key relevance, and so it was hypothesised that at an election immediately after a period in which they have exerted such relevance, we are likely to see a stronger presence of independents. This was confirmed for both independent candidates and voters. One result not included in the table because it was not a specific hypothesis concerns the importance of an independent presence, one of the five central premises in this book in terms of the electoral tradition of independents. It was found that this makes a difference to both voters and candidates, with both the number of independent candidates and the independent vote at the previous election having a positive effect on support for independents and the numbers running on this label (see Table 8.4 in the appendix for more details of this).

Conclusion

Relating these findings to the comparative world, we can say that independents are more likely to emerge in smaller populations, while geography and thresholds do not necessarily matter. Hence

independent candidates have been elected in large single-seat constituencies in Australia, Canada and the US. What contributes to
an independent presence is a conducive personalistic and localistic
political culture where attachments to parties are not as embedded
as elsewhere. Hence the proliferation of independents across some
South Pacific island states. Independents are obviously a protest vote,
particularly in systems with electoral market failure and where there
is a clear political vacuum. They are also an option that may be more
appealing in countries such as Australia, Ireland, the UK and the US
where extreme ideological parties have traditionally had little electoral
impact. Finally, a strong and persistent presence of independents, such
as in Russia or Ireland, suggests that they may be no flash-in-the-pan
protest vote, and that they may be indicative of a deeper political
division.

Relating the findings back to the central thesis of this study concerning the permissiveness of independents in Ireland, evidence was found
to support most of the five premises stated in Chapter 1. A tradition
and presence, electoral rules, political culture and relevance in parliament vis-à-vis government all matter, while the influence of the party
system is mixed. Given that most of these hypotheses are constructed
from single variables, it is best to be cautious over a decision to reject
or accept them. That the party system may have been found not to
matter as much as expected may be more a weakness in the indicators
used to measure this variable. What can be said is that the evidence
is generally supportive of most of the arguments made about the permissiveness of independents in Ireland. This is the dominant factor
that explains their significance. Having detailed the extent of this significance and considered a range of causes throughout this study, the
final chapter draws a number of conclusions about independents. It
also addresses a wider and perhaps more important issue, which is the
normative value of independents, and whether they are good or bad
for party democracy.

Appendix to Chapter 8

Statistical analysis

The analysis in this chapter is based on aggregate-level data from Dáil electoral constituencies, drawn from official publications of electoral statistics and from Christopher Took and Seán Donnelly's website electionsireland.org. The economic data was sourced from annual reports of the Irish Central Statistics Office (cso.ie). The variables for analysis are: territorial size of constituencies, size of electorate, effective threshold, intra-party solidarity, left-wing party support, electoral volatility, turnout, unemployment rate, proportion with a third-level qualification, proportion of ABC (employers, higher and lower professionals) and D (semi- and unskilled) workers, support for independents at the previous election, the number of independent candidates running, and a dummy variable measuring if independents were involved in the government formation process in the previous Dáil.

Table 8.3 contains summary statistics for these variables. Constituencies are pretty small in size, with the largest less than 6,000 square kilometres and the smallest just 28 square kilometres. The mean vote is a significant 7 per cent, reaching a high of over 40 per cent in some cases, a considerable feat in multi-member contests. The decline in both turnout and intra-party solidarity and the rise in electoral volatility in recent years are perhaps indicative of the declining linkages between parties and the electorate. There is considerable variation in the socio-economic indicators, evidence that tentatively supports the hypothesised socio-economic divide. With the measures of an independent presence being the support for independents and the numbers of independent candidates, these dependent variables are used in two separate regression models, which are detailed in Table 8.4.

Both models are ordinary least squares regressions, with the first column of figures based on the vote for independents as the dependent variable, and the second using the numbers of independent candidates. The reported coefficients indicate the change in each

Table 8.3 *Summary statistics per constituency level, 1981–2011*

Variable	Mean	Range
Size (km^2)	1,730	28–5,772
Electorate	54,995	26,158–88,522
Effective threshold (%)	15.6	12.5–18.75
Independent vote	7.3	0–42
Independent candidates	2.4	0–14
Intra-party solidarity	66.4	36–88
Left-wing vote	23.9	0–68
Volatility at previous election	16.2	0.5–50.5
Turnout at previous election	67.8	52–81
Unemployment rate	12.0	3.6–27.1
3rd level education	14.7	0.7–63
ABC occupation	21.5	1.3–55.4
D occupation	12.5	1.3–23.1

Author's figures calculated from various issues of *Election results and transfer of votes for Dáil and bye-elections*. Dublin: Stationery Office; Central Statistics Office accessed at www.cso.ie.

Table 8.4 *Models of independent significance*

Variable	Model 1 Vote	Model 2 Candidates
Size (km^2)	0.0003(0.0003)	−1e-5(1e-5)
Electorate	−1e-4(4e-4)*	−3e-5(2e-5)*
Effective threshold	0.01(0.23)	−0.37(0.09)***
Independent vote, election-1	0.36(0.04)***	0.04(0.02)*
Independent candidates	1.16(0.14)***	–
Intra-party solidarity	−0.08(0.05)*	−0.05(0.01)***
Left-wing vote	−0.13(0.03)***	0.005(0.01)
Volatility, election-1	−0.04(0.04)	−0.005(0.02)
Turnout, election-1	−0.08(0.05)	−0.03(0.02)
Unemployment	0.30(0.07)***	0.007(0.03)
Third-level education	0.10(0.05)*	−0.06(0.02)***
ABC	0.05(0.07)	0.07(0.03)**
D	0.23(0.10)*	0.02(0.04)
Independents in government	1.83(0.61)***	−0.39***
Constant	6.51(8.06)	14.25(2.97)***
N	415	415
R^2	0.45	0.19

Note: Standard errors are in parentheses. Significance levels: *$p < 0.05$, **$p < 0.01$, ***$p < 0.001$

Author's figures calculated from various issues of *Election results and transfer of votes for Dáil and bye-elections*. Dublin: Stationery Office; Central Statistics Office accessed at www.cso.ie.

dependent variable associated with a one-unit change in the independent variable (the vote for independents in model one, and the number of independent candidates in model two). The asterisks indicate which effects are likely not to be the product of random sampling error.

9

Conclusion

Introduction

The presence of non-party parliamentarians in a mature and stable party democracy is the puzzle that this study has sought to solve. While independents are present in transition and semi-democracies, and also at local levels of government, it is very unusual to have them in the national parliament of a mature democracy. That being said, the numbers choosing to run as independents, the electoral support they receive and the numbers elected are all on the rise in the comparative sense. This poses a number of important challenges to parliamentary democracy, primarily because of the manner in which it has evolved to become party democracy. The consequences are that without parties, such regimes would be unlikely to survive. Given their opposition to the party way of life, it seems logical to infer that independents threaten to undermine party democracy. For this reason, it is important to understand the contributing factors to an independent presence. This final chapter summarises the various arguments discussed in the previous eight chapters, but also considers the normative value of independents, taking into account the consequences they can pose for party democracy. This constitutes the latter section of this chapter, which assesses the merit of a number of accusations made against independents, based on the evidence used in this study.

Explaining independents' presence

It was shown throughout this study that independents' significance in Ireland is pretty much an outlier, as there are more independent parliamentarians in the Dáil than the combined total in all other Western democracies. It was also shown, however, that these independents are not a uniform category, and that their nature varies, both with time and context. This was further detailed in the contributions by independent politicians, both past and present.

269

Bax began his work on machine politics in Ireland with the words 'to many the Irish are almost a byword for political irrationality' (1976, 1). The presence in Ireland of a politician long considered irrelevant, if not extinct, in most democracies would seem to support this argument. However, this is not necessarily the case, as it has been shown that there is a strong rational thread running through the factors that explain the presence of independents. The overarching thesis to this study is that this significance is because the factors that act to suppress independents in other systems are absent in the Irish case. It is quite the opposite, in fact, as conditions are permissive of independents in Ireland and a range of factors facilitate their emergence, including political norms, electoral rules, an electoral tradition, the party system and their role in parliament. Because these all work to independents' advantage in terms of producing conducive conditions, there is a rational underpinning to their emergence. For example, Aldrich (1995, 145–6) describes three forces in nineteenth-century America that pushed politicians towards parties: people voted for party rather than candidate, the institutional electoral rules were favoured towards parties and there was little chance of having influence as an independent. As has been shown in this study, none of these forces are present in Ireland, which explains why some choose not to pursue the party path. It does not necessarily further their goals.

In a political culture where the candidate is to the fore, working in tandem with an open party system and a favourable institutional setting, it is logical to expect to see a greater independent presence than in systems with unfavourable conditions where independents are suppressed. When these are combined with an opportunity to play a role as kingmaker in the formation and maintenance of governments, and bring home the bacon for their constituencies, it is no wonder that independents have had a continued presence in Ireland. Indeed, given the increasingly marginal position of the backbencher, the limited opportunities to contribute to policy within the party, the high levels of party discipline and the increased importance of the personal organisation – over the party machine – in getting elected, the question could be changed from 'why independent' to 'why not more independents'? An aspiring party candidate might have to wait years to acquire any influence within a party, first having to secure a nomination, then an election and then bide time as a backbencher. Instead, a quick route to influence is to run as an independent and wait for a minority government (which has been the form of more than 50 per cent of administrations since 1981). Leaving the party does not have the negative impact that would result from such an act under a party-centred list electoral system or a plurality version using single-seat constituencies. A party dissident can retain his or her seat under STV. In addition, the option remains to rejoin the party in the future. The rationality of the independent status is perhaps best highlighted by former independent TD Jackie Healy-Rae. As is detailed in Chapter 7, he was a one-time Fianna Fáil councillor who failed to secure a party nomination for the 1997 general election, ran independent, was elected, and was then a crucial vote in getting the minority Fianna Fáil–Progressive Democrat government into power, a role he held again after the 2007 election. Had Healy-Rae remained within Fianna Fáil, and even been added to the ticket in 1997, it is most unlikely he would have ever held the influence he ultimately wielded over two administrations. Indeed, confirmation of this hypothesis came in the form of the many complaints from Fianna Fáil TDs about his influence. Following Healy-Rae's securing of EU Objective One funding for his constituency in 1998, one Fianna Fáil backbencher said, 'There is no point in being a Fianna Fáil backbencher anymore. Jackie Healy-Rae is running the show. He is running Fianna Fáil. It's kind of obvious. That's the way it seems … It is a terrible blow to every Fianna Fáil backbencher if Jackie Healy-Rae can do that. Jackie Healy-Rae has all the clout' (McGarry 1998).

Independents pop up in many parliaments from time to time but in almost all cases they comprise dissident party MPs. These have not been elected as independents and they usually join a party before the next parliament. In the few occasions where they decide to run as an independent, it is even rarer that they get elected. For example, in the lifetime of the 2010–15 British House of Commons, there were twelve different independent members, with just one of those elected as an independent MP. There were five independents at dissolution in 2015, with just one returned to the new parliament. This is what makes their presence in Ireland all the more unusual. Although a considerable number of independents elected in Ireland have a history of involvement in one party or another, this is not unexpected because party remains central to political life and is the first path of entry for most politicians. There is no independent organisation to join in most towns or in university, so it is only natural that those politically inclined gravitate towards parties. Everyone has a history, and while the media in Ireland tend to have a preoccupation about the gene pool of independents, this really is not of great concern to their independence. The so-called gene pool from which independents come does not always have a bearing on the party they would back in a minority government. In any case, none of these independents maintain their affiliation with a party once they leave. From this perspective, all the independents in

Ireland are 'pure' in the comparative sense of the term, as they run on their own and do not take a party whip if elected. As noted in Chapter 3, this is unlike many of the independents elected to the Japanese Diet, one of the few other national parliaments to which independents are regularly returned.

As an electoral, though not necessarily a legislative, phenomenon, independents have experienced a slight resurgence across liberal democracies in recent years. This has manifested itself in Martin Bell, the BBC war journalist, being elected in the UK in 1997, followed by Richard Taylor representing a local hospital group in 2001 and 2005. Bernie Sanders, who sought to be the Democratic nominee for the presidential election in the US in 2016, was elected as an independent to the US House of Representatives in Vermont from 1991 to 2007, before he was elected to the federal Senate in 2006 – replacing another independent, Jim Jeffords. There Sanders was joined by Joe Lieberman and, following the latter's retirement in 2013, former independent governor of Maine, Angus King, was also elected to the Senate. In Australia, independents re-emerged onto the federal stage in 1990, and in 2010 held a key role as kingmakers, replicating a position they have occupied at the state and territorial level in the same country in past decades.

The resurgence of independents in recent years in Ireland can therefore perhaps be viewed through this prism as part of a wider international rise of independents. However, it is stretching the comparative evidence too far to call it a rise, and in any case what is happening in Ireland is far greater than all these other countries combined. So while at the twelve Dáil elections between 1961 and 1997 the mean number of independents elected was just less than four, in 2002 it was thirteen, followed by a dip to five in 2007, before rising again to fourteen in 2011, following which support for them continued to rise in the run-up to the 2016 election, when twenty-three were elected. As discussed in Chapter 3, the Irish case is also different in that this is a resurgence of independents rather than a re-emergence, as they have had a continuous presence in the Irish parliament. In addition, as described in detail in Chapter 7, they have also been able to wield influence on a regular basis via the role they play vis-à-vis minority governments. Outside the Australian experience, independents occupying a role in the government formation process is a rare occurrence. This can make them irrelevant elsewhere, meaning people see little point to either run as, or vote for, an independent. So while tradition and norms act to suppress independents in other jurisdictions where politics is all about parties, this is not the case in Ireland, where independents are an embedded and recognised component of the country's political make-up, and even its culture. This is reflected in political satire, such as John B. Keane's *Letters of an Irish Minister of State* (1991), in which party TD Tull McAdoo runs as an independent. In more recent times, comedian Pat Shortt has played an independent councillor in a television comedy (*Killinaskully*) that ran for five series, and has written the diaries of another fictional independent, Maurice Hickey (2007). An award-winning comedy-drama, *The Running mate*, on the Irish language television station, TG4, in 2007 centred on a party councillor who runs as an independent against his one-time party colleague. While not all of these may be wholly positive portrayals of independents, the very fact that they are the subject of such satire at all is indicative of the presence independents have in the Irish political psyche. Far from being suppressed, they are cherished by some as the embodiment of the strength of localism and personalism over party. This is the next factor that is permissive of independents in Ireland, and was the subject of Chapter 5 on the independent voter.

In other countries, the norm of political behaviour centres on the party, which puts independents at a severe disadvantage. In Ireland, however, the personality of the candidate and what they can achieve for the locality are to the fore. Combined with a detachment from parties, this allows independents to compete on a more even keel with parties than is the case in other political systems. This political culture works in tandem with an equally facilitative electoral system to help independents, the fourth factor that is permissive of independents, which was the subject of Chapter 6. Electoral rules are one of the main agents of suppression for minor actors in most jurisdictions, but this is not the case in Ireland, which uses perhaps the most candidate-centred of all voting systems. However, the effects of STV are not wholly as expected, in particular concerning the consequences of the multi-member constituency. STV on its own does not produce independents, as is evident by their weakness in other jurisdictions using the same voting system. Rather, the operation of STV in tandem with other factors is what has a positive effect for independents. One of these factors considered in this study concerns the party system. Given the centrist, catch-all nature of the mainstream Irish parties, independents act in a rational, Downsian fashion to cater for groups and issues not represented by the parties. This was detailed in Chapter 2, where it was shown that there have been a wide range of different types of independents, depending on the issues of the day, but that they can rush in where parties are absent. Another aspect of the party system concerns its openness; that is, the fact that it does not have deep roots in terms of social cleavages – which was discussed in Chapters 2 and 8. The openness of the system has varied over time, and the more open the party system, the more likely independents are to emerge. The high levels of volatility among the Irish voter and declining levels of attachment in the early twentieth century are undoubtedly a contributory factor behind the rise of independents over this period. In general, the lack of cleavage-based competition is one reason why political competition has been more about personality and locality than ideology, but whatever the cause, it possibly affords independents a window of opportunity – although the evidence concerning this premise is mixed.

Taken together, we can see how these factors explain independents' presence in Irish party democracy. The party system, independents' record of electoral success, the political culture, the electoral system and independents' influence on minority governments combine to facilitate a culture permissive of independents. The party system, electoral behaviour and the voting system are structured in an open fashion to create possibilities for aspirant independent entrepreneurs. They do not need to be in a political party to have an impact. They can also tap into a historical tradition of support for independents, and can wield some influence in parliament, both of which indicate their relevance. This was never more evident than at the February 2016 Dáil election, when a record number of independents were elected, a record number voted for them, and they participated in the formation of government, ultimately occupying four seats in the new cabinet.

Generalising the findings beyond Ireland, the conditions under which independents emerge include favourable political norms, in particular a localistic and personalistic political culture, and an electorate detached from parties. This explains why independents are prevalent in newly forming democracies where party attachments are slow to form. While independents have had a slight emergence in mature democracies with dealigning electorates, this has been tempered by another relevant condition, a conducive electoral system. Given that STV is described as the most candidate-centred of all sets of electoral rules, it may well explain why parties are so reluctant to adopt this system. The party system is also a key factor. Where gaps in the electoral market appear, independents can represent voters not catered for by the parties. Equally, where party competition is not built on solid social structures, independents are at less of a disadvantage. With the erosion of the importance of social cleavages, this may contribute to an emergence of independents in some regimes. Finally, while it may be well and good to have conducive norms and institutions, if independents cannot have an impact, voters are unlikely to stick with them. Whether this is via patronage for their constituency or influence on government policy, independents need to offer a clear function and role to justify electoral support for them. This is especially the case given the party-centred nature of parliamentary democracy; independents need to be relevant.

One comparative arena in which independents are particularly present is the group of Pacific islands that lacks parties, as was discussed in Chapter 1. One of the arguments given for their absence is due to the 'premodern' nature of political development in this region, in that political competition is centred more on personalistic and tribalistic politics (Anckar and Anckar 2000), rather than party, ideology and social cleavages, as occurs in most 'modern' Western societies. As Dunphy (1995, 10–13) shows, it has been argued that the Irish political system exhibits features of premodernism, such as a 'peasant culture', where voters are attached to politicians rather than party or ideology and where clientelistic politics is to the fore. As in the Pacific, it can be argued that this culture is conducive to independents, and explains their persistence in Ireland. However, this thesis was not explored in greater detail in this study because there are a number of flaws in its reasoning. First, unlike the Pacific, Ireland has stable, durable and strong political parties that have dominated political competition, which we should not expect in a premodern culture. Further, the presence of independents has ebbed and flowed, and the economic development, or modernisation, since the 1980s, which in theory should not be conducive to independents, coincided with a steady rise in support for them. In addition, Ireland is not the only country to have high levels of clientelism and personalism, and yet the others where such features are present lack independents. Malta is a classic case of this, where despite a clientelistic and personalistic political culture in a smaller and more homogenous island than Ireland, and with a conducive electoral system, independents have zero political impact.

In the opening scene of the 1974 film *The Parallax View*, Senator and presidential hopeful Charles Carroll declares 'I've been called too independent for my own good' (Pakula 1974), his last words before he is assassinated. While an independent path may not have been rational for Carroll to pursue, this study has shown that a range of conducive conditions to run as an independent exist in Ireland, which makes their emergence a far more rational occurrence than in other political systems, especially if there is no party that caters for an aspirant's interests. Where in other systems such individuals would out of necessity have to join a party (Senator Carroll, for example), this is not the case in Ireland where independent-minded individuals can run, and be elected, as independents. As described by the collection of independents in Chapter 4, there is a range of motives explaining a decision to enter politics as an independent, but all the politicians recognise the contribution of different factors that permitted them to opt for an independent life. Under a different electoral system, a different set of political norms, in a parliament where they would be ostracised, or in a closed-party system, it is most likely these individuals would never have considered the independent option and consequently may not have even entered politics. So long as these conditions prevail, independents are likely to remain a core feature of the Irish political landscape.

Independents: good or bad?

This study has examined a number of factors behind the presence of independents in the Irish political system. However, the 'smoking gun' question that was briefly discussed in the introduction remains to be answered – what is the normative value of independents? To what extent are independents a positive feature of a modern democracy, or detrimental to its functionality? Just as the rise of populist parties has led some to fear the consequences for the stability of their respective polities, so too the presence of independents in Ireland has stimulated much discussion about their ability to undermine the functioning of the political system. As touched on in Chapters 1 and 7, the conventional wisdom among many commentators, political scientists and, not surprisingly, political parties, is that independents are bad for democracy. They see independents as virtual free-riders, who avoid the responsibility of governing, but at the same time wish to extract patronage from governments. They see independents as shirking responsibility by prioritising local over national interests, and adopting populist mantras that they know can never be adopted, but for which they will never be in a position to take responsibility. Such sentiment was summarised by Michael O'Leary, the chief executive of the Ryanair airline, following the February 2016 Dáil election:

> It's all very well for people electing the local lunatic … but we've got to be a bit more sensible … we need some stability. You can't elect either the local popularity contest [sic] or the local lunatic. Ultimately independents do nothing. Independents are grandstanders. They are not going to get into government. The worst governments we have had here are where they have been held to ransom by one or two independents … We can't keep voting for, and I've used the example, bankrupt property developers, to go in and run the country as independents. They're never going to run the country. We need sensible parties and parties with sensible policies. It's about time we as an electorate vote on the basis of sensible economic policies, not strangers promising us sweeties (RTÉ Radio 1, *Countrywide*, 16 April 2016).

Such concerns about independents were echoed in the memoirs of former Labour Party leader, Éamon Gilmore, who dismissed the possibility of a Fine Gael-led minority government in 2011, because it would have had to include 'a mixture of independents, many of whose national politics were either a mystery, or in marked contradiction to each other. And the country was in crisis, and needed a stable government, and fast!' (2015, 73). Likewise, in 2014 the political editor of the *Irish Times* claimed that if a large number of independent TDs were returned following the next Dáil election 'that would make the formation of the next government extremely difficult, if not impossible, and plunge the country into a phase of political instability, with unknown consequences' (Collins 2014). Independents are conscious of these concerns, and in the run-up to the 2016 Dáil election, they attempted to assuage fears about their influence. In one of his weekly *Sunday Independent* columns, independent TD Shane Ross claimed that:

The worst feature of Ireland's political culture is so-called party loyalty. The party system is Ireland's democratic demon ... The three big parties all play the same game. They are diseased. They have all bought into it. Party loyalty is the common thread. Loyalty to the citizens is a secondary consideration. The national interest comes in a bad third. The Dáil itself has been strangled by party loyalty (Ross 2014).

In the same column, Ross advocated the formation of an Independent Alliance (which he ultimately helped set up the following year) that could support a government if needed:

Contrary to anti-independent propaganda being spewed out presently, there would be no lack of stability. Independents would be a coherent group, united on core principles. A unique democratic vehicle would be created. Governments would not fall. We would not have an Italian situation ... Critics dismiss such heretical thoughts, insisting that legislation could be defeated regularly. Indeed it could. What would be more democratic? Independent TDs would be able to speak their minds in the Dáil, write their own speeches reflecting their own views and vote with their consciences. From time to time, legislation would be returned for improvement or repeal (Ross 2014).

Why did Ross feel the need to defend independents to this extent? Why are they held in such low esteem, as echoed in the sentiment of Michael O'Leary and Stephen Collins? Are the latter correct in their views concerning independents? There are a number of accusations that can be made against independents, some of which were outlined in the introductory chapter, and on which such negative sentiment is based. Six of the key criticisms of independents are detailed in the following section, which also includes an assessment of the merits of these particular arguments. The aim of this is to determine the value of independents for parliamentary democracy, and whether they pose a threat to the latter.

Criticisms of independents

1. Independents make it difficult to form a government
The first accusation against independents is that their being elected to parliament can deprive parties, or a combination of them, of an overall majority. This can lessen the possibilities concerning government formation, rendering the process more difficult. In addition, because they are oppositional politicians, independents might prefer to avoid responsibility and not help to form a government. Or, where they do wish to participate, their demands may be excessive.

It is true that whenever a single party fails to win an overall majority, government formation is that bit more difficult. However, it is not wholly clear why more independents would necessarily make the process more arduous, because negotiations between parties tend to be lengthier. If anything, independents can make the process of government formation somewhat easier, as they do not have to consult a parliamentary party or grass-roots members, which can sometimes be a stumbling block for, or at least slow down, inter-party discussions. This was particularly evident in 2016, when independents were willing to discuss forming a government before the votes had even been counted. In contrast, the two main parties took over six weeks before they began to talk, and when they concluded an agreement, it was independents who provided the necessary support to form a government. The other parties in the Dáil refused to back the re-election of Enda Kenny as Taoiseach, so without the independents there would have been a need for another election. In this way, independents' nonpartisanship that makes them amenable to coalition with most parties can help to resolve the stasis that results from electoral stalemate, preventing the frequent election cycles and changes of government that have occurred in Italy and Greece.

2. Independents cause instability
The second accusation concerns the level of instability that can ensue when minority governments look to independents rather than parties for external support. In the absence of a whip, independents are free to withdraw their support at any stage, and they can be under significant pressure from their local constituency to do so if the government

introduces unpopular initiatives with local repercussions. The consequence is that such a government might always be teetering on the edge, one step away from collapsing, with significant effects for the ability of the government to function and for the external perception of the stability of the national economy. Those who express such fears highlight the early 1980s as an example, when, as discussed in Chapter 7, there were three general elections in eighteen months in Ireland, as two minority governments reliant on independents survived less than one year, with one unable to get its fiscal budget passed.

Certainly, this threat of instability is a pressing issue that minority administrations have to face, and one which can undermine their ability to implement long-term strategies. It might also have the consequence that much of their time is spent in the form of day-to-day conflict management, the main aim of which is survival. Such a government might be likely to avoid the hard issues – those that are most in need of being resolved, but which could be more likely to contribute to its defeat.

This instability is also increased by the heterogeneity of the independents. It could be very difficult for a minority government to survive if they had to look to independents of different ideological hues. However, such arguments overemphasise the importance of ideology in Irish politics. Looking after the needs of their constituency tends to be the primary focus of most parliamentarians, and where a minority government helps independents achieve this goal, the latter tend to provide consistent support, as is shown in Chapter 7.

It would also be a mistake to assume that a reliance on independents necessarily implies a short-lived unstable arrangement. As discussed in Chapter 7, the reality is not quite so straightforward, because the key variable is management of independents. In the 1980s, they were mishandled, with the consequence that governments fell. When the support of independents is managed, as Bertie Ahern achieved in his 1997–2002 administration, the government need not be unstable, and this proved to be the then longest-serving government in peacetime history. Even when the Fianna Fáil-led government (2007–11) in the middle of the recent economic recession veered from one crisis to another, it was not the independents on whom it relied that were responsible for the instability, but rather internal dissensions within the governing party and with its coalition partners. So, yes, independents can create instability if they are ignored, but likewise we would expect any party to behave in a similar fashion if it too was ignored by its coalition partner.

In terms of a government's longevity, administrations looking to the support of independents are shorter than the average majority

279

government, but at two years and eight months are not short from an international perspective. This does not necessarily imply that such governments were not unstable, but one measure of stability is the support independents provide to governments in the Dáil. As was shown in Chapter 7, independents propping up a minority administration provide a level of support four times greater compared to independents in opposition. This suggests that independents can provide a level of stability, or at least support, to a government, and that it need not be short-lived, nor regularly defeated. Whether such governments survive because they are strong enough to almost compel independent support, or because their weakness means they avoid potential conflict with independents, is another issue, as is the assumption that instability caused by independents voting against a government is necessarily a bad thing.

3. Independents make parliament unworkable

The third accusation is that nothing will get done in parliament if there are too many independents. Their oppositional nature means that they can create legislative gridlock for minority governments. Independents' non-whipped status can also result in cyclical instability, with governments being constantly dismissed and formed as independents switch their preferences. While these two outcomes are theoretically possible, there is little evidence of their having occurred in Ireland. Certainly, independents have been quite oppositional in parliament, but as is detailed in Chapter 7, this is when their votes are not needed by the government. When independents' support is required, it is a different story. The more pressing factor why a minority government could find it difficult to get legislation passed is when it is considerably short of a majority, which was particularly the case for the government formed after the February 2016 election. In general, though, there is little to suggest that less legislation is passed by governments reliant on independents. There is more evidence of independents contributing to parliamentary instability, notably in 1927 (when there were two elections in four months), and the 1981–82 and 1987–89 periods. However, as discussed in Chapter 7, these are rather complex episodes that involve more than independents' volatility. Undoubtedly a key reason why independents in Ireland have so far not made the Dáil unworkable is because there has not been excessively large numbers of them elected. As was mentioned in Chapter 1, when this does happen, such as in the example used of Papua New Guinea, the work of parliament can be greatly disrupted. However, this may be more due to a politically unstable climate than just the presence of independents. In more stable environments, such as the Pacific island states where parties are absent, parliamentary life does proceed and political chaos is not necessarily the outcome.

In any case, we should also question whether a parliament that efficiently processes legislation is necessarily desirable. The aim of parliament should not be to rubber stamp, or rush through, government-sponsored legislation. A Dáil where legislation takes longer to process because of greater scrutiny by more independent-minded TDs, and where the government does not always get its way, is a more preferable outcome than an executive-dominated regime, which was for a long time the pattern in Ireland. One of the criticisms of the parliamentary system when the state faced bankruptcy and potential collapse in 2010–11, was that it had failed in its role: legislation was guillotined, opposition was stifled and anyone who challenged the government's newspeak was ostracised. Had there been more scrutiny and had things gone a bit slower in parliament, Ireland might well have been spared some of the ravages of the economic crisis.

4. Independents skew the allocation of national resources
The cost of the support independents provide to minority governments tends to be patronage for their respective constituencies. The democratic validity, and disproportionate nature, of this power, especially in relation to independents' influence on distributive policy, has been the source of some criticism, as it is claimed that this skews the allocation of national resources, without regard to priorities and needs (FitzGerald 2000). As former Taoiseach Garret FitzGerald said: 'Somebody's getting something for that county which really is a priority for elsewhere' (March 2002; broadcast on *Prime Time*, RTÉ 1, 26 January 2016).

As was discussed in Chapter 7, it is difficult to determine the true nature of independents' influence. Some of them in the past claimed responsibility for a lot of infrastructural expenditure.[1] However, an unknown quantity of this could already have been destined for the independent's constituency, irrespective of his or her influence. Independents may simply have been given advance notice by the government in order to appear as if the funding was due to their intervention. It could well be that independents' influence is overexaggerated, and is a quasi-charade tolerated by the government because it ensures the independents and their voters remain on side. Former Taoiseach Bertie Ahern, who negotiated agreements with four independents in two of his three administrations, admitted 'it was all a game' (Hickey 2015, 69). The independents issued threats, but so long as the government appeased them, they were kept on side.

Whatever independents get, criticisms of their pork-barrel politics ignores the reality that politics by definition is about the distribution of scarce resources. Everyone, from backbenchers to government ministers, to interest groups outside of parliament, is competing to get their hands on a slice of the national cake. Independents are no different, but what they get greatly pales into insignificance compared to that accruing to those inside government, particularly cabinet ministers. Former independent TD Tony Gregory thus claimed that 'in any government the ones responsible for maldistribution of economic wealth would have been government ministers who favoured their own constituencies'. There are many examples of this, but one in particular was found by the state broadcaster RTÉ in its analysis of the allocation of private housing grants in 2015. Mayo and Limerick, home of the Taoiseach and Minister for Finance, received double the national average of such grants.[2] It should also be said that the influence sought and achieved by independents is far less than that accrued by minor parties in government with similar numbers of TDs. For example, in the 1997–2002 government, the four Progressive Democrat TDs in the coalition had a far greater effect on the distribution of resources than the four independents supporting the minority administration.

5. Independents negotiate secret deals, which are neither accountable nor transparent

The accusation here is that the deals between parties and independents have sometimes remained secret, reducing the accountability and transparency of such arrangements. Most particularly, these include those negotiated by Bertie Ahern as Fianna Fáil leader with a number of independents in 1997 and 2007. Those critical of these agreements maintain that the cost of an independent's vote should be made public, to reveal the extent of the pork-barrel politicking.

However, the reason why many of these agreements have not been published is that confidentiality is often the cornerstone of high-level negotiations in any walk of life. If either side had to reveal the concessions they had to make, it might undermine support for such deals among their respective supporters. For example, perhaps one of the reasons why some independents have not published their deals with governments is not because they are given so much, but rather the opposite. If independents revealed the actual cost of their support they would be under significant local pressure to demand more, or not to back a government. By implication, having to make such deals public might cost governments more. Thus, Tony Gregory always intended to publish the details of his eponymous deal with Fianna Fáil leader

Charlie Haughey in 1982. Consequently, as detailed in Chapter 7, it was an extensive agreement, estimated to cost more than £200 million. Gregory needed to have such a package in order to defend his support for Haughey.

In any case, as detailed in the last section, because it is so difficult to determine what government expenditure is due to the influence of an independent, the publication or otherwise of independent deals makes little difference. Who knows what they really received in return for their support? For example, in the programme for government agreed between Fine Gael, Fianna Fáil and independents in May 2016, no mention was made of the costs of independent support. And although, as discussed in Chapter 7, independents were adamant that they were not concerned about patronage, there was much speculation in the media about what the independents had really delivered for their constituencies in unwritten agreements (see Kelly 2016; Leahy 2016).

6. Independents reduce cohesion and accountability in parliament
Another concern is that it could be difficult for any government to form a coherent national policy if it had to pander to a large number of independents, each with their own concern. The consequence could be that such policies are simply a mishmash aggregate of local or ad hoc interests. Of course, this does not necessarily imply that policies made by party governments in an environment where independents have no influence are necessarily coherent. It would also be naive to imagine that when formulating policy, Irish governments do not take account of local concerns, regardless of the presence or otherwise of independents.

In terms of accountability, independents cannot be held to account nationally as they contest only their local constituency. If independents were determining policy it would be difficult for voters to know who, and how, to hold to account. This is in contrast to parties, who are accountable by their running candidates in most constituencies. In other words, most voters get to cast their verdict on parties' policies, but not of those of individual independents. In this way, the presence of parties facilitates parliamentarians interpreting the nature of their mandate, and whether their policies are supported by voters (Gallagher 2010, 130). The argument here is that without a party running candidates in most constituencies, parliamentarians would not know what policies were preferred by voters (Aldrich 1995, 23).

There is certainly merit to this argument, but this would only hold if there was a government comprised entirely of independents who stood solely on an individual ticket. For example, if the cabinet comprised independent ministers who introduced national policies concerning health, agriculture and education, but the convention of collective responsibility was waived, as was the case in the Australian Capital Territory in 1998, only the voters in the local constituency could hold this policy to account; the national electorate would be unable to do so. In addition, such an independent minister would not know what kind of national mandate he or she had to make policy, nor what would be the mood of the nation regarding their implementation.

Because these criticisms of independents concerning efficiency and accountability are really only relevant in a system where independents constitute a sizeable proportion, if not a majority, of parliament, they are not really applicable in the Irish parliament.[3] In addition, such a defence of parties is based on a number of questionable and idealistic assumptions, namely whether voters cast preferences based on policy, are aware of party platforms, the nature of the mandate they give to parties, and whether they are capable of crediting or blaming parties for past performance (Bergman et al. 2003).

The final means of assessing the normative value of independents concerns measuring their impact on what constitutes good governance. Does the presence of independents undermine the ability of a political system to achieve these properties? There are a variety of measures of good governance, but one of the most widely used is the worldwide governance indicators dataset, compiled by the World Bank since 1996 (www.govindicators.org). Using a range of surveys on perceptions of governance, these are combined to produce six indicators of good governance that can be compared across country and time. They cover accountability, political stability, government effectiveness, regulatory quality, the rule of law and control of corruption. Examining their application in Ireland, periods of minority government rule reliant on independents had little effect on these variables, with the exception of the 2007–11 administration, when the decline in the quality of governance was the product of an economic recession, not necessarily independents' influence. In fact, rather than weakening the political system, it was suggested in the aftermath of the 2016 election that a minority government reliant on independents might actually strengthen parliamentary democracy, by making the government more accountable (Cannon 2016; O'Malley 2016). Since the data only goes back to the mid 1990s, and given the limited influence independents can have on these indicators, it is difficult to draw more conclusions about what they imply concerning the impact of independents on good governance.

Overall, from the discussion of the primary accusations against independents, it is difficult to conclude that they pose a threat to party democracy, at least certainly not in the numbers present in Ireland.

Many of the criticisms of independents lack an empirical basis, and are in some ways a product of a prevailing paradigm that party is good and non-party is bad. In part, this paradigm is a product of parties' domination of political systems, in order to negate any threat to their omnipotence. For example, many of those who condemn the party whip system for preventing the freedom of expression in parliament also criticise independents for not being able to speak as one voice, or for not being a coherent group and having different opinions. You cannot have both; either you welcome diversity, or you prevent its expression to assist stability. It was noticeable how this paradigm began to shift following the 2016 Dáil election when so many more independents were elected. The instability of minority governments and independent-mindedness of TDs that many commentators had warned against before the outcome were now being welcomed as an opportunity for a new politics where parliament, and not government, would be to the fore.

Whatever one thinks of independents, their facilitation – where anyone with limited resources can run for office, get elected and influence government – is a healthy sign of the openness of the Irish political system. You do not have to follow the well-trodden party path to enter politics, and the sheep who plough a lonely furrow do not get devoured. Rather, the capacity of the Irish system to enable independents to survive and even thrive facilitates its embracing of diversity and plurality; it allows more voices to be heard and strengthens the direct link between the citizen and the parliamentarian, which can only enhance representative democracy. So, while to most international observers independents' election in Ireland in February 2016 and resultant participation in government might seem an unusual phenomenon, they are a symptom of a functioning, not a failing, electoral democracy.

Notes

1 For examples of such claims, see a series of newspaper interviews in the *Irish Times* in 2000 with the four independent TDs supporting the Fianna Fáil–Progressive Democrat minority coalition (A. O' Connor 2000a, 2000b, 2000c; O'Regan 2000).

2 See 'Housing funds favour counties of senior politicians'; www.rte.ie/news/ investigations-unit/2015/0206/678283-housing-funds-favour-counties-of-some-senior-politicians/ (accessed 5 February 2016).

3 For more on how parliaments operate in the absence of parties, see Weeks (2015).

Appendix
Independent TDs 1922–2016

Independent TD	Constituency	Times elected independent	Years in Dáil as independent TD	Years in Dáil as party TD
Michael J. Hennessy	Cork East & North-East	1	1922–23*	*Cumann na nGaedheal TD 1923–32
Laurence O'Neill	Dublin Mid	1	1922–23	
Alfred Byrne	Dublin Mid	13	1922–28; 32–56	
William Magennis	NUI	1	1922–23	
Ernest Henry Alton	Dublin University	6	1922–37	
Sir James Craig	Dublin University	6	1922–33	
Gerald Fitzgibbon	Dublin University	1	1922–23	
William Edward Thrift	Dublin University	6	1922–37	*Cumann na nGaedheal TD 1927–38
Myles Keogh	Dublin South	3	1922–27*	
Darrell Figgis	Dublin County	2	1922–27	
James Cosgrave	Galway	1	1923–27	
John James Cole	Cavan	5	1923–27; 27–32; 37–44	
James Sproule Myles	Donegal	7	1923–43	
Bryan Ricco Cooper	Dublin County	2	1923–27*	*Cumann na nGaedheal TD 1927–38
John Daly	Cork East	2	1923–27*	*Cumann na nGaedheal TD 1927–32
Richard Henrik Beamish	Cork Borough	1	1923–27	
Andrew O'Shaughnessy	Cork Borough	1	1923–27	
William Redmond	Waterford	4	1923–27*	*National League/Cumann na nGaedheal TD 1927–33
Seán Lyons	Longford–Westmeath	1	1923–27	
Gilbert Hewson	Limerick	1	1927	
John F. O'Hanlon	Cavan	3	1927–33	

Independent TD	Constituency	Times elected independent	Years in Dáil as independent TD	Years in Dáil as party TD
Alexander Haslett	Monaghan	3	1927–32; 33–7	
Jasper Travers Wolfe	Cork West	3	1927–33	
John Good	Dublin County	4	1927–37	
Arthur Clery	NUI	1	1927	
Daniel Corkery	Cork North	1	1927*	*Fianna Fáil TD 1927–32; 33–7
Michael Brennan	Roscommon	2	1927–32*	*Cumann na nGaedheal/FG TD 1933–43
Joseph Xavier Murphy	Dublin County	1	1927–32	
Frank McDermott	Roscommon	1	1932–33*	*National Centre Party/Fine Gael TD 1933–7
Brooke Brasier	Cork East	1	1932–33*	*Fine Gael TD 1933–43
James Dillon	Donegal	5	1932–33; 42–53*	*National Centre Party TD 1933–37; Fine Gael TD 1937–44; 53–69
James Coburn	Louth	2	1931–37*	*National League TD 1927–31;Fine Gael TD 1937–54
Robert Rowlette	Dublin University	1	1933–37	
Joseph Hannigan	Dublin South	2	1937–43	
Thomas Burke	Clare	5	1937–51	
James Larkin snr.	Dublin North–East	1	1937–38*	*Labour TD 1943–44
Alfred Byrne jr.	Dublin North–East	5	1937–44; 48–52	
Patrick Cogan	Wicklow	3	1938–43; 48–54*	*Clann na Talmhan TD 1943–48
Philip Mahony	Kilkenny	1	1943–44	
Denis Heskin	Waterford	2	1943–48	
Ben Maguire	Leitrim	4	1939–51; 54–57*	*Fianna Fáil TD 1927–39
Oliver J. Flanagan	Leix–Offaly	4	1943–53*	*Fine Gael TD 1953–87
Tom O'Reilly	Cavan	1	1944–48	

Name	Constituency		Years	Notes
William Dwyer	Cork Borough	1	1944–48	
William Sheldon	Donegal East	5	1944–61*	*Clann na Talmhan TD 1943–44
Patrick O'Reilly (Castlepoles)	Cavan	1	1948–51	
Michael Sheehan (Ballintemple)	Cork Borough	1	1948–51	
Patrick Cogan	Wicklow	2	1948–54*	*Clann na Talmhan TD 1938–48
Charles Fagan	Longford–Westmeath	2	1948–53*	*NCP TD 1933; FG TD 1933–48, 1953–61
John Flynn	Kerry South	2	1948–52*	*Fianna Fáil TD 1932–43; 52–7
Noël Browne	Dublin South-East	2	1951–53; 57–58	*Clann na Poblachta/Fianna Fáil/National Progressive Democrats/Labour/Socialist Labour Party TD 1948–51; 1953–4; 58–65; 69–73; 77–82
Jack McQuillan	Roscommon	3	1951–58*	*Clann na Poblachta/National Progressive Democrats/Labour TD 1948–51; 58–65
Peadar Cowan	Dublin North-East	1	1951–54*	*Clann na Poblachta TD 1948–51
Michael ffrench-O'Carroll	Dublin South-West	1	1951–54	
Patrick Lehane	Cork South	1	1951–54*	*Clann na Talmhan TD 1948–51
Patrick Finucane	Kerry North	4	1951–54; 57–69*	*Clann na Talmhan TD 1943–51
Thomas NJ Byrne	Dublin North-West	3	1952–61	
Patrick Byrne	Dublin North-East	1	1956–57*	*Fine Gael TD 1957–69
James Carroll	Dublin South-West	2	1957–65	
George Edward Russell	Limerick East	1	1957–61	
Jack Murphy	Dublin South-Central	1	1957–58	
Florence Wycherley	Cork West	1	1957–61	

Independent TD	Constituency	Times elected independent	Years in Dáil as independent TD	Years in Dáil as party TD
Frank Sherwin	Dublin North-Central	1	1961–65	
Joseph Michael Sheridan	Longford–Westmeath	5	1961–81	
Seán Dunne	Dublin County	1	1961–65*	*Labour TD 1965–73
Joseph R. Leneghan	Mayo North	1	1961–65*	*Fianna Fáil TD 1969–73
Neil Blaney	Donegal North-East	8	1970–95*	*Fianna Fáil TD 1948–70
Michael Lipper	Limerick East	1	1977–81	
Seán Dublin Bay Rockall D. Loftus	Dublin North-East	1	1981–82	
Jim Kemmy	Limerick East	2	1981–82*	*Democratic Socialist Party/Labour TD 1987–2002
John F. O'Connell	Dublin South-Central	1	1981–83*	*Labour TD 1965–81; Ceann Comhairle 1981–82; Fianna Fáil TD 1983–7; 89–97
Tony Gregory	Dublin Central	8	1981–2009	
Seán Treacy	Tipperary South	1	1987–89*	*Labour TD 1961–87; Ceann Comhairle 1987–97
Tom Foxe	Roscommon	2	1989–97	
Johnny Fox	Wicklow	1	1992–95	
Mildred Fox	Wicklow	3	1995–2007	
Harry Blaney	Donegal North-East	1	1997–2002	
Jackie Healy–Rae	Kerry South	3	1997–2011	
Michael Lowry	Tipperary North	5	1997–*	Fine Gael TD* 1987–97
Tom Gildea	Donegal South-West	1	1997–2002	

Name	Constituency		Years	Notes
Séamus Healy	Tipperary South	4	2001–7; 2011–	
Marian Harkin	Sligo–Leitrim	1	2002–4	
Jerry Cowley	Mayo	1	2002–7	
Paudge Connolly	Cavan–Monaghan	1	2002–7	
Niall Blaney	Donegal North-East	1	2002–6*	*Fianna Fáil TD 2006–11
James Breen	Clare	1	2002–7	
Paddy McHugh	Galway East	1	2002–7	
Finian McGrath	Dublin North-Central	4	2002–	
Liam Twomey	Wexford	1	2002–4*	*Fine Gael TD 2004–7; 2011–16
Catherine Murphy	Kildare North	2	2004–7; 2011–15*	*Social Democrats TD 2015–16
Beverley Flynn	Mayo	1	2004–8*	*Fianna Fáil TD 1997–2004; 2008–11
Maureen O'Sullivan	Dublin Central	3	2009–	
Noel Grealish	Galway East	2	2009–*	*Progressive Democrats TD 2002–9
Thomas Pringle	Donegal South-West	2	2011–	
Tom Fleming	Kerry South	1	2011–16	
Michael Healy-Rae	Kerry South	2	2011–	
Shane Ross	Dublin South	2	2011–	
Mick Wallace	Wexford	2	2011–	
John Halligan	Waterford	2	2011–	
Mattie McGrath	Tipperary South	2	2011–*	*Fianna Fáil TD 2007–11
Denis Naughten	Roscommon–S Leitrim	1	2011–*	*Fine Gael TD 1997–2011
Tommy Broughan	Dublin Bay North	1	2011–*	*Labour TD 1992–2011
Luke Flanagan	Roscommon–S Leitrim	1	2011–14	
Stephen Donnelly	Wicklow	1	2011–15; 2016–*	*Social Democrats TD 2015–16
Michael Fitzmaurice	Roscommon–S Leitrim	2	2014–	

Independent TD	Constituency	Times elected independent	Years in Dáil as independent TD	Years in Dáil as party TD
Clare Daly	Dublin Fingal	1	2015–*	*Socialist Party/United Left TD 2011–15
Joan Collins	Dublin South-Central	1	2015–*	*People Before Profit/United Left TD 2011–15
Seán Canney	Galway East	1	2016–	
Michael Collins	Cork South-West	1	2016–	
Catherine Connolly	Galway West	1	2016–	
Michael Harty	Clare	1	2016–	
Danny Healy-Rae	Kerry	1	2016–	
Kevin 'Boxer' Moran	Longford–Westmeath	1	2016–	
Katherine Zappone	Dublin South-Central	1	2016–	

Note: This includes only those elected as an independent candidate. Where a former party TD is elected as an independent, their years as an independent begin from when they left the party. 'Times elected independent' includes by-election victories. 'Years in Dáil as party TD' includes years before and after life as an independent TD.

*Denotes they were also a party TD.

References

Interviews

Bertie Ahern, Taoiseach (1997–2008) and Fianna Fáil TD for Dublin Central (1977–2009), 27 January 2015.

Niall Blaney, independent TD for Donegal North-East (2002–6), 17 December 2008.

Patrick Byrne, independent TD for Dublin North-East (1956–57), 12 December 2014.

Phil Cleary, independent MP in Australian House of Representatives (1992; 1993–96), 23 March 2010.

Lucinda Creighton, independent TD for Dublin South-East (2013–15), 11 December 2014.

Stephen Donnelly, independent TD for Wicklow (2011–15), 27 January 2015.

Charlie Flanagan, son of Oliver J. Flanagan, independent TD for Laois-Offaly (1943–54), 17 December 2008.

Mildred Fox, independent TD for Wicklow (1995–2007), 12 December 2014.

Noel Grealish, independent TD for Galway West (2009–), 11 December 2014.

Bob Katter, independent MP in Australian House of Representatives (2001–11), 6 April 2010.

Seán Dublin Bay Loftus, independent TD for Dublin North-Central (1981–82), 27 May 2008.

Finian McGrath, independent TD for Dublin North-Central (2002–), 13 April 2004

Mattie McGrath, independent TD for Tipperary South (2011–), 11 December 2014.

Denis Naughten, independent TD for Roscommon–South Leitrim/Roscommon–Galway (2011–), 28 January 2015.

David Norris, independent Senator for Dublin University (1987–), 17 May 2004.

Rob Oakeshott, independent MP in Australian House of Representatives (2008–13), 30 March 2012

Shane Ross, independent Senator for Dublin University (1981–2011) and independent TD for Dublin South and Dublin Bay South (2011–), 10 May 2004.

Liam Twomey, independent TD for Wexford (2002–4), 9 April 2004.

Andrew Wilkie, independent MP in Australian House of Representatives (2010–), 15 February 2012.

Tony Windsor, independent MP in Australian House of Representatives (2001–13), 6 April 2010.

Publications

Aars, Jacob, and Hans Erik Ringkjøb. 2005. 'Party politicisation reversed? Non-partisan alternatives in Norwegian local politics.' *Scandinavian Political Studies* 28(2): 161–81.

Abedi, Amir. 2004. *Anti-Political Establishment Parties: A Comparative Analysis.* London: Routledge.

Åberg, Martin, and Christer Ahlberger. 2015. 'Local candidate lists: historical artefacts or a novel phenomenon? A research note.' *Party Politics* 21(5): 813–20.

Abramson, Paul, John Aldrich, Paul Paolino and David W. Rohde. 1995. 'Third-party and independent candidates in American Politics: Wallace, Anderson, and Perot.' *Political Science Quarterly* 110(3): 349–67.

Adrian, Charles R. 1959. 'A typology for nonpartisan elections.' *Political Research Quarterly* 12(2): 449–58.

Ahern, Bertie. 2009. *Bertie Ahern. The Autobiography.* London: Hutchinson.

Alasia, Sam L. 1984. 'Big man and party politics: The evolution of political parties in Solomon Islands.' *Pacific Perspective* 13(2): 72–84.

Aldrich, John. 1995. *Why Parties? The Origin and Transformation of Political Parties in America.* Chicago: University of Chicago Press.

Alighieri, Dante. 1996. *The Inferno of Dante: A New Verse Translation by Robert Pinsky.* London: J. M. Dent.

Allen, Neal, and B. J. Brox. 2005. 'The roots of third party voting.' *Party Politics* 11(5): 623–37.

Anckar, Dag. 2000. 'Party Systems and Voter Alignments in Small Island States.' In *Party Systems and Voter Alignments Revisited*, ed. Lauri Karvonen. London: Routledge, 261–83.

Anckar, Dag, and Carsten Anckar. 2000. 'Democracies without parties.' *Comparative Political Studies* 33(2): 225–47.

Andren, Peter. 2003. *The Andren Report: An Independent Way in Australian Politics.* Canberra: Scribe.

Avlon, John. 2004. *Independent Nation: How the Vital Center Is Changing American Politics.* New York: Three Rivers Press.

Ayearst, Morley. 1971. *The Republic of Ireland: Its Government and Politics.* New York: New York University Press.

Bailey, Kenneth D. 1994. *Typologies and Taxonomies: An Introduction to Classification Techniques.* London: Sage.

Bale, Tim, and Torbjörn Bergman. 2006. 'Captives no longer, but servants still? Contract parliamentarism and the new minority governance in Sweden and New Zealand.' *Government and Opposition* 41(3): 422–49.

Bartholdi, J. J., and J. B. Orlin. 1991. 'Single transferable vote resists strategic voting.' *Social Choice and Welfare* 8(4): 341–54.

Bax, Mart. 1976. *Harpstrings and Confessions: Machine-Style Politics in the Irish Republic*. Essen: Van Gorcum.

Beales, D. E. D. 1967. 'Parliamentary Parties and the "Independent" Member, 1810–1860.' In *Ideas and Institutions of Victorian Britain: Essays in Honour of George Kitson Clark*, ed. Robert Robson. London: G. Bell and sons, 1–24.

Bean, Clive, and Elim Papadakis. 1995. 'Minor parties and independents – electoral bases and future prospects.' *Australian Journal of Political Science* 30: 111–26.

Bélanger, Éric. 2004. 'Antipartyism and third-party vote choice: A comparison of Canada, Britain, and Australia.' *Comparative Political Studies* 37(9): 1054–78.

Bell, Martin. 2001. *An Accidental MP*. London: Penguin.

Beller, Dennis C., and Frank P. Belloni. 1978. 'The Study of Factions.' In *Faction Politics: Political Parties and Factionalism in Comparative Perspective*, eds Frank P. Belloni and Dennis C. Beller. Santa Barbara: ABC-Clio Press, 3–17.

Berens, Charlyne. 2005. *One House: The Unicameral's Progressive Vision for Nebraska*. Lincoln: University of Nebraska Press.

Bergman, Torbjörn, Wolfgang C. Müller, Kaare Strøm and Benjamin Nyblade. 2003. 'Dimensions of Citizen Control.' In *Delegation and Accountability in Parliamentary Democracies*, eds Kaare Strom, Torbjörn Bergman and Wolfgang C. Muller. Oxford: Oxford University Press, 651–706.

Berry, Richard. 2008. *Independent: The Rise of the Non-Aligned Politician*. London: Imprint Academic.

Bogdanor, Vernon. 1984. *What Is Proportional Representation?* Oxford: Blackwell.

Bolleyer, Nicole, and Liam Weeks. 2009. 'The puzzle of non-party actors in party democracy: Independents in Ireland.' *Comparative European Politics* 7(3): 299–324.

Bottom, Karin, and Colin Copus. 2011. 'Independent politics: Why seek to serve and survive as an independent councillor?' *Public Policy and Administration* 26(3): 279–305.

Brancati, Dawn. 2008. 'Winning alone: The electoral fate of independent candidates worldwide.' *The Journal of Politics* 70(3): 648–62.

Bréadún, Deaglán de, and Mary Minihan. 2011. 'Healy-Rae and Lowry Claim Credit for Changes.' *Irish Times* (9 April).

Brennan, Geoffrey, and Loren Lomasky. 1997. *Democracy and Decision: The Pure Theory of Electoral Preference*. Cambridge: Cambridge University Press.

Brennock, Mark. 1998. 'Keeping the Independent TDs Happy.' *Irish Times* (12 December).

Browne, Noël. 1986. *Against the Tide*. Dublin: Gill and Macmillan.

Browne, Vincent. 1982. 'Fine Gael – Almost as Bad.' *Magill* (1 March).

Busteed, Mervyn A. 1990. *Voting Behaviour in the Republic of Ireland: A Geographical Perspective*. New York: Oxford University Press.

Cannon, Ciaran. 2016. 'Why Minority Governments Are the Best Way Forward in the National Interest.' *Irish Independent* (2 March).

Carbone, Giovanni M. 2003. 'Political parties in a "no-party democracy."' *Party Politics* 9(4): 485–501.

Carey, John M., and Martin S. Shugart. 1995. 'Incentives to cultivate a personal vote: A rank ordering of electoral formulas.' *Electoral Studies* 14: 417–40.

Carty, R. K. 1981. *Electoral Politics in Ireland. Party and Parish Pump*. Ontario: Wilfried Laurier University Press.

Casey, Harry. 1991. 'Champagne Corks Pop as the Foxe Supporters Celebrate Hospital Deal.' *Connacht Tribune* (22 February).

Cashin, Paul A. 1995. 'Real GDP in the seven colonies of Australasia, 1861–1991', *The Review of Income and Wealth* 41(1): 19–39.

Chubb, Basil. 1957. 'The independent member in Ireland.' *Political Studies* 5: 131–42.

Clark, Alistair, and Lynn Bennie. 2008. 'Electoral reform and party adaptation: The introduction of the single transferable vote in Scotland.' *Political Quarterly* 79(2): 241–51.

Coakley, John. 1987. 'The Election in Context: Historical and European Perspectives.' In *How Ireland Voted 1987: The Irish General Election of 1987*, eds Michael Laver, Peter Mair and Richard Sinnott. Dublin: Poolbeg Press, 153–73.

———. 2003. 'Independent Politicians.' In *Encyclopedia of Ireland*. Dublin: Gill and Macmillan, 515.

———. 2010a. 'Appendices.' In *Politics in the Republic of Ireland*, eds John Coakley and Michael Gallagher. London: Routledge and PSAI Press, 434–70.

———. 2010b. 'Society and Political Culture.' In *Politics in the Republic of Ireland*, eds John Coakley and Michael Gallagher. Leichhardt, NSW: Routledge, 37–71.

———. 2010c. 'The Foundation of Statehood.' In *Politics in the Republic of Ireland*, eds John Coakley and Michael Gallagher. London: Routledge and PSAI Press, 3–36.

———. 2012. 'The Rise and Fall of Minor Parties in Ireland.' In *Radical or Redundant. Minor Parties in Irish Political Life*, eds Liam Weeks and Alistair Clarke. Dublin: The History Press.

Coleman, Marie. 2009a. 'Joseph Xavier Murphy.' In *Dictionary of Irish Biography*. Cambridge: Cambridge University Press.

———. 2009b. 'William Archer Redmond.' In *Dictionary of Irish Biography*. Cambridge: Cambridge University Press.

Collet, Christian. 1999. 'Can They Be Serious?: The Rise of Minor Parties and Independent Candidates in the 1990s.' Unpublished PhD dissertation. University of California, Irvine.

Collins, Stephen. 1991. 'From MacEoin to Reynolds: County Longford Politics, 1960–2000.' In *Longford: Essays in County History*, eds Gerard Moran and Raymond Gillespie. Dublin: Irish Academic Press, 240–61.

REFERENCES

——. 1996. *The Cosgrave Legacy*. Dublin: Blackwater Press.

——. 2014. 'The Rise and Rise of Independents.' *Irish Times* (1 November).

Copus, Colin, Alistair Clark and Karin Bottom. 2008. 'Multi-party Politics in England: Small Parties, Independents, and Political Associations in English Local Politics.' In *Farewell to the Party Model? Independent Local Lists in East and West European Countries*, eds Marion Reiser and Everhard Holtmann. Wiesbaden: Springer, 253–76.

Copus, Colin, Alistair Clark, Herwig Reynaert and Kristof Steyvers. 2009. 'Minor party and independent politics beyond the mainstream: Fluctuating fortunes but a permanent presence.' *Parliamentary Affairs* 62(1): 4–18.

Copus, Colin, Melvin Wingfield, Kristof Steyvers and Herwig Reynaert. 2012. 'A Place to Party? Parties and Nonpartisanship in Local Government.' In *The Oxford Handbook of Urban Politics*, eds Karen Mossberger, Susan E. Clarke and Peter John. New York: Oxford University Press, 210–24.

Costar, Brian, and Jennifer Curtin. 2004. *Rebels with a Cause: Independents in Australian Politics*. Sydney: UNSW Press.

Cowley, Phil, and Mark Stuart. 2009. 'There was a doctor, a journalist and two Welshmen: The voting behaviour of independent MPs in the United Kingdom House of Commons, 1997–2007.' *Parliamentary Affairs* 62(1): 19–31.

Cox, Gary. 1987. *The Efficient Secret. The Cabinet and the Development of Political Parties in Victorian England*. Cambridge: Cambridge University Press.

Curtin, Chris, and Tony Varley. 1995. 'Community Action and the State.' In *Irish Society: Sociological Perspectives*, ed. Patrick Clancy. Dublin: Institute of Public Administration, 379–407.

Curtin, Jennifer. 2005. *Getting Elected as an Independent: Electoral Laws and Party Favouritism*. ed. Democratic Audit of Australia. Canberra: Democratic Audit of Australia.

Daly, Susan. 2016. 'Two Healy-Rae Brothers Elected to the Dáil.' *TheJournal. ie* (28 February).

Dangerfield, George. 1952. *The Era of Good Feelings*. London: Methuen.

Dempsey, Pauric. 2009. 'Richard Sidney Anthony.' In *Dictionary of Irish Biography*. Cambridge: Cambridge University Press.

Denver, David, Alistair Clark and Lynn Bennie. 2009. 'Voter reactions to a preferential ballot: The 2007 Scottish local elections.' *Journal of Elections, Public Opinion & Parties* 19(3): 265–82.

Dolan, Anne. 2009. 'Byrne, Alfred.' In *Dictionary of Irish Biography*. Cambridge: Cambridge University Press.

Donohoe, Miriam. 2000. 'Independent TDs Insist on Abortion Referendum.' *Irish Times* (4 July).

——. 2007. 'Flynn Agus Na Fianna.' *Irish Times* (30 June).

Downs, Anthony. 1957. *An Economic Theory of Democracy*. New York: Harper and Row.

Dunphy, Richard. 1995. *The Making of Fianna Fáil Power in Ireland, 1923–1948*. Clarendon Press: Oxford.

297

Ehin, Piret, Ülle Madise, Mihkel Solvak, Rein Taagepera, Kristjan Vassil, and Priit Vinkel. 2013. *Independent Candidates in National and European Elections*. Brussels: Policy Department, European Parliament.

Ehin, Piret, and Mihkel Solvak. 2012. 'Party voters gone astray: Explaining independent candidate success in the 2009 European elections in Estonia.' *Journal of Elections, Public Opinion & Parties* 22(3): 269–91.

Farrell, Brian. 1987a. 'Government Formation and Ministerial Selection.' In *Ireland at the Polls, 1981, 1982, and 1987: A Study of Four General Elections*, eds Howard Penniman and Brian Farrell. Washington DC: American Enterprise Institute, 131–55.

———. 1987b. 'The Road from 1987: Government Formation and Institutional Inertia.' In *How Ireland Voted: The Irish General Election 1987*, eds Michael Laver, Peter Mair and Richard Sinnott. Dublin: Poolbeg Press, 141–52.

Farrell, David M., Malcolm Mackerras and Ian McAllister. 1996. 'Designing electoral institutions: STV systems and their consequences.' *Political Studies* 44(1): 24–43.

Farrell, David M., and Ian McAllister. 2006. *The Australian Electoral System: Origins, Variations, and Consequences*. Sydney: University of New South Wales Press.

Farrell, David. 2015. *Outlook for the Political Landscape in Ireland 2015–2017*. Dublin: Davy.

Faulkner, Pádraig. 2005. *As I Saw It: Reviewing over 30 Years of Fianna Fáil and Irish Politics*. Dublin: Wolfhound Press.

Felle, Tom. 2004. 'Independents Give Bertie Another Option Outside PDs.' *Irish Independent* (18 June).

Ferriter, Diarmaid. 2009. 'Oliver J Flanagan.' In *Dictionary of Irish Biography*, Cambridge: Cambridge University Press.

Fine Gael. 2016. *A Confidence and Supply Arrangement for a Fine Gael-Led Government*. Dublin: Fine Gael.

FitzGerald, Garret. 1991. *All in a Life: Garret FitzGerald, an Autobiography*. Dublin: Gill and Macmillan.

———. 2000. 'Gregory Deal a Precursor to Destructive Localism of Politics.' *Irish Times* (19 August).

———. 2003. *Reflections on the Irish State*. Dublin: Irish Academic Press.

Fitzpatrick, David. 2014. *Descendancy: Irish Protestant Histories Since 1795*. London: Cambridge University Press.

Gallagher, Michael. 1975. 'Disproportionality in a proportional representation system: The Irish experience.' *Political Studies* 23(4): 501–13.

———.1976. *Electoral Support for Irish Political Parties, 1927–1973*. London: Sage.

———.1978. 'Party solidarity, exclusivity and inter-party relationships in Ireland, 1922–1977: The evidence of transfers'.' *Economic and Social Review* 10(1): 1–22.

———. 1982. *The Irish Labour Party in Transition, 1957–82*. Manchester: Manchester University Press.

————. 1985. *Political Parties in the Republic of Ireland*. Manchester: Manchester University Press.

————. 1989a. 'Local elections and electoral behaviour in the Republic of Ireland.' *Irish Political Studies* 4(1): 21–42.

————. 1989b. 'The Election Results and the New Dáil.' In *How Ireland Voted*, eds Michael Gallagher and Richard Sinnott. Galway: Centre for the Study of Irish Elections and PSAI Press, 68–93.

————. 1993. *Irish Elections 1922–44: Results and Analysis*. Dublin: PSAI Press.

————. 1999. 'Politics in Laois-Offaly 1922–92.' In *Laois: History and Society. Interdisciplinary Essays on the History of an Irish County*, eds William Nolan and Padraig G. Lane. Dublin: Geography Publications, 657–89.

————. 2000. 'The (Relatively) Victorious Incumbent under PR-STV: Legislative Turnover in Ireland and Malta.' In *Elections in Australia, Ireland, and Malta under the Single Transferable Vote*, eds Shaun Bowler and Bernard Grofman. Ann Arbor: University of Michigan Press, 81–113.

————. 2003. 'Stability and Turmoil: Analysis of the Results.' In *How Ireland Voted 2002*, eds Michael Gallagher, Paul Mitchell and Michael Marsh. London: Palgrave, 88–118.

————. 2005. 'Ireland: The Discreet Charm of PR-STV.' In *The Politics of Electoral Systems*, eds Michael Gallagher and Paul Mitchell. Oxford: Oxford University Press, 511–32.

————. 2010. 'Parliamentary Parties and the Party Whips.' In *The Houses of the Oireachtas: Parliament in Ireland*, eds Muiris MacCarthaigh and Maurice Manning. Dublin: Institute of Public Administration, 129–52.

Gallagher, Michael, and Lee Komito. 2010. 'The Constituency Role of TDs.' In *Politics in the Republic of Ireland*, eds John Coakley and Michael Gallagher. London: Routledge and PSAI Press, 230–62.

Gallagher, Michael, Michael Laver and Peter Mair. 2011. *Representative Government in Modern Europe*. 3rd edn. New York: McGraw-Hill.

Gallagher, Michael, and Michael Marsh. 2002. *Days of Blue Loyalty: The Politics of Membership of the Fine Gael Party*. Dublin: PSAI Press.

Gallagher, Michael and Liam Weeks. 2010. 'Ireland'. In *Elections in Europe. A Data Handbook*, eds Dieter Nohlen and Philip Stover. Nomos: Baden-Baden, 987–1026.

Gallo, Carlo. 2004. 'Russian Duma Elections in the Territorial Districts: Explaining Patterns of Proliferation of Independent Candidates, 1993–1999.' Unpublished PhD dissertation. London School of Economics and Political Science.

Garvin, Tom. 1987. 'The Road to 1987.' In *How Ireland Voted 1987: The Irish General Election of 1987*, eds Peter Mair, Michael Laver and Richard Sinnott. Dublin: Poolbeg Press, 4–8.

Gendźwiłł, Adam. 2012. 'Independent mayors and local lists in large Polish cities: Towards a non-partisan model of local government?' *Local Government Studies* 38(4): 501–18.

Gilligan, Robbie. 2012. *Tony Gregory*. Dublin: O'Brien Press.

Gilmore, Éamon. 2015. *Inside the Room: The Untold Story of Ireland's Crisis Government*. Dublin: Merrion Press.

Girvin, Brian. 2006. *The Emergency: Neutral Ireland, 1939–45*. London: Macmillan.

Gregory, Tony. 2000. '1982 Deal with FF Was Not "Horse-Trading."' *Irish Times* (2 September).

Griffith, Gareth. 2010. *Minority Governments in Australia 1989–2009: Accords, Charters and Agreements*. Sydney: NSW Parliamentary Library.

Hale, Henry E. 2005. *Why Not Parties in Russia?: Democracy, Federalism, and the State*. Cambridge: Cambridge University Press.

Hamilton, Alexander, James Madison, John Jay and Jack N. Rakove. 2003. *The Federalist: The Essential Essays*. Boston: Bedford/St. Martin's.

Hanley, Brian. 2014. 'Tony Gregory.' In *Dictionary of Irish Biography*. Cambridge: Cambridge University Press.

Hansen, Martin Ejnar. 2009. 'The positions of Irish parliamentary parties 1937–2006.' *Irish Political Studies* 24(1): 29–44.

———.2010. 'The parliamentary behaviour of minor parties and independents in Dáil Éireann.' *Irish Political Studies* 25(4): 643–60.

Hart, Jennifer. 1992. *Proportional Representation: Critics of the British Electoral System, 1820–1945*. London: Clarendon Press.

Hayton, David. 2004. *Ruling Ireland, 1685–1742: Politics, Politicians and Parties*. London: Boydell Press.

Hennessy, Mark. 2015. 'Coalition Can Get Re-elected with Independents.' *Irish Times* (26 February).

Herbert, A. P. 1950. *Independent Member*. London: Metheun.

Hickey, Donal. 2015. *The Healy-Raes. A Twenty-Four Seven Political Legacy*. Killarney: Rushy Mountain Books.

Hijino, Ken Victor L. 2013. 'Liabilities of partisan labels: Independents in Japanese local elections.' *Social Science Japan Journal* 16(1): 63–85.

Hirczy de Mino, Wolfgang, and John C. Lane. 2000. 'Malta: STV in a Two-Party System.' In *Elections in Australia, Ireland and Malta under the Single Transferable Vote. Reflections on an Embedded Institution*, eds Shaun Bowler and Bernard Grofman. Ann Arbor: University of Michigan Press, 178–204.

Hogan, James. 1945. *Election and Representation*. Cork: Cork University Press.

Horgan, John. 2000. *Noël Browne: Passionate Outsider*. Dublin: Gill and Macmillan.

Hug, Simon. 2001. *Altering Party Systems: Strategic Behavior and the Emergence of New Political Parties in Western Democracies*. Ann Arbor: University of Michigan Press.

Humphreys, Joe. 2002. 'Independents Stake Their Claims.' *Irish Times* (21 May).

The Irish Times/IPSOS MRBI. 2015. *Poll Report. May 15 2015*. Dublin.

Ishiyama, John, Anna Batta and Angela Sortor. 2013. 'Political parties, independents and the electoral market in Sub-Saharan Africa.' *Party Politics* 19(5): 695–712.

Jensen, Harold John. 1998. 'The Single Transferable Vote in Alberta and Manitoba.' Unpublished PhD dissertation. University of Alberta.

Joyce, Joe, and Peter Murtagh. 1983. *The Boss: Charles J. Haughey in Government.* Dublin: Poolbeg Press.

Junzhi, He. 2010. 'Independent candidates in China's local people's congresses: A typology.' *Journal of Contemporary China* 19(64): 311–33.

Karvonen, Lauri. 2010. *The Personalisation of Politics: A Study of Parliamentary Democracies.* Colchester: ECPR Press.

Katz, Richard S. 1980. *A Theory of Parties and Electoral Systems.* Baltimore: Johns Hopkins University Press.

Keane, John B. 1991. *The Celebrated Letters of John B. Keane.* Cork: Mercier Press.

Keith, Bruce E., D. B. Magleby, C. J. Nelson, E. Orr, M. C. Westyle, R. E. Wolfinger. 1992. *The Myth of the Independent Voter.* Berkeley: University of California Press.

Kelly, Fiach. 2011. 'Revealed: Secret Deals for Lowry and Healy-Rae.' *Irish Independent* (9 April).

———. 2016. 'Independent TD Got Funds for Runway in Government Deal.' *Irish Times* (20 May).

Kelly, Matthew. 2006. 'Cooper, Brian Ricco (1884–1930).' In *Oxford Dictionary of National Biography,* Oxford: Oxford University Press.

Kenny, Shane, and Fergal Keane. 1987. *Irish Politics Now. 'This Week' Guide to the 25th Dáil.* Dingle: Brandon.

King, Simon. 2000. 'Parties, Issues and Personalities: The Structural Determinants of Irish Voting Behaviour from 1885 to 2000.' Unpublished PhD dissertation. University of Oxford.

King-Hall, Stephen. 1951. 'The Independent in Politics.' In *The British Party System,* ed. Sydney D. Bailey. London: Hansard, 101–13.

Klein, Axel. 2001. 'Japan.' In *Elections in Asia and the Pacific : A Data Handbook, Volume II: South East Asia, East Asia, and the South Pacific,* eds Dieter Nohlen, Florian Grotz and Christof Hartmann. Oxford: Oxford University Press, 334–94.

Knight, James, and Nicolas Baxter-Moore. 1972. *Northern Ireland – The Elections of the Twenties.* London: Arthur McDougall Fund.

Kukovic, Simona, and Miro Hacek. 2011. 'Non-partisan candidates and lists at Slovenian local elections, 1994–2010.' *World Political Science Review* 7(1): 350–75.

Lago, Ignacio, and Ferran Martínez. 2011. 'Why new parties?' *Party Politics* 17(1): 3–20.

LaPalombara, Joseph and Myron Weiner. 1966. 'The Origin and Development of Political Parties.' In *Political Parties and Political Development,* eds Joseph LaPalombara and Myron Weiner. Princeton: Princeton University Press, 3–42.

Laver, Michael. 2004. 'Analysing structures of party preference in electronic voting data.' *Party Politics* 10(5): 521–41.

Leahy, Pat. 2016. 'Independents playing both sides of political fence.' *Irish Times* (14 May).

Lee, J. J. 1989. *Ireland 1912–1985: Politics and Society*. New York: Cambridge University Press.

Lipset, Seymour Martin, and Stein Rokkan. 1967. 'Cleavage Structures, Party Systems, and Voter Alignments: An Introduction.' In *Party Systems and Voter Alignments: Cross-National Perspectives*, eds Seymour Martin Lipset and Stein Rokkan. New York: Free Press.

Mackenzie, W. J. M. 1957. 'The export of electoral systems.' *Political Studies* 5(3): 240–57.

Mair, Peter. 1987. *The Changing Irish Party System: Organisation, Ideology and Electoral Competition*. London: Frances Pinter.

Manning, Maurice. 1972. *Irish Political Parties: An Introduction*. Dublin: Gill and Macmillan.

———. 1999. *James Dillon: A Biography*. Dublin: Wolfhound Press.

Mansergh, Nicholas. 1934. *The Irish Free State: Its Government and Politics*. London: Allen and Unwin.

Marsh, Michael. 2010. 'Voting Behaviour.' In *Politics in the Republic of Ireland*, eds J. Coakley and M. Gallagher. London: Routledge and PSAI Press, 168–97.

Marsh, Michael, and Richard Sinnott. 1999. 'The Behaviour of the Irish Voter.' In *How Ireland Voted 1997*, eds Michael Marsh and Paul Mitchell. Boulder: Westview Press, 151–80.

Marsh, Michael, Richard Sinnott, John Garry and Fiachra Kennedy. 2008. *The Irish Voter: The Nature of Electoral Competition in the Republic of Ireland*. Manchester: Manchester University Press.

Maume, Patrick. 2009a. 'Bryan Ricco Cooper.' In *Dictionary of Irish Biography*. Cambridge: Cambridge University Press.

———. 2009b. 'Neil Blaney.' In *Dictionary of Irish Biography*. Cambridge: Cambridge University Press.

McCullagh, David. 1998. *A Makeshift Majority: The First Inter-Party Government, 1948–51*. Dublin: Institute of Public Administration.

———. 2010. *The Reluctant Taoiseach: A Biography of John A. Costello*. Dublin: Gill and Macmillan.

McDonnell, Duncan, and Marco Valbruzzi. 2014. 'Defining and classifying technocrat-led and technocratic governments.' *European Journal of Political Research* 53(4): 654–71.

McDowell, Robert Brendan. 2001. *Grattan: A Life*. Dublin: Lilliput Press.

McGarry, Patsy. 1998. 'Kerry TD Running the Show Says FF Deputy.' *Irish Times* (18 November).

McGee, Harry. 2012. 'Lenihan Offered Healy-Rae 1m in Return for Support.' *Irish Times* (19 March).

Meehan, Ciara. 2010. *The Cosgrave Party: A History of Cumann Na nGaedheal, 1923–33*. Dublin: Royal Irish Academy.

Meredith, J. C. 1913. *Proportional Representation in Ireland*. London: E. Ponsonby.

Milne, Robert Stephen. 1966. *Political Parties in New Zealand*. Oxford: Clarendon Press.

Mitchell, Arthur. 1974. *Labour in Irish Politics, 1890–1930: The Irish Labour Movement in an Age of Revolution*. Dublin: Irish University Press.

Mitchell, Paul. 2001. 'Divided Government in Ireland.' In *Divided Government in Comparative Perspective*, ed. Robert Elgie. Oxford: Oxford University Press, 182–208.

Moser, R. G. 1999. 'Independents and party formation: elite partisanship as an intervening variable in Russian politics.' *Comparative Politics* 31(2): 147–66.

Murphy, Gary. 2010. 'Interest Groups in the Policy-making Process.' In *Politics in the Republic of Ireland* eds Michael Gallagher and John Coakley. London: Routledge and PSAI Press, 327–58.

Nicolson, Harold. 1946. *The Independent Member of Parliament*. London: Hansard Society.

Norris, Pippa. 2006. 'Recruitment.' In *Handbook of Party Politics*, eds Richard S. Katz and William Crotty. London: Sage, 89–109.

Ó Fathartaigh, Mícheál. 2001. 'Is the West Awake? Clann Na Talmhan. A Study of 1939—51.' Unpublished BA dissertation. Trinity College Dublin.

O'Byrnes, Stephen. 1986. *Hiding Behind a Face: Fine Gael under FitzGerald*. Dublin: Gill and MacMillan.

O'Connor, Alison. 2000a. 'Blaney Claims the Government Has Agreed to Pay £8m for Bridge.' *Irish Times* (7 August).

———. 2000b. 'Gildea Getting Benefits for Donegal.' *Irish Times* (8 August).

———. 2000c. 'The Importance of Being Powerfully Independent.' *Irish Times* (10 August).

O'Connor, Kevin. 1990. 'Haughey Buys Vote for £500,000.' *Sunday Independent* (11 February).

O'Day, Alan. 2004. 'Redmond, William Archer (1886–1932).' In *Oxford Dictionary of National Biography*. Oxford: Oxford University Press.

O'Leary, Cornelius. 1979. *Irish Elections, 1918–77: Parties, Voters, and Proportional Representation*. New York: St. Martin's Press.

O'Malley, Eoin. 2008. 'Government Formation in 2007.' In *How Ireland Voted 2007. The Full Story of Ireland's General Election*, eds Michael Gallagher and Michael Marsh. London: Palgrave, 205–17.

———. 2011. 'Government Formation in 2011.' In *How Ireland Voted 2011. The Full Story of Ireland's Earthquake Election*, eds Michael Gallagher and Michael Marsh. London: Palgrave, 264–82.

———. 2012. 'Wipeout! Does Governing Kill Small Parties in Ireland?' In *Radical or Redundant: Minor Parties in Irish Politics*, eds Liam Weeks and Alistair Clark. Dublin: History Press, 94–109.

———. 2016. 'Minority Government Could Be the Best Outcome.' *Irish Times* (27 February).

O'Regan, Michael. 1998a. 'Blaney to Decide His Position on Constitution.' *Irish Times* (18 April).

———. 1998b. 'Coalition Labours Hard to Keep Independents on Side.' *Irish Times* (13 April).

———. 2000. 'Healy-Rae's Bonanza of Projects for South Kerry.' *Irish Times* (9 August).

———. 2008. 'Cowen to Meet Independents to Discuss Deals with Ahern.' *Irish Times* (13 May).

———. 2014. 'Jackie Healy-Rae: A Colourful, Wily, Grass-Roots Politician.' *Irish Times* (5 December).

O'Sullivan, Donal. 1940. *The Irish Free State and Its Senate: A Study in Contemporary Politics*. London: Faber & Faber.

Oakeshott, Rob. 2014. *The Independent Member for Lyne: A Memoir*. Sydney: Allen & Unwin.

Olson, David M. 1965. *Nonpartisan Elections: A Case Analysis*. Texas: Institute of Public Affairs, University of Texas.

Orr, Graeme. 2010. *The Law of Politics. Elections, Parties and Money in Australia*. Annandale: Federation Press.

Owen, D., and Jack Dennis. 1996. 'Anti-partyism in the USA and support for Ross Perot.' *European Journal of Political Research* 29(3): 383–400.

Pakula, Alan J. 1974. *The Parallax View*. USA: Paramount.

Papadakis, Elim, and Clive Bean. 1995. 'Independents and minor parties – the electoral system.' *Australian Journal of Political Science* 30: 97–110.

Pedersen, Mogens N. 1982. 'Towards a new typology of party lifespans and minor parties.' *Scandinavian Political Studies* 5(1): 1–16.

———. 1983. 'Changing Patterns of Electoral Volatility in European Party Systems, 1948–1977.' In *Western European Party Systems: Continuity and Change*, eds Hans Daalder and Peter Mair. Beverly Hills: Sage, 29–66.

Rae, Douglas W. 1967. *The Political Consequences of Electoral Laws*. New Haven: Yale University Press.

Rafter, Kevin. 1993. *Neil Blaney, a Soldier of Destiny*. Dublin: Blackwater Press.

———. 2000. 'Foley Suspension Would Strengthen Independents.' *Irish Times* (15 February).

Rafter, Kevin, and Shane Coleman. 2007. 'The Kingmakers.' *Sunday Tribune* (27 May).

Ragin, Charles C. 1987. *The Comparative Method: Moving beyond Qualitative and Quantitative Strategies*. London: University of California Press.

Reed, Stephen R. 2009. 'Party strategy or candidate strategy: How does the LDP run the right number of candidates in Japan's multi-member districts?' *Party Politics* 15(3): 295–314.

Regan, John M. 1999. *The Irish Counter-Revolution, 1921–1936: Treatyite Politics and Settlement in Independent Ireland*. Dublin. Gill and Macmillan.

Reilly, Benjamin. 2002. 'Political engineering and party politics in Papua New Guinea.' *Party Politics* 8(6): 701–18.

Reiser, Marion, and Everhard Holtmann. 2008. *Farewell to the Party Model:*

Independent Local Lists in East and West European Countries. Nomos: VS Verlag.

Renwick, Alan. 2011. *House of Lords Reform.* Newcastle: Political Studies Association.

Robinson, Lennox. 1931. *Bryan Cooper.* London: Constable.

Rochon, Thomas R. 1985. 'Mobilizers and challengers.' *International Political Science Review* 6(4): 419–39.

Rodrigues, Mark, and Scott Brenton. 2010. *The Age of Independence? Independents in Australian Parliaments.* Canberra: Parliamentary Library.

Rosenstone, Samuel J., R. L. Behr and E. H. Lazarus. 1996. *Third Parties in America: Citizen Response to Major Party Failure.* Princeton: Princeton University Press.

Ross, Shane. 2014. 'Independents Can Offer Stability and a Return to Truly Democratic Principles.' *Sunday Independent* (7 December).

Russell, Meg, and Maria Sciara. 2009. 'Independent parliamentarians en masse: The changing nature and role of the 'crossbenchers' in the House of Lords.' *Parliamentary Affairs* 62(1): 32–52.

Sacks, Paul M. 1976. *The Donegal Mafia. An Irish Politcal Machine.* New Haven: Yale University Press.

Sartori, Giovanni. 2005. *Parties and Party Systems: A Framework for Analysis.* Colchester: ECPR Press.

Sawer, Marian. 2004. *Above-the-Line Voting—How Democratic?.* Canberra: Democratic Audit Unit.

Sharman, Campbell. 1999. 'The representation of small parties and independents in the Senate.' *Australian Journal of Political Science* 34(3): 353–61.

———. 2002. *Politics at the Margin: Independents and the Australian Political System.* Canberra: Department of the Senate.

———. 2013. 'Limiting party representation: Evidence from a small parliamentary chamber.' *Legislative Studies Quarterly* 38(3): 327–48.

Sherrill, Kenneth. 1998. 'The dangers of non-partisan elections to democracy.' *Social Policy* 28(4): 15–22.

Sherwin, Frank. 2007. *Frank Sherwin: Independent and Unrepentant.* Dublin: Irish Academic Press.

Shortt, Pat. 2007. *I Will in Me Politics. The Maurice Hickey Diaries.* Dublin: O'Brien Press.

Sifry, Micah L. 2003. *Spoiling for a Fight: Third-Party Politics in America.* London: Routledge.

Singleton, Gwynneth. 1996. 'Independents in a multi-party system: The experience of the Australian Senate.' *Papers on Parliament* 28: 61–82.

Sinnott, Richard. 1995. *Irish Voters Decide: Voting Behaviour in Elections and Referendums since 1918.* Manchester: Manchester University Press.

———. 2010. 'The Electoral System.' In *Politics in the Republic of Ireland*, eds Michael Gallagher and John Coakley. London: Routledge and PSAI Press, 111–36.

Smith, Raymond. 1985. *Garret. The Enigma*. Dublin: Aherlow.

Smith, Rodney. 2006. *Against the Machines: Minor Parties and Independents in New South Wales, 1910–2006*. Sydney: Federation Press.

Strom, Kaare. 1990. *Minority Government and Majority Rule*. Cambridge: Cambridge University Press.

Taagepera, Rein, and Martin S. Shugart. 1989. *Seats and Votes: The Effects and Determinants of Electoral Systems*. New Haven: Yale University Press.

Tillie, Jean. 1995. *Party Utility and Voting Behaviour*. Amsterdam: Het Spinhuis.

Ungoed-Thomas, Jasper. 2008. *Jasper Wolfe of Skibbereen*. Cork: Collins Press.

Varley, Tony. 1996. 'Farmers Against Nationalists: The Rise and Fall of Clann Na Talmhan in Galway.' In *Galway: History and Society*, eds Gerard Moran and Ray Gillespie. Dublin: Geography Publications, 589–622.

———. 2010. 'On the road to extinction: Agrarian parties in twentieth-century Ireland.' *Irish Political Studies* 25(4): 581–601.

Veenendaal, Wouter P. 2013. 'How democracy functions without parties: The Republic of Palau.' *Party Politics* published online November 25: 1–11.

Walker, Brian Mercer. 1992. *Parliamentary Election Results in Ireland, 1918–92*. Dublin: Royal Irish Academy.

———. 2011. 'An Irishman's Diary.' *Irish Times* (12 March).

Webb, D. A., and R. B. McDowell. 1982. *Trinity College, Dublin 1592–1952, An Academic History*. Cambridge: Cambridge University Press.

Webb, Paul. 1996. 'Apartisanship and anti party sentiment in the United Kingdom: correlates and constraints.' *European Journal of Political Research* 29(3): 365–82.

Weeks, Liam. 2008a. 'Independents in Government. A Sui Generis Model.' In *Newly Governing Parties. In Power for the First Time*, ed. Kris Deschouwer. London: Routledge, 136–56.

———. 2008b. 'We Don't like (to) Party: Explaining the Significance of Independents in Irish Political Life.' Unpublished PhD dissertation. Trinity College, Dublin.

———. 2009. 'We don't like (to) party. A typology of independents in Irish political life, 1922–2007.' *Irish Political Studies* 24(1): 1–27.

———. 2010a. 'Membership of the Houses.' In *The Houses of the Oireachtas*, eds Muiris MacCarthaigh and Maurice Manning. Dublin: Institute of Public Administration.

———. 2010b. 'Parties and the Party System.' In *Politics in the Republic of Ireland*, eds Michael Gallagher and John Coakley. London: Routledge and PSAI Press, 137–67.

———. 2011. 'Rage against the machine: Who is the independent voter?' *Irish Political Studies* 26(1): 19–43.

———. 2012. 'The Dog that Did Not Bark. Why Did no New Party Emerge in 2011?' In *Radical or Redundant. Minor Parties in Irish Political Life*, eds Liam Weeks and Alistair Clark. Dublin: History Press, 7–26.

———. 2013. 'Rational, reverential or experimental? The politics of electoral reform in Oceania.' *Australian Journal of Political Science* 48(4): 383–97.

———. 2014. 'Crashing the party. Does STV help independents?' *Party Politics* 20: 604–16.

———. 2015. 'Parliaments without parties.' *Australasian Parliamentary Review* 30(2): 61–71.

———. 2016. 'Independents and the Election. The Party Crashers.' In *How Ireland Voted 2016*, eds Michael Gallagher and Michael Marsh. London: Palgrave, 207–26.

Weeks, Liam, and Alistair Clark. 2012. *Radical or Redundant. Minor Parties in Irish Political Life*. Dublin: The History Press.

Weeks, Liam and Aodh Quinlivan. 2009. *All Politics is Local: A Guide to Local Elections in Ireland*. Cork: Collins Press.

Weiner, Myron, and Joseph LaPalombara. 1966. 'The impact of parties on political development.' In *Political Parties and Political Development*, eds Joseph LaPalombara and Myron Weiner. Princeton: Princeton University Press, 399–435.

White, Graham. 1991. 'Westminster in the Arctic: The adaptation of British parliamentarism in the Northwest Territories.' *Canadian Journal of Political Science* 24(03): 499–523.

———. 2006. 'Traditional Aboriginal values in a Westminster parliament: The legislative assembly of Nunavut.' *The Journal of Legislative Studies* 12(1): 8–31.

White, Lawrence William. 2009a. 'Daniel Morrissey.' In *Dictionary of Irish Biography*. Cambridge: Cambridge University Press.

———. 2009b. 'Thomas Burke.' In *Dictionary of Irish Biography*. Cambridge: Cambridge University Press.

Whyte, John H. 1974. 'Ireland: Politics without Social Bases.' In *Electoral Behaviour: A Comparative Handbook*, ed. Richard Rose. New York: Free Press, 619–51.

Windsor, Tony. 2015. *Windsor's Way*. Melbourne: Melbourne University Press.

Wright, G. C., and B. F. Schaffner. 2002. 'The influence of party: Evidence from the state legislatures.' *American Political Science Review* 96(02): 367–79.

Wright, Gerald C. 2008. 'Charles Adrian and the study of nonpartisan elections.' *Political Research Quarterly* 61(1): 13–16.

Yeats, William Butler. 1990. *The Poems, Edited by Daniel Albright*. London: Everyman's Library.

Index

Ahern, Bertie 45, 77, 109, 114–15,
    209–10, 218, 231–3, 235–40,
    242, 246, 251, 279, 281–2
Ahern, Dermot 114
Alberta 178
American Samoa 13
Ancient Order of Hibernians 34
Andren, Peter 22, 149, 191
Anthony, Richard 49, 216
Anti-Austerity Alliance 226
anti-party sentiment 11, 78, 150–1,
    157, 160–1, 163–5, 168–70
Army Wives' Association 27
Association of Combined Residents'
    Associations 105
Australia 3, 9, 11, 18, 22, 28, 54,
    56–7, 59–63, 67, 89, 149–50,
    158–60, 162, 173, 178, 186–93,
    195–203, 207, 228, 265, 272,
    284
Australian Capital Territory 187, 189,
    193, 196, 284
Austria 56

Ball, John 145
Barrett, Seán D. 140–6
Barry, Anthony 7
Beamish, Richard Henrik 38
Belgium 56, 159, 254
Bell, Martin 272
Blaney, Harry 77, 236–8, 259
Blaney, Neil 45, 49, 73, 77, 85, 219,
    222, 230–4
Blaney, Niall 239, 248
Blind Men's Party 26
Boland, John 106
Breen, Dan 44
Brennan, Michael 214

Brennan, Paudge 85
Brennan, Séamus 237
Broughan, Tommy 78–9
Browne, Noël 22, 43, 107, 219–20,
    224, 229–30
Bruton, John 235
Bulgaria 56, 58
Burke, Edmund 101
Burke, Patrick 216
Burke, Thomas 17, 41, 223
Burma 186
Business Men's Party 39
Byrne, Alfie 16–17, 34–5, 67, 214–15,
    224, 246
Byrne, Alfie Jr. 35, 223–4, 246
Byrne, Kevin 105
Byrne, Patrick 35
Byrne, Thomas 35

Callely, Ivor 114
Canada 3, 11, 13–14, 22n, 57, 59, 67,
    150, 159–60, 178, 186, 207,
    265
Canney, Seán 80, 227–8
Carlow-Kilkenny 35, 82–4
Carroll, James 217–18, 246
Cavan 36, 38, 67, 128
Cavan–Monaghan 82–3
Chile 102
Christian Democratic Party 27, 102–4
Cine Gael 27
City Workers' Housing Association 26
Clann na Poblachta 35, 103, 208
Clann na Talmhan 41, 208, 216
Clare 17, 41, 82–3, 151, 237
Clare Farmers' Party 41
clientelism 16, 91, 121, 130, 143, 151,
    275

Cogan, Patrick 70, 223, 225, 229–30
Cole, John Copeland 36, 38
Cole, John James 36, 38, 216
Collins, Joan 79
Collins, Michael 85, 110
Collins, Stephen 277
Connolly, Catherine 226
Connolly, James 110
Connolly, Thomas 103–4
Cooper, Bryan Ricco 36–7, 67,
    214–15
Cork 27, 36, 38, 40, 82–5, 95–6, 99,
    111, 130, 134
Cork County Farmers' Association 40
Corkery, Daniel 44
Cork Progressive Association 27, 38,
    40
Cosgrave, James 34
Cosgrave, Liam 224
Cosgrave, William T. 35, 213–16,
    224–5
Costello, John A. 223–5, 228–9
Costello, Séamus 129
Cowan, Peadar 225, 229–30
Cowen, Brian 109, 115, 240–2, 249
Craughwell, Gerard 79
Croatia 12
Cumann na nGaedheal 35, 37, 39–40,
    49, 70, 208, 213–15, 249
Cyprus 56, 138, 254
Czech Republic 56

Daly, Clare 79
Daly, John 214
Democratic Left 43, 116, 119, 235
Democratic Socialist Party 222
Denmark 3, 11, 56–7, 59, 159
Department of Education 130
Department of Finance 145
Department of Health 227
Department of the Taoiseach 238
de Valera, Éamon 36, 41, 110, 210,
    215–17, 223, 225, 229–30
Dillon, James 16, 34, 216, 223–5,
    228–9, 246
Donegal 16, 24, 36, 38, 41, 45, 82–4,
    104, 236–7
Donegal Progressive Party 27, 38, 50
Donnelly, Stephen 46, 116, 125
Dowling, Brendan 141
Doyle, Michael 35
Dublin 82–6, 99, 103–11, 118, 126–8,

130, 133, 139, 141, 143, 215,
    218, 231
Dublin Bay Loftus, Seán 76, 91, 102–9,
    112, 219–21, 246
Dublin City Council 102, 109, 112,
    126
Dwyer, William 40

Ecology Party 27
elections
  by-elections 80–2, 116, 120, 126,
      128, 132, 202, 215–16, 230,
      237, 246
  Dáil
    (1922) 26–7, 40, 44, 54, 67
    (1923) 26–7, 37, 39, 67–9, 72,
        213
    (1927) (June) 26, 67–70, 72, 213,
        280
    (1927) (September) 26–7, 34,
        39–40, 69–70, 280
    (1932) 27, 35, 39, 49, 69, 72,
        210
    (1933) 41, 69–70, 72, 217
    (1937) 37, 41, 44, 69–70
    (1938) 70, 72, 217
    (1943) 27, 69, 72, 216
    (1944) 27, 72, 217
    (1948) 27, 51, 69, 77, 223, 239
    (1951) 27, 73, 225, 228, 246, 248
    (1954) 27, 40, 230
    (1957) 27, 73, 84, 103
    (1961) 27, 77, 217
    (1965) 27, 73
    (1969) 27, 73, 104
    (1973) 27, 44, 73, 104–5
    (1977) 73, 75, 98, 106
    (1981) 45, 73, 76, 84–5, 106, 109,
        219
    (1982) (February) 27, 43, 76, 108,
        129, 230
    (1982) (November) 27, 248
    (1987) 27, 221
    (1989) 27, 47, 76, 233
    (1992) 27, 46–7, 75, 151, 236,
        248
    (1997) 27, 47, 75–7, 84–5, 151,
        158, 235–6, 259, 271
    (2002) 27, 46, 75, 77, 128, 133–4,
        151, 164, 183, 248
    (2007) 27, 75–7, 114, 116, 120,
        128, 158, 205, 239, 248

elections (*cont.*)
  Dáil (*cont.*)
    (2011) 27, 35, 46, 51, 55–6, 59,
      77, 115–16, 122, 125–6, 132,
      157–8, 184, 248
    (2016) 24, 28, 35, 51, 55–6,
      76–80, 84, 109, 115–16, 124,
      126, 158, 162–3, 166, 184, 208
  European Parliament 11–12, 18, 42,
    45, 46, 56, 58, 80–1, 91, 138
    204n1
    (1979) 94, 105
    (1999) 46
    (2004) 134
    (2009) 128
    (2014) 77
  local 80–1
    (1974) 76
    (1979) 76, 129
    (1991) 123
    (2004) 120
    (2009) 132
    (2014) 77
  presidential 81–2
    (1997) 46
  Seanad
    (1977) 93
    (1982) 101, 198
    (2011) 140
    (2016) 2–3
electoral systems 18–22, 49, 53, 65,
  150–1, 167, 172–204, 252,
  256–7, 261–4, 273–6
  alternative vote 173, 187–91
  double ballot 174, 176
  first-past-the-post 174
  list 4, 6–7, 12, 19, 24, 56, 58, 187,
    191–2, 201, 270–1
  single-member plurality 59, 176
  single non-transferable vote 59,
    64–6
  single transferable vote 21, 40, 65,
    71, 113, 151, 155, 172–204,
    258, 271, 273–4
'Era of Good Feelings' 12–13
Estonia 12, 56, 59, 150–1, 186, 254
European Union 22n1, 56, 129,
  134–40, 145, 151–2, 237, 271
  European Parliament 22, 77, 94,
    105, 133–40
  see also under elections
Evicted Tenants' Association 26

Falkland Islands 13
Fanning, Aengus 95
Farmers' Party 34–5, 40–1, 213, 215
Fathers' Rights Responsibility Party
  27
Federalist, The 6, 13
Ffrench-O'Carroll, Michael 229–30
Fianna Fáil 2, 16, 20, 23, 26, 38, 42–5,
  49–50, 52, 70–1, 73, 75, 79–80,
  85, 96, 98, 102, 106–8, 110,
  114, 120–1, 138, 164–5, 170,
  176, 184, 208–10, 213–19,
  221–3, 226–36, 239–41, 243,
  246–7, 249, 258, 271, 279,
  282–3, 285
Figgis, Darrell 44
Fine Gael 2, 7, 26, 34–5, 38, 41, 47,
  49–51, 71, 73, 75, 79–80, 85,
  94, 106–10, 114, 120, 138, 165,
  170, 176, 208, 210–11, 217–23,
  226–31, 235, 242, 249, 258,
  277, 283
Finland 3, 56
Finucane, Patrick 217, 228
Fís Nua 27
FitzGerald, Garret 8, 94, 100, 106–8,
  151, 217, 219–22, 230–1,
  234–5, 281
Fitzmaurice, Michael 78–9, 227
Five Star Movement 78
Flanagan, Luke Ming 51, 54, 246
Flanagan, Oliver J. 17, 51, 217–18,
  223–5
Fleming, Brian 108
Fleming, Tom 79, 90n3
Flynn, Beverly 240, 246
Flynn, John 223, 229–30
Fox, Mildred 77, 236–9, 246,
  248
Foxe, Tom 47, 233–5, 246, 248
France 56, 174, 176

Galway 78, 82–4, 109, 239
Geary, Paddy 141
gene pool independents 29–30, 52,
  65–6, 110, 271
Germany 56, 158–9
Gibraltar 186
Gildea, Thomas 77, 235–9
Gillard, Julia 63
Gilmore, Éamon 277
Good, John P. 39–40

governments
 1923–27 (Cumann na nGaedheal)
  213
 1927 (Cumann na nGaedheal)
  213–15
 1927–32 (Cumann na nGaedheal)
  215–16
 1932–33 (Fianna Fáil) 210
 1943–44 (Fianna Fáil) 216–17
 1948–51 (Fine Gael–Labour–
  National Labour–Clann na
  Poblachta–Clann na Talmhan)
  223–5, 242, 246–8
 1951–54 (Fianna Fáil) 228–30,
  246–7
 1961–65 (Fianna Fáil) 217–19, 247
 1981–82 (Fine Gael–Labour)
  219–21, 242
 1982 (Fianna Fáil) 230–3, 247–50
 1987–89 (Fianna Fáil) 221–3, 247
 1989–92 (Fianna Fáil–Progressive
  Democrats) 233–5, 247
 1994–97 (Fine Gael–Labour–
  Democratic Left) 210
 1997–2002 (Fianna Fáil–Progressive
  Democrats) 235–9, 246–8
 2002–7 (Fianna Fáil–Progressive
  Democrats) 210
 2007–11 (Fianna Fáil–Progressive
  Democrats –Green) 210,
  239–41, 246–9
 2011–16 (Fine Gael–Labour)
  210–11, 213
 2016– (Fine Gael) 225–8
Grattan, Henry 144
Grealish, Noel 35, 78, 227, 240–1
Greece 278
Green Party 120, 164–5, 170, 208,
  223, 226, 235, 239
 see also under Ecology Party
Gregory, Tony 8, 42–3, 76–7, 108
Guernsey 13

Haaugaard, Jakob 11
Halligan, John 79–80, 227–8
Hanafin, Mary 114
Hare, Thomas 177
Harkin, Marian 91
Harney, Mary 223, 239–41
Harradine, Brian 63
Harty, Michael 227
Haslett, Alexander 36

Haughey, Charles 8, 43, 45, 104,
  106–8, 126, 128, 130, 219, 222,
  230–6, 239, 247, 283
H-Block candidates 45, 106, 219
Healy, Séamus 51, 78, 227, 246
Healy-Rae, Danny 1–2, 227
Healy-Rae, Jackie 2, 77–8, 210, 218,
  235–42, 248, 250, 251n1, 271
Healy-Rae, Johnny 2
Healy-Rae, Maura 2
Healy-Rae, Michael 1–2, 227
Hederman, Carmencita 76, 104
Hennessy, Mark 108
Hermon, Lady Sylvia 55
Heskin, Denis 41
Hewson, Gilbert 214
Hillery, Patrick 108
Hogan, Phil 114
Holohan, Richard 35
Hungary 3, 12, 56–7, 59
Hyland, Barbara 16

Iceland 22n1
Identity Ireland 28
Immigration Control Platform 27
Independent Alliance 28, 51, 79–80,
  109, 113, 115–16, 167, 200,
  227, 277
Independents 4 Change 51, 53n4, 79,
  200, 226
India 186
Irish Democratic Party 28
Irish Farmers' Association 42
Irish Housewives' Association 27
Irish National League Party 35
Irish Parliamentary Party 34, 214
Irish Republican Socialist Party 27, 42,
  45
Irish Times 27, 29, 39, 70, 171n4,
  216–18, 231, 277, 285n1
Irish Women's Citizens' Association 26
'Irish Worker' League 27
Irish Workers' League 27
Isle of Man 186
Israel 22n1, 254
Italy 56, 78, 179, 278

Japan 4, 11, 18, 22, 22n1, 28, 54,
  56–7, 59–62, 64–6, 89, 159–60,
  255, 272
Jeffords, Jim 271
Jersey 13

Jinks, John 215
Johnson, Thomas 214

Kazahkstan 4
Keane, John B. 273
Kemmy, Jim 17, 107, 219–22, 230, 232–3
Kennedy, John F. 103
Kenny, Enda 210, 226–7, 278
Kerry 1–2, 78, 82–3, 236–7
King, Angus 56, 272
Kiribati 13

Labour Party 20, 26, 42–3, 46, 49, 50, 52, 72–3, 79, 82, 92, 99, 106, 110, 116, 119, 139, 165, 170, 186, 208, 210–11, 214–16, 219, 221–2, 226, 230, 233, 235, 242, 258, 277
Laois-Offaly 82–3, 151
Larkin, James 232
Larkin, James Sr. 43
Latvia 254
Lehane, Patrick 228
Lemass, Seán 36, 141, 217–19, 229, 247
Leneghan, Joe 217–19, 249
Lieberman, Joe 272
Lipper, Michael 73
localism 2, 16, 18, 46–8, 80, 124, 148–9, 151–3, 155–7, 163–5, 167–8, 170, 175, 257–8, 265, 273–4
Longford 44, 48
Longford–Westmeath 48, 82–4, 218
Louth 82–3
Lowry, Michael 47, 78, 85, 210, 227, 235, 239–42, 246, 248–9
Luxembourg 89, 159, 254
Lynch, Brendan 105

MacBride, Seán 103–4
McCabe, Fergus 111
MacCarron, Daniel 104
McCreevy, Charlie 120
MacDermot, Frank 41
McGrath, Finian 78–80, 91, 109–16, 227–8, 239–40, 249
McGrath, Mattie 78
Mack, Ted 149
McQuillan, Jack 44, 229–30
Maguire, Ben 44, 216, 223

Maher, T.J. 42
Malta 3, 11, 56, 138, 155, 173, 186, 195, 200, 202, 254, 275
Manitoba 178
Manning, Vincent 105
Marshall Islands 13
Martin, Micheál 114
Mayo 82–4, 282
Meath 82, 84
Micronesia, Federated States of 13
Mill, John Stuart 177
Minnesota 12
Mitchell, Jim 107
Monaghan 16, 34, 36, 82, 84, 127
Monaghan Protestant Association 36, 38
Monetary Reform 27, 51
Montalva, Frei 102
Moran, Kevin 'Boxer' 227–8
Morrissey, Daniel 49
Murphy, Catherine 91, 116–26
Murphy, James Xavier 38–40, 69
Murphy, John A. 92–102
Myles, James Sproule 36

National Action 27
National Centre Party 35
National Farmers' and Ratepayers' League 35, 41
Naughten, Denis 78, 80, 227
Nauru 13
Nebraska 12
Netherlands 56, 159, 161, 254
New South Wales 187–92, 196–7
New Vision 27
New Zealand 3, 11, 22n1, 28, 56–7, 59, 67, 158, 160–1, 186, 202, 204n2
Nighthawks 108
Noonan, Michael 226
North Central Community Council 42–3
Northern Ireland 36, 44–5, 55, 92, 101, 105, 186, 190, 201–2, 204n2, 225, 232, 237
Northern Territory 188
Northwest Territories 13
Norway 22n1
Nunavut 13

Oakeshott, Rob 22, 63
O'Connell, Daniel 67, 99

O'Connell, John 106
Official Sinn Féin 42
O'Hanlon, John F. 67, 214
O'Hanlon, Rory 234
O'Higgins, Kevin, 53n1
O'Higgins, T.F. 104
O'Leary, Michael 276–7
Orange Order 16, 36
O'Reilly, Patrick 223
O'Shaughnessy, Andrew 38
O'Sullivan, Maureen 91, 126–33, 227, 231, 246
O'Toole, Joe 114

Pakistan 186
Palau 13
Papua New Guinea 10, 280
Parallax View, The 275
Parnell, Charles Stewart 102
party system 1, 4, 14, 19–20, 22–3, 25, 34, 52–3, 55, 66–7, 70–1, 73, 89, 105, 125, 138, 164, 207, 252–9, 261–5, 270, 273–7
People Before Profit Alliance 27
People's Convention 27
personalism 13, 48, 149, 151, 153, 155–7, 163–5, 168, 170, 257–8, 263, 273, 275
Plunkett, David 145
Podemos 78
Poland 12, 56
political culture 18–21, 43, 119, 125, 148–52, 155, 167, 172–3, 195, 200–2, 252, 256–8, 263, 265, 270, 273–5, 277
  see also under clientelism; localism; personalism
populism 17, 78, 121, 276
Portugal 56, 145, 159
Pringle, Thomas 226
Progressive Democrats 34–5, 120, 164–5, 170, 208, 221–3, 233, 235, 239–40, 242–3, 271, 282, 285n1
protestant 24, 35–8, 51–2, 67, 70, 93, 110, 153, 177

Queensland 188
Quinlan, Patrick 95, 98
Quinn, Fergal 79

Rafferty, Mick 111, 132
Ratepayers' Association 26, 178
Redmond, William 34–5
Renua Ireland 78–9
Reynolds, Albert 107, 235
Rice index of cohesion 211–12
Romania 12, 56
Roscommon 44, 47, 51, 78, 82–3, 233–4
Roscommon–Galway 78
Ross, Shane 46, 53n3, 79–80, 227–8, 277
Russia 12, 14, 18, 149, 255, 259, 265

Sanders, Bernie 56, 78, 272
Scallon, Dana Rosemary 46
Scotland 12, 178, 186, 189, 201, 202, 204n2
Sheldon, William 36, 38, 41, 223–5, 228–9
Sheridan, Joseph 48, 73, 84, 217, 218, 249
Sherlock, Joe 219
Sherwin, Frank 22, 24, 166, 217–18
Shortt, Pat 273
Sinn Féin 27, 37, 44–5, 78, 99, 101, 103, 114, 165, 170, 178, 235
Sinn Féin the Workers' Party 219, 230, 247
  see also under Official Sinn Féin; Workers' Party
Sinnott, Kathy 133–40
Sligo–Leitrim 44, 82–3
Slovakia 12, 58
Slovenia 58, 254
Smith, Paddy 218
Social Democrats 78–9, 116, 118, 120, 122, 125–6, 226
Socialist Labour Party 42, 219
Socialist Party 138, 235
South Africa 186
South Australia 187–91, 196–7
Spain 58
Spring, Dick 233
Sweden 58
Switzerland 22n1, 57, 254

Tarand, Inderek 12
Tasmania 63–4, 174, 176, 187–9, 192–3, 196–8, 253–4
Tax Reform League 27
Taylor, Richard 272

Tipperary 51, 78, 82–5, 235
Town Tenants' Association 26
Transcendental Meditation 27
Treacy, Seán 222, 233
Trinity College, University of Dublin
        37, 90n2, 92, 140–6, 247
Trump, Donald 78
Tully, John 35
Tuvalu 13

Uganda 14
Ukraine 4
unionism 35–9, 52, 93, 216
Unionist Party 34, 36, 39
United Kingdom 3, 11–12, 14, 18, 22,
        28, 34, 55–7, 59, 66, 113, 150,
        153, 159, 174, 176–8, 186,
        223–5, 265, 271–2
United Left Alliance 27
United States of America 3, 7, 11–13,
        18–19, 22n1, 46, 52, 56–7,
        59, 78, 102–3, 113, 150, 158,
        160–2, 176, 186, 265, 270,
        272
University College Cork 92–101

University College Dublin 95, 102
Unpurchased Tenants' Association 26

Victoria 187–9, 191, 197

Wallace, Mick 53n4, 79, 113
Waterford 34, 41, 82–3
Western Australia 187–9, 191, 197
Westmeath 44, 48, 84
Wexford 35, 79, 82–4
Whitaker, T.K. 97, 142
Wicklow 46, 70, 82–4
Windsor, Tony 22, 63
Wolfe, Jasper Travers 214
Woods, Michael 106
Workers' Farming Association 26
Workers' Party 43, 116–19, 219, 222
Workers' Unemployed Action Group
        27, 51
World Bank 284
Wycherley, Florence 85

Xenophon, Nick 63

Zappone, Katherine 80, 227–8

Lightning Source UK Ltd.
Milton Keynes UK
UKOW06n1816110917
309006UK00010B/57/P